The Long Shadows

The Story of Jake Erlich

ANDREW ERLICH

A TRUE-LIFE NOVEL

The Long Shadows, The Story of Jake Erlich by Andrew Erlich

ISBN: 978-0-9774089-9-3 (Paperback)
ISBN: 978-0-9774089-8-6 (E-book)

For information regarding permission, write to: Multicultural Publications at info@TheLongShadowsBook.com

Library of Congress Control Number: 2012907519
Printed in the United States of America

Book Designer: Michelle Radomski
Copyeditor: Courtney Wilhelm

Multicultural Publications
Scottsdale, Arizona

This book is dedicated to my Uncle Jake and
my parents, Myer and Ruth Erlich—great story tellers.
It is also dedicated to all those people who
have struggled with being different.

Acknowledgments

I would like to thank my wife, Robin, my son, Ben, my daughter, Danielle, and my mother, Ruth, for their patience, love, and support over the years as I wrote this novel. I am grateful to Bobby Davidoff, Susan Davidoff, Ray Klein, Michelle Bartlett, Rhoda Goodman, and Diane Barshop for their valuable feedback. I would like to thank my mother-in-law, Edna Pindler, for sharing her memories of early Hollywood.

My coach, Lori DeBoer, was instrumental in introducing me to writing and motivating me to keep at it. This work would not have been possible without the generosity of Jake's friends and the children and grandchildren of his friends who shared their recollections, stories, photographs, and home movies. In particular, I would like to thank Diana Serra Cary of Northern California; Bob Phillips, Betty Snyder, Fred McDaniel, and Cita Schuster of El Paso; and Marise McDermott, Amy Fulkerson, and Sarita Rodriguez of the Witte Museum in San Antonio. I also appreciate the help I received from Circus World Museum in Baraboo, Wisconsin and the John Ringling Circus Museum in Sarasota, Florida. I am grateful to Dr. Michael Tomar, Christian Gerstheimer, Michelle Villa, Laura Zamarripa and Jeffrey Romney of the El Paso Museum of Art, and photographer Marty Snortum for their efforts to share Jake's art with the world. I also want to thank Eric Pearson, of the El Paso Community Foundation, and Sally Gilbert and Norma Geller of Impact | Programs of Excellence for their help in telling my uncle's story. Last but not least, I would like to acknowledge Sean Garrison for his guidance and counsel, Michelle Radomski for her work laying out this book, Ilisa Keith for her efforts to publicize it, Laura Mitre for her formatting and Courtney Wilhelm for her editing.

PROLOGUE

Wisconsin Historical Society - Image ID 22991

Hotel Dieu Hospital - May, 1952
'Round my Indiana homestead wave the cornfields,
In the distance loom the woodlands clear and cool,
Oftentimes my thoughts revert to scenes of childhood,
Where I first received my lessons - nature's school.

Our polar-opposite voices, mine a brawny baritone and hers a sweet soprano, blended together. The melody filled the old hospital ward with whispered music. The young nurse gently put her hand on my forearm. It felt good. Then we both closed our eyes and continued to harmonize.

But one thing there is missing in the picture,
Without her face it seems so incomplete,
I long to see my mother in the doorway,
As she stood there years ago, her boy to greet.
Oh, the moonlight's fair tonight along the Wabash....

"What's going on in here?"

We abruptly stopped singing, opened our eyes and looked to the doorway. The angry face of Sister Mary Katherine, the nun in charge of the night shift, peered back at us out of the darkened hallway. Liz sank into a wooden chair next to my bed and clutched her hands tightly in her lap, like a school girl in the principal's office for the first time. We both knew the old nun was by the book. She was infamous for not putting up with nonsense from patients and for firing young nurses at the drop of a hat. Word around the ward was that she wasn't always that way. When Sister Mary Katherine was young, just starting her work in hospitals, she was tolerant and kind like Liz. But after the Spanish Flu Epidemic of 1918 and all she had to deal with, they say she hardened. God knows all the struggles I've been through have changed me. I wondered what, if anything, about me had not changed.

"Good evening, Sister," I answered. "Nurse Reardon suggested we sing to cheer me up. It was such a wonderful idea. You see, I have been feeling kind of blue," I answered.

Liz looked down and didn't say a word.

"Humph," the old nun replied, suspiciously looking over the spectacles that were propped on the end of her nose. "Just keep it down. There are sick people in this place." She shook her head.

"Yes, ma'am, I promise." As she walked away we could hear her long, black robes brush against the linoleum and the gold chain and crucifix she wore around her neck jangling on the front of her habit. When the nun was safely out of earshot, the young nurse stood up and walked over to the huge bed my parents had loaned Hotel Dieu for me to sleep in because their hospital beds would never have fit me.

"Thank you for bailing me out, Mr. Erlich. I don't think Sister Mary Katherine would have taken too keenly to the fact that you were trying to cheer me up. If she ever got wind that I told a patient about how homesick I've been—if you'll excuse the expression—there would be hell to pay."

"It was nothing." I noticed that my nurse looked troubled; more troubled than I'd ever seen her look before. She had been working the graveyard shift for just a few months. What with my frequent hospitalizations for all the damned transfusions I needed, my awful insomnia, and things being mostly quiet on the ward during the late hours she worked, we had become acquainted. Her name was Elizabeth Reardon. I called her Liz.

That night I wasn't sure if Liz was bothered by the run-in we'd just had with her boss or if something else was on her mind. She sat down again and leaned forward. Liz wore a starched nurse's uniform complete with a white apron and cap, bobby pinned to her curly brown hair. The cap had a thin, navy blue stripe across the front that indicated her neophyte status among the nurses at Hotel Dieu Hospital. Liz Reardon was the youngest and kindest of the many nurses who tended to me. That may explain why I'd grown so fond of her. She had understanding brown eyes, the color of the rich, black coffee they serve in the pie car on the circus train and a sweet voice, well suited for someone who works tending the sick. The fact that she only stood five feet tall and must have weighed no more than a hundred pounds dripping wet originally made me skeptical she could care for someone my size. Liz was polite and proper to a fault with Midwestern sensibilities. She always smelled clean and fresh; the way mesquite trees in the Upper Valley did after a July monsoon.

"You look worried, Liz," I said.

"I'm the one that's supposed to do the nursing here," she replied.

"Come on, what's the matter?" I asked.

Liz glanced away. It wasn't at all like her to avoid my eyes.

"I shouldn't be talking with you about my personal business, Mr. Erlich."

"Liz, I've told you before, please call me Jake. Maybe I can help."

"I don't think anybody can help."

"Why don't you try me?"

Liz hesitated for a minute. "Mr. Erlich . . . I mean Jake, I honestly don't think you can relate." She smiled. I looked at her but didn't say a word. After a minute of uncomfortable silence she finally spoke. "I . . . I really need this job. I can't risk losing it. At first, I didn't even want to take it, but I had to. I'm an only child. Since my dad died, my mom depends on the money I send every month."

"There was a time when I had to help my folks out, too. And I do know what it's like to be forced to do something you really don't want to do," I said haltingly.

"You do?" Liz sounded surprised.

I was stunned at my openness. I guess her honesty elicited the same in me. Up until that moment, our conversations had been cordial, playful, and even interesting, but never personal.

"This job is my first post out of nursing school. It might not seem like a big deal to someone like you who has traveled all over, but to me west Texas is a world apart from Indiana." Liz walked away from me toward the one window in my room and glanced out of it into the darkness. Then she turned around. "I'm a shy person and I'm having trouble making friends," she said quietly. "As hard as I've tried, I just don't feel like I fit in here."

I know what that's like, I thought. The look of worry on her face began to dissipate a bit. She seemed a little lighter, as if each word she shared with me had a weight of its own that she no longer had to bear alone.

"I've lived most of my life on the road. I never really got used to it," I replied, feeling I needed to help her but not sure how. I paused and looked directly into the young nurse's dark eyes. "Liz, are you lonely?" I asked quietly, reaching out and taking her tiny hand in mine. She pulled away and sat back down in the chair. I felt I'd overstepped my bounds. I was intruding. *How would I answer that same question if she asked me?* I wondered. Not waiting for that possibility to unfold and uncomfortable with the silence, I continued to speak. I was surprised by the words that impulsively flew out of my mouth. "I know what it's like to be lonely"

She didn't respond but looked at me quizzically.

"Jake, I look forward to our nightly chats. I really do. And I don't want to offend you." I nodded uncomfortably wondering where she was headed with this. "Tonight is the first time you have shared anything with me about yourself but still . . . " She paused mid-sentence.

The young nurse had no way of knowing that for most of my life I'd been a very private person. Outside of my family, I don't think I'd ever opened up to anyone.

"What's on your mind, Liz?" I asked, pressing her.

She hesitated. "I understand you're seriously ill and all, but how can someone like you . . . ? " She spoke in an insistent, irritated tone I had not heard her use before. I realized that there must be much more to this young nurse than the sweetness and youth that met the eye.

Up until that instant, spending time with her had been easy and uncomplicated. I would just listen and occasionally make a sage suggestion about how she might handle some minor situation. But I guess it was really a one-way relationship. Now, suddenly, I had an awful intuition that I was going to be compelled to do something I didn't want to do. I did not like that feeling at all.

"What do you mean, someone like me?" I responded with my own irritation.

She hesitated. "Well, you are a rich movie star and a world-famous circus celebrity. With all due respect, how can you possibly know what it's like to be lonely?"

"Do you really want to know?" I asked pushing back. Liz nodded. "It's not such a happy tale. I don't want to offend or upset you. I don't think you realize what you are getting yourself into."

I was certain that if I really unburdened myself on this young nurse and told her even a fraction of what I'd been through, it would drive her away. Maybe that was why I had never really shared my story with anyone else. And then there were all the contradictions, ironies, and inconsistencies in my life. How could I possibly explain them to someone else when I didn't understand them myself? What would another person think if I told them how often I worried that I'd never truly lived, yet I also frequently felt so bad I just wanted to die; or that I craved liberty, yet for most of my life, I was terrified of the unknown?

When your worst fears come true and you're actually dying, I always thought you'd experience a certain freedom to say and do whatever you want. But now that I was dying, I didn't feel free. I still wanted to hold back.

"I'm waiting," Liz said, challenging me to explain myself.

What have I gotten myself into? I wondered. Sure, I could just send her away, change the subject, or buy more time in some other manner, but I knew that would torpedo our friendship. I looked forward to my nightly discussions with Liz and didn't want to jeopardize them by not answering her. I hated the prospect of lying awake alone and pondering how many days, nights, and minutes of life I had left. It seemed there was no way out. I hesitated.

"If . . . if . . . if what I say bothers you, please tell me and I'll stop," I said, more anxious than I thought I would ever be speaking to someone half my age. I couldn't believe what was happening. For the first time, I was actually going to tell someone my story. Perhaps there was something in my story she needed to hear?

"Don't worry about me," she insisted.

"One more thing; even though I've lived a mostly public life, I'm really a very private person. I'd appreciate it if what I say stays between us."

"You have my word on that, Jake," she answered. At that instant I was so uneasy that if I could have, I would have jumped out of bed and run out of that hospital to avoid talking about myself.

"Liz, do you still want to listen to this?" I asked, trying to give her and me one final chance to avoid what I knew would be very unpleasant.

"Yes, sir. I do." The young nurse nodded.

"If you could just help me sit up a bit . . . " I grabbed Liz's forearm and inched my enormous torso up the back of the bed. Then she bunched half a dozen pillows behind me. I sighed. "Thanks, that's much better," I said. I questioned how sharing my secrets and stirring up all those awful memories could possibly help anyone, least ways me. But it was too late. Liz looked at me expectantly, waiting for me to begin.

"Well, here goes." I took a deep breath. "I think as good a place to start as any, is at the beginning of the end of the story. It was 1936, just around this time of year. The circus was in New York for our month-long opening run at Madison Square Garden. Things were going bad for me—really bad. I had a lot on my mind—too much. You might say I'd reached the end of my rope. As I often did, I had been walking in the darkened menagerie to clear my head before I left the circus. I couldn't put off the decision any longer. I clutched the sideshow contract in my right hand, unsure what to do about it. That night, I particularly needed some peace and quiet. That's not what I got."

CHAPTER 1
Gargantua the Great

Hertzberg Circus Collection, Witte Museum, San Antonio, Texas

"Hey, you gigantic, ugly son of a bitch."

The menacing voice stopped me in my tracks. More frightened then enraged, I clenched my fists and slowly spun around to face him. But there was no one there. I must be losing my mind, I thought.

Then I heard it again, louder and more threatening. That time, as if dragged by a tiger into the brush, the raspy voice yanked me across the dimly lit menagerie, all but vacant at that late hour. That's when I saw the rube, looking like a drunken lunatic, shouting at a seemingly empty, hand- carved red and blue animal cage. The whole scene was eerie and strange. I knew he was asking for trouble, because I recognized whose cage it was. He continued to scream but there was still no response from the darkened confines. Then, out of the shadows, as if from another dimension, Gargantua lunged at the bars with such force that he would have broken through them if his leg wasn't chained. The gorilla shook those bars with all his strength, hurling primate invective at his tormentor, like it was feces: "Oooh, oooh, aaah, aaah," Gargantua roared. Then he pounded his chest.

The rube taunted him again, mimicking his cry. "Oooh aaah, I'll give you something to holler about, you flea-bitten monkey."

I was incensed at the rube for tormenting Gargantua, but I didn't know what to do. I had an ominous premonition he was planning to hurt the gorilla. Still, I was shocked and couldn't believe my eyes when he reached into his pocket and took out a baseball-sized rock.

What kind of a maniac would do something like that? I thought. Then the rube wound up and hurled the rock between the bars, into the cage, striking the gorilla on the arm. Gargantua shrieked. I felt an overpowering need to protect him. I knew what it was like to be hit by rocks. That's when I charged him. I don't remember much after that. Everything went black.

The whole episode was like a bad dream. They told me I smacked him hard—really hard. They said that at a full gallop, I planted my left shoulder squarely in his upper back, just below his neck. The next thing I knew, Clyde Ingalls, Frank Buck, and two roustabouts were pulling all four hundred pounds of me off him.

"He could have taken his head off!"

"The rube crumbled like a paper doll."

"You should have seen it. He hit him like a freight train!"

From every direction a chorus of anonymous accusers filled the air.

"Now . . . in the backyard!" Ingalls ordered, slamming his half-smoked stogie into the dirt. He was furious. He had my contract, now torn and bloody, in his right hand. The two of us hurried out of the menagerie. I looked back at the figure crumpled on the ground and wondered if he was dead. As we walked away from the scene of the crime to whatever my fate would be, my left shoulder and my neck ached. My head throbbed. Under my torn pants I could feel that I had scraped and bruised both of my knees when I crashed down on the ground with the rube.

"What in the hell has gotten into you, Jake? You could have killed him," he thundered as we walked. "For your sake and ours, you better hope to hell that son of a bitch's okay."

"He hurt Garganatua. He threw a—"

"I don't give two shits what he did. It's not your place to protect that gorilla. It's not your place to protect anyone. All you're paid to do is sit on your keister and let the fans gawk. If that's not enough for you I'll give you your walking papers right now." He stopped to glare at me. "You could have maimed that guy, or worse! What the hell were you thinking?"

"I don't know. I don't know," I said, stopping and looking down at him. Ingalls kept moving. I hurried to catch up. "I just lost control. I blanked out. It's never happened like this before."

What's happening to me? I thought. I felt frightened and guilty. *What have I done?*

"There's no excuse for what you did," Ingalls said as if reading my mind. "We're hurting. We're hurting bad. We can't afford a lawsuit. Do you want to put the nails in our coffin? The Gentry Brothers, Sparks, Cole, Robbins, 101 Ranch, and Sells-Floto and in the past two months, Al G. Barnes and The Hagenbeck-Wallace Show; they've all gone belly up. If it wasn't for that snarling simian, the biggest thing since Jumbo, we'd be on the street as well, eating in soup kitchens." Ingalls shook his finger at me.

"Gargantua doesn't snarl, Clyde," I said nervously. It was easier for me to defend the gorilla than myself.

"Just shut up!" Ingalls shouted. "I have to think about what to do now." He paced back and forth in front of me, took his hat off and began nervously running his fingers through his thinning hair.

Ingalls and I stood alone just outside the empty, three-ringed arena where the main acts performed in the old Madison Square Garden. That space, which had been packed with circus performers, animals, clowns, musicians, and fans just a few hours before, was like a graveyard. I hung my head, wishing I could melt into the grimy sawdust and peanut shells that lined the floor. My knuckles were raw and my knees must have been bleeding because my pants were sticking to them. My head felt like it had been hit with a roustabout's sledgehammer. As if I'd been living in one of those cages in the menagerie, I couldn't get the smell of urine-soaked hay out of my nose.

"That's just what we need—a full-on scandal. I can see the headlines now: 'The Great Gargantua Goes Wild as Freak Cripples Fan.'" My boss kicked the dirt and sent fragments of sawdust flying in every direction. Clyde was about five and a half feet tall with a big beer belly, dressed in his signature seersucker suit and straw hat. To anyone who watched as he scolded me, it must have seemed comical. I bit my lip and didn't say a word. Clyde Ingalls, who the public knew as the colorful and always-affable manager of Ringling Bros, Barnum and Bailey's sideshow, the largest and most famous freak show in the world, could be very scary. In nine years with the circus, this was the scariest I'd ever seen him.

"What's gotten into you?" he asked, pacing back and forth in front of me again. "First you disappear for three days in Milwaukee. Then you're a month past due to sign your contract for next season. Now you attack a customer." He shook his fist up at me. "Should I call the men in white coats to take you to Bellevue in a straitjacket? Or maybe you want to end up in a mud show, or worse? You've got a home here. You're a flea's dick away from losing it."

I felt numb. I didn't know what to say or do, so I just shook my head mechanically, as if I agreed with him.

"You goddamned better straighten up," he said, slamming his hat into his thigh. "I'll let you know when the suits figure out how to clean this mess up."

XXXX

When Ringling Bros played in New York, just like in most of the other cities where we performed, I would stay on the circus train with the other performers, but not that night. After all that had happened, I needed to escape from my home away from home. I couldn't bear to face my friends. I was ashamed and humiliated at how badly I'd lost control. So I checked into The Algonquin Hotel in midtown.

Later that night, I remember stepping toward an open window in my hotel room. I leaned out of it, a bit too far. Feeling the muggy coolness, I looked down. Despite what had happened a few hours before, it wasn't like me to be impulsive. *What am I doing?* I thought. More numb than alarmed, I carelessly leaned farther out of the window. *Just a little bit more and you'll lose your balance; top-heavy, you'll tumble into space. That would be an easy solution to my troubles,* I thought. The sight of the street twelve stories below made me shaky. Even so, something compelled me to climb out onto the ledge. I looked down and asked myself unanswerable questions. *Why wasn't I born a man of normal dimensions like all the others? Why can't I just step into a store and buy a pair of shoes or a shirt like every other man? Why can't I ever sleep in a normal size bed? Why can't I find a woman to love me?*

In the moonlight I saw the shadowed wood and steel skeleton of a new art deco building going up across Forty-Fourth Street. I wondered what kind of a drunken architect designed me. *Was there some kind of a mistake in my blueprints? How could any architect possibly have expected me to stand up?* I thought that it was just a matter of time until my flawed foundation would crack and, in an awful crash, my girders would collapse.

In those days, I could never get enough of the Manhattan skyline. Looking back on it, as big as I am, I must have been fascinated and comforted by things like tall buildings that made me feel small. But that night, so long ago, the view from the open window of my hotel room in The Algonquin was dangerous. The bottomless sadness that from time to time terrified me had disappeared for a while, but that night it came back with a vengeance. I couldn't think my way out of it or ignore it. Like those massive structures that surrounded me, it demanded my attention. I willed myself to step back from the danger. I did. But that had the opposite effect of what you might think. Moving backward, the image in my mind transformed. I was no longer passively falling into space but running to the window and jumping to my death.

Well it was as if Thanatos, the god of death, had devoured my fear and left me horribly energized with an overpowering will to die. *How long would it take me to hit the ground?* I wondered. I imagined the grizzly thud my eight-and-a-half-foot frame would make when it shattered on the sidewalk. Since I was seven years old I'd always been a spectacle. Would my death be just another show, and a free one at that? Would my giant body lying on the sidewalk in a bloody heap draw a crowd like I did in the sideshow?

That wasn't the first time I had seriously thought about suicide. I originally contemplated killing myself when I was sixteen, shortly before I moved to Hollywood. It had been a terrible summer what with all the taunts and teasing, and that horrible experience down by the river.

In the past, something always stopped me, someone, some twist of fate. But that night, in my empty hotel room, I was alone. No one would intervene. No one from Ringling Bros even knew I was there. I did that deliberately. In the past, I could never go through with it. I would think about my parents and how hard they had worked when they first arrived in this country. I'd think of my big brother, Ben. If I ended it all, he'd try but wouldn't be able to use that sharp mind of his to make sense of anything so senseless and tragic. He'd end up dropping out of college to care for my distraught parents. My baby brother, Myer, would lose that cheerful innocence of his. No one in my family would ever be the same. They would all be devastated by my death. Suicide would bring shame upon my family. If I killed myself, Rabbi Roth wouldn't even allow them to bury me in the B'nai Zion Cemetery.

But there in that lonely hotel room I was immune to fear of shame. Looking back on it, that awful night my emotions were raw and my racing thoughts were more lethal than ever. I knew that at any second they had the unrestrained strength to hurl me out of the window. I wasn't sure if any concerns and hesitations I had about taking my life really mattered anyway. The storm that was raging in me did not allow me to see beyond the pain I was experiencing that moment; that there might possibly be more to my life than I could have imagined. At that time, all I could think about was what had taken place earlier that night and if I would be fired from my job in the sideshow, the only place a freak like me came close to fitting in. If I lost that job, what would I do? What could I do? I'd be a burden to my family. Without work, depending on them like I did when I went blind . . . I would never let that happen again.

If Clyde Ingalls canned me, I'd have no choice. Sooner or later, one way or another, I knew I'd end it all. *Why put off the inevitable?* I asked myself. I felt trapped. I couldn't breathe. There was no air in the damned hotel room. I stepped toward the open window again. Now I was outside of myself, watching the whole scene unfold as it were a film starring someone else. The sound of a ruthless voice coming from somewhere in my room frightened me. *A freak like you doesn't deserve to live. All you do is cause problems.* I couldn't block out the blood-thirsty thoughts. Then I reached for the open window frame with both my arms, the way someone does who is trying to escape a burning building. I pulled myself closer. There was no turning back. *It would be so much easier for everybody if you were dead.*

XXXX

Not wanting to believe what almost just happened, I slammed the window and stepped away. When I finally got back into the two beds the hotel staff had pushed together for me, I was too confused and exhausted to be terrified. Willing myself to sleep wasn't an option. I kept flashing back to the awful incident a few hours earlier. I still couldn't believe what I had done. I worried that after all those years, a dangerous, rogue gorilla in me that I always feared but didn't really understand had finally broken free from his cage. When would I attack again? Who else would I hurt?

Lying there in bed, the memories of what had happened started to come back in intrusive staccato bursts: the feel of my shoulder crashing into the drunk's spine; the sickening smell of whiskey coming from his bloody mouth as he laid there, half-dead in the sawdust. I decided to get up and take a walk. I dressed quickly and made my way downstairs.

It was about three a.m. when I turned left out of the hotel lobby onto Forty-Fourth Street. I moved as if in a dream toward Madison. A ghostly breadline materialized out of the steam that escaped from manhole covers and the shadows cast by dim streetlights on the sidewalk in front of St. Andrews. The whole thing was haunting; a Hieronymus Bosch painting come to life on a three-dimensional concrete canvas. The ragged ones stood three abreast, a tattered army crusading for soup. The line of hungry, vacant eyes waiting for the rescue mission to open at sunup snaked almost around the block. Some of those standing there were bums in patched clothing. Some were wearing shabby business suits and ties. Here and there one of them held a child by the hand. I looked at them with sympathy for their plight while several of those poor specters looked up at me with what I assumed was envy. I imagined they would have longed to sleep in a secure and comfortable place like The Algonquin, to dine in its fine restaurant, and to wear the clean, new clothes I sported, even if the price they would have to pay for those luxuries was to live and work as a freak of nature. At that moment on the chilly sidewalk, I don't think it was so much my height that created the chasm between me and the people in the breadline. Rather, it was money and the food, shelter, and security it buys in a world haunted by hard times.

I turned left on Sixth Avenue and headed toward the park. About half way down the block I passed an Apple Annie selling fruit for a few pennies.

"Won't you buy an apple, mister?" she pleaded. I reached in my pocket and gave her a dollar.

"Keep the change," I said. When she handed me the small bruised fruit it got lost in my massive hand. She never looked me in the eyes but gazed down at the sidewalk as if she could see through it. *She must have been hitting the bottle pretty hard*, I thought. The Apple Annie's one-time fine clothing, now gray, told a sad story of better times. Her cheeks had circles of pink rouge on them. She was a tragic caricature of a Ringling clown.

"You take care, ma'am," I said quietly. Walking away from her, I stashed the apple in my coat pocket and imagined what her life must have been like before the Crash. I thought of my mother. I imagined if life had taken a few other tragic twists and turns and she, God forbid, was forced to sell apples on the street to strangers in order to survive. The image made me cringe. After another six blocks, I couldn't walk any farther. Emotionally spent and completely drained, I sank into a bench at a bus stop.

It's funny how memory works. You look back and remember some oddball things and not others. But I recall, as clear as a harvest moon over Waco Tanks, sitting there and staring at my long legs and huge feet resting in the gutter. Then I fell fast asleep.

CHAPTER 2

New Shoes

The Erlich Boys, El Paso circa 1914

I can honestly say that I spent my life beating the odds. I was born prematurely in July of 1906 in Denver, Colorado where my father, mother, and older brother, Ben, had emigrated from Poland. My paltry three-and-one-half-pound birth weight frightened the family, who worried I wouldn't survive. The special medical attention I required taxed my poor parents, who barely spoke any English. Although at times I've been certain it would have been much easier for everyone if I hadn't, I did beat the odds, surprised the doctors, and survived. My birth was followed by the birth of my brother, Myer, in 1911.

In 1912, when the family moved to El Paso, I was an average, normal little boy who looked like any other six year old. My health was the last thing on my parents' minds. I was wiry and fresh-faced, with a Milky Way of freckles. My mother told me I had inquisitive, friendly blue eyes that defined my soon-to-be-angular mug. My thick, wavy brown hair was neatly combed. I remember how Mama gave us our haircuts. She particularly complained about my hair: "That mane looks like a nest for a family of *tecolotes* (owls)." I loved how Mama made pictures with her words. In the Erlich family, you'd typically be treated to a complete spice rack of languages: Spanish, Yiddish, Polish, and heavily-accented English.

Mama's exotic looks and jalapeño personality seemed to fit with a savory mixture of languages. She was full figured, had red hair, and sleepy blue eyes set deep in a face with a peaches-and-cream complexion. I'm sorry to say that her face would soon be marred by wrinkles of worry and crow's-feet from too many sleepless nights.

The first inkling that things weren't right with me came early one morning right after I turned seven. By then we were living in Sunset Heights.

"Look, Papa, look!" Ben roared as he and I raced down the hall and barged into the bathroom where my father was shaving.

"Where's the fire?" Papa asked, his face full of shaving lather as he set his straight razor on the sink. Hearing Ben's excitement, Mama came quickly from the kitchen, where she had been cooking breakfast, and gazed at the scene unfolding in our tiny bathroom.

"Look!" Ben demanded. We were positioned back to back with the somber countenance of rivals about to duel. It was plain to see that I stood two inches taller than my ten-year-old brother, Ben. "This isn't fair. I'm supposed to be bigger."

Mama and Papa didn't seem happy. I remember that when Ben had gone through growth spurts they celebrated. They even recorded a history of those passages with a grease pencil on the bathroom wall. But this time things were different. My growth would never be a source of pride and delight. As I remember it, Mama and Papa looked worried. I took it all in.

I would soon also outgrow my mother. Within a year, I would outgrow my father as well. My parents didn't scare easily. Papa had survived as a Jew in the Russian Army, faced down Boxers during the rebellion in China, and immigrated to the United States with twelve cents to his name. He'd worked in Rocky Mountain boomtowns like Leadville and Silverton, selling to silver miners out of a pack on his back. Mama was his equal. When my father left for America, she had to fend for herself in Poland, raising Ben on her own for two years until they had amassed enough savings to immigrate. In the face of crisis, my parents remained dignified and resourceful. But what they were up against with me was different.

It was right after they realized I was taller than my big brother that the incident with the shoes took place. Even though I was only about seven and a half at the time, I recall everything vividly. It was Sunday, at sunset. Shadows slowly draped the untamed cholla and tumbleweeds in my family's backyard. Those shadows made their way through our borderland window above the apron-front farm sink and slowly robbed our little kitchen of light. That's when Papa raised his voice. It seemed to me, hunkered in a kitchen chair, as I watched him pace back and forth like an interrogator, that he didn't speak but roared.

"Are you sure those shoes don't fit?" Papa stopped and peered down at me. He was strong but seldom stern. He had gentle blue eyes and the kind of good looks that turned heads. His first job in the United States was as an artist's model. Papa had ridden in the Russian Cavalry and his presence on horseback was so striking that he stood out in the crowd. He had huge forearms and gentle hands with dexterous fingers, which suited him for his work as a watchmaker. His demeanor was formal but our family mostly knew him to be warm and loving. So I was startled when the thunder of his question bounced off the ceiling and walls and rattled the black cast-iron frying pan and the purple ceramic pot that hung next to the doorway. It's funny how a parent's anger can come back in an instant with a photo's clarity.

For what seemed like an eternity, the only sound in that kitchen came from the tick-tocks of the handmade gingerbread clock on the mantle above the stone fireplace in the next room. Sitting there in the center of the kitchen, at the family's secondhand tiger's oak table, I avoided his eyes.

I remember squirming on the chair and picking at my patched, gray knee pants. They were held in place by cut-down black suspenders that originally held up my father's, then my brother's, trousers. The blue hue of my short-sleeved shirt had all but disappeared. My clothes were thread-bare, but clean and well-pressed. The only part of my wardrobe that weren't hand-me-down were my shoes, because my feet were bigger than my big brother, Ben's.

"I can't believe it. That's not possible—your mother just bought them," Papa bellowed.

The tone, rather than the words, wounded me. It was not a superficial injury, the type that came from tripping on one of the clumps of red *caliche* that dotted our unpaved street or from being thumped by an itinerant elbow from Ben. I'd heard my father speak harshly to others, but never to me; he didn't have to.

I was an aware, sensitive boy, a good son, and a helper. I was the type of kid who would think before reacting, almost always measuring my responses; a young dam that cautiously released water to irrigate, not destroy, the valley below. I automatically tuned into what I thought others expected. That would become a real problem for me. I knew my parents had high hopes for their sons. Throughout my life, I've never wanted to disappoint them. Though I was only a child, like the desert tortoises in the nearby Franklin Mountains, I understood how to blend in. As a child of immigrants, that innate ability—one I would soon lose—served the family well. I was gentle, like my father; all the more reason to be upset by his uncharacteristic display of what I read as hostility. I never got into trouble. When Ricky Feuille invited neighborhood boys to play with matches and smoke Camel cigarettes behind the Bernat's house, I was the only one to refuse. Whenever mischief beckoned, I imagined the look of sadness in my mother's eyes. Throughout my life, I've felt that, at times, my conscience has hog-tied and handcuffed me. As a child, it was as if I had a premonition that foretold the anguish I would soon cause my parents. Looking back after all these years, I see that that uncanny ability to see the future robbed me of my boyhood.

Be still, I remember ordering myself, as I waited for what my father would do next. Trying my best to be a good boy, I sat on my hands. I pressed my palms into the wooden breakfast room chair so hard that I almost levitated.

"Look at me when I talk you!"

I remember my father's voice like it was yesterday. I looked up at him, but only for an instant. I couldn't bear to see him angry. I never could. I noticed that he was only using English. Languages have a special way of communicating feeling. English is good at icebox coldness. A pleaser by nature, I was devastated that my father was displeased. Invisibly, I trembled.

"Let me see them," Papa ordered. I reached down and picked up the shoes from their place by my stockinged feet and presented them to him. That was the third new pair of shoes I had gotten in the past six weeks. Generally, my mother was the parent in charge of shoes. When my shoes got too tight, I went to her. Papa took hold of those shoes, examined them for some anomaly, and muttered to himself. He resumed pacing.

I wondered why my father, a man whom I respected and adored, a man who worked from sunrise to late at night six days a week in our little family store, would not only be interested, but mad about my shoes.

Does he think I'm not telling the truth? I remember asking myself. Truth was important to the Erlichs. And it has always been important to me. I recalled the day my father lectured and spanked my big brother after he lied about a case of eggs purchased especially for Passover that had gone missing. Ben had appropriated them as a secret weapon to heave at the neighbor boys in a dirt-clod fight.

"In German, *Erlich* means honest," he'd said. Although I was an innocent bystander, he'd lectured both of us. When Papa enunciated the word "honest," I had thought of our name as a badge of honor. I visualized my family as Apache Indians in the Sonoran Desert, brandishing our war shields, announcing to everyone who we were and what we stood for.

"When you don't tell the truth you bring shame not only on you but on your family," my father warned. Looking back, I can say I feared shame more than I feared my father's belt, which on occasion I'd seen him use on Ben.

Though it was wintertime and not at all warm in that unheated kitchen, I began to sweat. "Papa, my shoes don't fit anymore," I insisted. "I'm not lying to you. I swear."

"I know, I know," my father said, in a quieter but still stern voice. Papa stopped pacing and kneeled in front of me. I noticed that his brow was wrinkled and a bluish-purple vein above his right eyebrow throbbed. Thankful to be distracted for a few seconds, I watched it move. Papa further unlaced my barely scuffed, black high-top Buster Brown shoes and loosened the tongue. With a firm, determined grip, he took the shoe in his right hand and slid my foot partway in, just past my toes and instep. I remember how Papa pushed harder; I had to avert my eyes. I was embarrassed, but not sure why.

I looked down and saw my father's brown oxfords, which he cleaned and spit-shined daily. I was fond of those shoes. I remembered all the nights I had peered out from under my bedcovers at Papa's shoes. He would come home late as usual from work and tiptoe into the room that Ben, Myer, and I shared. Then he would bend over and give us each a *kush* on the forehead. I looked forward to the predictable, soothing squeak my father's shoes made on our wooden bedroom floor. It was a talisman of safety, a blessing, a sound that reminded me things were secure in that dimly lit room. When I heard that sound, I could let myself fall backward through space into sleep. That's a feeling I haven't had too often in my life. That evening sitting in our kitchen I wondered how my father saw my shoes. From the look on his face, and the way he was straining, they seemed more like a curse.

Over the years, when I recall how my father struggled with those shoes, it reminds me of the tale of Jacob's wrestling match with the angel that I'd learned when I was a little boy in *chader*—Jewish School where we went to study Monday through Friday after school and on Sunday. In that Bible story Jacob scuffles with a seraph and won't stop grappling until the angel blesses him. Watching this unfold, God laughs. He changes Jacob's name to *Israel*, which means "you who struggle with God and prevail." Though Papa was single-minded and strong, it was impossible for him to have known that was the beginning of a lifelong wrestling match with an invisible menace he would not and could not win.

"Papa," I asked, trying my best to connect with him and lessen the distance I felt growing between us, "when your shoes didn't fit, did your father get mad?" My father was so focused on what he was doing that he didn't say a word.

I knew I must have done something very wrong. Only two Mondays before, after school, Mama and I had gone to Givens and I had picked out a pair. In those days it was the only place to buy kids' shoes in El Paso. Two months before, when Mr. Silverman measured my feet, he couldn't believe that I was only in the second grade. I liked the attention and felt proud to be big for my age.

Upon our return, Silverman looked surprised and muttered, *"Das ist ungaublich."* My mother shot him a disapproving look. When she paid Mr. Silverman, pulling coins from her purse, she'd looked at me and frowned. "These have to last you until *Pesach,*" she said.

I remember worrying that the salesman must have given me a smaller pair by mistake or maybe when I had walked through a puddle of water in front of the Azar's house on the way home from school the day before they had shrunk.

"Stand up on that foot, Jake." Papa tried and tried to force my foot into the small opening, but it was no use. He pushed so hard his face turned red. I pushed, too. I felt that forcing my foot into that tight leather shoe was imperative for the family's survival. I knew that shoes were expensive. I imagined that if my parents spent all of their butter and egg money on me, Ben and little Myer would have to go without. Maybe the family would starve. I knew I was lucky to even have shoes. After all, some of the kids at Vilas School went barefoot.

"Ouch, that hurts, Papa," I said, no longer able to keep silent. Papa sighed, sat up, and wiped the sweat from his brow. I felt guilty that I'd hurt my mother and father by not wearing my shoes at least until spring, as I knew I ought to. I was comfortable with *oughts* and *shoulds*. In those days they defined my world, like the North Star. "I'm sorry; sorry I made you buy those awful shoes for me, Papa," I started to cry.

Papa reached up and put his right hand on my shoulder. I knew he wanted to comfort me, but he must have felt strangely unequal to the task. I know Papa was uneasy with his sense of inadequacy in the face of my sadness.

"*It's nicht gaferlach mien kind*. It's not so important," he said. But I didn't believe him. My father didn't know how to tell me that he wasn't angry; he was frightened. Papa just sighed, picked up the shoes, and stared out of the window into the moonless night. I stood there for a few seconds, waiting for him to turn around. Then I silently retreated to my bedroom. I wondered if Papa would give me a *kush* that night.

The next day, Mama and I made our way to Givens.

"You two, again?" Mr. Silverman said in a loud, overly familiar voice.

I avoided his eyes by watching the salesman's belly shake as he spoke. I smiled to myself and thought, *It moves like the jelly on top of Mama's gefilte fish.*

For the second time in a month, my mother and I sat silently in front of the eager seller of shoes. Silverman had been selling shoes and boots in west Texas since the turn of the century. He was like a walking ledger, a veritable shoe maven. If you asked him, he could recite by heart the shoe sizes and preferred styles of most of the men, women, and children that made up the tiny but growing Jewish community in El Paso, Texas. But he had never encountered a customer like me.

Silverman measured my feet, shook his head as if he were having a conversation with some unseen audience, and quickly disappeared through the worn, velvet curtains that hid the stockroom. Within a few seconds he came through those curtains with the exuberance of an actor bounding on the stage for an encore. He cradled several boxes as he made his way to where Mama and I sat.

Silverman presented the same style high-tops that I had just outgrown. I looked up to see my mother biting her lower lip, which I would come to recognize as a telltale sign that she was worried. The pride I had felt at being "big for my age" a few short months before had disappeared. It was replaced by foreboding. Not knowing what to do, I closed my eyes tightly and descended, inside; a lifelong way I had of escaping. Sitting in Givens, embarrassed and worried, I sought refuge in an inner world where I longed to find something to soothe me. But no comfort materialized out of that murkiness.

As if he couldn't tolerate the vacuum, Silverman filled it with chatter. "This is a first for us," he said, looking over his spectacles and down his nose. "I mean I've never sold so many shoes to one *kleiner bocher* (little boy) in so short a time. Chaa, Chaa." He laughed with a German accent. I wondered if he was laughing or struggling for air. "What are you feeding this boy, Mother Erlich?"

I squirmed and Mama's jaw clenched. Silverman's loud voice was a magnet for attention in that small store. He, like many others over the years, seemed unaware of my increasing anguish. Another mother, this one towing a little girl who wore a yellow bonnet, craned her neck to see what all the fuss was about. The cashier and another salesman, like deserters from the Foreign Legion, left their posts to see what was happening. That was the first time I remember drawing a crowd. I couldn't wait to get out of there. I felt mortified. At that point, I would rather have gone barefoot.

Unfortunately, I would become a constant visitor to Givens Shoes. Within a few years, Givens could no longer accommodate me; I would bust out of even the largest shoes in El Paso. At great expense for any family, I would have to have shoes custom made.

XXXX

Two months and four pairs of shoes later, I sat on Dr. Epstein's leather-covered exam table. In those days, he was the best doctor in town. My mother and father flanked me, sitting on uncomfortable iron chairs that had been painted white. I was nervous. I subtly scanned my parents and sensed their apprehension.

"Dr. Epstein came by the store last week. I sold him a *zeiger*. He should be on time," said my father, trying to lighten the mood in the sterile examination room. "Then again, maybe the watch is already *kaputt*." He smiled at me. I forced myself to grin back.

"Once in Poland during an influenza outbreak, when I got deathly ill, they made me take kerosene," said Mama, frantic for something to talk about. I recall that I grimaced, imagining what kerosene tasted like. I wondered if Dr. Epstein would prescribe it for me.

"Weh es mir, Dora!" said Papa, rolling his eyes. "Are you trying to scare the poor boy?"

Mama folded her hands and looked down. I watched. *Something's the matter. Papa never leaves work for something like this*, I thought. It was rare for me or anyone in the family to even visit a doctor. It only happened when someone was very sick. Mama had told us boys that when she and Papa were children, neither of their families had *geld* for doctors or medicine. Babies were born at home, delivered by midwives. Often, children got very sick and even died without ever seeing a doctor or going to a hospital.

"Dr. Epstein will have an answer for us," my father said, directing his comment at my mother. A forced smile came to her lips. She slowly looked away and out of the third-story exam room window in the Blumenthal Building onto the plaza below. I tried to see her face. I noticed that she opened her purse, took out a linen hankie, and dabbed at her eyes.

"Mama, what's going on? I don't feel sick. Why are we here?" I asked. "When we came last week, why did the nurse take my blood?"

Just then, Dr. Epstein entered the examination room. That middle-aged physician had prematurely gray hair. He walked with the stooped shoulders of a man who often bore the heavy burden of bad news. Epstein wore a stethoscope around his neck and carried a manila file in his right hand. He placed the file down on the exam table next to me and carefully opened it as if it were a prayer book. Then he put his right hand on my knee and looked over at my parents. He made no small talk but immediately spoke in a grave tone. If his words had a color they would have been gray like the stones in the cemetery.

"I have never had a patient like this." My eyes darted back and forth from the doctor to my mother and then my father. "If Jake was my boy, I'd take him to Los Angeles, maybe Chicago . . . to a specialist," said Dr. Epstein, shaking his head.

Los Angeles or Chicago; I'll miss school, I thought. I liked school. The thought of leaving home, El Paso, and Doogan—our new police-dog puppy—made me queasy.

"*Was ist* a specialist?" Mama asked.

"In my training I did study about this type of syndrome: monstrous growth, consistent with that of giants," Epstein said, ignoring Mama's question.

Two words, *monster* and *giant*, pierced my ears like bullets. This would be the first of many callous doctors I would come to dislike; doctors who would want to poke, prod, and measure me like some kind of prized specimen; doctors whose callous words would almost destroy the only man I ever met who was taller than me.

I was dizzy. My heart began to pound. I felt my throat closing.

"If he keeps growing like this, by his eighth birthday he'll be close to six feet. I don't know what's going to become of him. We're not looking at the development of a normal child here."

I remember he talked as though I wasn't even there.

"What's going to happen with his schooling?" asked Mama.

"Mrs. Erlich, this is serious," Epstein rebuked her. "School should be the least of your concerns at this point. I'm worried about him."

I started to feel strange, almost like I was eavesdropping on a conversation about someone else.

I thought my father looked pale. "Dr. Epstein, is there nothing you . . . ?"

"I'm sorry, Mr. Erlich. There's nothing more I can do."

My ears buzzed. I got up off the examination table, unable to contain myself, and moved away from Epstein and my parents. My thoughts raced. *I'm not like the normal kids. Something must be wrong with me.* I moved toward the window, as if to fly right out of it.

"Jake, sit still! You're distracting me. Mind your manners," Papa commanded.

I forced myself to sit down on the exam table. My thoughts ran in no particular direction other than away, like the lizards that Doogan chased in the yard. My parents and Epstein continued their conversation. I tried to listen but all I could hear was my heart thumping. *I can't breathe*, I thought. The room grew dark, almost black. That was my first panic attack.

I had to escape. I jumped to my feet and ran to the door. Before anybody could grab me, I bolted. I almost knocked down the nurse standing in the hallway as I charged by her. Then I sprinted through the waiting room that was full of patients and dashed down the stairs and out onto Oregon Street.

I ran. I ran past the benches in the plaza and the tiled fountain with the two sleeping, olive-green alligators. I ran across the train tracks and by the St. Regis Saloon, where the old cowboys drank.

I was going at full steam when I flew off the curb at Stanton and Mills. I saw a huge mass of white out of the corner of my eye. Instantly I glanced up from the pavement and froze. The old white horse that pulled Kapilowitz's dairy wagon was rearing backward to avoid trampling me. I only hesitated for an instant. I didn't stop as I normally would to apologize for much more minor offenses than that one. I just looked back over my shoulder and heard my father's friend yell *"paskunyak"* and some other Polish cuss words that my parents used when they were furious.

After another few minutes I finally did stop. I was dog-tired. My shirt was soaked with sweat. When I began walking up the incline on Mesa Street towards Sunset Heights and our home, I plotted how I would pack a bag, some food, and run away. I could sleep in the plaza at night and go to school on my own. There was no way I would leave my brothers and Doogan to see some strange doctor in Chicago or Los Angeles or wherever.

Looking back on my life, that was the first time I tried to run away from the inevitable. Running away would become a constant theme in my life. I often wonder how a seven year old could possibly comprehend the cyclone of feelings that came with the abrupt doctor's terrible decree; feelings that were punctuated by words like "giant," "abnormal," and "monster"—words I would hear all too often in my life. Kids have trouble with emotions. Hell, so do adults.

It was dark by the time my parents got home. When I heard them approach, I looked up from my place on the wrought-iron bench on the front porch. I was sobbing, bewildered. Doogan was curled at my feet. I wanted my mother and father to make it all better. They sat down on either side of me, as they had in Dr. Epstein's examination room. My mother hugged me and drew me close. *"Sha, sha mein kind."*

"Jakey, I swear to you we'll do whatever it takes to get to the bottom of this," my father said.

If only Mama's hug and Papa's promise could have stopped the nightmare. My parents took me to many specialists in Los Angeles, Chicago, New York, any and everywhere they heard there was someone who might help me. But all of those doctors were unable to fulfill that most ancient of healing rituals. No physician could even name my condition, let alone explain or stop it.

CHAPTER 3

The River with Two Names

Watercolor, Jake Erlich

It was the kind of scene I might have easily missed looking out from the open vestibule on Car 96 of Ringling Bros fast-moving train. But as I've come to understand, in dreamtime everything is slowed down, so I could see the weathered wooden horse in detail. The faded shades of red, black, and orange made it look like a circus relic, abandoned long ago. This strange sight made me sad at its neglect, and curious as to how and why he was left there. It appeared awkward, discarded in dry, yellow grass on a high cliff overlooking the ocean.

That refugee from a midway merry-go-round was lifeless. I was surprised when the inert object stirred. First I saw the vitality in the deep-blue eyes that flashed, then in the thick, black mane, which wafted in the morning breeze.

I was awestruck at his resurrection from dead wood to breathing steed. The cedar stallion took two steps toward the cliff. Not hesitating, he stepped into the abyss. I was frightened for him.

I wanted to scream, "Stop!" but the word was frozen in my throat. Before gravity grabbed and hurled him downward to the pounding surf and jagged boulders, he unfolded powerful, feathery wings. Transformed into Pegasus, he flew across the cobalt sea and white caps far below. Overwhelmed, tears welled up in my eyes. I strained to see where he went. Almost as much as I needed to breath, I knew I must find out what happened to him next . . . but—a loud jangle from the telephone jarred me back to my bed.

I was half-awake, disoriented from my dream and hungover after too little sleep. I realized that awful noise was the wake-up call I'd requested when I finally made it back to The Algonquin from my late-night walk.

XXXX

By the time I got out of the cab at Madison Square Garden it was already mid-morning. I was worried and scared. There would be hell to pay for leveling that rube the night before. *I really hurt him*, I thought. *Maybe I killed him.*

As I made my way into the performers' entrance at the rear of the building, there was, as always, a great deal of hubbub. Vendors' trucks were competing for places to unload their wares: stocks of food for the troopers, animals, and fans; boxes full of balloons, candy, pendants; and lizards to re-supply the butchers. Everywhere there were people: troopers, some in costume, some in civilian dress; hard-working roustabouts carrying crates of this and that to repair and replace whatever that well-oiled machine had broken the night before. There was even an Indian elephant sunning himself, tied to the loading dock.

Surrounded by all of that commotion, I fearfully scanned the crowd and visualized a swarm of G-men waiting to haul me away in handcuffs. And if the cops didn't get involved, I was sure the circus would can me. I wonder why I hadn't run away and avoided that mess or just holed-up in my hotel room. But at some deep level I knew I didn't have any choice but to come back. Though I felt somehow imprisoned by my job in the circus, the ritual and responsibility of predictable, daily work had always soothed me. There was no place else I could or would go. *The only way I will ever leave Ringling Bros is boots-first.* Over my years in the sideshow that was a frequent thought.

"Good morning, Jake." A roustabout with a worn, gray knit hat pulled down around his ears, a cigarette clinched tightly between his yellow teeth, and a coil of frayed rope around his shoulder, stopped to chat with me. His easy demeanor let me know he knew nothing about what had happened the night before; I hoped no one else knew.

"Good morning, Hank," I said, hurrying past

He looked surprised. Typically I would have stopped, but not that day. Because of my recent outburst and the crappy way I felt, I was in no mood to talk to anyone. I quickly made my way to the dressing room that the freaks shared in the Garden. At two hours before the matinee I hoped I was early enough to avoid seeing any of the other sideshow performers who typically didn't arrive that early. Even though we were a tight-knit group, a family so to speak, lately being around them made me anxious. At that point, I wasn't really sure why.

I was relieved that the dressing area was empty. So as quickly as I could, I got in the cowboy costume I would wear for the matinee's opening spec. While using the mirror to tie my blue calico bandana, I heard someone behind me. I scanned the mirror to see who it was but there was no one. I gazed into the mirror once again.

"Congratulations! I hear you're a cross between Max Schmeling and Joe Stydahar. Score one for the freaks."

Immediately recognizing the telltale German accent, I turned around and looked down. There he stood, all twenty-four inches of him. Harry Doll, the famous circus personality and *pater familias* of the Dancing Dolls family of little people, was my closest friend in Ringling Bros. He approached me and put his tiny right hand on my knee.

"You're a regular monster of the midway; a protector of damsels in distress, midgets, and now, menagerie monkeys."

I looked away. His attempt at humor embarrassed and irritated me. Normally Harry would make me laugh, but that day I didn't even want to see him.

"What's wrong, Jakey? You don't seem like yourself." Harry was typically very perceptive.

"Ah, it's nothing." I briefly glanced at him and quickly shifted my gaze to the mirror. In retrospect, I think it would have been good for me to unburden my self. I wanted to tell him; I really did. I wanted to come clean about how I was thinking of leaving the circus; to report about Gargantua and the rube; and about how I almost jumped out of a twelfth-story window the night before; I wanted to tell him about everything but I just couldn't.

"By the way, I have a message for you from the boss," Harry said, interrupting my thoughts. "Ingalls wants to see you before the show today. Is it about the rube? What got into you?"

I realized that Harry wasn't going to back off. When he was curious about something he was like a bulldog that smells meat.

"I gotta go now, Harry. There's no time. We'll catch up later," I said, too anxious to stay there a second longer.

"Whatever you like, Jake," Harry said with resignation.

I just didn't want to get into things with Harry or anyone else, for that matter. As a kid, I learned *"La ropa sucia se lava en casa."* It's an old Spanish saying: "Dirty laundry should be washed at home."

I learned that proverb from Kika, the maid who helped Mama with our house. That old woman had been around for as long as I can remember.

The last time I saw her I was fifteen. She was smiling with her toothless grin, standing at the threshold to my room, holding a breakfast tray she made up especially for me.

Kika was born and raised on a *ranchito* in the hardscrabble mountains outside Chihuahua City. She walked with a limp, dragging her left foot behind her. Her lifeless leg was the result of some childhood fever that had gone untreated for lack of a doctor and the funds to pay one if he'd miraculously materialized. As I recall, Kika's gray hair was drawn back tightly in a bow, which accentuated both her round face—an artifact of her *mestizo* heritage—and the quarter-sized mole on her left check.

"Señora, tal vez le hicieron mal de ojo," Kika had said to my mother some years before at the outset of my horrendous growth.

I remember how Mama listened intensely to her, nodded and responded: "Yes! Yes! Perhaps it was a *Kina Hora* (evil eye)," she said, referring to an identical Jewish version of that Mexican belief.

Mama and Kika subscribed to the same superstition. One originated with white and blue gauze-covered Bedouins huddled in an ancient date palm oasis, the other among Mayans clad in scarlet macaw feathers crouched in an emerald jungle. Both Mayans and Bedouins, like Mama and Kika, had strained to explain the inexplicable. My father, the rational one, called these explanations *buba misas*: a grandmother's foolishness. At first, so did I. But I felt so bad in those days that I wondered if there was something to that "evil eye" business. Perhaps someone had put a spell on me.

I recalled the tray that Kika balanced on her belly that morning when I was fifteen. It was a loving attempt to get me to eat. The *azafata* was laden with a special breakfast I normally loved: steaming Mexican hot chocolate that smelled of cinnamon, almonds, and cocoa and handmade flour tortillas so fresh they melted the marigold butter she had slathered onto them into shiny riverlets.

When I turned my head away in disgust, Kika looked hurt. She was doing her best to make sense of the mean mask I wore over my adolescent sadness: *"Ay mijo, tal vez tu tristeza nació de un susto* (Oh, sweetheart, maybe your melancholy was born from a great fright you suffered)," she said.

"Tal vez," I replied, my anger only slightly diminished by guilt. When she put the tray down on my dresser, I angrily motioned for her to take it away. She stepped closer to hug me but I moved back, afraid that if I let

Kika get close I would start to weep and never stop. My tears would wash her, my parents, our meager belongings, and every house in Sunset Heights away in a flash flood of pent-up sorrow. Kika looked at me once again. Slowly, like in my dream, she stretched her right palm up to caress my cheek but she couldn't reach it.

"Ay, Dios mío," she called out, shaking her head with a smile that was equal parts grief and wonder. Then Kika picked up the tray with my uneaten breakfast, slowly turned around, and walked out of my room. I watched her limp away. The sound of her dragging foot echoed in my mind as I climbed back into bed to hide from the day.

Most people, besides my family, have no idea that I spent a lot of my life hiding. I was feeling down then, too. So down I was barely eating. As a matter of fact, I hadn't eaten much since that whole awful incident down by the river. I mentioned the river before; this is as good a time as any to tell you what happened.

It was 1921. I was just fifteen years old, already seven and a half feet tall and still growing. Summer's blast furnace had really begun to scorch El Paso and business was slow, so Papa gave Ben and me time off from working at the store. Mama had taken Myer, who was seven, with her to the synagogue where she and some other ladies from the Sisterhood were cooking a community meal to welcome Philip Roth, our new rabbi. She left Ben in charge. It didn't take him long to realize that was a perfect opportunity to get a break from the monotony and heat.

"Come on, don't be a pill. I'm so bored," Ben pleaded.

"Mom and Dad told us it's too dangerous," I resisted.

"If you don't come along I can't go. I promised I'd keep an eye on you."

"I don't wanna go," I insisted.

"Are you becoming a hermit like one of those weirdoes who live in caves in the Sierra Madres?" Ben taunted me.

"We swore we wouldn't go. Don't you remember?"

As I saw things, I wasn't a goody-two-shoes; more than anything, I just wanted to stay home and avoid people. It seemed that everywhere I went in those days, kids and adults teased me. Sometimes their taunts were downright cruel and insulting. They'd play mean tricks; even trip me. So whenever possible I preferred to stay home and keep to myself.

"I know. I know," Ben replied. "But what Mama and Papa don't know won't hurt them. Come on, Jake, you know how much fun it is and how pretty it is down there. Please, I beg you."

I looked up to my "big" brother. I liked his company and wanted to please him, so reluctantly, I let him talk me into it. If I knew what would soon transpire, I never would have gone.

Within the hour, Ben and I had made our way through the neighborhood. We walked by Vilas Elementary School, passed the Schroeder's corner grocery and the Chaldean's barber shop, and descended two flights of rickety wooden steps that led to a rocky mesa. After we hiked down it, we hurried passed the railroad siding next to the icehouse and found ourselves on the well-worn path to the Rio Grande.

The desert foliage dramatically changed as we approached the river. As if by magic, stands of Desert Willows, Salt Cedars, and Russian Olive trees appeared. Ben and I scrambled through the reeds, red flowers, and honeysuckle. We saw multicolored hawks, falcons, and cranes, not ordinarily spotted in town. As we got closer to the water, I could smell the river and the scarce moisture it gifted to the dry desert air. Just the fragrance had a cooling effect.

When we got to the water's edge, we both peeled down to our rough, cotton summer underwear. Ben didn't hesitate. He jumped from the saw grass on the edge into the stream, laughing and splashing as he landed in the brown water. Then he stood up and plodded downstream, almost knocked over by the current. Fifty yards down river, he joined two boys he recognized from school. Growing up, I often wished I had as many friends as my brother.

I sat down on the bank. A few seconds later I shooed a horsefly from my nose and wanted to be somewhere else. While I determined what to do next, the words "Rio Grande" rhythmically repeated in my mind.

Throughout my life, when anything was labeled big, like that river, it immediately tugged at my attention. On the Mexican side they called the same stream *Rio Bravo*: the fierce river. On opposite banks of the river with two names, sometimes children would fire rocks from homemade slingshots and catapult insults in English and Spanish, but not that day.

Sometimes the river was full and fast-moving. But at other times it seemed to dry up. When it almost dried up, as it had the winter before, I imagined that its life had moved underground, its spirit descending to where no one could see it. I liked the fact that the Rio Grande/*Rio Bravo* didn't always match its name. Just like me, the river did not fit with the names people called it—whatever language they spoke.

Sitting there with my knees folded up to my chest, I sensed that the river was alive, ever changing. At least for those few minutes, I felt at peace, calmed by the flowing water. Back then, peaceful times like that were islands in the stream for me; few and far between.

Somewhere up river, the last of the huge winter snow packs in the mountains of Colorado and New Mexico had melted. That, plus two weeks of strong, nightly summer monsoons made the water flow fast and free, almost flooding the banks. That day, it truly looked like a big, fierce river.

I turned my head to see that Ben and his friends had waded farther downstream to hunt for crawdads in the shade of an old oak whose branches hung out over the shallows. It was really hot. The water looked so inviting but it was too dangerous.

"Hey, Jake!" I turned and recognized a group of five boys and a girl from the neighborhood approaching. I stood up and cautiously walked toward them. You might say back then I was too trusting or pretty naive. But I think I was still innocent. Three of the boys were classmates from school. One was younger—about thirteen—as was the girl. When I got closer they began to run away.

"The giraffe, the giraffe!" the ragtag group of teenagers squealed as they galloped off in mock terror.

I think that whenever something like that happened—and it frequently did—it hurt like a punch in the gut, shattering the illusion I wanted to believe; that I might fit in with the others.

Caught up in the moment and wanting to be accepted in the new game, I chased them like a lion cub after blue wildebeest. I pursued my quarry in a gangly canter, feeling the afternoon breeze warm my face.

Winded, I finally cornered them about a hundred yards down river. They huddled under a Palo Verde tree on a bed of its fallen yellow flowers. It's been so long, I cannot remember most of their names.

A skinny boy with patched overalls and buck teeth stepped forward and pointed. "Look! It's Ichabod Crane."

Then the girl—she had freckles and pigtails—jumped out from behind one of the boys and barked, "How's the weather up there, Jake?"

Everyone laughed.

Emboldened, a chubby blond boy, a head shorter than everyone else, put his hands on his head. His outstretched fingers formed his unworldly idea of a jungle animal's ears. Then he swaggered in front of the pack. "Is it a boy? Is it a girl? No! It's a giraffe."

Soon the others picked up the chant. "Giraffe . . . giraffe . . . giraffe!" they bellowed.

Frozen, unable to flee or fight as any animal would, I just stood there. Eisenbeis—I do remember his name—stepped out from behind the others and sized up the frenzy.

He was a sixteen-year-old bully and the biggest boy in the neighborhood besides me. I'd seen him beat a boy so bad it left him unconscious. Eisenbeis was the type I tried to steer clear of. He ran around wild because his father was a drunk and his mother left him when he was little. So when he approached me as if to help, I didn't know what to make of it. But at that moment my hope for an ally made me too trusting. Against my better judgment, I hesitated.

When he got close enough, I saw a blank stare in his gray eyes, as if he was glaring at someone else. Isn't it funny that I can still remember the color of that bastard's eyes? When I realized what was happening, it was too late. Eisenbeis socked me in my groin. Then he shoved me. I was reeling from the pain and wanting to vomit. I had no idea that Tito, his henchman, was crouched on hands and knees behind me to ensure I would fall backward.

I tumbled, taking the brunt of that hard fall on my left hip. I crashed into the ground with a seismic thud. For the next six weeks I would carry a jagged purple, black, blue, and at times grotesque green bruise, the size of a small meteorite, on my hip; a memento of lost innocence—a tattooed reminder of just how malicious some kids can be.

I looked up from where I'd fallen to mean stares and crooked adolescent fingers that all pointed at me.

Don't get the wrong idea; not all the kids in my school were cruel, some—many, in fact—were gentle and kind. But those jackals were as mean as they come and they're the ones that fill this riverside memory.

I was all alone. Ben was nowhere in sight. He and his friends had wondered farther down river out of earshot. I couldn't think. It felt like I had swallowed a volcano. If I breathed too deep it would erupt, sending a cloud of ash a hundred miles high, spewing shattered pieces of myself all the way to Santa Fe.

As I scanned my surroundings I felt almost numb. The light on the riverbank was unreal, dream-like. But the pain from the bone-dry stickers that had punctured the flesh of both of my hands when I'd fallen brought me back, making me remember that I was alive. For a kid, crying in front of your peers is never a good idea but at that moment I didn't have any choice. My tears slowly started to flow. They must have stained my face a sandy brown as they merged with the dust that had come to rest on me.

Freed from my paralysis, I got to my feet and wiped my eyes. If only I could have gone back in time and helped myself through that turbulent time. I would have urged myself to punch and kick Eisenbeis before he got the drop on me. But it was too late for that.

"Never run from predators. It makes them think you're prey." I remembered the words of the old fireman that taught Ben and me to box on Sundays behind the firehouse. "Stand your ground!"

So I stood there facing them. But when a rock flew by my right ear I panicked, turned, and ran toward the river. I tripped in the reeds and scampered to my feet. A barrage of stones soon followed. Having to dodge rocks that were thrown at me when I was a kid would become all too common. Ugly scars on my right knee, chin, and in the small of my back were proof that sometimes, just like with Gargantua, the stones hit their mark.

I was trapped: on the one side, my rock-throwing tormentors, on the other the treacherous Rio Grande. A rock hit me hard on the back of my right shoulder. My only escape was the river.

Not even thinking of my parents' admonition, I ran down the bank into the water. When I was only knee-deep I slipped on green moss. I fell forward. Rocks continued to land all around me. Luckily, the river was at its widest where I had entered. Soon I was out of the range of their rocks, but they continued to hurl insults.

"Kill the Kraken! Kill the Kraken!" They screamed.

I couldn't believe what was happening. I couldn't think. I needed to escape. I dove under the murky water, propelling my giant frame far from those verbal harpoons. All that swimming helped to dissolve my panic. Gradually I surfaced, with just my head, eyes, and nose above the surface. I felt like a storybook creature, a great white whale coming from the depths. As I swam, I treasured the feeling of the water containing my huge body. I stretched my long arms and legs in the river and thrust myself forward. I felt buoyed and weightless.

The water was warm but refreshing. It had a distinct smell and taste; not salty like the ocean, but slightly metallic, woody. After about two minutes, I had reached the middle of the stream. I couldn't hear their insults any longer. I felt invigorated, reborn, and safe. Relieved to be free of danger, I finally relaxed.

Then a crocodile of an undertow took hold and dragged me down below the surface. I felt the river close its jaws around me. Desperate to free myself, I sank deeper and deeper into its belly. I swallowed water. I couldn't breathe.

Then all at once, I felt my head jerk back and my hair yanked upward as if someone or something wrenched me between worlds.

XXXX

At first I couldn't see anything. All I remember was the deafening sound of crickets. When I finally could focus, I saw Ben and his two friends looking down at me, outlined by a tapestry of topaz sky and billowy white clouds. I sat up and vomited ugly river water and bile.

"What happened?" I asked.

"You almost drowned. What the hell were you doing in the middle of the river? You know how dangerous it is out there," Ben said. I was ashamed to tell my brother and his friends about my run-in with Eisenbeis and the others. "You're damn lucky that *mojado* (wetback) came along *and* saved you," Ben continued.

I pushed myself up to my hands and knees.

"What *mojado*? Where is he?" I asked.

"He's gone," Ben said.

A few minutes later, I learned that in payment for his good deed the angel who saved my life had stolen my shoes. I don't know why he took them; they must have been too big for him. Maybe he just claimed the giant shoes as a memento. Maybe he'd try to sell them in the *mercado* (market). Maybe he kept them to pass on to his kids as a family heirloom.

I can laugh about it now but back then I was mostly ashamed. And I don't know if I was more scared that I might easily have drowned or that my parents would find out what had happened. When we finally got home, the bruises where the rocks hit me started to hurt like crazy. Those bruises took a long time to heal but the depression that came on full force after that incident never has. In fits and starts it comes and goes, but like the river with two names it never really disappears.

CHAPTER 4

The Giraffe

Hertzberg Circus Collection, Witte Museum, San Antonio, Texas

Let me finish telling you what happened at Madison Square Garden. Where was I? Oh, yes.

After I left Harry in the freaks' dressing area, I walked down the hallway and found the staircase. Slowly I climbed down the dimly lit stairwell to the basement where they kept the menagerie and where, in venues like the Garden, we set up the sideshow. I felt like a desperado fleeing to his hideout. But instead of a posse, I wanted to dodge Ingalls, the threat of being fired, and the pressure to make a decision about renewing my contract. I also wanted to avoid any circus friends with their questions about what went down the night before.

For my purposes, there was no better place to disappear than the menagerie. Before the incident with the rube it was my favorite place in the circus. There was something about that space; so full of squawking, growling animal life and feral smells that made me forget about myself.

It was 1936 and by then I'd been with Ringling Bros for ten years. At thirty, you'd think I'd know my own mind or at least have some sense of direction. In those hard times the circus was a sure bet. I got shelter, three squares a day, a fair salary, and I was a celebrity to boot. But I was miserable. Yet, when I thought of leaving I'd get scared like a kid. I felt as confused and down as I did before Papa and I had made our fateful trip to Hollywood.

When I stepped into the menagerie that morning, the first thing I did was take a look around. *This was the scene of the crime that will most likely end my circus career*, I thought.

Immediately I heard the roars and growls and breathed in the odors I'd come to love. They let me know that even in the midst of a big city the place was full of wildness. That day it reminded me of a wild place in me.

I glanced to the front of Gargantua's cage, sure I would see the rube's corpse where I had flattened him. Instead I spotted my friend Frank "Bring 'Em Back Alive" Buck speaking to a tall drink of water. When I approached the pair, Buck turned toward me. From the look on his face I couldn't tell if he was surprised or upset that I was interrupting his hunt.

"Way to go last night, mate," the lion tamer said. The woman he was talking with looked up at me and smiled.

Without thinking, I smiled back. *She must be another of Buck's fawning chippies*, I thought. It seemed like every place we played he had women. They were attracted to him like flies to sugar.

"That was one bad fellow who deserved his comeuppance," Buck said. Sometimes the lion tamer's personality matched his appearance, dashing and full of bravado. But he could also be kind and caring, not only to the animals he ran but also to his friends. He was a lean six-footer, mustached, and ruggedly handsome in his custom-tailored, khaki lion tamer's costume and brown safari jodhpurs.

"Maybe you could plead my case to Clyde Ingalls. I think he's going to fire me," I replied.

"Don't be silly, Jake. We've all got a soft spot for that gorilla. Just about everybody who works with Ringling Bros knows what Gargantua went through; taken from his mother when he was just a baby and that drunken sailor that threw acid in his face on the voyage from Mombasa. That son of a bitch left him with a scowl," he said, turning toward what I assumed was his starstruck paramour. "Please forgive my French, ma'am." The young woman nodded. "And if it wasn't for Gargantua, this show would really be hurting. So don't you worry," he added, stepping forward and patting me on the forearm.

"Who is your friend?" the woman asked.

"Oh, I'm so rude. Let me introduce you two. You know the social niceties aren't my strong suit. I don't have too much call for them on the savanna," Buck added, making a sweeping gesture to the right as if we could glance in that direction and see the African plain, complete with a herd of zebras. "Valerie McPhearson, this is my dear friend and the gentlest giant, Jake Erlich, also known as Jack Earle."

She looked up at me and extended her hand, which got lost in mine. The woman had a firm handshake.

Val was in her early thirties and about five foot nine. She had long auburn hair and wore a paint-stained brown artist's smock. I imagined the smock camouflaged her curves, long legs, and an expensive French outfit she wore underneath it. Her eyes were bright green and big; the kind a man could get lost in. They sparkled. I would come to realize that woman's beauty was intoxicating and healing. Like Orpheus's music, it made me forget, at least for a while, all my troubles. But like all drugs, I would pay a price for it.

"Val is here doing a sculpture of Gargantua for her art class at NYU," Buck explained.

I glanced across to the gorilla's cage. He was an altogether different creature from the enraged beast I'd seen the night before. Now Gargantua slept peacefully on a pile of light-green and yellow straw in the front of his cage.

I looked down to Val's rough first attempt at his likeness, resting on a small card table in front of her. On the right side of the sculpture was a mound of untouched brown clay.

To this day I don't know why I said anything, but I did. It was like the words sprang out of me with a life of their own:

"Do you mind if I take a crack at sculpting one of the animals?" I asked.

"Be my guest," she answered, clearly surprised by my request. She wasn't the only one; Buck gave me a curious look as well.

"I never thought of you as an *artiste*, Jake," Buck said. "But if you must, which one of the beasts will you use as your model?"

"I think I'll try the giraffe," I said.

"Why am I not astounded by that choice?" Buck retorted sarcastically.

When I picked up the clay no one uttered a word. The two of them just watched me kneading it.

"I'll tell you something you might not know about giraffes," Buck finally said, filling the vacuum.

Or that we might not want to know, I thought but would never say.

He was my friend but there was a certain formal distance I maintained with "the dangerous great white hunter who faced down man-eaters," especially when he was around one of his conquests. At that point, Buck did not consider me a threat.

"It goes all the way back to the early thirteenth century, when the Ming emperor commanded adventurers to search the world for riches," he began.

I shot a look over at the young lady as if to say: *You have to excuse him, Miss. My friend Frank fancies himself a history professor.*

Valerie winked at me and then turned to face Buck. I thought of my mother's admonition to avoid women who wink at you. *Oh, he's got a pigeon here*, I thought. Little did I know who the real the predator was.

"The adventurers sailed the globe with a fleet of three hundred ships and thirty thousand men. They visited thirty countries and returned home with treasures; precious stones, pearls, ivory, coral, lions, and leopards. But the most exotic gift was from the Chief of the Kingdom of Malindi in Africa," Buck explained.

"What was it?" Val asked.

"A giraffe," Buck said, pointing to my sculpture. As Buck spoke, I deliberately lost myself in the warm, pliable clay I worked between my fingers. "Jake, are you with us?" Buck's voice stirred me from my trance, bringing me back to the menagerie.

"Oh, I'm sorry; I got carried away. You were saying something about the giraffe."

"Yes, the Malindi called him *Ch'ilin*. As Frank spoke, I continued to manipulate the malleable clay in my hands. "Well, believe it or not, the Chinamen also used the word *Ch'ilin* in their language," Buck continued.

Valerie reached out and took Frank's hand coquettishly. "So don't keep us in suspense, Frank. What does *Ch'ilin* mean in Chinese?" Valerie asked.

"It's the name of a very special, mythic creature that only appears in visions to those who are most pure," Buck answered.

By then I had finished my sculpture and set it on the table next to Val's. I looked up at the penned giraffe I had been using as a model.

"Jake, you and the *Ch'ilin* have a lot in common," Val said, smiling warmly at me.

"We both eat plants?" I joked, a bit embarrassed by her attention.

"No, seriously; you both see the world from above," Val added.

You know, I've come to think we all have our own personal menagerie in us with our own Gargantuas and giraffes. Sometimes we're proud of our menagerie and sometimes were ashamed. For most, our giraffes and gorillas are invisible to everyone else. They just live in a very dark place within us that only we know. But for others, their menagerie is not only visible but dramatic and draws disturbing attention.

The young woman stepped closer to me and began circling the small artist's table to get a better look at my primitive attempt at sculpture.

Even now, I wonder what she saw in me and why I tried so hard to get to know her.

"Wow, that is really good," she said, her gaze going back and forth between the giraffe in the pen, the clay giraffe on the table, and me. "I mean, I'm impressed. This is really good," she repeated. "Who have you been studying with?"

"No one," I said laughing. "This is the first time I've done anything like this. I'm no artist," I said, dismissing her compliment.

"I cannot believe that. You're a natural." She touched my hand, as she had touched Buck's. Buck stepped forward and grabbed her hand. Though she was no longer touching me, it still felt electric. The admiration in her voice was unmistakable. I liked it.

"Hey, Jake, if you don't make it in the sideshow, or as a boxer who beats up rubes, you could give sculpting a try," Buck said.

His words stung. Normally I would not personalize the jokes he told at my expense. But that time it was hard to ignore his banter. The crack about not making it in the circus and beating up rubes was hitting below the belt. His words zeroed in on what, at that moment, were my two biggest dilemmas: my attack on the fan the night before and my future in Ringling Bros. If I knew then what I know now, I would have understood that Buck's insensitive comment was a reflection of jealousy.

"I hate to go. I'm having so much fun with you fellows, but I have to run," Valerie said, interrupting the jousting she'd just caused. "I'm due at a Junior League charity luncheon at the Waldorf," Val said, looking at her jeweled wristwatch. "I will talk to you soon," she said, taking hold of the gorilla she had been sculpting and putting it in a small cardboard box that was resting under the table. I picked up the giraffe I had just made. Val quickly began to unfold the legs on the small table and stowed it under Gangantua's cage. She turned back as she started to walk away.

"Say, Mr. Erlich, may I keep the giraffe?"

"I think Ringling Bros might have an issue with that," I replied, impressed by my spontaneity. Val chuckled. Buck just stood there and watched.

"No, you silly man. I'm talking about the sculpture. There are some people I want to show it to."

"Help yourself," I replied.

She walked back to me, took hold of the thing, put it in the box with hers, and turned to walk away again. I wondered what she would do with my sculpture. It turns out I would never see it again.

"Ta-ta, gentlemen," she said. "I'll be in touch."

As I watched Val walk away, I noticed Clyde Ingalls walking toward us across the menagerie at a fast gate. He had a determined look on his face. When he got closer, I saw a piece of paper clutched in his right hand. *He's got my contract*, I thought. I felt trapped. There was no place I could hide.

"I hope he didn't spot me," I said to Buck as I jumped to the side of the giraffe's pen.

"What's the problem, Jake?" Buck asked, looking up at me.

"I just don't want to see him right now," I replied. I was embarrassed to tell Buck the truth; that I wasn't sure about signing up for another season.

"You're edgy cause of that idiot last night, right?"

I peeked around the enclosure to spy on Ingalls. He was halfway across the menagerie and headed right for us. I quickly moved a few steps to get behind Gargantua's cage. It offered more cover from my pursuer. The gorilla turned his head and looked out at me from behind the bars with a curious expression and went back to chewing on a piece of straw. Buck followed behind me.

"Please don't tell the old man you saw me," I said, looking down at him over my right shoulder.

Then I dashed away toward the nearest exit, a door in the wall of the basement that prop men and janitors used. That exit led to a narrow, shadowy passageway that ended who knows where. Sometimes when you're running from something, you don't stop to worry about where you're headed or if you will fit. The ceiling was only about seven feet high, so I had to walk bent over. It didn't matter, since I was relieved to be getting away from Ingalls.

That feeling of using a back way, a behind-the-scenes space to hide out reminded me of all those alleys in El Paso I had taken when I was a kid.

In those days I was more and more withdrawn; in full retreat. Back alleys were my best friends, helping me avoid people. Taking alleys became a habit, a reflex for survival, providing the illusion that I could escape other people and my sadness.

One of my favorite alleys was located behind our family's Fewel Street home. That sanctuary ran for almost half a mile down the steep hill that stretched from Sunset Heights to Mesa Street.

About a quarter mile down from our house, just before the alley intersected North Oregon Street, a huge old willow tree that looked like it hadn't been trimmed in ages rested up against the fence at the rear of the Krohn place. I imagined that in 1598, when Juan de Oñate and his party of explorers first gave *El Paso del Norte* its name, they rested under that tree.

When I wanted to avoid people I would retreat to that willow and lay down under it. Sometimes when I rested there I would close my eyes, squeezing them so tightly that I'd see golden and scarlet flecks of light. Then I'd breathe in the cool shadiness, remembering, if just for a while, that I was part of the same life force that animated the tree. I liked how it towered over me. Often I'd focus on the detail of its bark, trunk, leaves, and branches. I imagined its growing roots descending deep. They led me to secret underground caverns with civilizations where I would be considered small and my worries would dissolve. As far as I knew, trees were never judged. They never felt alone or that they didn't fit in. Trees became my good friends. I'm embarrassed to admit it, but sometimes I even spoke to them.

XXXX

The narrow alleyway I'd been using to escape from Clyde Ingalls came to an end at a small door that looked plum-color in the limited light. I pushed hard and it flew open into blinding, mid-morning Manhattan sunshine. As I bent even lower at the waist and stepped out onto the sidewalk, I began to feel the stares.

After a stint in silent pictures and ten years with the circus, I had come to expect the attention. When I was on stage I'd even grown a bit numb to it. But up close and personal like that, I always found the gawkers jarring. Given the fact that I was wearing my Western costume, I drew the scrutiny of more New Yorkers staring up at me than normal.

To escape, I jumped into the first available cab I saw. "Fulton Fish Market, please," I said. There were still two hours before I would be required to line up in the backyard for the matinee's opening spec. I wanted to spend that time as far away from Ingalls as possible.

As we drove along, I was relieved by the sight of the Brooklyn Bridge, the cool breeze, and the telltale smell of fish. When I exited the taxi at the waterfront, I walked on the ancient pier. Everywhere I looked there were wooden cartons full of fish on mounds of crushed white ice—all kinds of fish: haddock, halibut, cod, snapper, blue-fin tuna, shrimp, scallops, lobster, and crab. I couldn't get enough of places like the Fulton Fish Market. The unique sights, sounds, and smells it exuded that morning got me to ignore the unwanted attention of strangers and took my mind off myself.

I loved the scene of the fishmongers marketing their wares. Just like the menagerie, there was a unique freshness, life, and mystery about that place. That day, the East River reflected the brilliant sunshine back in my direction in a million tiny diamonds of light. I ambled up to the railing, enjoying the dancing colors displayed by those shimmering, liquid prisms. A tugboat pushing a huge garbage barge north cruised upriver against the tide.

That tiny tugboat, pushing a weight that seemed larger than it could bear, reminded me of the struggle I was having about whether to stay or leave the circus. The sight of that tug and the smell of fish also made me think of another transition in my life, heralded by another boat. It took place during a life-altering trip that was supposed to be a vacation in California four years before I joined Ringling Bros.

CHAPTER 5

The Neptune

Jake dressed as Santa, El Paso circa 1916

After that awful experience with the other kids down by the river, the sadness hit me really hard and escaping it became a daily struggle. It didn't make any difference that Ben beat the hell out of Eisenbeis behind the reservoir. That melancholy was like a storm that lingered; a cold front that covered the sun for days.

I couldn't sleep. I couldn't eat. I felt so tired. Moving was a chore. Everything took too much effort. I didn't even want to brush my teeth. If I weren't for Mama and Papa and not wanting to worry them I would have never left my room. I began to think that it would have been better if the Mexican who stole my shoes had just let me drown.

How would my father react if he knew the awful things I was thinking? I wondered. *You're worthless. All you do is cause your parents pain. You'll never amount to anything. I wish you had never been born.*

I snarled at myself. I imagined punching the ugly head with its protruding jaw, bulbous nose, and pimpled adolescent skin that glared back at me from the mirror above my dresser. Thinking better of it, I smashed my fist into my thigh instead. I wanted to cry but I couldn't.

Every night I woke up sweating and unable to breathe. As alone as I felt with all of that pain, I don't think I did a very good job of hiding it from my family. My older brother told my folks that I'd been taking back alleys to avoid people. That must have been the last straw. A few days later they came up with the idea for the trip to California.

"A change of scenery; maybe some fishing. That will be good for you," Papa explained.

Little did Papa or I know how eventful that trip would be.

XXXX

Two weeks later, when Papa and I finally packed up the family's Model T Ford for our trip, I just went through the motions. For all I cared, we could have been going to Fabens to pick up a crate of cantaloupe.

We departed after sundown on Saturday, driving through the night to avoid the treacherous desert heat. For two hours, quiet had filled our car like run-off from a summer rain had deluged the arroyo we passed alongside the road back in Canutillo. Somewhere just west of Las Cruces, Papa tried to break the awkward silence, but I wasn't interested in talking. I was so cramped. Cars weren't built for seven-and-a-half footers like me, so I had to press my knees tightly into my chest or drape my feet across the seat toward Dad.

"Did I ever tell you how we ended up in El Paso?" Papa asked.

Normally he was a man of few words and even fewer vacations. But now he was taking me on one and struggling awkwardly to make conversation. Papa's words were forced. His behavior was out of the ordinary. It made me uncomfortable, as if his attempts to talk to me added to the heaviness I already felt in my chest. Strangely, I started to feel angry. I imagined myself pushing his words back at him so hard that they would fly past his face and out of the car window. Then they'd bounce along the highway until they finally rolled to stop by some Okie's worn-out mattress, abandoned by the side of the road. Papa continued to speak.

"Yes, Papa," I finally answered, looking out my window, not knowing what else to say. "But tell me again," I said, reflexively polite.

Although I've always loved and respected my father, would not have hurt him for the world, and valued honesty, I was lying to him. I had about as much interest in listening to that *misa* (story) as I had in taking that damned trip to California. When I was younger, I loved his stories. It never bothered me that I'd heard them all before. I was just grateful to spend time with him and to connect any way I could. Although I never had any children of my own, I now realize how important it is for a father to connect with his son. It was particularly important at that time of painful transition in my life.

By the time he had finished his story, we had driven into Lordsburg and needed to stop for gas, a toilet break, and a soda pop.

Back then, the culinary options for Jews who kept kosher, like us, were limited. Sure, there were lots of choices in New York or Chicago but not where we were. There wasn't even a deli in El Paso, let alone food for us in the badlands of New Mexico; so Mama had packed sandwiches of leftover brisket on *challah*, purple plums, and some of her pecan cookies.

We ate our supper without speaking, sitting on the charred stumps of two oak trees by the side of the road. Papa seemed to be wary of our surroundings. He kept glancing from the road to where our Ford was parked, as if expecting someone. I was just beginning to understand why people constantly need to be looking over their shoulders.

"I'm going to get some sleep," I said as we pulled out of the filling station. I was determined to avoid any further conversation.

I looked away from him and out my window. My attention was drawn to the Big Dipper and then to the North Star. They were so clear in the dark desert sky. By the time we hit the Arizona state line it was past midnight. Despite the darkness, the nighttime temperature still hovered at an uncomfortable one hundred degrees.

My clothes clung to my sweaty body. I reached my right arm out the open window to try to escape the claustrophobic heat in that confining car. Even though I knew what to expect, I was surprised by the temperature of the sirocco. It scorched me. The burning wind divided around my arm, a colossal peninsula of flesh and bone; my outstretched fingers, fiords.

Just outside of Phoenix, I woke with a start as our car skidded off the road. It was lucky for us my father hadn't been driving very fast.

"I'm sorry, Jakey. I must have dozed off," Papa said.

A few minutes later he pulled the Model T to the side of the road to get some rest. He parked under a stand of saguaro cactus silhouetted by the light from a late-rising sickle moon. Papa immediately began to snore.

I was restless and couldn't sleep. I looked over at him and wondered what would become of me. I still didn't understand why we had come on that trip. Money was tight and vacations were rare. Why did he take me and not Mama and my brothers? Why had he chosen that time for our road trip? After a while, the questions and concerns that were filling my head were drowned out by a symphony of palo verde beetles, cicadas, and crickets. I drifted off into a dreamless sleep.

If it hadn't been for a flat tire just outside of Indio where boards, not asphalt, served as the road, we would have made it to Santa Monica—or as some of my parents' friends called it, the Coney Island of the West—by morning. Instead we arrived at noon.

I would learn that my father was a practical man. He had a clearly defined agenda for our trip. I had no idea that fishing wasn't the primary purpose of our holiday.

As soon as we checked in to the beachfront hotel where we were to stay, Papa suggested we take a walk on Santa Monica's bustling streets. We were supposed to be looking for a fishing store to buy gear for our excursion the next day. I was tired, but Papa insisted.

We walked up Ocean Avenue towards Wilshire Boulevard. People constantly stared at me. Papa seemed oblivious; he just ignored all the attention. I wished I could have. He stopped and spoke in English and Yiddish with passersby on almost every block. At first I just stood by in silence, clenching my jaw and gritting my teeth, wishing I'd never come on that trip. I hated all the attention. When people stared at me like they did that afternoon in Santa Monica, I wished to be invisible; that I would actually disappear. But after two hours of trudging all over Santa Monica and encountering an infinite number of gaping strangers, I'd had enough. I couldn't take it anymore. My head throbbed with one of my all-too-frequent headaches.

We were walking away from a small grocery store. He had spent ten minutes chatting with the business's apron-clad owner who had been sweeping the sidewalk. I stopped abruptly, spun around, and looked down at Papa.

"We've been walking for two hours. You've stopped and talked to more people than a Tammany Hall politician: Polacks, Hungarians, *Galizianas*, even *Litvaks*. Here's a bait and tackle shop we've already passed three times," I snarled, pointing to a sign above a store. "Papa, what in the Sam Hill is going on?"

He smiled sheepishly.

"Jakey, do you still mind the people?" Papa's question took the wind out of my sails long enough for me to think about what had been happening on our walk.

"Do you mean to tell me that all this searching for fishing gear was just to get me out with the crowd?" Even though I glared down at him, my father, like little David sizing up Goliath, stood his ground.

"Just answer my question," he said firmly.

"I can't believe . . . !" Exasperated, I took a deep breath, inflating my cheeks like a blowfish. I sighed, hesitated, then closed my eyes and shook my head in frustration. Finally, sensing what Papa needed to hear, I tried to placate him. "Well I . . . I . . . I guess I don't mind them. Well anyway, not as much as I did before." I struggled to hide my sarcasm, sure I didn't sound convincing.

Papa looked up at me and unloaded both barrels of what he'd been thinking.

"You've got to toughen up, kid. Just because they are looking doesn't mean that they are laughing at you or that they know anything about you."

Without uttering another word, Papa spun around on his heels and entered the fishing store. For about a minute I remained frozen, staring in disbelief at the empty space where he had stood an instant before. Back then my father knew just what to say to exasperate me, particularly when he said something I really needed to hear.

XXXX

That night, after a dinner of herring, corn beef, and cabbage stuffed with rice and raisins at a nearby kosher restaurant, Papa and I returned to the boardwalk. Then we stepped onto the beach, took off our shoes and socks, and rolled up our trousers. The tide was out. I ran a zigzag pattern out to where tiny waves lapped up on the beach and back to Papa. He strolled in the hard-packed sand closer to the shore. After two days of driving through the desert, the cool, salty air felt refreshing. The beach and the boardwalk were crowded. People flocked to the seashore for a moonlight swim, to enjoy the steel Ferris wheel on the pier, to indulge in frozen bananas dipped in chocolate and peanuts, to spoon on the beach, or to Charleston at one of the popular casinos.

After a while, Papa spoke to me from his heart about not wasting energy and time on what strangers think, about not giving up before even starting, about accepting what can and cannot be changed. I tried to listen, I really did, but the constant swish of the surf, the bright lights and mirrored music of the pier's merry-go-round, the laughter, and the sounds of an orchestra escaping through a half-open ballroom window in a nearby casino grappled for my attention. Looking back on it, I didn't want to listen to what Papa said. The distractions helped me avoid the painful realities and challenges he pushed me to face.

XXXX

Each morning I relished the chugging, almost meditative sound of the diesel engine that propelled our rickety old fishing boat through Santa Monica Bay. Before sunrise, Papa and I, along with twenty other men and a half-dozen boys, sailed from the pier on the *Neptune*.

On the second morning, I recall glancing back from my place by the railing on the starboard side of the bobbing boat and drinking in the orange-and purple-hued daybreak sky. I watched a black plume rising from the smoke stack disappear in the breeze. A swarm of cackling seagulls flew just below it, looking for a snack of discarded bait or fish entrails that wouldn't be served until afternoon.

A fine salt spray covered my face. Being out in nature like that gave me a needed break from my self-consciousness. Although I still got stares from the other fishermen, my surroundings were so dramatic that they almost drowned out my need to blend in. If I noticed someone looking my way I could easily divert my attention to the ocean, the sky, my gear, or the schools of fish I imagined swarmed under the sea.

Later, as I baited my hook with a slippery sardine, Papa cast his line into the white-capped fishing bed where the *Neptune* was anchored. I carefully cocked my right wrist to my ear. My rented fishing rod flexed. As I whipped my arm forward, the baited line flew a third of a football field farther than my father's had.

"You seem to be standing a bit straighter today, Jake," Papa commented as he rewound his fishing reel.

I didn't respond. I didn't know if he was right or it was just wishful thinking. It would take a few more years, but I would come to recognize that changes in my posture reflected changes in my mood. I normally felt tense and withdrawn, so I tended to hunker down. Perhaps I avoided standing tall because I was frightened to get a glimpse of what more anguish might exist beyond the uncontrollable reality I'd experienced since I turned seven. Maybe I constricted myself and didn't stand tall in some futile hope that that would stop me from growing; that I could will myself to be ordinary and end the nightmare before things got worse.

XXXX

That day, like we did each afternoon, when the *Neptune* docked, Papa and I gave our catch— bonita, red snapper, and albacore—to poor folks who gathered where the fishermen came ashore. As we disembarked, I carried the burlap bag that held the prizes from our day at sea. It was wet with a salty smell of ocean.

Once we were on the pier, an old gray beard with an olive complexion approached me. He walked with a limp like Kika. Then the old man snatched the bag from my hand. As he limped away, I heard him mutter "*Evaristo* (Thanks)." The strange sound of that word dissolved into the hustle and bustle of the Santa Monica Pier in late afternoon.

I turned around to find Papa. When I reached him I noticed that two odd characters had joined the crowd. Their apparel and the way they stared at us made them stand out. Instead of wearing sweaters and bait-stained denim and khaki like the others, these gentlemen were dressed for high tea. I think I was so aware of their clothing because I'd been envious. You see, I'd always worn hand-me-downs. The taller and thinner of the two wore a charcoal-gray suit and a black fedora on his balding head. The short and rotund one sported a coffee-colored houndstooth suit, a chocolate-brown derby, and a neatly trimmed moustache. He puffed on a half-smoked panatela.

Though I was drawn to the fine, big-city clothing they wore, something about them put me off. The two oddballs stared at me in a manner that made the hair on the back of my neck stand up. They were eyeing me with hunger and anticipation, just like the rest of the crowd was eyeing the burlap bags that the *Neptune's* passengers were schlepping ashore. I would shortly learn that those two were looking for a different kind of a meal.

"Papa, the men in the suits are staring at us," I said, elbowing my father.

"Just ignore them," Papa replied. Before he could finish his thought the two well-dressed strangers pounced.

"Excuse me sir," said the short one. I took a step back. "Can we please have a word with you?"

For an instant I imagined the cigar smoker looked like the *Neptune* would have if it were reincarnated as a man and stood upright. The tall one seemed to be measuring me with his eyes. Papa stepped in front of me, taking a protective stance.

"Why, what's this about?" he asked in a prickly tone.

"You seem kind of touchy," the short one said.

I saw Papa clench his fists. "What business is it of yours how I seem?! You two best back off from my boy and me or you'll be sorry," Papa threatened. He's always been so protective.

"I'm so sorry if we have offended you, but we have a business proposition," said the small one.

"Who the hell are you and what do you want?" Papa challenged with the same tone I'd seen him use with snake-oil salesmen who, from time to time, came into the store.

"My name is Zion Meyers," said the taller of the two.

"And I'm Jerry Ash," added the shorter one.

It turns out they were talent scouts and silent comedy film pioneers who represented Century Comedies and Universal Pictures. "We work with Carl Laemmle, the studio president. Maybe you've heard of him?" Ash continued.

Papa looked back at me and in a tone he normally saved for German Jews who looked down on the rest of us, he muttered: "*Er es groisachti* (He thinks he is a big to-do)."

"If you don't mind, what is your name, sir?" Meyers asked.

I saw the muscles tighten in Papa's jaw. For a moment, he stood there in silence as if to say: I do mind.

Finally he answered: "My name is Mr. Erlich, and this is my son, Jacob."

"So you just came to Los Angeles for a fishing trip, Mr. Erlich?" Myers was making a statement with his question but I wasn't sure what he was trying to say.

"That's right . . . and we don't want to be bothered. I'm not interested in buying whatever it is you're selling.

"Please hear us out, sir," Ash continued. "I'm sorry if we offended you with our attention but when you come to the moving picture capital of world, how could you ever think you wouldn't get noticed? Since you got to town, the tom-toms have been pounding."

Papa looked at me in a silent appeal for a translation of that Jazz Age metaphor but I had no idea what it meant either.

Sensing our confusion, Ash rephrased his remark. "Since you two arrived, word has spread like wildfire about a boy giant."

Meyers took a half step forward. "People in our line of work would kill to sign somebody up who can pull the kind of attention your boy can!"

"Nobody else has talked to you about the flickers?" Ash added.

"The flickers have not been such a big deal for us," Papa shot back. "Please *geh weg* (go away). We're not interested in you or your movie business." Papa grabbed my arm and we started to march down the pier toward Ocean Avenue. I felt embarrassed. I towered over Papa, yet he was treating me like a child.

As I felt Papa tug me along, I wanted to stay and hear what those two had to say. *Wow, the movies*, I thought. *Why was Papa so harsh? After all, they hadn't done anything so bad.*

I turned around to see Myers and Ash looking at each other in amazement. It turns out that Los Angeles was full of people who were constantly scouting for new and unique talent to help their movies stand out from all the rest that rolled out of Hollywood. The town was full of actors who would have given their eyeteeth for such an opportunity.

Like cheetahs who've gotten a scent of prey, they ran after us. I heard their footsteps just behind us. Papa and I stopped. He turned around to face our pursuers, his face red.

"Please, Mr. Erlich . . . hear what we have to say. It's a great opportunity for this *bocher* (young boy) and your family. All we ask is fifteen minutes," Ash pleaded.

That was a one-in-a-million chance. At that instant I didn't stop to think about the downside, about how scary it would be to leave my family in El Paso, to move to Los Angeles alone and to work in pictures. Somewhere deep inside I didn't feel frightened. I just felt desperate. I understand that sometimes fate uses desperation to make itself heard. For the first time in my short life I had the opportunity to reach for the brass ring. When would somebody like me ever get a chance like that again? No matter what Papa thought, I couldn't let it pass me by.

"I think we should listen to what they have to say," I said.

Papa turned to look at me. We were both surprised at my audacity. You see, in those days, neither of us was accustomed to me speaking up like that. Asserting myself would be a lifelong challenge.

Papa must have seen the determination in my eyes. He looked away and grumbled a word or two in Yiddish and stared out over the railing on the pier to the ocean. He looked as if he were waiting for something or someone, perhaps a tramp steamer from Shanghai that carried a mysterious passenger who would tell him how to resolve his ambivalence about what to do next.

"Okay, okay, but just fifteen minutes is all." Papa finally agreed.

To this day I don't know why Papa changed his mind. Maybe it was his destiny, too. I felt relieved. Ash and Meyers looked like they just received a stay of execution from a firing squad. Papa locked like he was still ready to pull the trigger.

The four of us ducked into The Crab Catcher, a seedy restaurant at the end of the pier. The first thing I noticed when we entered that place was the smell of stale beer and the two drunken sailors at the bar, their heads pillowed on their arms.

An apron-clad waitress with curly blonde hair and very red lips led us across the sawdust-covered floor to a small table in the back. From the moment we sat down with the well-dressed cheetahs I sensed Papa's impatience. Three of us ordered cherry pie and coffee; Papa just waived his hand curtly: "Nothing for me."

For about five minutes no one said a thing. After Papa's initial outburst, Ash and Meyers seemed to be cautious, politely avoiding any semblance of a hard sell. They just sat there and looked at us as they ate their pie.

I looked up at the thick, black fishing net and white buoys that hung from the roof of the darkened restaurant serving as ersatz maritime décor. When Papa took out his Hamilton pocket watch to check the time, I saw myself as a huge swordfish, frantically thrashing about in that net.

What Meyers and Ash didn't know was that when Papa said we only had fifteen minutes, he meant business. Now there were only ten minutes to go. Soon Papa would say time was up. *Hurry up you schmendriks*, I thought. Finally, Ash put down his fork and wiped his lips with the napkin.

"Mr. Erlich, we would like to offer your son a contract to try him out working as an actor in pictures at Century Comedies. We can make him a star. Someone like your boy would be perfect for—"

"Huh?!" my exhale was punctuated by a question mark and shock. The whole thing felt unreal, like a dream.

"Whoa, whoa!" Papa almost yelled, as if he were still in the Russian Cavalry. For a moment I imagined him atop a runaway horse that had his ear shot off, sawing at the reins, and trying to stop his stampeding mount.

I felt sick. I felt I was about to cry. I put my hand over my face. *He's going to ruin it. He's going to ruin it. I don't know what it is yet, but he's going to ruin it*, I thought. Patience was a virtue I had yet to learn. Suddenly, I confronted the loss of a destiny I hadn't even known I had just a half hour before.

"My son's not an actor, much less a professional actor," Papa argued.

I stopped myself from slamming my hands down on the table. I felt wild. "Papa don't you remember, I've had a year of drama at El Paso High?" I pleaded.

"Don't worry about that," said Meyers. "We can teach him to act. He'll make a good living. Anyway it's only for one picture. If you or Jake is unhappy after we finish shooting, then you can stop. But if he likes it—and you like it—this could be the beginning of something big."

"What do you have to lose?" asked Ash.

"Yeah, Papa, what do we have to lose?" I added for emphasis.

Papa held up his hands. My father could be stubborn, especially if he felt forced into something. But I couldn't hold myself back. I experienced a unique feeling I'd never had; certainty about what I wanted to do. That kind of certainty would be in short supply when it came to making my decision about staying or leaving the circus.

After a minute, Papa looked at me and then at the two men. He looked down at his folded hands on the gingham tablecloth. Then, as though it weighed fifty pounds, he slowly lifted his head.

"This is a *ganza* (big) decision. I need to think about it and talk to the Missus. I will contact you within the week." Papa abruptly stood up and extended his hand.

Myers and Ash looked uncomfortable. After all, they were so close to closing the deal. I bet it was unnatural for them, but they must have sensed the need to go slow with someone like Papa.

At that moment I was elated, flying, but I bit my lower lip almost until it bled. That forced me to come back down to the real world. I reminded myself that Mama would be more difficult to convince than Papa.

On the taxi ride back to our hotel I couldn't believe what was happening to me. I was so anxious my head spun. I could barely think, let alone listen to Papa speak.

"I don't know, Jakey. The movies . . . such a big city . . . what about school? We'll have to call Mama."

I took a deep breath as he spoke. I whiffed the scent of something sweet yet distant, like the aroma of the first tiny honeysuckle blossom in the desert in late winter. You can't see it, yet you're sure it's there. You might say that for the first time since I was seven, I smelled hope.

XXXX

That night, sleep was definitely out of the question. But that sleeplessness was different than what I had experienced earlier in the summer. I wasn't haunted by memories of what Epstein and the other doctors had foretold for my future or by the traumatic memories of cruel taunts and teasing. I was thrilled but also frightened.

Earlier that night, Papa had challenged me. He recalled how I had spent the summer hiding in my room and how, in my effort to avoid people, I had even skipped out on my job as a lifeguard at the reservoir. Later, tossing and turning in the cramped hotel bed, I played and replayed Papa's words. They were like a song in my head, the kind you can't forget.

"How will you ever handle all the attention?" he'd said to me.

Papa was right; I loathed attention. Yet, the December before, when I wore the raggedy Santa suit in front of my parents' store, I remember how I felt absolutely carbonated. That mangy costume felt comfortable. When I did my Saint Nick impression, the ragtag group of children and not a few adults swarmed me on the sidewalk. The commotion brought out Morris Thurmond, the photographer whose studio was across the street. When he set up to take my picture, about a hundred shoppers—Mexicans, Texans, and a few Tigua Indians—all rushed to be in that shot. The three hours I spent in costume went by like three minutes. I felt free in a way I'd never felt before. I never told Papa or Mama, but I couldn't wait for next Christmas. That's kind of strange for a Jewish boy.

I wondered if playing roles in Hollywood would make me feel like that. I started to drift off. If Mama blessed this whole business, which was very unlikely, I couldn't imagine what life in the movies would really be like; just like later when I couldn't imagine what life would be like without the circus. How would I learn to act in front of a camera? Would my bosses be kind? I had only been away from my mother and father once. That was just a weekend trip with the Kahn's when I was eight and went with them and Abbie to their cabin in Cloudcroft. Since there was no way I'd fit in their bunk beds, I had to sleep on the floor. Those two days I was up there with them in the mountains, I cried myself to sleep. How could I ever live on my own without my family?

The last thing I remember that night in our hotel in Santa Monica was a gray image: me under bright lights in a brown cowboy outfit, complete with boots, sheep skin chaps, silver-engraved six-guns, a tin star, and a ten-gallon hat. Just before I fell asleep, I thought I heard the crisp, booming sound of a movie director's voice: "Roll 'em."

XXXX

At about seven o'clock the next morning, we called Mama from the pay phone in the hotel lobby. I bounded down the three flights of stairs well ahead of Papa, carrying *Treasure Island* in my right hand. I was so anxious for him to make the call; I figured reading would help me pass the time. Books have always helped me to calm down. But that morning I couldn't concentrate enough to read even one sentence. I waited impatiently for Papa by the stairs.

It seemed like it took him two weeks to reach the lobby. When he finally did, we walked past the registration desk and Mrs. Tomasic, the hotel owner's mother. She seemed to perennially stand guard from her post; her small, ancient frame almost hidden by the overstuffed green and orange floral couch where she always sat in the middle of the room.

Mrs. Tomasic put down her *Daily Forward*. How could I ever have imagined that newspaper would write articles about me in the future? She looked us up and down as if we were thieves in the night, and grunted, "*Guten Tag*." Without so much as a smile, she lifted her paper and began reading again.

At that early hour, besides the desk clerk and a skinny bellhop whose pants were too short, Mrs. Tomasic was the only person in sight. I was relieved. I didn't want a pack of strangers eavesdropping on my parents' discussion about my future.

Papa approached the public telephone that was mounted on the middle of a beige wall at the rear of the lobby next to a magazine rack. He lifted the large black receiver and rapidly depressed the metal lever that had supported it two times.

"Operator, operator," he demanded. An instant later I heard Papa say, "I want to make a station-to-station collect call to El Paso, Texas. The number is 4256."

Papa replaced the receiver and looked over at me where I was standing about four feet behind him. I took a step closer. Mama would have just opened Geneva for business. I imagined her standing in front of the open safe, counting out the U.S. currency and Mexican pesos she would use to make change for customers. At that hour, Ben would be washing the windows and Myer would be dusting the glass showcases in the store.

The phone rang. "Yes, yes my name is Erlich, Isadore Erlich," Papa said. "Hello *Mamala*, it's *Yitzhak*. No, nothing is wrong! We are having a wonderful time. But I have something very important to tell you . . . No! I promise nothing is wrong . . . Jakey is right here . . . Yes, he's fine."

I inched closer and struggled to make out what they were saying, but not so close as to make my father feel I was intruding. I held the book in front my nose, but even Long John Silver couldn't hold my attention. Papa lowered his voice to prevent me from hearing. I knew he was telling Mama about the meeting with Meyers and Ash and their offer.

I imagined that Mama's scream of disapproval was so deafening it pierced the distance and traveled across three states from Texas to the Pacific Coast without the need of Mr. Graham Bell's invention: *"No . . . No way . . . never . . . not over my dead body will I let my little boy move to such a God-forsaken place with strangers—actors no less! Hollywood. Puey."* I could just see her spitting as she enunciated the word. *"He's just a child. How do you know these two talent scouts aren't* ganuveem *(thieves)*?"

Papa's voice brought me back to the real world.

"I know I know, but he's been so sad. When he finishes school if something should happen to us, how will he make a living in El Paso?" Papa asked.

In order to keep my fearful fantasy about Mama's response at bay, I anxiously tried to weave together the entire conversation from the few fragments I heard.

"Yes, of course . . . but maybe the movies would be a place where his height would help him."

I found myself pacing back and forth.

"Ya, ya, I'm worried about it as well. Who would watch him? Show people?"

"Papa!" I roared. He was about to murder my movie career. The sound of my own voice startled me. It woke up the bellhop, who had fallen asleep where he was standing. It got the clerk to raise his head from the numbers he was inscribing in the ledger. It so unnerved Mrs. Tomasic that she looked up from her newspaper and angrily opened it to the next page. But Papa just ignored me and went on talking. I wanted to grab the phone from Papa's hand and beg Mama to let me accept the offer and move to Hollywood.

"Certainly, but he'll never be happy working in the store. It's not for him," he continued. Papa was right. "I hate to say it, but . . . " His voice trailed off so I couldn't hear the rest of what Papa said.

Then there was an uncomfortable, and what felt like unending, silence. Papa listened for several minutes, nodding his head in agreement as the words that would determine my fate were magically transported across space. I watched Papa, but visualized Mama slicing and carving the idea of me moving to California and finally, in a fatal *coup-de-grâce*, stabbing it in the heart. I looked down at the hotel lobby's warped wooden floor and mourned for the loss of my future.

"We'll take the first train tomorrow morning. Don't worry about the car. The Gattagnos are out here on vacation. I'm sure they wouldn't mind driving the Ford back and saving the train fare . . . Ya, I love you, too!" Then he hung up.

Slowly, Papa turned to gaze up at me, understanding my need for an immediate answer. He looked mischievous. "I'm not sure, Jakey. We'll see what Mama says when we get home," he said with a sly smile and a wink.

It wasn't like my father to wink. He wasn't a winking sort of a man.

"Papa!"

Reborn with hope and possibility, my mind danced. I started to ask him a question.

"*Sha*!" Papa held up his right hand to stop my onslaught. "Not another word until we get home."

I bit my tongue and galloped to the stairs, taking them two at a time. When I reached our room, I was so wound up that I ran into the closed door and dropped my book. Questions that my excitement had kept at bay began to come to me, first in a trickle, than in a flood.

If I move to Hollywood, where will I eat? Where will I sleep? Inside the room, I spun around and around trying to remember where I stashed my suitcase. I noticed that my spinning quieted my questions, though just for an instant. The questions resurfaced, louder and more intrusive. *Will they stare at me? Who will look after me? What if I get sick? What if I make a mistake? Will they yell at me? Will they laugh?*

I spun faster and faster, whirling like some kind of a dervish, intoxicated on the divine. I crashed into the bedside table and sent the lamp flying. Moving so fast, fueled on excitement and the need to flee my reservations, I couldn't stop or calm myself. I collapsed on the bed, breathless and uncertain about the promise of a future I never dreamed possible.

Even if I could have spun as fast as a Sufi and answered the torrent of all those questions with the wisdom of a *gaon* (a Talmudic Scholar considered a genius), I could not have foretold the hard knocks and danger that lay ahead, the least of which was Papa's anger at me because of the lamp I had just destroyed.

CHAPTER 6
The Grand Parade

"Burlesque," Jake Erlich

It was the scent of orange blossoms and coal dust that I remember most the instant Mama, Papa, and I got off the train in City of the Angels. If it hadn't been for the distraction of those intoxicating smells, I was so claustrophobic I would have trampled the swarm of travelers that encircled me as we crept down the platform. Once finally inside the terminal, I recall one wall of the baggage claim area of Union Depot as being covered with a colorful mosaic, the likes of which I'd never seen before. Its shiny turquoise, gold, and scarlet tiles chronicled settlers of all sizes and shapes exploring and building the new world that was to become California.

I wondered what that new world had in store for me and I for it. I was determined to make the most of this golden opportunity to make my way in the world and make my parents proud of me. I wasn't afraid of hard work, but what terrified me was not fitting in yet again. Looking back on it now, my plan was very simple: I would do what I was told to make it in movies. I was lucky it would work out so well, but I almost got myself killed. My experience in Hollywood would get me to see that being a man required much more than being a good boy.

I had been anxious ever since Mama had shocked me with her positive attitude, approval, and out-and-out insistence that I move to Hollywood and begin working in movies. In later years Mama would tell me how she didn't sleep a wink or even eat after the phone conversation when Papa first broached the idea. As soon as she hung up the telephone that morning, she had run to the *schul* to seek Rabbi Roth's sage counsel. Through her fear, tears, and once even uncharacteristically raising her voice to the rabbi in disagreement, she finally accepted—painful as it was for a worried mother—that the move to Los Angeles was about what was best for me, and not what was comfortable for her and Papa.

I stared out the window during the cab ride from the train station to the small boarding house where we would stay. At that time, Hollywood, which had once been a full day's wagon ride from the center of town, was still a youthful and pristine community; a sweet suburb more than the city it would become.

I was fascinated but also worried. To me, everything felt new, different, and threatening. In retrospect, I know it was there that I played a part in the golden age of silent films, or as they would later call it in the history books, the "Grand Parade." But back then I was a nervous wreck. I hated the fact that there was nothing I could do to prepare for whatever awaited me in my new career. I just had to wait.

To take my mind off of things, Mama, Papa, and I spent the next few days sightseeing. To be honest, touring the town didn't help a bit. I was overwhelmed. If I could have, I would have camped out on the doorstep of Century Studios. Though I tried, I could not stop worrying about what was going to happen on my first day of work. It's funny that it takes getting old or sick to appreciate each new moment for all it has to offer.

"Don't concern yourself, son," Papa had reassured me. "Those men who make the flickers are professionals. They know you're a novice. They'll ease you into things. Nothing will happen in your new movie career until you've got a firm grip on the reins and you're ready for it."

As Papa always says, *"mensch tracht unt Gott lacht* (men talk and God laughs)."

XXXX

"Wake up, Jake. It's time to go," Papa said at six thirty in the morning exactly five days after we arrived.

Pulling the covers over my head intensified the chill and gooseflesh on my uncovered feet and legs that hung over the end of the boarding house bed. My custom-made divan would not arrive for another month. It took about that long for me to get accustomed to those cool California mornings.

"You don't want to be late for your first day at the studio, do you?" Papa's voice echoed his excitement for this new opportunity.

Not feeling that there was anything at all auspicious about that early hour, I turned away from him and rolled over. My anxiety had marched back in force, and that morning I was not in the least inclined to wrestle with any of my demons.

"I feel sick to my stomach," I moaned. "Just let me sleep."

Papa didn't buy into my excuse. "Not on your life, mister! If you don't get your *tuchas* out of bed in the next minute, I'm going to pour a pitcher of cold water on your head."

He was determined. In part, Papa's determination was driven by an intense work ethic. Flu, fever, diabetes, even broken bones didn't keep him away from the store. He never missed a day of work until his coronary in 1948. But that morning, Papa wasn't only driven by his work ethic; he knew how important that opportunity was for me. He wasn't about to let me wreck it because of a bellyache—feigned or real.

I must have realized that, because at that moment my certainty that he meant business got the better of my anxiety. I sat up. "All right, all right; just give me a minute."

"The clock is ticking. You've got thirty seconds left," Papa threatened.

Did I mention he was always a stickler for punctuality? I stretched and shook my head from side to side, as if stretching and shaking were antidotes for the massive uneasiness that swooped down on me as I slept. I willed myself to get out of bed and hurriedly dressed.

In the apartment's little kitchenette, my mother had prepared a big breakfast of fried eggs, kippered herring, toast, and coffee.

"Not this morning, Mama." I rushed past her to the door, sure if I smelled the fish I would vomit.

When Papa emerged from the boarding house a few minutes later, he looked surprised to see me waiting for him on the sidewalk.

Soon Papa and I were walking down Sunset Boulevard, making our way toward Poverty Row, where Century and a swarm of other small movie studios were located. We both looked dapper in the black suits and neckties we had bought especially for that trip at Bellman's Dry Goods back home.

"You can't go wrong with black," Sam Bellman had said. "It's an investment, good for weddings, funerals, and *Bar Mitzvahs*."

Now he could add that a black suit is just right for a young man's first day making silent pictures. Papa's suit came off the rack. Mine had to be custom-made. My father insisted we get dressed up, at least for my first day on the job. "First impressions, Jakey . . . we don't want them to think were *greenas*, right off the boat."

XXXX

A few minutes after we stepped out of the boarding house, I spied them trailing us like a pack of coyotes. Half of them were in the street and half on the sidewalk. Some were pointing at me. The old feelings rushed me. I frantically looked back then down at my dad. He didn't seem to notice. Scanning the street, searching for a place to run to and hide until dark, I spotted an alley between a druggist and a five-and-dime. Just as I started to break away, Papa grabbed me. He yanked my arm, and with it my attention.

"Come on, Jakey! You've got to get used to this. Just ignore them. Somehow you've got to get ahold of yourself. You might as well start right now."

He just stood there, holding on to my arm, with people staring at us.

"Just give me a minute, Papa." I looked back at my pursuers once again, turned away, and tried to forget about them. This was an inauspicious beginning to my movie career. "I'm ready now," I said after I'd composed myself as best I could.

Papa and I continued walking toward the studio. "Think about it, *boychik*. If you were normal size and you saw a man walking in the street that was twice as big as you, wouldn't you stare too?" Papa asked.

I grumbled some inaudible answer and diverted my attention to the young palm trees that lined the broad boulevard. In those days, they barely came up to my knees. As we walked, we passed California stuccos in pale green. I particularly admired the Spanish style architecture of the bride's-breast pink and salmon colored residences. But as we approached Poverty Row, things changed. In jarring contrast, every structure, whether it was a bungalow, fence, or wall, was painted dark industrial-gray.

Century Comedies, where even in my wildest dreams I could never have envisioned myself working, was situated on the southeast corner of Sunset and Gower, about a mile from where we were staying. The exact address was 6100 Sunset. On the west side of the street stood Christie Studios and there was an Italian restaurant called The Napoli on the north side of the intersection. The food was very good, but I would come to wish I had never eaten one meal there.

In the old days, the Century Studios property was a rambling farm complete with a huge barn and outbuildings. When Julius Stern and his brother Abe bought and turned it into a movie studio, they tore down just about everything but the barn and rebuilt a bunch of structures. When we finally reached the entrance to the main office, housed in a small bungalow, adrenaline began coursing through me.

Papa ambled through the door first. As I had to do in most doorways, I bent over to make my way inside. But in my excitement, I miscalculated and smacked my head hard. When I was no longer seeing stars, the first thing I remember was a sweet, smoky odor. Soon I would learn that that was the sharp smell of raw film.

The bungalow's unpainted interior contained two desks piled high with papers, long black pieces of film, photos, and newspaper and magazine clippings. Unlike our home in El Paso, which was always impeccably neat, that place was unbelievably cluttered. It was such a mess that I thought if Mama were there she would have grabbed me by the arm and taken me home on the next train.

"What do you want?" asked the woman seated behind one of the desks.

Papa and I froze in our tracks. I would learn that that crotchety woman was Kitty, the secretary to the Stern Brothers. She was about Mama's age and spoke with dramatic flair in a nasal New York accent. Kitty was a block of a woman, as tall as she was wide. She had a pointy nose and chin to match, which made me think of her as a witch who guarded a bridge in some German fairy tale. She wore a plain black dress that was so large I imagined that under it she stored her broom, her cauldron, and a squad of evil gnomes who did her nasty bidding.

"What do you want?" she asked again in a now impatient tone.

I wanted to leave and come back another time.

Papa shook his head as if tasting a shot of strong *schnapps* and tried to remember the purpose of our visit. The woman in the black dress put me off; I thought she was rude and I didn't like her. First impressions can be deceiving. Mine certainly were about Kitty.

"Ahem," he made a noise to clear his throat. "I'm Mr. Erlich and this is my son, Jacob. We have an appointment with Julius Stern. We were referred by Mr. Meyers and Mr. Ash."

"Of course." Kitty knew exactly who we were and why we were there. Her belligerence was just for show, a weird initiation rite for newcomers to Century Comedies. "Please have a seat. Mr. Stern will be here soon."

As commanded, Papa sat down in one of two wooden, canvas-backed picnic chairs placed in front of one of the desks. Because of my dimensions and all the furniture I had broken in the past, I had gotten quite adept at assessing whether or not a chair could hold me. That time, because of my nervousness, the novelty of the surroundings, and Kitty's intensity, I forgot to look before I sat. The chair collapsed. I tumbled backwards. I felt more embarrassed than hurt by that fall.

Kitty ran to my side and bent down. "You poor thing, are you okay?"

Papa stared at me in amazement. I felt mortified and unsure whether or not I could trust her. I knew that I was blushing in the shade of *Purim* carnival: candy-apple red.

"You shouldn't worry. People fall out of chairs all the time here," Kitty said with a disarming sarcasm and a coquette's wink, extending a hand to help me to my feet. I refused it.

"I'm fine! I'm fine!" I protested to the woman who would become my ally, confidant, and friend.

Kitty would teach me the ins and outs of Century Comedies. You see, she had been working at the studio since it opened, and had become the Stern's right-hand man. As such, she truly knew the ropes.

I rolled to my right and looked up at Papa and Kitty and was startled to see a strange little bit of a man who seemed to have materialized out of thin air. I felt awkward as a newborn giraffe when I clambered to my feet.

"Stern is my name; Julius Stern," he said, introducing himself. He had a German accent and a voice that was so commanding I felt my heels click together of their own accord as he spoke. I would meet a lot of memorable, tough people during my time in Hollywood, but Julius Stern was among the most memorable and the toughest.

Stern was in his midforties, barrel-chested, and bald. He wore thick spectacles that magnified the small brown eyes set deep in his orange-shaped head. He and his brother were sticklers for the rules of fashion. No matter the time of year, Julius was always formally dressed with starched collar and necktie. Since it was summer, he wore a straw boater and white shoes.

"Let me show you around the place," he said, opening the bungalow's rear door.

"Mind your head," I heard Kitty say with a chuckle.

Thinking she was a royal pain, I gritted my teeth and did my best to ignore her. Then Stern, Papa, and I stepped into the back lot and my future. We moved along on a raised wooden walkway painted white that snaked past several framed bungalows. In front of one of them I saw a stack of round silver cans.

"Those tins contain our bread and butter," Stern said. "They each hold a finished movie."

I was flooded with all of the new sights and sounds. We walked a bit farther to a large building. Coming out of it I saw spear-carrying gladiators, harem girls, and a backdrop of an alpine meadow strewn with edelweiss that two painters expertly carted by us.

"That's our prop department," Stern explained. "It's huge. It has to be. We need a lot of backgrounds and props because we produce all kinds of serials. You name it: Westerns, jungle adventures, mysteries, even animal flickers. Speaking of animal pictures, here at Century we've even got our own zoo with our own bull handler." Then we walked by the largest structure at the studio. "You know, this old barn was part of the original property. It's so big I run several crews in there at the same time," he said.

I was impressed by the immensity and scale of all that I saw. I had never been exposed to anything like it before. I wanted to stop the tour and start working as soon as I could. If I knew what was shortly to take place, I would have been more patient.

We moved to an area with two huge, windowless sound stages. On their respective doors, one had a large painted letter *A* and the other a large painted letter *B*. Stern opened door A and we entered.

The space was huge. Several movie crews were working at the same time. We stopped and observed one of them. A half-dozen musicians played for a romantic interlude, acted out by two young actors. I noticed Papa was looking away; he seemed embarrassed. I imagined myself playing the part of the dashing leading man, embracing the pretty ingénue. That's how naive I was in those days. The scene was framed by blinding lights and captured on film by a hand-cranked Lytax camera and crew of ten.

Everyone we passed stopped to stare at me. I liked the fact that an instant later they returned to what they were doing, as if I wasn't even there.

After we left the sound stage, we continued walking for another five minutes, during which Stern didn't say a word. I wondered what he was thinking. Maybe he was having second thoughts about his talent scouts' decision to hire me. We wound our way back to the building that contained the prop department. But this time we entered it and stopped in front of a rack with suits, coats, uniforms, and capes. Though the costumes gave off a very musty smell, just looking at them filled me with anticipation: I wondered which ones I would wear and when they would teach me to act. A short woman with a wrinkled, yellow tape measure draped around her shoulders sat in front of the rack. She looked like a cross between a gypsy queen and somebody's grandmother. The woman gazed up at me with a look of astonishment that quickly transformed into panic.

"This is Mrs. Romanov, the mistress of the wardrobe. She will get you set with today's costume. Then you'll put on your makeup. I want you at Stage B to begin shooting in an hour," Stern said.

"An hour? What, do you think I'm Moses at the Red Sea? I don't do miracles. There's nothing on the rack to fit him," Mrs. Romanov protested.

"Get goldilocks—you know, that blonde—to help. Whatever it takes but make it happen," Stern ordered.

"Stage what? Put on my makeup? I need . . . Papa, can't we? I thought I would . . . " I objected. I was overwhelmed but too nervous to be terrified.

Mrs. Romanov grabbed a small ladder resting on a wall behind the rack of costumes. Without so much as a by-your-leave, she opened it in front of me, climbed to the fifth rung, and began to measure my arms and shoulders. Before I could utter another word of dissent, Stern had spun around and disappeared into the crowd on the wooden walkway.

I wanted my father to rescue me, but he was as surprised as I was. He looked at me with a helpless grin that said: *You're on your own, Jakey.*

I thought for sure that first day all I would do was take a tour of the studio, learn the lay of the land, and maybe get some pointers on how to act in movies. But there had been no real tour and not even a minute of orientation and certainly no pointers. Soon I would be shooting the first scene in my first film. I didn't have the slightest idea who my character was, what the story was about, how to act on camera, or what in the hell I was doing there. I wasn't ready. I was totally lost and what's more, I didn't even have my costume.

A few seconds passed as a mute Mrs. Romanov scrambled off the ladder and angrily shuffled through the clothing on the rack. I came to the awful realization that it was just my first day on the job and I was already causing big problems.

Then the old woman coughed, spit on the ground, roughly signaled for me to follow her, and guided us to another nearby building. Inside was the cubbyhole—more accurately, the closet—that would serve as my dressing room. It would have been small for an ordinary sized man; for me, it was miniscule.

A few minutes later, Blanche Payson, a six-foot-two, two-hundred-pound Amazon who had worked as a police woman in Los Angeles before her stint as an actress at Century, stood in my dressing room. She extended one arm to shake my hand. In the other hand she held a banged-up beige cosmetics case. I recall she had the strongest grip of any woman I'd ever met. As a matter of fact, it was stronger than those of most men I knew.

Blanche explained that Julius had tasked her with giving me a crash course on the basics of donning movie makeup. For the next fifteen awful minutes I was initiated to the mysteries of being vamped. As Papa looked on, Blanche roughly painted thick, white, lead-based greasepaint all over my face. That awful stuff came in paper-wrapped, six-inch-long solid cylinders. The first time she rubbed it on me, it actually hurt. Then Blanche used a toothpick to apply a dab of lip rouge to the inner corner of each of my eyes. After that, she used her pinky finger to carefully apply purple eye shadow. She finished by patting my entire face with white powder. I coughed after inhaling some of that heavily leaded dreadful dust.

By then, Mrs. Romanov had returned with my costume and hung it on a small rack that ran along the rear wall of the dressing room. My first costume consisted of worn dungaree coveralls and a scratchy canvas shirt done in a Scottish Plaid. I was to use my own shoes until the studio could special order some to fit me.

Blanche and Papa stepped out and I changed into the outfit Mrs. Romanov had just delivered. As I dressed, I gazed out of the single source of light in the cramped room. It was a tiny block of smoky glass in the rear wall. I imagined squeezing myself through it and high-tailing it to the Hollywood Hills.

"Hurry it up, princess!" Blanche yelled.

When I came out of the door I was embarrassed for them to see me in costume. The pants looked two sizes too short and the shirt was so small I could barely button it. Papa politely smiled. Blanche wasn't so kind. She shook her head and snickered.

"Follow me!" she demanded as she lit out down the wooden path. "It's time to lose your virginity." Blanche started out at a brisk pace.

Papa didn't look pleased. We both jogged to keep up. Soon we stood in front of Sound Stage B. Blanche threw the door open with authority and marched in. Papa followed and I brought up the rear, hoping to not be seen.

The massive space was dimly lit by twin skylights. When I had just about reached the dozen or so members of the film crew who were huddled together, I tripped on a cable and plunged into a small utility table that was holding a stack of blue plates that I later learned were used as props. I whacked my shin on the way down. A crescendo of shattering ceramics and my shriek of pain announced my clumsy crash landing on cold concrete. *So much for staying invisible*, I thought. In unison, the entire group turned and moved toward me. If I could, I would have shrunk into the floor.

"That's quite an entrance. Can you do it again for the camera?" Fred Fishbach, the director of my first film, asked. Everyone but Papa and I laughed. "You must be Big Jake," he said in a voice that was at once booming and friendly. "We won't hold your clumsiness against you."

I know he was trying to make me feel welcome, but I felt anything but that. Fred Fishbach was an experienced moviemaker who had worked for Mack Sennett at Keystone. He was tall and muscular and reminded me of what a Notre Dame fullback would look like in the flesh. He dressed conservatively in gray wool trousers, a white shirt, and dark cravat. If I close my eyes I can still see him in the white visor with green felt lining that he always wore on set to reduce the glare from those damned klieg lights.

There was something about Fishbach that got you to trust him. I liked him from the get go.

"Nice to meet you, sir," I said timidly, holding out my hand to greet him.

"Well, what the kid lacks in grace he makes up in manners," Fishbach said.

"I'm Jake's father," said Papa, holding out his hand as well.

"Well, I can see that when it comes to social graces the apple didn't fall far from the tree. But how in the hell did such a little man produce this Paul Bunyan?"

"That's a long story," Papa said. I'd seen him handle similar questions he wanted to deflect in that manner before.

"Well, hopefully some day when we have more time you'll tell me, but for now we have other fish to fry. Jake is up in the next scene."

Papa and I walked back behind the camera. Despite the fact that the camera operator and lighting men and all their helpers—who I would later learn were called grips—focused like diamond cutters on their tasks, I was certain they were studying and judging my every move, just waiting for me to make a fool of myself again.

XXXX

I had been trying my best not to think about it. I really had. But standing there waiting for my first time in front of a movie camera, all I could think about was the fact that Papa and Mama were going home to El Paso the next day. Mama and Papa had already been in Los Angeles for almost a week and had to get back to my brothers—particularly my little brother—and the store.

Standing in that chilly soundstage with an aching shin, I came face to face with the reality that I would soon be alone with all those peculiar strangers working in this weird new business. I hadn't even shot a frame of film and already a crowd had followed me in the street, I had smacked my head, I had fallen out of a chair, and my new coworkers saw me trip and break dishes. I wanted out . . . to quit . . . to go back on the train with my folks.

"Erlich, come over here." It was Alf Goulding, the assistant director and one of the gag men. I hesitated suspiciously, having no idea who he was. "I won't bite," he said noticing my reticence. "I just want to help you."

It turns out Goulding really did want to help me. He had previously worked as an actor and had compassion for what it was like to be the new guy on the set.

In those days in silent comedies, there were no real writers, just gag men like Goulding. Gag men would write their ideas for the funny parts in a particular scene that the actors would later bring to life in the movie.

I looked around in hopes that Goulding was calling somebody else.

"Erlich, on the double." Goulding was a little shorter than Papa but very thin, with a head of busy blond hair and a ruddy complexion to match. He was a regular Beau Brummel; everything the man wore matched. "Kid, today you'll be filming a stunt." Goulding said. I had no idea what a stunt was and I was too embarrassed to ask. "Four men playing the roles of detectives will boost you up to the open lintel so you can eavesdrop on the conversation between some bank robbers taking place inside a hotel room," he said.

Then he went on to tell me I was to squeeze myself through the tiny opening and fall to a mattress out of sight on the other side. Then the director would stop filming. A group of grips would hoist me up and I would do the same thing from the opposite direction, coming out of the opening over the door in the next room.

"The bits sure to get a laugh," Goulding insisted.

When I heard his description of what I was supposed to do, I got nervous. Perspiration poured off of me. It was too late to run away. Soon, hoisted, squeezed, and contorted, I would be the center of attention.

"I might not even fit through that tiny opening," I muttered to Papa.

"Okay boys, take your places for the scene in the hotel hallway," the director ordered. I walked to the door with four large men. I thought I would throw up or crap in my pants. But as terrified as I was, my excitement soon took over.

"Hold the hammers," Fishbach commanded. The carpenters, who had been building sets on the soundstage, stopped what they were doing. "Ready, action, camera!"

Wow, my first time in front of a movie camera, shooting the first scene in my very first picture! I want to remember this moment, I said to myself.

Before I knew it, four actors grabbed my legs and boosted me up. They all appeared to be *schtarkers*, but they had misjudged my tonnage. Apparently crushed by the load, they started to sway to the right, then to the left, then to collapse backward. To avoid falling, I did the only thing I could. For dear life, I grabbed the outside of the scenery flat painted to look just like a hotel room door. In my death-grip struggle to hold on, I began to swing my feet. When my right foot slammed into the canvas-thin scenery, I booted a hole in it the size of a steer's head.

"What's this?" I heard a banshee echoing across the room. "Have you forgotten? We have a budget! Do you think we're full of money? Such a waste . . . a waste!" It was Stern, bellowing through a megaphone. "Erlich, I expect you to get it done in one take! Do you hear me? One take!"

Terribly embarrassed yet again, and more afraid of my new boss than any plunge, I dropped back to earth. When I slunk back to Papa, I saw he was standing next to Kitty, who must have come on to the set while I was doing my scene. She looked at me with a smile. After our earlier interaction I would have never expected her kindness.

She motioned for me to bend down. I did. She put her lips next to my ear and whispered softly. "If you wanna make it in pictures, kid, you need to toughen up. Sometimes Mr. Stern can be a real horse's ass. You need to learn when to ignore what he says and when to take him seriously."

Stern worked us actors like dogs. On second thought, he was probably kinder to his dogs. Because he and his brother Julius were such slave drivers, Century Comedies was prolific and made a lot of money. We'd crank out a movie in less than a week. We called them "five-day-wonders." They made Century Studios rich and the rest of us poor *schleps* exhausted.

Each of our movies cost only about $3,000 to make, but the producers had taken in about $50,000 from investors to cover costs. Then Universal made $300,000 when they distributed our films. You can see there was a lot of money in the picture business. But contrary to what everybody and their cousin thinks, not for me. I started out earning forty dollars a week. Soon they raised me to seventy-five dollars a week. That was a good wage for a kid who was barely seventeen. But it didn't make me rich and they made me earn every penny.

By the time we wrapped that first day and I'd scrubbed the greasepaint off my face and changed back to my own clothes, it was past eight o'clock. Let me tell you, getting that makeup off was a royal pain. In all my time in Hollywood, I never got used to the theatrical cold cream we had to use for that chore. It got so I would dread the sight of the big blue cans of that foul-smelling goo.

That night after work, I was a new kind of tired. I was sore. I mean I was bruised in places I didn't know I had places. In retrospect, being so drained was a very good thing; a gift. When we got back to the apartment, I was so French-fried that I fell fast asleep before supper and before I could *dre a kopf* (worry) about my parents' departure the next morning.

CHAPTER 7

Musso and Frank

Lobby card circa 1923

Bang, bang, bang.

A jackhammer pounding on the apartment door woke me at five thirty a.m. "Wake up, Jake," I heard Mrs. Scheiner, the landlady, holler. "It's time to get ready for *arbeiten*."

I struggled to lift my hundred-pound eyelids. When I finally did, I felt like Hap Arnold flying in thick Atlantic fog. But I had no instruments, no plane, not even a damned map to guide me. When I rolled out of bed, it hit me hard: I was alone.

An hour before, without making a sound, Mama and Papa had left for the train station. Lunatic-frantic, I searched the apartment for any traces of my parents: a piece of clothing in the closet, a suitcase under the bed, even a smell. I knew that they were going. We had talked about it since we arrived in town. We had already discussed the rent being paid for the next two months, about me writing to them and my brothers weekly, and how I would take a trip home in December for Myer's *Bar Mitzvah*.

But those memories didn't soothe or even stop my rush to find clues of their departure. It made no sense, but still I searched. It was as if I believed that if I could figure out exactly where, how, and when they disappeared into the darkness, maybe I could will them back. But they were gone. The only evidence I found of them ever having been there was a note in my father's handwriting and a twenty-dollar bill they left for me on the little table in the kitchenette.

Dear Jakey,

Be a good boy!

We love you,

Mama and Papa

P.S. Remember, a good name is worth more than gold.

I had never felt so alone. Luckily, my parents had raised me with a strong sense of responsibility and commitment. I'm sure you can tell from the little I've already shared that responsibility and commitment have always been both my anchor and my sail; they keep me stuck or they get me moving. That morning it was the latter.

Within a few minutes, I was dressed and out the door. A moment later I was back in my room. I had forgotten my sweater; I promised Mama I would take in case it got chilly.

XXXX

By Thursday night, the end of my first week in Hollywood, I was banged, bruised, and bumped, but I had finished my first movie, *A Corn-Fed Sleuth*, the tale of a hayseed who came to the big city to seek fame and fortune. You might say it was autobiographical.

What I remember most about that memorable week happened late on Friday afternoon. Archie, Century's PR man, had just finished shooting some publicity pictures of me when I felt a tug on my pants leg. It was Kitty. Over the past week, my initial harsh judgment of her had begun to change.

"Hiya, kid. How was your first week in pictures?" she asked.

"Okay, I guess. I hope Mr. Stern, Fishbach, and the other fellows on the crew liked my work," I said, searching for a compliment or some morsel of approval.

You see, all week long I did the gags the gagmen wrote and followed the director's instructions. I even did most of my scenes in one take, but nobody told me I did a good job, much less complimented me. Over that week, and during my first year in Hollywood, seeking the approval of others was a constant.

"Come with me. I wanna show you something," Kitty said as she stepped out of my dressing room and onto the wooden path.

She waddled at such a brisk pace that I almost had to run to keep up with her. After a few minutes, we stood in front of a bungalow on the other side of the lot that I had not noticed before. Kitty and I entered, walked to the back of the building, and descended a flight of rickety stairs. The dimly lit, Tampa-Jewel-smoke-filled basement served as Century's projection room. It had two rows of empty chairs, behind which stood a non-descript man next to a card table that supported a small, hand-cranked movie projector. I thought I recognized Fishbach and Goulding with their backs to us sitting in the second row.

"Is that who I think it is?" I whispered. Kitty nodded.

"Roll it, Roland." Goulding ordered.

The scratchy numbers four, three, two, one appeared on the screen, followed by the title, *A Corn-Fed Sleuth*. Over the next twenty minutes, for the first time ever, I watched myself on film. From the opening scene where my tiny mother paddled me, to the final shot when I returned the stolen loot, I was riveted. Not so much by the story, but more—much more—by my image.

There was something other-worldly about seeing yourself projected on a small screen in a darkened room. I wondered what it would be like to see that image on a huge, bigger-than-life screen in a real movie house. I couldn't wait for my friends and family to get a load of this.

I was also captivated by seeing the other players react to me. That was a first. In my seventeen years of life I'd never before thought of others responding to me. I was always reacting to everyone else, trying to wedge myself into their lilliputian world, a place I didn't fit.

When the scene of me squeezing myself through the hotel door lintels played, Roland, the man operating the projector, laughed out loud. I noticed that Kitty giggled, too. I was too green to understand why, but I liked how that made me feel.

Later, I would come to appreciate what I enjoyed so much about acting in flickers. Even though they were just slapstick comedies, they gave me the power to connect with and impact others.

Something else, something very strange—and another first for me—happened as I watched that footage. Ever since I was seven, when I met someone or encountered a new group, I automatically focused on how different I was than everyone else. Watching me painted onto that silent film screen with the other actors, I recognized, if just for twenty minutes of gags, how much I was like the others, just taller. I got the chills as the screen went black and the movie ended.

Flap, slap, flap, slap, flap, slap. I heard the percussive sound of celluloid popping against a metal movie reel, a noise that would become more and more familiar. Roland stopped winding the projector and switched on the lights. Other studios were using projectors powered by electricity, but because Julius Stern was such a skinflint, we still used an old-fashioned version at Century. By then, Fishbach and Goulding had stood up, turned around, and approached us.

Goulding yawned and stretched. "I promise, Jake, it's the wallpaper that put me to sleep and not the acting," he said with a wink.

"Great job, Jake." Fishbach added. "Kitty, I think we've got us the making of a new star; if we can only convince Stern."

When I heard the name *Stern*, my stomach started to churn. *What was he talking about? Why did Stern need convincing? I had just gotten started in the movie business. Was my job already in jeopardy?*

As if she sensed my concern, Kitty took my massive pinky finger in her hand and squeezed it reassuringly.

XXXX

Ahuga, ahuga.

As promised, the next morning, Zion Meyers, one of the talent scouts who discovered me on the Santa Monica Pier, was outside my boarding house honking.

When he dropped by the set on the Thursday before, Meyers had made the date. "To celebrate wrapping *A Corn-Fed Sleuth*, we'll go to Musso and Frank on Hollywood Boulevard. It's a hot watering hole for the film crowd. Be ready at twelve-sharp on Saturday."

I had been eagerly awaiting my Hollywood outing ever since Meyers mentioned it. Whenever I wasn't busy working, all kinds of fantasies of the sites and celebrities I would see ran through my head. So when it came time to go, I bolted out of the apartment and ran down the stairs. As I flew out of the front door, I realized I had forgotten my sweater again and turned to go back and get it.

Ahuga, ahuga.

Meyers honked the horn on his new sapphire Packard again.

The heck with the sweater, I thought, and hurried to the curb and got in the car.

"Hey Jake, how's tricks? I'm sure glad we talked your Pop and Mom into letting you stay," Meyers said as we pulled away.

"Me too!" My knees were pressed, better said smashed, up against my chest. I could barely fit in the tiny front seat.

"Before lunch, I wanna take you on a little tour of Hollywood." Meyers drove east down Sunset toward Western. As we passed Vermont, he looked over at me and then back at the road. "Jake, they're really charged up about you at the studio."

I sensed the excitement in his voice. "What about Stern?" I asked modestly, unsure whether or not I should bring up what had been troubling me since I heard Fishbach's comment the day before.

"Why do you ask?"

"Yesterday afternoon, Fishbach said something about Stern needing to be convinced about me. Is there a problem?"

"It's no big thing. Don't worry, sport. There are some conditions to the deal, but we'll talk about that at lunch."

I felt queasy. I hated when anyone said "Don't worry" or "We'll talk about it later." Based on my experience with doctors, whenever I heard those words I would cringe and wait for the other shoe to drop. I also wondered what deal Meyers was talking about.

"Don't worry, sport," Meyers repeated. "I've got a contract right here for your next flicker." Meyers tapped the breast pocket in his blazer. "It's a formality; just waiting for your John Hancock." As we crossed Figueroa he looked at me again. He took his right hand off the steering wheel and patted my forearm as if to congratulate me. "They wanna call it *A Howling Success*. I say, strike while the iron is hot!"

Meyers was still looking at me. The traffic had stopped suddenly because a farmer in a small truck full of flowers four cars in front of us had a flat.

Ka-Pow!

Meyers smacked into the back end of an elegant, fresh-from-the-showroom-floor, ebony Pierce-Arrow Touring car. Luckily, we hadn't been driving too fast. It was just a fender-bender, so nobody was hurt. That's why Meyers and I were both shocked at what happened next.

The two cars in the crash pulled to the curb. The driver of the Pierce-Arrow, a muscleman of a chauffeur, flew out of the limo. When he surveyed the damage to his limousine, he ripped his black-billed cap off his head, threw it down in the street, and stomped on it with his boots. Wounded-grizzly-bear-mad, he glared at us. Then with both fists ready for war, the chauffer charged Meyers' side of the car.

"Get out of there, you little weasel!" he demanded.

If Meyers's window hadn't been shut, I'm certain the chauffer would have punched my new friend where he sat. Meyers turned pale. He tried to sink under the dashboard to escape from the danger. "Stand up, Jake!" Meyers, now huddled on the floor, spoke in a demanding whisper.

I couldn't understand why he wanted me to stand up. What did it have to do with me? The chauffer pounded more violently on the window. Then he began to pound on the roof.

"Please, stand up!" Meyer's terrified tone let me know that he was no longer demanding, he was begging.

Still confused, I didn't move. When the chauffer saw his quarry stall, he put his boot on the door of the car and tried to pry it open. Luckily, Meyers had locked it. I wondered if the enraged limo driver would pull the new Packard's door right off its hinges.

Meyers elbowed me again. "Stand up, you idiot! Can't you see? This gorilla wants to kill me!"

Up until that instant I always thought of myself as peaceful. I still do. I've always seen myself as a lover, not a fighter. But when the gravity of that situation finally sunk in, I realized I didn't have any choice. I opened the Packard's passenger door and swung my legs out onto the pavement. Slowly, I unwound all four hundred pounds of me.

The chauffer stared up. I watched his clenched-for-battle jaw unhinge. Judging by the look of disbelief and terror on his face, he must have thought ten feet of titanic muscle and bone was glaring down at him from the sidewalk. Along with the blood, the enraged expression on the chauffeur's face had drained, replaced by what I can honestly say was a look of pale panic. He spun around, fled to his wounded limo, jumped in and sped away, burning the rubber of his rear tires. I bet that poor fellow messed his pants in the process.

When I got back in the car, Meyers looked shaken. "Whew, that was a close call," he said. "Thank you, Jake. I owe you big time!" He took a linen hanky out of the front pocket of his blazer and wiped his brow. I smiled to myself. *Maybe there is something to this giant stuff, after all*, I thought.

I believe that was one of the first times I was genuinely happy to be as big as I am. As you'll hear, that was not the last time a bully who crossed my path got his due. Looking back on it, I think I must have experienced what a huge Great Dane puppy does after his first full-grown bark. But as pleased as I felt, I was still worried about Stern.

"If you don't mind, Jake, let's cut the tour short. I need a drink," Meyers said.

At the next intersection, we made a U-turn and headed back to the restaurant. Prohibition had been in full swing for three years and I wondered where and how he'd get the hooch.

XXXX

With its bubbly crowd, mahogany paneled walls, and luscious menu, Musso and Frank would eventually become one of my favorite haunts. Although it was only a little past noon on a Saturday, the place was already jumping.

My friend took two long snorts from the leather covered flask he carried in the inside pocket of his sport coat as soon as we sat down in our booth. "Look over there, Jake; by the door." I turned my head and saw a portly young man that was dressed to the nines talking to the host. "That's Roscoe Arbuckle, better known as Fatty Arbuckle. In the old days before the scandal he acted in some of Fred Fishbach's pictures at Century. Two years ago the guy even signed a million-dollar deal. That was before this fickle town tried to crucify him. But people don't know the real scuttlebutt."

"What are you talking about?" I asked.

"Well, I'm sure you read about the drunken party in San Francisco and the starlet who supposedly died after Arbuckle raped her."

I nodded. Even though I was just fourteen when all that happened, and my parents tried their best to shield me from such things, that story got a lot of play in the papers, even in a small town like El Paso.

"Well, that's not what happened," Meyers continued. "That girl died as a result of a female medical procedure."

"A female medical procedure?" I had no idea what he was talking about.

"Do you know what an abortion is, Jake?"

"That girl had an abortion?" I asked. My big brother had told me about abortions but that was the first time I ever heard of anyone actually having one.

"She had a botched abortion that led to an awful infection that killed her. And rather than bring that to light, they sold Roscoe down the river. He was just in the wrong place at the wrong time."

I looked over my shoulder and caught a glimpse of him being seated at a table. Despite believing I knew the score, I was still pretty naive in those days, so I was stunned to hear about the dark side of Hollywood. I kept glancing at the fallen star but doing my best to not stare.

"People forget Arbuckle was acquitted. To the public and many people in this business, he's still guilty as sin. One more thing: at the trial, your director, Fred Fishbach, was the only one in this town with balls enough to testify for Arbuckle as a character witness," Meyers continued.

I wasn't at all surprised to hear that about Fishbach's character. You could just feel how solid he was by working with him. I wanted to work with him again soon. I'm sad to tell you that within a few years, Fishbach, who was only thirty-six, died from cancer.

Meyers and I sat in silence for a few minutes.

"I feel like a tourist," I admitted, unabashedly excited to spot a famous movie actor, albeit one with a tarnished reputation.

"Jake, if you look down this row to the booth at the very back of the restaurant, there's Charlie Chaplin and Paola Negri sitting together," Meyers said, picking up on my comment.

Nonchalantly, I turned around and, in the far corner of the room, saw a non-descript man with curly brown hair sitting with a woman whose features were obscured by a cloche.

"Chaplain; wow! Ever since I saw him in *The Little Tramp*, I've been a big fan." I was tempted to get up, walk over, and ask the funny man for his autograph. *I can't* wait *until I tell Ben and Myer about this. They'll never believe it.* In all my years in Hollywood I don't think I ever totally got over being starstruck.

"I just love this place," Meyers said as he took another drink of gin. "Bottoms up," he added, knocking back what was left in the flask. I took a swig of my root beer. "The studio is having a party at the end of the month at the Ambassador. Once you've got two more pictures under your belt, you're sure to be invited."

"I'm . . . I'm not so sure . . ."

I wasn't at all certain I'd be in Hollywood long enough for that to happen. First off, I wasn't convinced there would be a second movie. And if I was to really have a career in pictures, the very thought of going to an adult Hollywood party caused me skyrockets of forbidden fantasy and guilty crash landings. Visions of too much whiskey, wild flappers dancing on top of pianos, and a late-night phone call to Mama and Papa from the Hollywood Police filled my head.

"We have your son in solitary confinement," the imaginary officer said in an Irish brogue. *"It took a division of our best to bring him in. He's looking at thirty to life."*

A waiter in a white waist-length coat put a delicious-looking hamburger and hash browns in front of me and a plate with parsley-covered Dover sole and scalloped potatoes in front of Meyers. I was thankful to be awakened from my daydream by a luscious-looking lunch.

You may have noticed that I talk about food a lot. That may have come from having parents who grew up so impoverished they never had enough to eat. Then again, it may be because I was raised in west Texas at the turn of the century in a family that could barely make ends meet. For us, eating in fancy restaurants was something we just didn't do. That's not to mention that my appetite was fueled by the fact that I was growing like crazy.

You can see why I picked up that scrumptious hamburger like it was a fragile thing of beauty, but after I savored the taste of just one bite, I put the burger back on my plate. I was surprised, but at that moment something was more important than eating. I couldn't wait any longer; I had to talk about Stern's comment.

"Mr. Meyers . . . "

"Come on, Jake . . . call me Zion."

"Okay, Zion, I think . . . I think," I stuttered nervously, "I think we're putting the cart before the horse."

"What do you mean?" asked Meyers as he put down his fork.

"Well, before the accident I told you that I was worried about Stern. Is he . . . is he . . . is he going to fire me?"

Meyers listened intently, nodding his head. I wasn't sure if he nodded to let me know I was, in fact, getting canned, or to communicate he understood what I was saying.

Without asking for clarification, I continued: "You said that he did have some concerns. What concerns?"

Meyers laughed. This time he shook his head. Then he wiped his mouth with his napkin, cut up some fish, and chewed it slowly, appearing to savor the taste. He wiped his mouth yet again. "Yum, yum, yum. Delicious . . . the best in town." Waiting for him to respond was absolute torture. Meyers paused for a few seconds. "Here's the straight talk, kid," he finally began. "Take it from me—I've been around this town a long time. For a rookie, you did great on *A Corn-Fed Sleuth.* The problem is not about your acting. It's whether or not you can work with a little kid."

I had absolutely no idea what Meyers was talking about. He sat back in the booth and continued.

"The star of your next picture is a four-year-old girl. Her name is Baby Peggy and she's big box office. Have you heard of her?"

I had heard the name but I had absolutely no idea who she was. Back then, I was too embarrassed to demonstrate my ignorance so I just nodded.

"Stern has a lot of time and money invested in that tyke. She's a golden goose for him and he wants to keep it that way," he explained. "So he needs to be damned sure you two hit it off. She's been making pictures at Century since she was a year and half old."

I shook my head in amazement. Only a year and half old! *That's unbelievable!* I thought, reflecting on how difficult the first week on the job had been for me—and I was seventeen. I wondered how a child could ever take direction.

"In the past, Baby Peggy's always been a real trooper," Meyers continued. "Normally, she does whatever the director says. Baby Peggy's a phenom; like a little old lady in a child's body. Everything was fine until the last picture, when she had a run-in with a nasty pelican that went after her." Meyers paused and put his fork and knife down on his plate. "For the first time she almost came unglued. Her dad calmed her down. He fancies himself a horse and dog trainer; says the same techniques work with kids. Well, I don't know about that, but what I've observed firsthand on the set is that his daughter is either terrified of him or she craves his approval or both. Well, whatever goes on between Baby Peggy and her daddy, Stern is on pins and needles. See, sport, Stern's not worried about a scared little girl. He's worried about a little girl who won't work."

I sat there in that booth, unsure about how I felt. On the one hand, Julius Stern was offering me a second movie; on the other, my future in pictures didn't depend one iota on how good I was at my job, but on whether or not some spoiled movie star would get along with me.

"Stern wants a powwow with you and Baby Peggy on Monday at the studio. He wants to watch the chemistry. If the kid gets upset, your goose is cooked. If not, you're in the money. They've got a whole slew of movie ideas for you two; even a couple of fairy tales."

Despite the challenges I had faced and missing my family during the previous week, and now my worries about Baby Peggy, the idea of doing more pictures was utterly seductive. I picked up my hamburger and devoured what was left.

His words . . . *they've got a whole slew of movie ideas for you two* . . . kept running through my head. I was so excited and starstruck that all I could think about was working in silent pictures and belonging in Hollywood. I just had to keep working in movies. I would do whatever it took to have that kid like me. Having recently come from such a dark and depressed place, I was too hungry to stop and think that there might be some gravel in the oatmeal. That wisdom would only come with time and broken teeth.

About fifteen minutes later as I was washing down my last bite of banana cream pie with a great cup of java, Meyers jumped up and said, "Wait here, Jake. I have something important to show you. It's a surprise."

I sat back and stretched my legs alongside the outside of the booth, thinking about the upcoming meeting with Baby Peggy and what I could do to make sure things went smoothly.

A few minutes later, Meyers returned carrying a cordovan leather briefcase. I wondered what it contained. He methodically cleared the remaining dishes, utensils, and whatever else was on that table out of the way. Then he opened the case and removed a large, folded, poster-size piece of thick paper. As if he were opening a present he'd waited all year for, he slowly unfurled the paper and carefully set it down in the middle of the table facing me. It was a large advertisement they used in movie houses, called a lobby card. The poster measured about four feet by three feet and had a red and yellow border. Each margin contained a black art-deco radio tower crowned with a radio-wave-emitting globe. The words *International News* with a smaller subheading, "The World Before Your Eyes," were splashed in India ink across the top margin.

The lobby card's center headline, the largest of the three, grabbed my attention: "World's Tallest Boy" with the caption: "Hollywood's latest acquisition is Jack Earle, a walking Woolworth Tower . . . Hollywood, California." In those days the Woolworth Tower was the tallest skyscraper in the world. For a moment, I just stared at the poster's printed words.

"Is this Jack Earle fellow competition I have to worry about?" I asked cautiously.

Meyers laughed. "No, no, Jake. Jack Earle is you.

"What do you mean? That's not my name!" I felt very confused.

"Look, Jack Earle is your new name . . . your stage name." Meyers went on to explain that in Hollywood, just like on the great white way, actors were given catchy names that were easy for the average Joe to pronounce and remember.

The coining of my stage name, sometimes also spelled Earl, demonstrated that the powers that be at the studio were invested in my future. But my new name was significant for other reasons. Looking at that poster and my newborn handle, Jack Earle, all I could think about were heroes whose names were changed. There was Abram who became Abraham, and Jacob who became Israel. Then there were all those Indian braves in the Zane Grey novels who went on vision quests and were awarded new names by the Medicine Man. For me, there was something more than publicity to this new moniker business. Each of those heroes got a new name after a struggle. They each got a second chance, a clean slate, a reprieve from the warden. But in every story, after each of them got their new name, they weren't done with their battles—far from it. It wasn't that easy. From what I could recollect, every one of the owners of a new name had more—many more—dues to pay.

CHAPTER 8

The Durbar Spectacular

Hertzberg Circus Collection, Witte Museum, San Antonio, Texas

I never finished telling you what happened as a result of decking that rube in Madison Square Garden. I think when I left off I was gazing at a tug in the East River after fleeing Ingalls and the need to make a decision about my future in the circus—if I had any future.

Well, that afternoon I arrived back at the circus with only about five minutes to spare. Thank goodness I was already in costume or I would have been late and in even more hot water, if that were possible.

The cop at the performers' entrance was tasked with checking identification and keeping out the riffraff and runaway kids who dogged us everywhere we played. I wish I needed ID. All that flatfoot had to do was take one look at me and he knew I belonged, so I breezed right past him without even stopping.

Walking through the entrance to that building never failed to amaze me. Today was no different. Even though I was seriously thinking of leaving the circus, performing in Madison Square Garden always made me feel a sense of awe and wonder. For a performer, playing for a New York audience in those hallowed halls absolutely meant you were in the big time. That was a thrill I would miss if I left the show.

As quickly as I could, I made my way to the backyard. That's what we called the area just outside, where the acts entered and exited the Big Top or, in this case, the arena. I walked by Fred Bradna, Ringling's Ringmaster and Equestrian Director.

Bradna was an institution. He'd been with the circus as long as anyone could remember. He was unmistakable with his pencil-line moustache, red-frocked velvet coat, white pants, calf's skin gloves, black top hat, and the silver drum-major's whistle he wore around his neck. Although Bradna was a small-framed, short man, he was born with natural gifts you would assume were the birthright of a bigger person; great charisma and a booming voice that could silence a Big Top full of thousands or get a circus crew jam-packed with egotists to march in time and perform on cue.

When I walked by him, Bradna looked me up and down with the same critical eye he employed with Ringling's prized Percherons. The Ringmaster carried a clipboard to ensure that all the acts assembled in the backyard lined up in the right order.

"I was beginning to wonder if you were gonna make it or not today, Erlich. Please don't tell me you're turning prima donna on me," he said, looking for my name on his list.

I just nodded and kept walking, searching for my assigned position in the multitude of performers and animals that, if placed in a straight line, would have stretched for several city blocks. Looking back on it, one of the things that kept me in the circus was how well-ordered things were and that I knew just where I belonged.

As I approached, my eye was immediately drawn to a dozen or so regally robed elephants and a company of drummer girls in gorgeous purple satin costumes. In those days, we were Madison Square Garden's biggest money-maker, and from the looks of the elaborate Durbar spec we were about to present, you could easily see why we drew such large crowds. I knew my station in the lineup: just in front of Gaspaux's rhinestone-and-feather-clad Arabian Show Ponies and behind Lew Jacobs and the other clowns. My place in that assembly of men and beasts was at least one point of certainty in my circus life. I nudged myself into position and felt a tug on my trouser leg.

"Where the hell have you been, Jake? Do I have to worry that you're hitting the bottle?" I heard Harry Doll ask.

I looked down at him.

"Harry, it's been many years and I've never let you down yet, have I?"

"No, you haven't. But there is always a first time," he shot back. "Even before you decked that rube last night, you've been acting stranger than a one-legged man in a sack race."

There was a long, uncomfortable pause. I felt that I had offended him earlier that day in the dressing room and hoped he would forgive me. Neither of us seemed to know what to say next. Then, bridging the growing distance between us, Harry broke the silence. "You know, this is sort of an anniversary. It was ten years ago, here in the Garden, when the circus started their 1926 run, that I first met you. Do you remember?"

"You're so romantic," I joked, trying to lighten the mood. The serious look on Harry's face let me know he didn't appreciate my levity.

I didn't say it, but I would never forget that night. The unpleasant experience I had during my first performance with the circus was inscribed in indelible ink in my memory. Clyde Ingalls, whom I'd only met a few weeks before in El Paso, dressed me up in an outlandish, scratchy wool outfit that included gold buttons, gold epaulets, a red satin hat that was sixteen inches high, and patent leather platform shoes. I was so damned high in the air that I had to keep moving my toes to make sure it was my feet down there. That first night, standing in the sideshow tent, when I heard the talker holler "Doors!" and the stampeding crowd approached, my knees started knocking. Every fiber in my being had screamed "Run!" Then, for the first time, I heard the voice of the man who would become my best friend.

"Take it easy, Jake!" I had looked high and low for the source of the thin yet vibrant sound. I couldn't figure out where it was coming from until I dropped my gaze a very, very far distance down to the sideshow platform next to mine and Harry had smiled up at me. "Welcome, Jake, and don't worry. There are more freaks out in the crowd then there are up here," he had said with the authority of the well-seasoned trooper that he was. I smiled back at him. Though he was a little man, there was something powerful about his presence and his words that calmed me down and helped me to face the onslaught.

That first performance in the sideshow was the beginning of a beautiful friendship that had lasted for years. You can see why the thought of telling him I was about ready to leave the circus was eating me up inside.

"Okay, big man, enough with the nice memories. The show's about to begin so assume the position," Harry ordered. Like one of the finely trained, plume- and sequin-clad equine specimens just behind us in line, on command I bent down on my right knee. Resting my right elbow on my knee, I spread my fingers wide and turned my open palm to face the ceiling. I looked like a waiter who forgot his tray. In some kind of bizarre scene from *Gulliver's Travels*, Harry sat squarely in the middle of my hand.

Two shrill calls from Bradna's whistle pierced the early afternoon air. The animals in line, sensing the excitement, roared, neighed, growled, and announced their presence however they could. Though most of the troopers had done this dance so many times it was second nature, they were never nonchalant. An adrenaline-generated murmur filled the backyard. The show was about to begin and everyone was keyed-up. Over my years with the circus, I think I must have gotten addicted to that adrenaline. That was something else that kept me hooked on the place.

I carefully stood up, hoisting Harry over my head. He looked like a little emperor, enthroned next to my right ear. One minute later, Bradna blew his whistle again. That was the cue for Ringling's big brass band to begin the show's drum and bugle overture. Like Hannibal's Legion, the colossal collection of costumed performers and beasts that was to be the circus's opening Durbar Spectacular slowly moved forward through the arena entrance.

Once inside that space, I immediately felt the thrill of it all. There was so much stimulation in that place: perfume of peanuts and popcorn, heat from the multi-colored spotlights, heart-walloping music, the explosion of what seemed to be a million photographers' flashes, murmuring applause, and a blurring of faces all whooshing by on an absolutely electric current of excitement.

Marching around the circus's three rings was special for me. There was something otherworldly; for lack of better words, something sacred about it. When I marched in the spec I felt connected to primitive mask-clad Indians dancing around a winter campfire and to Romans racing their chariots in the Colosseum. In the spec, we carried on a timeless, trance-inducing choreography by tramping around and around in circles.

More often than I'd like to remember, I'd been painfully bruised when one of Gaspaux's ponies stepped on my Achilles. So that night as we started to move out and one of those Arabians stepped a little too close for comfort, I picked up the pace.

Harry and I marched along in uncharacteristic silence. He knew that something was wrong and I wouldn't or couldn't talk about it. Trying to escape the tension, I looked away from him, up at the rigging for the trapeze. In just a few minutes, my friends the Codonas would be flying high above the crowd doing death-defying triple summersaults The audience's attention would always be glued to them. I think that's because trapeze artists fulfilled the need we humans have to be free of our limitations, including gravity, time, and thought. In just a few years, the overwhelming danger of that pursuit would hurl Lillian Lietzel, Fred Codona's wife, to her untimely death. She would take her husband's sanity along with her. After Lillian fell to her death, Fred became terribly depressed. Finally he married another flyer. That was a disaster. The marriage ended up on the rocks. At a meeting in Long Beach at the divorce lawyer's office, Codona pulled out a gun. When it was over, he had killed his ex-wife, her mother, the divorce lawyer, and himself. I'm not proud to admit it, but when that all went down I understood just how down Fred Codona must have been.

During that afternoon's spec in Madison Square Garden, after I looked at the rigging for the trapeze artists, I turned my attention to the center ring. There I saw the huge steel cage that housed Frank Buck's big cats. The lion tamer was another death-defier, sure to grab the rubes attention. I imagined his Bengals as our deadly passions; Buck's whip, chair, and gun our meager will.

That afternoon I must have looked at the acts with different eyes; the eyes of a man who knows his time somewhere is limited. The reality that I would be leaving soon either of my own accord or against my will was sinking in. I remember worrying that when I left or was canned, I'd feel like a refugee; displaced, never fully at home anywhere else. I loved the circus but I also hated it. I would truly miss my friends in the show. And to be honest, besides the rubes, who at times made my life a living hell, I liked having an audience.

As I continued walking around the rings, I looked up to the packed stands and watched fans enter while others exited the arena. Looking back at it from this hospital bed, it makes me think of all those people who at that very instant were coming into and leaving this world; some would see a great show; some would detest their experience; some would be forced to leave before they were ready; others would leave early of their own accord.

XXXX

"There's somebody waiting for you at the exit, Jake," Harry said, "He looks pretty anxious to see you."

I looked to the green curtain and saw Clyde Ingalls peering right at me. I wanted to run, but there was nowhere to go and no way to avoid the confrontation I had been dreading. As we approached, he aggressively stepped forward. "May I have a word, Jake?" he asked, loud enough to be heard above the throng.

"I've got to take care of this, Harry." I stepped out of line and lowered my little friend carefully to the ground.

Harry walked on and was swept away with the rest of the procession. I was scared of the tongue-lashing and ultimatum I was sure to receive. I was still ambivalent about what I wanted to do. Leaving would be a big gamble. Where would I go? The Depression enveloped the world with no sign of letting up. If I left how would I support myself? And if Ingalls let me stay, what prospects might I miss? How much time did I have to waste?

"Hello, Jake. Have you been avoiding me?"

I had no idea what to say to him. "Well . . . Well . . . " I stammered. "Clyde . . . Clyde, you were furious with me last night and, to be honest, I was very embarrassed by what I did." Unable to look him square in the eye, I stared over his right shoulder as if I were speaking to someone standing behind him.

"Look, Jake, I've put that behind me. That rube ended up with a bad bruise on his butt and on his ego. A lot of your friends say he had it coming. Our lawyers gave him two C-notes and he decided to forget the whole damned thing. As far as that affair goes, I just need your promise it will never happen again; and I mean never!" Ingall's demeanor shocked me. I had expected him to tear off my head and hand it to me on a platter, but he was levelheaded and calm.

"Absolutely. I give you my word," I answered reflexively, grateful for the apparent reprieve. I felt relieved, but I also knew I still owed him my decision about my future in the circus.

"I know you have not made up your mind yet about next season. With the way things are in the world, for the life of me I can't figure out why." *Here it comes*, I thought. "We're in the middle of worst hard times any of us can remember. Men are begging for work, getting their food in bread lines. You're in the Big Red with the largest and most respected of any freak show. If you're not careful you'll end up in a mud show or worse." He shook his index finger at me. I just listened, nodded my head, and wished I were a million miles away. "You're the only one in the troop who hasn't signed up for next season. I need to know what you plan to do by next Monday before the show, and no later. If I don't have a signed contract, I will assume you are resigning as of next season. Do you understand, Jake? Have I made myself clear?"

"Crystal clear," I answered, now making direct eye contact but just for a few seconds. "You'll have my answer by then."

I turned around and started to walk away. That had not gone at all as I anticipated. I felt shell-shocked. *What other unexpected surprises are in store for me?* I wondered.

"One more thing, Jake." I turned around, expecting the other shoe to drop. "That dame I saw you and Buck talking to in the menagerie—you know, the artist. She had a messenger drop this off for you before the matinee." He reached up, handed me a small envelope, and walked away.

Without any hesitation I tore it open and read the note on the sweet-smelling monogrammed stationary.

Dear Mr. Erlich,

It was such a pleasure to meet you today. I know it is last minute, but my husband and I are hosting a soiree this Wednesday evening at our home in the city. I would love for you to come. There are some people attending whom I would like you to meet. Frank Buck is coming. There is no need to RSVP. I know that you are not done until about nine, so if you would like, just get here when you can. Our address is:

376 Madison.
Your new friend,
Val McPhearson
P.S. I do hope I see you there.

I reread the note several times. Surprise and anticipation washed over me just like stormy waves in Santa Monica. I didn't want to admit it, but I hoped there was something written between the lines. My jitters about Val's note didn't make any sense. Even though I had just met her, I felt as eager for the party as a kid counting down the days to his birthday. What's more, she was married. Yet I was all twisted up inside. I hadn't felt that way about anybody since I left Hollywood. Recalling what a fiasco that turned out to be, I was determined not to make that same mistake.

CHAPTER 9

Madame Lya

Jake and friends, including Lya Graf (seated on the wing)

Wisconsin Historical Society - Image ID 10860

"Damn it!"

A new roustabout on bucket brigade must have missed it, I thought, scraping freshly dropped manure from my shoes. My logic was of little consolation. I had been thoughtlessly rushing to avoid the long lines at Western Union and now I had to pay the price for my carelessness. Once my shoes were as clean as they were going to get, I raced to Lexington Avenue and the nearest telegraph office.

"For the love of Mike!" I growled when I saw the eighteen others who had beaten me to the punch. *That's just what I need to start my day—a half-hour wait in line with a bunch of palookas being serviced by one Methuselah of a clerk*. Just the thought of it made my back ache.

The other customers looked like a regular rogue's gallery. They were as different from one another as night is from day. But when I walked into the place, they all did the same thing: In a simultaneous ballet of rudeness, all eyes turned and stared at me. Then, as if collectively trying to erase their bad manners, in unison they quickly looked away. I was accustomed to how herd-like people could be in demonstrating and then attempting to hide their lack of manners. As time had gone by, I thought I'd gotten better at ignoring that kind of negative attention. But for some reason, that morning it particularly irked me.

Because of the mess on Monday night and my dithering about whether to stay or leave the circus, I had woken up on the wrong side of the bed. Add to that the horse shit on my shoes and the prospect of an hour-wait in line and you have a recipe for my foul mood and my short fuse. It's not hard to fathom why I had a hell of a time ignoring their discourtesy. I wanted to be anywhere else but in that crowded Western Union office, but I didn't have a choice.

That morning at 8:30 a.m. on the dot, as I did on the fifteenth and the thirtieth of every month, come rain or shine, I collected my check at the pay-car, cashed it, and made my way to the nearest Western Union office. Like clockwork, every two weeks I would then wire my folks money. Ever since they went *mahulla* (bankrupt) after the Crash, Mama and Papa needed my help to make ends meet. Even though things were going a bit better for them, I still sent a little something every time I got paid. Looking back on it now, I can say that needing to help my folks gave me a reason to put up with the lousy things I had to endure on the road; not the least of which was my loneliness, occasionally stepping in fresh manure, and long waits in line.

I just wanted to send my money order to my folks, make it through the rest of that day with no more aggravation, and attend Val's party that evening. My jaw was clenched as I stomped through the crowd in the Western Union office toward the wooden tables in the back where they kept the forms for money orders.

That's where I found her. She was standing on tiptoes between two tables, trying to get hold of one of those forms. The little woman could barely reach the counter, let alone the cubbyholes where the documents were stashed. She had her back to me, but there was no mistaking her. I can just picture Lya now.

She was always a sharp dresser. As a matter of fact, that morning Lya was the best dressed person in the place. She wore a conservative knit suit of gray wool, a black cloche, and gray and black gloves. When Lya stretched her three-and-one-half-foot self to reach the necessary paper-work for a money order, I noticed her black patent leather high heels and her finely shaped, tiny calves.

Lya was so intensely involved with trying to get ahold of that form that, unlike the others, she hadn't even noticed me come in. Encountering my little friend was a pleasant surprise on what was already a most unpleasant morning. Just the sight of her gave me a lift; Lya had that way about her.

I was relieved that my mood lightened a bit I didn't want my friend to see my dark side. In those days I still worked particularly hard at hiding it. It must have made me feel a bit ashamed. That probably explains why when my gloominess would descend I'd disappear for a few days. Thank-fully those times had been few and far between. But recently they had been increasing. I wondered how long I could keep my moods a secret. Up to that point the worse thing any of my chums in Ringling Bros could say about me was that I was shy. My conversation with Harry the previous day in the dressing room was the first time I had ever spoken frankly with any of the other freaks about my melancholy.

I reached over Lya's head, down onto the counter, and took a hold of the form she was struggling to reach. "May I be of service, *fräulein*?" I asked, clicking my heels together just behind her.

She spun around and glared up at me. "I don't have time for foolishness, Jake," Lya said in her strong German accent. Then she grabbed the form out of my hand in a way that put me off more than the stares of the people in line. I wasn't used to that kind of rudeness from her. Normally when we met she was the first one to smile. She was typically playful and even a little coquettish, but never curt like that.

Lya Graf was another one of the sideshow's little Germans. When she first came to Ringling Bros two years before, Daisy Doll—Harry's sister—had introduced us. After that, the Dolls, Lya, and I became inseparable. When we went off the lot to dinner or the movies we always got stares. I guess the coming together of opposites always draws attention. It's magnetic. One reporter in Chicago saw Lya and me together at a fundraiser for orphans at the Palmer House. The picture his photographer snapped of us turned out to be front page news in the next day's *Tribune*. The headline that accompanied it read, "The Oddest Couple: World's Tallest Man and World's Smallest Woman." When my friends pointed it out and teased me, I laughed to cover my embarrassment. But Lya didn't think it was so funny. She got angry. "You think it's a joke?" Lya asked as she stomped away from the rest of us.

She was an exotic, brunette beauty with prominent cheekbones, porcelain skin, perfectly proportioned features, and an exquisite, curvaceous figure. Sometimes she moved with a combination of elegance, grace, and earthiness. At those times she seemed absolutely sultry. But at others she seemed asexual, like a kid sister.

That morning in the Western Union office, I was surprised by her angry ebony eyes. As a matter of fact, I don't think I'd seen her that angry since the incident with the newspaper headline in Chicago.

That wasn't the first time we'd run into one another in a telegraph office, each of us wiring money; me to my family in Texas and her to her people in Dresden. I guess family obligations are cross-cultural.

"I know it's just a little every couple of weeks," she said once in the Davenport telegraph office, "but my family depends on me." Her father was a tailor and her mother an accountant, but they barely made ends meet for themselves and Lya's two younger, normal-sized brothers who still lived at home. Things were tough after the Great War in Berlin. "I wouldn't think of not helping them out," she had told me that day. I knew just what she meant.

Though Lya was easy to talk to, we never talked about anything too personal. Still, she was one of those people that make you feel special. Lya was more than a friend. She was intuitive and smart. I imagined her to be a shrewd counselor who, if the need arose, could help me get a different take on things. Sometimes I observed people asking Lya's advice. When they did, I noticed that she never told them what to do. She just listened. But the way she listened was different than when others, even my friends, listened. Lya listened more deeply. So far I had resisted the temptation to do so, but when she listened to me she made me want to open up more. *There's something unique about her that's much more impressive than her diminutive size,* I concluded back then. It wasn't only me. Others recognized her wisdom as well.

"She has the gift," Harry had said. He told me how she had used a dream he shared with her to help him make the right decision about a movie offer to star in an upcoming Todd Browning feature film. That movie turned out to be the smash hit *Freaks.* It made him a bundle and led to a role in *The Wizard of Oz.* At the urging of Harry and Daisy, Lya began to use her forte to make a few extra dollars in the sideshow as "Madame Lya, Fortune Teller: Seer of the Stars and Reader of the Crystal Ball."

Looking back on it, Lya was one of my closest friends in Ringling Bros. I miss her. Yet back then, the thought of telling her about my plans to leave the circus made me nervous, so I kept putting it off. But something told me she already knew. She was such an old soul, with insight beyond her years. It's too bad what happened to her.

I fondly recall the time we spent together and I wish, I really wish, I had appreciated it more. There were late nights over coffee and cigarettes while playing gin rummy in the pie car, and conversations in the backyard before our shows began and after they finished When you have the perspective that comes with time . . . oh perspective; it can be a blessing or a curse. Anyway, with hindsight you know what was important and what was a waste of time. You look back and you realize you had people around that you took for granted. You see that you were never as alone as you thought you were.

But that morning in May of 1936 in the Western Union office in Manhattan all I could focus on was Lya's intensity. She was a freak, like the rest of us in the sideshow, but Lya was a freak in a different way, too. But it's not what you might think. The word *freak* had a special significance for all of us in the sideshow. It meant we were troopers, earning a living in the circus. But that word meant even more than that to me.

When I think of that word, I remember an incident with my parents' dictionary while I was home on a break from Ringling Bros. One day during that trip, it must have been in the winter of 1932, I was sitting at Papa's old, oak, rolltop desk at Geneva Loan and worrying if I was going to break his uncomfortable office chair. I was thumbing through my folks' dusty *Webster's Dictionary*. They hardly ever used that damned book; it seemed brand new. But that day they finally did have need of it. They were addressing a letter to my mother's brother, Uncle Label, who had immigrated to Scotland. My parents had asked me to look up the correct spelling of *Glasgow*. I think the dictionary intimidated my folks. I wondered why they ever bought that book in the first place. Looking back on it, I think they were, like many immigrants, insecure and sensitive about their use of English. They wanted at least the semblance of a reliable literary resource, a linguistic weapon they could call upon in case the need arose to defend themselves. Unlike the pitches of other snake-oil salesmen who preyed on immigrants, when it came to the huckster who sold them their first and last dictionary, they were easy prey.

That morning, sitting in Geneva Loan as I tried to find the correct spelling of *Glasgow*, I accidentally—if you believe in accidents—came across the word *freak*. Among the synonyms and dictionary definitions, I found that a freak is someone who has special, other worldly, magical powers.

Well, my friend Lya was the first freak I met who fit those words. There was, indeed, something magical and other worldly about her. As a matter of fact, I had been thinking that maybe some of her other worldly magic might help me interpret the dream I had about the merry-go-round mount who became a Pegasus. But with all that was going on, I hadn't gotten around to it. *Maybe waiting in line together today at the Western Union office will be an opportunity to do just that*, I thought.

"I'm sorry, Lya. I was just trying to help you out," I said, staring down at my little friend and trying to smooth over any feathers I had ruffled.

"Don't worry, Jake. It's not arms and legs. I've just got a lot on my mind," she answered.

"I don't mean to intrude, but what are you worried about?" I asked.

"I really don't want to talk about it," she said. Then she opened her purse and removed a fountain pen. "Would you give me a lift?"

"Sure." I picked her up and set her down on the counter. Then she sat down on the granite countertop and began to fill out the form. I heard a snicker and turned to see two of the rubes in line pointing at us. When she finished, she nodded at me. I lifted her up and set her down on the ground.

"Danke shoen." Despite her thank you, there was a bite in her voice. We made our way to the back of the line. As we walked, her high heels made a loud clickety-clack sound on the marble floor.

"What's going on with you?" she asked frankly, avoiding any pleasantries. "You haven't seemed yourself lately." *Was my sadness that apparent?* I wondered. "I'm worried about you," she continued. Her eyes were so concentrated I thought they would burn a hole right through me. "The little voice in my head that I've learned to listen to has been telling me things are *nicht gut* (not good)."

"What do you mean?" I asked.

"You know what I mean, Jake." She cut right through my subterfuge, like a sharp knife through Swiss cheese. When she was straightforward like that with others I admired her for her honesty, but when both barrels of her directness were aimed at me I wanted to duck. Reflexively, I looked to the door as if I were planning out the easiest path to escape her questions.

"You've been moping around for weeks. Even though you're trying to not show it, I can feel your moodiness like an arthritic elbow feels the rain."

I wondered if I hadn't really taken that morning's scowl off my face and what she was referring to was my sour puss. Maybe I wasn't doing such a good job of hiding my melancholy. I was worried and embarrassed that somehow, with her second sight, she might be aware of what I had done on Monday night.

"This line is moving slower than molasses in January," I said, trying to change the subject.

"And what's this I hear about you attacking a fan in front of Gargantua's cage?"

I felt cornered. There was no way out. "I have a lot on my mind, too," I replied, shrugging my shoulders.

"So what's eating at you?" She was relentless.

"Well, to tell you the truth . . . "

"That's what I've come to expect from you, Jake."

Trying to bullshit my way out would never work with her. Lya was too perceptive for that. In an instant, I decided that was as good a time as any to tell her the truth. "I've been struggling with whether or not to leave the circus."

"What?" she looked amazed at what I had said. Lya put her hands on her hips and continued. "Are you that unhappy?" She snapped at me again.

The look on my face must have been a combination of pain and puzzlement. I would have expected a more compassionate or even a more curious response but not her hostility. Lya questioned me like a prosecutor and a preacher; as if she already knew the answers to her questions before she asked them and like she was going to give me a sermon. Her manner put me off. If I didn't have to send that damned money order to my parents I would have stormed out of the telegraph office. Hostility or not, I decided to tell her what was on my mind.

"I'm tired of the rubbernecks and the questions about my personal life. I'm tired of not fitting in." The look on my face changed from puzzlement and pain to anger. Emphasizing my words, I raised my voice and pointed at her. The man in line in front of us turned to watch and listen to what must have looked like a very odd scene. I immediately lowered my voice and spoke in an angry whisper. The rube got the message and turned back around. "I've had it with being an exhibit in a sideshow. I'm tired of sleeping on a cramped train, walking through mud, crapping in an outhouse and stepping in manure. There's got to be more for me in this life."

"You know, Jake, Ringling Bros has been very good to us." Her voice was softer now. I felt like a yo-yo. An instant before, I had felt repelled. But when her tone changed I had calmed down a bit and felt drawn to her. "Other freaks like us are shut-ins or working for abusive mud shows." *She sounds like Clyde Ingalls*, I thought. But she was more caring. "I came to accept things as they are a long time ago. This is where I am, where I'm supposed to be, and where I want to be. And what's more, I don't really have any choice," she said.

The busybody who had tried to eavesdrop on our conversation a few minutes before took a step toward the front of the line and Lya and I both stepped forward into the vacant space.

"I have many souls who depend on me." As she spoke, I thought about my mother and father and how they depended on me. "I don't have time for self-indulgence," Lya said as we waited. "It's just a waste of time, Jake."

"Well, I hope I do have a choice; some other options in this life besides the circus. I don't want to waste any more time. That's what I'm afraid I've been doing. I'm struggling with this. Can you help me?" I put my hand on Lya's shoulder. My palm covered her entire shoulder and my fingers went almost half way down her back. She backed away. "Can you share some of your wisdom, Madame Lya?"

Other than my parents, my brothers, and a few friends in Hollywood, that was the first time I'd ever really asked anyone for help. Lya looked up and paused. She took a step toward me.

"I don't have any special insight, Jake. I'm just practical and I use common sense."

"Well, I guess I'm not the most practical person and when it comes to common sense . . . it's not so common, at least not with me." I forced a laugh.

"I really don't have any wisdom about what you should or shouldn't do about the circus, Jake. But I think you know how I feel about the subject," Lya said as she looked away.

There were several seconds of silence. To avoid the discomfort the quiet stirred in me, I turned to the large window to my left and felt the warmth of the morning sun streaming through the plate glass. Then I turned to my right and saw all sizes and shapes of the shadows cast by the people in line on the bare white wall to my right. I immediately looked back to Lya.

By now more of the people ahead of us had been served and we moved closer to our destination. Lya's lack of a response to my question about my future in Ringling Bros made me anxious. I really couldn't tolerate the silence any longer. Maybe my question about leaving the circus had hit a chord with her. Maybe I had put her on the spot and she was uncomfortable, too. In my nervousness, I attempted to make conversation to fill the vacuum. I struggled to find something to say and awkwardly changed the subject from my career to my dream life. Maybe she would respond to that. I knew she liked to talk about dreams. At least we would be talking and not just standing there.

"I had a dream that has been troubling me. Can I share it with you?"

"Sure, Jake, if that's what you really want to talk about," Lya answered.

I wasn't sure if she was being accommodating or sarcastic. I sighed and proceeded to tell her about my dream: the wooden horse stepping into nothing, his transformation into Pegasus, and his flight across the sea to the horizon. I loved that dream. I knew it had to be significant.

Lya listened intently. Then she paused and quietly turned to face the lineup of shadows on the wall. "You see those shadows, Jake?" I nodded, turning again to the black silhouettes. "All we know about this world, each other and ourselves, is shadows . . . superficial, two dimensional, dim reflections. Shadows are all we ever know, and yours, my friend, is quite a long shadow. I think there is a giant sleeping somewhere in there that is starting to stir. It's time to wake him up."

I had no idea what in the hell she was talking about. "What about the horse and Pegasus?" I asked.

"It's artifice. Just artifice."

"What?" I asked. I was bewildered.

"Next." I heard the clerk's gruff voice.

It was Lya's turn to purchase and send her money order. She turned away from me and walked up to the counter. I felt unsatisfied, confused, and angry. Her interpretation of my dream was anything but comforting. I was more unsettled than before she began to speak. I wished I'd never opened my mouth and asked for her help.

When Lya finished her business, she turned, walked to the door, and left. She hadn't even said good-bye.

Why was she so dismissive and abrupt? I felt like I'd just gotten stood up, that I'd been abandoned, that I didn't get what I needed. I mean, I had finally confided in Lya and she had not responded. In retrospect, I think she did respond. I just didn't like what she had to say. In just a few days I needed to give Ingalls my answer, and I was no closer to a decision than I had been when I left the sideshow the night before. As she walked to the door, all I could focus on was the clickety-clack sound her high heels made on the marble floor. I had unfinished business with that little woman and I knew, sooner or later, I'd have to deal with it.

CHAPTER 10

Uptown

Hertzberg Circus Collection, Witte Museum, San Antonio, Texas

Lya's unusual behavior at the Western Union office and the impending deadline for my circus contract troubled me for rest of the day. I couldn't get any relief. So at half past nine when Buck and I exited the cab we'd shared from the Garden in front of Val's brownstone, I was looking forward to the party as a needed distraction. Her home was in the upper fifties on Madison Avenue in a very swanky neighborhood.

"Pretty uptown, wouldn't ya say, Jake?" Buck asked as we climbed the outside steps.

The butler's condescending squint put me off and should have been the first hint I didn't belong. "Good evening, gentlemen," he said with a dismissive tone.

Stepping into the stylish three-story residence didn't make me any more comfortable. I had never seen such elegant furnishings. Everywhere I looked there was carved mahogany, chiseled stone antiques, crystal chandeliers, exotic Ottoman rugs from some pasha's harem and walls full of paintings—some classical, some in strange, upsetting styles I'd never seen before.

So this is how the other half lives, I thought. The place looked more like a museum full of rich people than a home.

Val's townhouse was a striking contrast to anything I'd ever experienced. My folks' place in El Paso was very simple, my apartment in Hollywood had been minimal, and to say my accommodations on the circus train were spartan would be an overstatement. My discomfort in those ritzy surroundings grew ten-fold the moment I stepped into the place and all eyes seemed to stare at me.

The throng of guests who filled Val's home walked with the confidence of those who never work, worry about paying bills, or even perspire. They just go from polo match to polo match and party to party. *This group could easily have stepped out of a Fitzgerald novel*, I thought. The men were attired alike in dinner jackets and ties. Some wore monocles. The women were all dressed in evening gowns, mostly in black. Some wore gloves. Looking at all those fancy people made it hard to believe that the streets of New York were full of homeless, hungry beggars.

"The guys look like a pack of penguins," Buck said with a laugh. "Some of them have got to be fore-flushers without even two nickels to rub together."

Buck and I wore plain, dark, threadbare suits and could easily have been mistaken for the help. Almost to confirm my suspicions, a waiter passed with a tray of exotic looking hors d'oeuvres but didn't even stop to offer us any. Buck grabbed him by the arm.

"Whoa there, sonny," he said with authority. Then he scooped up what appeared to be a shrimp and put the whole thing in his mouth. He spit the tail into a cocktail napkin and stuffed it into the waiter's shirt pocket. "Would you mind getting us some highballs?" he asked. "Then again, my friend here already has a set." Buck laughed and glanced up at me. The waiter looked as uneasy as I felt.

"That's very funny, Frank, but hardly original. You need to get some new material," I said as the waiter disappeared.

I'm sure any bantering with Buck that night was my attempt to hide just how awkward I felt in that alien setting. I looked around the room and noticed that out of the sixty or so people that were milling about, most of them were staring at me. Even though I'm sure they saw themselves as refined, cultured, and superior, they still gawked, just like the rabble had in the telegraph office that morning.

Then, without so much as a by-your-leave, Buck charged off toward a young flapper in a low-cut gown with a slit up the side. He moved like a leopard.

Now abandoned and standing alone in that crowd, I wanted nothing more than to shrink into the expensive tongue and groove oak floor. If it weren't for my desire to see Val I would have left immediately. Instead, a grand piano situated toward the back of the living room near the open terrace windows drew my attention. But for some reason I just stood there and didn't move toward it.

Why did I ever come to this damned shindig? I wondered. *I should have listened to my intuition and just gone back to the circus train.*

I was barely thirty years old when I attended that party. Back then I saw myself as a full-grown, mature man. Looking at the world from this hospital bed, I realize that growing up and maturing are not about age, but about experience and whether or not you learn from it. You might think it's strange to hear a giant like me talking about growing up. I guess you can look at growing up from more angles than there are in a geometry book. Well, to be honest, in many ways at thirty I was still a kid with a lot to learn. One of the things I had not yet gotten a handle on was how important it was to listen to myself. As a result, I did many foolish things, like attending Val's party, where I ended up feeling like a pork chop at a rabbi's convention.

But here's the rub; despite everything that happened to me, after all these years, I can't say I truly regret having gone to that party. There's something to be said for foolish choices that you can't truly appreciate until you get some distance. You see, as a result of attending Val's party, a lot happened that would never have occurred if I hadn't gone.

Finally, I moved across that crowded living room toward the piano. But I surprised myself and hurried by the ebony Steinway, then out of the huge, open terrace doors into the warm spring night and what I hoped would be some solitude. On the huge balcony, the first thing that caught my eye was a score of potted outdoor shrubs, which had all been trimmed in the shape of animals.

"Here is that highball, sir," said the young waiter who had come outside searching for me.

I smiled down at him and took the drink. *I have more in common with the server than any of Val's highfalutin friends*, I thought. As I glanced down to thank him, I noticed I was standing next to a shrub that resembled a giraffe. When I looked back the server was gone.

There would be no solitude on the balcony. It too was full of gawkers. Nobody smiled. Nobody said hello. It was as if I was on my sideshow platform at the circus, and they were a really tough audience. A few minutes later, unable to get comfortable outside, I stepped back into the smoky living room. That time I didn't hesitate but went directly to the piano and sat down. Ever since I was a little boy and I started playing with the used instruments in my father's store, I have loved making music. I guess that's why I spent all those hours teaching myself to play the piano and the saxophone. That came in handy during my days in vaudeville. I closed my eyes and stretched my fingers out on the cool, ivory keys. The feeling was familiar and comforting. First I played Bix

Beiderbecke's "In the Dark" and then Kern's "Ol' Man River." The music helped me to forget just how out of place I felt.

The next time I looked up, a pair of smoldering, chocolate eyes sheltered by one continuous brow, were embracing me. Those eyes, set deep in an angular face with pouty lips and the nose of a Russian empress, belonged to a young woman who looked like she had seen more than her fair share of pain. She appeared tough yet feminine, and wore her woven brown hair in a bun with a crown of sweet-smelling gardenias. The young woman's colorful jewelry and clothing stood in stark contrast to the staid black worn by all the others at the party and made her look like a walking *piñata* at a gathering of widows.

"You play so nicely," she said with heavily accented English and no hint of a smile. The strange-looking woman dropped her gaze. "*Ay*, your hands almost cover the whole keyboard."

"Two octaves, sixteen keys." I answered softly.

"*¿Qué* (What)?"

I couldn't tell if she couldn't hear me or she didn't believe what I had said.

"Each of my hands covers two octaves; sixteen keys," I explained in a bit louder voice. Since I was sitting at the piano, when I looked up I stared directly into her eyes. "*Muchas gracias* for the compliment about my playing," I answered.

"*¿Hablas español* (Do you speak Spanish)?"

"*Seguro que sí* (I sure do)."

She reached out her hand and I did as well. The woman looked down at my extended fingers, studying them for several seconds as if they were some kind of a strange aquatic animal she'd found on the beach. Then she took hold of my hand and rubbed the thumb of her other hand across one of my knuckles. I didn't want her to stop. My legs quivered. At the time, I had no idea who this woman was, but she was like no one I'd ever seen. There was something strange, alluring, and dangerous about her. I liked it. I felt heady.

She was attractive, but to tell you the truth back then I was so hard up that if somebody's toothless grandma had done the same thing I might have gotten aroused. I now understand that that night, to that exotic looking woman, I was just a big toy. She was amusing herself. But compared to other women who would soon cross my path, her playing was innocent.

"My name is Frida," she said in a whisper that felt strangely intimate. "You must be *el gigante* from *el circo*; the one who did the sculpture of the *jirafa*. Val told me you might come."

I looked over her shoulder and saw a squatty, stout man with a dark complexion and distinguished gray hair walking with Val toward us. Val was a vision of grace and loveliness. I could see her green eyes halfway across the room. They popped, accentuated by her simple beaded black gown. Val also sported a flapper's black headband that made a chic statement. She appeared to stand out from the other women in black but not so much as to be unique or unconventional like Frida.

"Hiya, Jake." She smiled warmly. "Thank you so much for coming." I stood up from the piano and smiled back, forgetting that I didn't belong. "I see you have met my dear friend, Frida Kahlo." Val put her hand on my forearm and glanced over at her friend.

I'm not sure if Val was just being cordial or marking her territory. The interest Val and Frida had directed my way was unsettling. I think that those two women were competing for something that had nothing to do with me.

At first I couldn't place Val's friend. But when she mentioned her last name, I immediately recognized the seductress I'd been chatting with. I often wonder what would have happened if I got tangled up in that tornado.

I realized that the squatty, stout man with Val must be Frida Kahlo's equally famous husband, Diego Rivera. Val then formally introduced us. I extended my arm. He gently shook my hand, looked down to the ground, and said nothing. Rivera's palm was sweaty. Since my days in Hollywood, I haven't been overly impressed by celebrities. But I must admit I was taken with Diego Rivera and Frida Kahlo.

A week before I met them at Val's party, I had read a piece in the *Herald* about Kahlo and Rivera and their art. In '34, I actually got to see "Man at the Crossroads," Diego's infamous mural in the lobby of the newly constructed Rockefeller Center. That happened just before Rockefeller's minions took pickaxes to it. Supposedly they destroyed that magnificent piece because it contained an unapproved image of Lenin. The following year I also saw a few of Frida's paintings at a gallery in Chicago. The article in the *Herald* had reported that they were in New York for the second-ever special exhibition at the New Museum of Modern Art.

Rivera had a jowly pockmarked face. For an instant I imagined that deep down between the folds of fat on his face, archeologists might discover an ancient Aztec ruin. He had dark eyes—every bit as small as his mate's were big—hat were hidden behind silver, wire-rimmed, octagonal glasses with lenses as thick as soda pop bottles. You could instantly see his indigenous roots in his body and feel them with his presence. He wore a poorly fitted, wrinkled, black linen suit that looked like he'd slept in it the night before, a belt thick enough to hold cartridges, and scuffed, clunky, black miner's shoes. Rivera's sloppy appearance and shorter stature served as an immediate foil for the finely manicured, tall sixty-year-old man who stood next to him. I wondered who he was.

"Oh, silly me, I forgot to introduce you to James. Jake, this is my husband," Val said. With that, the sixty year old reached out his hand and stared intensely into my eyes as if he were trying to read something written in them. James McPhearson had the cool bearing of a tuxedo-clad patrician who was accustomed to being in charge. His hand was dry and cool as a cucumber. I wondered why Val hadn't introduced her husband first.

"Val has told me all about you, Mr. Erlich. Welcome to our humble abode."

Humble, I thought, laughing to myself. "Thank you for inviting me." I answered meekly.

"I hope you enjoy yourself. Now if you will please excuse me, old chap, I have something I need to attend to." As he walked away, I thought he looked more like Val's grandfather then her husband.

"Jake, there are so many people at my party I want you to meet." Val squeezed my hand. "There are artists and friends . . . but before I forget, I have some wonderful news. A lot has happened since I met you."

Whatever wonderful news she was talking about, it didn't matter. She didn't have to say another word. You see, whatever Val was selling, I was buying. At least that's what I thought at the time. I looked at her and imagined being introduced to a whole new group of wonderful friends that weren't freaks.

"Do you remember I told you I wanted to show your sculpture to some acquaintances?" I nodded. "Well, I showed it to Frida and Diego. They demanded I immediately take it to that little man over there. Do you know who he is?"

She pointed to a small-framed, fortyish man sitting across the room on a love seat. He was drinking from a champagne flute and engrossed in conversation with a blonde woman with a full head of hair. She was twice his size and resembled a combination of a big-bosomed opera singer and a horn-helmeted Teutonic goddess. I imagined that at any moment she'd begin belting out an aria in German and one of those massive breasts would plop out of her low-cut gown, smack the smarmy looking bald man in the middle of his head, and knock him unconscious.

"No." I didn't have the slightest idea who he was or why I should care.

"He is a dear friend of ours. His name is Gustav Peters. He is the curator of the New Museum of Modern Art. Well Gustav, Diego, Frida, and I all agreed, you've got raw talent, Mr. Erlich; innate ability; a gift. I spoke to my husband. He immediately called John Ringling, another dear friend."

Is there anybody these people don't know? I thought. To be honest, at that moment I felt a bit intimidated by being in the court of the high and mighty McPhearsons. That would have been a really good time for me to have remembered Papa's admonition that "a good name is worth more than gold."

"John Ringling and my husband want to offer you a scholarship to art school the next time the circus winters in Florida. What do you think about that?"

I couldn't think and I couldn't speak, but it had nothing to do with the fact that I had just been offered a scholarship to art school. I'm embarrassed to admit it, but at that instant all I focused on was how it felt to hold Val's hand. To me, that night at that fancy party, art was still an abstraction and art school wasn't real. The only reality at that instant was the smell and touch of the beautiful woman with an old man for a husband standing next to me. But something about Val's proposal did attract me. I wasn't thinking about her offer in terms of my future as an artist. The only thing that enticed me about art school was that it was a means to get to know her.

Then I had a pang of guilt. *Val's a married woman*, I said to myself. It was as if I feared I'd climbed too high. If the fall didn't get me, then some other divine retribution certainly would. I reeled myself back in.

"Thank you, ma'am, but it was a fluke. I'm really not an artist," I said. I had seen myself through many different lenses: awkward child, giant outcast, Jew, freak, son, brother, friend, silent film comedian, but never as an artist, and least of all as a lover of a married woman.

"*No estoy de acuerdo* (I disagree). *Eres talentoso* (You're talented). I know talent when I see it." Rivera wagged his finger, as if this movement would jackhammer his point.

"You really think so?" I pivoted from feeling guilty to needing approval; an aspect of my personality of which I've never been proud. Then I bit my tongue so as to control myself and be more in command of my feelings and my words.

"*Sin duda* (Without a doubt)," Rivera continued. His voice grew more forceful.

Val and Frida nodded in agreement. In that instant, I saw my worry about whether to stay or leave the circus from a new perspective. If I left, it was a sure bet that John Ringling would revoke the generous offer Val just described, and I'd most likely never see her again. I didn't fully grasp it then, but I was falling for her in a big way.

But me . . . in art school? I just couldn't picture it. I was more confused than ever. Too many thoughts raced through my head for me to fully process any one of them. I felt shaky.

"I want you to meet Gustav," Val said as she floated across the room with Frida. An instant later, Frida limped back and whispered in my ear.

"I think we will be *amigos*. My father's best friend was a *largote* (big man). They played chess together. Do you play chess?" she asked.

"As a matter of fact—" But before I could answer she kissed me on the cheek and hobbled away toward Val. "She is so wonderful. I mean . . . I mean, Val is so wonderful." I worried that Frida's husband, who was still standing next to me, had misinterpreted whom I was talking about.

"Don't worry, Jake," Diego reassured me, stepping closer. He moved with a slow and measured pace. "I know what you mean. Val is wonderful. But it's such a waste. *Sabes, una calientota con un viejo que es tan frio como rico* (You know, a hot-blooded woman with an old man who is as cold as he is rich)."

I felt taken aback. Why was he telling me intimate things about Val? Even though I didn't know her very well, I still felt defensive of her and suspicious of the famous Mexican artist who was treating a relative stranger like me as a confidant. I looked across the room at Val.

For me, meeting her had been magical. But now, I don't know how magical it really was. Perhaps we met solely by chance. But so much of life is chance; how we decipher it and what we do as a result. Maybe that's where art comes from. Looking back on my life, I wished there had been more to my romances; that they matched my sweet imagination. It would take a while until I understood that I'm what you call a *romantic*. Real romance takes two, not just one with a vibrant fantasy life and a strong will.

Rivera cocked his head up and stared intensely at me. "Jake, Val tells me you worked in silent pictures. Tell me about the *viejas* in Hollywood? I hear those woman are fast and free," he said, almost licking his chops.

"I didn't have much to do with all of that," I replied sheepishly.

"I can't believe it . . . " He looked at me incredulously. "You're young and a motion picture star. They must have been on you like flies on *cajeta* (toffee)."

"Not really," I replied.

"How can that be? *¿Como es posible que eres conservador como un Victoriano o un norteño* (How is it possible that you're conservative like a Victorian or someone from northern Mexico)?" Rivera shook his head and looked puzzled.

"*¿Quién sabe* (Who knows)?" I replied, not wanting to disclose any more intimate details.

Actually, during my Hollywood days and during my time with the circus I wasn't innocent, but I certainly wasn't what you'd call a worldly man. I'd been to a cathouse or two, but that was so mechanical. I mean, the only time I'd ever fallen for anybody was once for a waitress in Hollywood. Some men are *mujeriegos* (womanizers) like Rivera and Buck. But as for me . . . well, some are meant to be married. Suffice it to say, I'm one of them. It is sad and one of my true regrets that that has never come to be.

"So how did a man like you ever stay so innocent?" Rivera asked sarcastically, evidently not believing what I had said.

It's something I'd thought about before. I'd been blessed with old-fashioned parents, an upbringing with good strong values, and kind, decent people who looked out for and sheltered me in Hollywood and the circus. But in retrospect, I think there was more to my innocence than that. Somewhere along the line I recall someone saying that innocence can be a thin disguise for fear. Maybe that was the case with me.

At thirty, in many ways I was still a boy with my manhood in a padlocked strongbox. Believe it or not, by nature I'm a pretty mild-mannered guy. It must not seem like it, especially after I told you how I clobbered that rube in the menagerie, but in those days I wasn't used to and avoided getting riled up like the plague. I guess that's why when I came anywhere close to feeling too strongly about anything or anyone, and God forbid, demonstrating it, particularly to a woman, it scared me six ways to Tuesday. Since I was young I knew that if I lost control I would do a lot of damage. Come to think of it, with all of my mom's worry about me and my health, I never once even raised my voice to her. Myer and Ben did, but not me. Besides the one time when I threw some flowers, I don't think I've ever felt angry at any female. I never, ever used those paints on my palette. Until I met Val, I didn't even know they were there. For that I'll always be grateful to her.

Rivera and I stood there silently for about a minute. Evidently he finally got the message that I really hadn't had any wild experiences with floozies because he changed the subject.

"You know, I think I saw one of your pictures before. *¿Dónde lo he visto* (Where have I seen you)?" Diego asked, stroking his chin. "*Ya, ya, recuerdo* (Now I remember). I saw you at the Omar Movie Theater in Mexico City in the winter of '24, *con la niñita*, the little girl. *¿Cómo se llama* (What was her name)?"

"Her name is Baby Peggy," I answered. "We made many movies together."

"*Era una maravilla* (She was a marvel); so tiny and such a good actress." If you would indulge me, kind *caballero*, I would love for you to tell me about that little movie star."

Rivera was persistent. If he couldn't get me to open up one way, he'd try another. I looked down at the odd looking Mexican muralist and thought back to that morning in 1923 when I was barely seventeen, and first met Baby Peggy.

CHAPTER 11

Baby Peggy

Jake and Baby Peggy in Jack and the Beanstalk, courtesy, Diana Serra Cary

As I recall, I met her on a cool, foggy morning. It was the time of year that Angelinos call the June Gloom. Zion Meyers and I arrived early and sat down in front of Stern's desk. Hoping I wouldn't break the chair that time, I was much more cautious then I had been when I parked myself in the same place two weeks before.

After safely seating myself, I heard a loud, sarcastic sigh of relief from Kitty, who was busy shuffling papers behind her desk. Her attempt at levity didn't lighten my mood. In a lame effort to lessen my anxiety, I engaged Meyers in small talk but it didn't work. I was about to lose my breakfast; my nerves were getting the better of me. Remember, as Meyers had made clear when we had lunch at Musso and Frank a few days before, there was a lot riding on that meeting.

"Have you talked to Jakey about the little girl?" Kitty asked.

"I told him a bit, but why don't you fill him in?" Meyers suggested.

I awkwardly turned my chair to face her.

"Well, she's what you call *adorable* . . . as cute as a button and smart as a whip. You won't believe how she minds . . . a natural for show business," Kitty said.

Since Meyers had first mentioned her name, I was worried big time that that kid held the key to my future. All weekend I scoured the town trying to see the child sensation on the silver screen. The only one of her films I could find playing anywhere was at a small movie house on Western. It was a two-reeler called *The Sheik*, a spoof on the Valentino classic of the same name.

I was surprised by just how good an actress Baby Peggy was. Compared to me, she seemed like a polished professional. I still can't figure out how someone so young could deliver a performance like that.

Maybe she was an actor in a past life, I thought. Unless you're a believer in reincarnation or you buy the idea of karma that so many of the swamis, mediums, and spiritualists who held court in Hollywood in those days tried to sell, I won't bother you with all my ruminations about who I must have been or what I must have done in previous lives to have merited being born into my unusual circumstances.

Seeing Baby Peggy's movie didn't really help much with my nerves that morning in Stern's office. I still had no idea what to expect when we met in person. I mean, I was usually good with kids. *Maybe this one will turn out to be a spoiled brat of a movie star. Maybe she's a fraidycat,* I thought. There was no telling what would happen when a little child met somebody my size for the first time.

"Before Baby Peggy's success in pictures, her parents were as poor as church mice," Kitty said. "The daddy was an out-of-work, knock-around cowboy, making a few dollars here and there doing stunts on horseback and, once in a while, acting as Tom Mix's double." When I saw that Kitty mimed holding onto a set of reins, I smiled. "Well one day, Marian, the mama—who happens to be an absolute doll—brought her nineteen-month-old to the set on the Century lot with a friend. It so happened that her friend had previously worked on one of Fred Fishbach's features. When he laid eyes on little Peggy he felt his prayers had been answered. You see, for some time, Fishbach had been scouring the town searching for a toddler to play alongside his star, Brownie the Wonder Dog. He was immediately taken with how well behaved the toddler was and how she obeyed her mother. That little bit of a girl fit the bill perfectly." Kitty sat forward and in her enthusiasm raised her voice. "It was a real flash of inspiration. When that flicker premiered the audience buzzed about the adorable tyke. The movie was a big hit. Now, a little more than two years later, Baby Peggy's a big box office hit. I mean she's as big as Jackie Coogan."

"Oh, don't bring that name up again," Meyers pleaded with a sarcastic tone. I turned to look at him.

"Why not?" I asked.

Meyers shook his head. "It's a sore subject around here," he added, and went on to explain that Fred Fishbach had also discovered Jackie Coogan. But Julius Stern in his infinite wisdom had taken a pass and had been kicking himself ever since.

"Well the Montgomerys—that's Baby Peggy's family," Kitty continued, "are now rich as Rockefeller. They even have their own horse ranch in The Valley. There are rumors floating around town that Uncle Carl Laemmle wants to offer her a big contract for features at Universal."

"I've seen her on the set. She works hard," Meyers added. "It's no way for a child to live. No playing. No bike. No friends. All the time she's up against scary—and I kid you not—dangerous stuff. Imagine a kid that age jumping out of a burning building, nearly being run over by a train, almost drowning in the surf, or being chased by dogs and bears. Until her last picture and the fiasco with that nasty pelican, I never saw her flustered, not even once."

After all, I've got to be scarier than a seabird, I thought. I glumly visualized the little girl taking one look at me, bursting into tears, and racing out of room, taking my movie career with her. I was so wrong. At that point, I had no way of knowing what a little soldier she was. But back then in Stern's office, waiting for that meeting, I pictured the worst and I had the knots in my stomach to prove it. As I sat there, I started to resent the idea that my future well-being depended on passing muster with a four year old. I had not even met Baby Peggy and I already didn't like her.

The door to the office flew open. Stern, followed by a young couple with a little *mazik* in tow, waltzed in. Stern stomped to his desk and sat down like some kind of potentate reclining on his throne. Baby Peggy broke away from her mother, galloped over to Kitty, and gave her a bear hug. Then she glanced back at her father as if she'd realized she'd broken a cardinal rule.

"I love your sailor suit, darling," Kitty said, admiring the little girls outfit. I rolled my eyes. *I bet that sailor getup cost a pretty penny*, I thought. Then the little girl started to bury her face in Kitty's skirt. She hesitated, glanced up at her father again, and then ran back to his side where she appeared to stand at attention. Baby Peggy had an impish little nose and lively brown eyes. Her hair was black and cut in short bangs. Her appearance was at once endearing and comical. The little girl had an animated, million-dollar smile outlined by two dimples. That smile broadcast her charisma to me and everyone else in Stern's office. No wonder she was a star.

Baby Peggy's mother, Marian Montgomery, with her chestnut hair worn in a pompadour, svelte figure, and luminous blue eyes, was in her mid-twenties and plainly pretty. There was warmth about her that made me feel she was someone I would like to get to know. Marian Montgomery, like Kitty, would turn out to be a good friend who helped me navigate the treacherous shoals of romance.

Baby Peggy's father, Jack, looked older and had rugged, cowboy good looks. Actually, he was a real life *vaquero* who, at thirteen, had run away from home in Illinois, bought a ticket to Alberta, and began his wild and wooly life as a cowpuncher. Whereas Marian had a peaches-and-cream complexion, Jack's skin was a dried, west Texas riverbed of patches and cracks.

"Mr. and Mrs. Montgomery, this is Jack Earle, the fella I was talking about," Stern spoke in serious tone from his perch behind his desk.

For a few seconds I hesitated. Everyone looked at me expecting some reaction. Then it hit me. Stern was talking about yours truly. I still wasn't accustomed to my new stage name. Finally, I stood up and extended my hand toward Jack and Marian. I wondered what would happen next. Should I say something? Should I wait for the little brat to approach me?

Stern, Kitty, Meyers, and the Montgomerys were silent. I felt the pressure growing to do something. Stern frowned. Obviously uncomfortable with the glacial progress of our meeting, he impatiently stood up and walked over to Baby Peggy.

What now? I thought.

"Come here, sweetheart. Talk to the nice giant," he said, grabbing hold of the little one's arm.

Why in the hell is he introducing me to a child—or anybody else—as a giant? I felt embarrassed and angry.

Baby Peggy started to pull back. Next I imagined she would run screaming from the room. But that's not what happened. Her father shot the little girl a demanding look and she stepped forward. I would soon learn that to Jack Montgomery, who compared child rearing to breaking wild horses, obedience was of the utmost importance. He equated it with love. Although I have come to have serious doubts about Jack Montgomery as a father and husband, he did become a confidant. It's funny how we look past or blind ourselves to our friends' flaws, even the serious ones.

Standing there at attention next to her father, Baby Peggy had the demeanor of a toy soldier. I knew that I needed to do something to cement my connection with that little girl other than rely on, what I would later learn, was her father's brand of intimidation. So I reached into my pocket and pulled out the silver dollar that my brother Myer gave me for luck when I left El Paso. I stepped closer, showed it to her, and then quickly palmed the silver dollar, making it disappear.

"Where did it go?" she asked.

"I dunno. It's gone," I answered.

With a flourish, I reached down and made it appear that I had pulled the coin from her ear. "You had it all along!" I said, thinking of the nest egg I'd hoped to begin building in Hollywood and how those plans might be dashed if this kid and I didn't hit it off.

"No, I didn't!" she said, laughing. Baby Peggy broke ranks and acted like the little girl that she was and not the little adult her father expected her to be. She began jumping, attempting to reach the coin I held in my hand. I handed her the silver dollar. I was surprised that she immediately gave it to her father.

"Mr. Earle, this is Baby Peggy," Jack said, pocketing the coin.

In a Little Lord Fauntleroy gesture, she formally extended her miniscule hand and it disappeared in my paw. I had won her over. Strange as it may sound, that brief interaction with Baby Peggy was a turning point in my life, a bend in my river.

I felt relieved and sat down. I actually began to like that child. In the relatively brief time we would work together, we formed a strong bond. If I knew then what I know now, I could have saved my young friend a lot of pain.

"It's a pleasure to meet you, Peggy," I said.

She giggled mischievously. Baby Peggy and I would go on to make several pictures together before she got her big break at Universal and left Century Studios for good. In the early twenties she went from making seventy-five dollars a week to a phenomenal million dollars for three features.

Many years later, I would run into her and learn that the fates had turned and times had become tough for the onetime *wunderkind* and her family. Her father's abrasive, tough-guy personality, coupled with relationships with show business swindlers, led to the loss of her leading roles and her family's wealth. As I recounted the story to Rivera at Val's party, I remember being rattled. *If it could happen to a big star like Baby Peggy*, I thought, *it could happen to anyone.*

That critical meeting with Baby Peggy jump-started my motion picture career. I was amazed at how well it turned out; but I wasn't the only one.

"She's outgoing. But I have never seen her be this outgoing with a stranger," a surprised Marian Montgomery had said.

"Maybe, for once, the child feels safe," Kitty injected from across the room, shooting an *I told you so* glance at Stern, who seemed stunned at how well things were working out.

Before the Montgomerys departed that morning, Baby Peggy approached and stood in front of me. Then she stepped on my right shoe and held out her tiny arms. I looked to her parents for a translation.

"She wants you to pick her up," her mother decoded.

When I lifted her up, I was surprised as she stood on my thighs and turned to face her parents, Kitty, and Stern. As if at a command performance, she bowed to stage left, bowed to stage right, and then curtseyed.

Baby Peggy and I made many blockbusters, including *Hansel and Gretel* and *Jack and the Beanstalk*. There was something absolutely singular about bringing opposites like us together on the screen. It engaged the public's imagination and pocketbook. Come to think of it, of the almost fifty films I made at Century Comedies starring alongside some of the top-rated comedians of the era, it didn't surprise me that Rivera had remembered one of the handful of hits I had made with Baby Peggy.

XXXX

"So I was right! I did see you and that little girl," Rivera said in a self-satisfied tone. Talking about Baby Peggy made me melancholy. I missed her, her parents, Kitty—and my innocence. I sat down on the piano bench and Rivera sat next to me. "So how did you get from silent pictures to Ringling Bros?" Rivera asked.

"That's a long story." I felt pressured. I really didn't want to discuss anything else that might make me blue, so I was relieved to see Frank Buck approaching us. Hopefully he'd save me from any more of Rivera's prying about my personal life and his inappropriate comments about Val.

My circus friend had returned from his quest for the lady faire empty handed. From where he sat, Rivera stared up at Buck imperiously. Then he abruptly turned to face me again. I wondered what kind of unpleasantness had occurred between those two. *There must have been a woman involved*, I thought.

"Hiya, Frank," I said. Rivera didn't say a word to him.

"Let's talk more about *las películas*," he insisted, ignoring Buck.

The pressure was off. I felt much more comfortable talking about silent pictures than about Val or my personal life. I started to tell them about Julius Stern.

Rivera interrupted me. "Of course you are going to tell us about a boss." Buck moved closer to the piano. Rivera eyed him cautiously. "The bosses *siempre se aprovechan de sus trabajadores*; they always take advantage of the workers."

"You goddamned bohemian. What kind of Bolshevik bullshit are you trying to feed him?" Buck aggressively pointed his index finger at Rivera.

Here it comes, I thought. The lion tamer and the artist glared at one another. *There's going to be an ugly scene, or worse*, I worried.

Rivera stood up aggressively. I held my breath waiting to see what would happen. Then Rivera did the unthinkable: He smiled at Buck. "*No te preocupes* (Don't worry), Jake, I know this *peti*-bourgeois *cabrón*. Val introduced us many moons ago."

Buck took a step toward him and gave him a bear hug and a hearty slap on the back. My tension about fisticuffs was immediately replaced by pernicious curiosity about just how long and why Buck and Val had been friends. Could it be that they really were lovers? Were my first impressions about Val and Buck, when I met her a few days before in the menagerie, correct? I couldn't believe I was beginning to feel pangs of jealousy for a woman I barely knew.

"Please go on with the story you started before you were so rudely interrupted, Jake," Rivera insisted. It took a concerted act of willpower to pull myself away from my suspicions and continue with my tale.

I went on to tell them about Stern and *Peg O' the Mounted*, a film Baby Peggy and I starred in that was scheduled to be shot in Yosemite National Park. When Stern saw the budget, in a fit of apoplexy he uttered his much-quoted reply: "A rock is a rock and a tree is a tree; drive twenty minutes and shoot the damned thing in Griffith Park."

In the same picture, the plot called for Baby Peggy to be stalked by a pair of mountain lions. The only lions we had in the studio zoo were African. You know, the ones with the busy manes, I said. Nonetheless, Stern ordered the director to use the lions he already had on hand. In his own words: "Shave those flea-bitten cats. Disguise the goddamned things. Do whatever you have to, but use them." And they did.

Things got quiet as Rivera and Buck appeared to form mental images of the shaved lions. Then Rivera made a loud noise. It wasn't a cackle or chuckle but a full *carcajada* of a belly laugh. For an instant Buck resisted, but then he joined him. I'd never seen him laugh that freely before. Their laughter was contagious. Soon I laughed too. We laughed so hard my side ached, and I forgot about my jealousy and worry about whether I should stay or leave the circus. The laughter united the three of us and made us bold. It launched us like free-falling, center-ring tumblers, each dependent on the other, but each alone, somersaulting off a lofty human pyramid through fiery rings into empty space.

Now it was more than laughter; it had holy fervor, a life of its own. Soon the three of us were laughing so hard, tears rolled down our cheeks. It was healthy, torrential laughter, a relief, a paroxysm. The laughter shook me to my foundation; a cathedral whose domes and spires have cracked, upended by a rampaging Titan; gravity now freeing centuries' worth of tears and trapped prayers.

We kept laughing until our tears flooded Val's fine oak floor. Then they flowed out past the snooty butler, onto Madison Avenue, and finally into a nearby storm drain. I imagined that later that night a tugboat captain on the Hudson couldn't understand why the river mysteriously rose or how the water had become so salty.

XXXX

The three of us stood there in an exhausted silence. After the cathartic release that just occurred, the quiet was almost meditative. Despite our laughter and how it temporarily connected us and the momentary freedom I experienced, I still felt lonely. I wondered where Val had gone and when she would return.

Emboldened by a deeper sense of intimacy with Rivera and Buck, and reminded of my melancholy, I couldn't stop myself and I told yet another story. As I began to speak I noticed that we had drawn a crowd of about twenty people.

For a person who had come to hate the stares of strangers, I must admit, that occasionally on the sets in Hollywood, and at times like that night at Val's party, I actually enjoyed being noticed. I wondered if I left the circus, would I ever feel the warmth of the spotlight on my face again? To be honest, I thought I'd miss performing. That's always been the paradox for me: on the one hand, I wanted to belong and loved being the center of attention, and on the other, I hated people staring at me. I guess it was because of why I thought they were staring. You see, I was afraid they looked at me not because of who I was, but because of what I was.

But that night, I continued to entertain the crowd. I told them how I'd been injured in 1925 doing a stunt during the filming of *A Royal Pair*. As I spoke, I noticed that Rivera's eyes opened wider, like he listened through them. Buck's bent elbows now rested on the baby grand, his palms pillowing his face.

He had a strange look for a death-defying lion tamer. It was the same innocent wonder I'd seen on the little faces in the orphanages and children's hospitals I'd visited over the years. When I told those kids tales of kind giants who would never harm a child they wore the same expression as Buck did.

I recounted how while filming that movie I'd fallen from the tiny running board of a speeding Model T Ford, crashed into the asphalt, and was knocked out cold. As I told that story I noticed that Val's guests pushed closer. I felt like I almost belonged, like a black who passed for white. If I'd been more aware during those days in Hollywood, I would have seen that fall as a pretty clear sign, a symbol, an ill-omened preview, of what would soon darken my world. But what good are signs or symbols if you don't understand them or you are not paying attention?

As I described what happened during the filming of *A Royal Pair* to my new friends that night, I relived it too. Please excuse my French, but that accident scared the piss out of me. After I left Hollywood, when friends tried to talk me into going back to the flickers, I'd think of that accident and other even more dangerous things that happened to me. But by then the Golden Age of silent films had passed. Talkies were all the rage. In those days I worried that even if I did go back to pictures I wouldn't fit in. It seems like that was the story of my life. I mean, in the thirties, after the Crash, some said the Golden Age of the circus was gone, too. Maybe there was no future for me there either.

Where did I belong? Where would I end up? I wondered.

XXXX

Rivera asked what happened after I had fallen from the Model T and was knocked out. I told him and rest of the crowd gathered around the piano that when I came to, the first thing I saw was Stern standing over me, bellowing through his damned megaphone. I scanned my audience and paused for dramatic effect.

Looking back on my life, I think that dramatizing things or making a joke out of them has helped me forget just how bad they really were.

After a few seconds, I proceeded with the story, telling them how Stern had shouted at me to get up and shoot the scene again. Several of those gathered around the piano laughed, others even clapped as if they'd seen a performance. It *was* a performance of sorts. A show where I took a story that was sad and scary and made people laugh at it, while never letting any of them see how I felt under all that greasepaint. I guess that's the mark of a true performer, especially the clowns.

As I watched Val's guests applaud, I wondered at how fast the last ten years had gone since I had left Hollywood. I questioned whether or not I would survive another ten years. After all, every sawbones I had ever visited sang the same tune; I was living on borrowed time. I laughed to myself, marveling at how I had ever ended up at a swanky party like that and wondered if I'd ever be invited to one again; especially if I left Ringling Bros and gave up my credentials as a bona fide celebrity.

The crowd, that only a few minutes before had made me comfortable, now made me claustrophobic. It was suddenly hard to breathe. I looked for the fastest way to get out of there. That's when I saw Val glancing at me over Buck's shoulder as they both walked out onto the terrace. I looked away.

CHAPTER 12

Ruby

Still from one of Jake's silent pictures, circa, 1924

Doctors have told me that in this life I've experienced my share, if not more, of wounds. As you, no doubt, have seen, I have the scars to prove it. But some of the wounds and scars I remember most aren't visible to the naked eye. I carry them in my heart. I wish I were a bigger man than that; that I could say I've forgotten all about them. But for me, even with time, the scars from some experiences have never totally disappeared.

I believe that in life, everybody develops according to their own innate schedule, by their own time clock. But when it came to women, my clock had never even been wound.

My first ill-fated try at romance came in late 1924. We were about to finish shooting *Hansel and Gretel*. I had been at Century Studios for over a year, and had several pictures under my belt. I was starting to get the hang of Hollywood and the movie business. In those days, when Baby Peggy and her mom had errands, Jack and I often lunched at The Napoli, the little Italian dive just across the street from the studio.

A young waitress named Ruby had been working there for about two months. She frequently waited on us. Her curly red hair, Catalina-harbor green eyes like Val's, her freckles, the gentle curve in her hips, how she moved . . . if you know what I mean, Ruby got my attention. If only I could have seen past her looks. For most men, that's an ability that, only—if ever—comes with age.

"I think that there waitress is flirting with you, boy. I do believe she's sweet on you, Jake," Jack teased.

"Oh, come on . . . there's no way," I disputed stiffly.

"Why don't you ask her on a date?"

"No. I don't have time for that tomfoolery."

"I thought you were Jewish, but you talk like a Mennonite."

"Besides, she's too pretty for me," I said, ignoring Jack's sarcasm. You see, truth be told, I was very shy and insecure and had no idea about my impact on the fairer sex. I'd never even been on a real date. I'd never so much as kissed a girl.

"Come on, Jake, are you joshin' with me? This is the simon-pure. You're a catch, buddy: bright, kind, good looking and a movie star to boot."

Back then I didn't really see myself as others saw me. You could say my melancholy and worry about being different fogged up any mirror I looked in. It's such a mystery how our beliefs about ourselves often have nothing to do with the real world. It's taken me a lifetime to recognize who I am. But back then, when it came to women, I didn't even have a clue.

"What do you have to lose?" Jack asked. "What's the worst that can happen?"

Well, worse than that did happen.

Over the next few weeks I ate just about every meal at The Napoli and I always sat at one of Ruby's tables. Other than small talk about the weather, I hardly said a word to her. I wanted to talk with Ruby; find out about her and tell her about me. But every time I tried to say anything it was as if I had come down with an exotic disease that robbed me of my speech. I didn't fancy myself a cake-eater, but when I was around that skirt I couldn't utter a word.

After one of my dinners, anxious to not appear like a drugstore cowboy, I took out a crossword puzzle from that day's *Times* and started to work on it.

"Whatcha doin?" Ruby asked.

"Just a crossword puzzler from the paper." I was shocked. She actually spoke to me. Maybe Jack was right. Maybe I had a chance with her. "Would you like to see?" I asked, eager for some way to continue the conversation.

"No, no thanks. All I ever care to look at in the paper is the funnies. Even when I buy a *Photo Play* I just look at the pictures of the stars," she said, wiping up the table in front of me. Frustrated, I buried my face in the puzzle. But Ruby kept talking. "Don't you ever eat at home?" Ruby teased. "It seems that you're always here."

I was speechless. She's actually trying to make conversation with me. Like a sap, I just smiled and raised my shoulders. All I could think about was how good her perfume smelled and whether or not she had a boyfriend. She looked at me and laughed. Then Ruby shook her head so hard I thought the pencil she kept tucked over her right ear would fall on the table where I was sitting. That torture seemed endless.

The next day at lunch, after a heart-stopping smile and a wink from Ruby and more of a sales job from Jack, I got my gumption up. *Today's the day I'll finally put a stop to my suffering and ask her out*, I thought.

"You go get her, sport!" Jack insisted.

I stood up and moved to the restaurant door, flung it open, and went outside. A minute later I came back with a bunch of winter roses that I bought at the flower stand on the corner. As I recollect, they were the color of ripe pumpkins. I was so nervous, I thought I was going to faint. It's funny to look back on it, but in those days the conversation I was about to have with Ruby was as serious as a heart attack. I sat down at the counter where she was refilling salt shakers.

"Hiya," she said.

"Hiya." I wanted to run away; but I made myself sit there. I really wanted to, but I couldn't speak. I just stared at her and felt dejected. *Here I go again*, I thought. I'd never done anything like that—you know, asking a girl on a date—before, and it was scaring the hell out of me. God, it's hard to believe I was so painfully bashful.

"Is there something you need?" she asked in a tone unmasking peevishness I hadn't seen before or that I'd chosen to ignore. I didn't know much about Ruby and she didn't know much about me. I was young and single and compelled to do what other young, single men do. So I ignored the warning signs. I wish I hadn't. Like I said before, when I was young I often ignored signs that warned me to stay away from people I really wanted in my life. That shortcoming has hurt me plenty. Anyway, I was finally able to come up with something to say.

"Do you . . . do you . . . " I stuttered.

"Do I what?" she asked.

"Would you . . . would you . . . like to go out with me for a soda sometime?" I set the roses on the counter.

"Is that what this is all about?" She put her right hand on my shoulder. Her touch sent tingling through my flesh and muscles all the way to my bones and beyond. That was the same feeling I had when Val had touched me at her party. Well, Ruby looked over at my friend Jack, picked up the roses, and chuckled.

"Why sure, Jake, that'd be swell." I glanced over at Jack, who gave me a wry smile as he clasped his hands in a victory salute.

All told, Ruby and I went out just three times. For our first date we went to the zoo in Griffith Park.

"The zoo is a good bet, Jake. You can walk around and not feel too much pressure to talk." Marian—you remember, she was Baby Peggy's mom—had recommended it when I asked for her advice. I thought it was a great idea.

I'll never forget how excited I was getting ready. That was the very first time I'd gone out on a date like other people my age. It felt like it was a significant accomplishment; like I was overcoming a hurdle that had stood in my way and hindered me from being normal.

On the bus ride to the park I was about to succumb to one of my fits of being unable to speak, but Kitty had helped me come up with a list of things we could talk about to break the ice. It was like she gave me a how-to guide or one of those connect-the-dots coloring books that the kids love. The first topic on the list was favorite animals.

"I like the monkeys. We absolutely must see them," Ruby insisted.

"Sure," I replied, trying my best to fit on the bus's tiny bench seat.

For a minute we sat in an awkward silence. She seemed fidgety. When I looked back on it later, I realized she had never asked me about my favorite animal. I had to volunteer that information myself. "My favorites are the giraffes," I offered.

Ruby didn't respond. She just kept patting her palms on the tops of her thighs and looking at the other passengers that were staring at us. *That went over like a lead balloon*, I thought. Next I asked about her family.

"That's kind of personal," she said curtly. Ruby was as interested in what I had to say as Aimee Semple-McPherson would have been in drinking a shot of gin. Then I moved to the next question on Kitty's "guaranteed to break the ice" list.

"Do you have any hobbies?"

"No, I just work."

I was beginning to feel like a dentist. Thank goodness the bus turned onto Crystal Springs Drive. A few minutes later we were at the Griffith Park bus stop for the zoo.

"This place is packed," she commented as we walked into the front entrance. I couldn't tell if she was complaining or just trying to make conversation.

I smiled. "You can say that again. The monkeys are this way," I said after getting directions from the ticket taker.

Within ten minutes we reached the chimpanzee cage. A crowd started to gather around us. One young father wanted Ruby and I to pose for a picture with his wife and baby.

"Do they always stare at you like that? You're getting as much attention as the animals." Ruby half laughed, scanning the crowd and moving closer to me in an affectionate sort of way.

Recalling that afternoon, I think I was hoping that Ruby's comment and her closeness meant she genuinely liked me. In those days all I hoped and dreamed of was to have someone to talk to. But as my Papa often said: "If hopes and dreams were candy and nuts nobody would be hungry next *yontif* (holiday)."

"It . . . it . . . " I stuttered, "it goes with the territory, you know." Without even thinking if she was safe, I felt the floodgates start to open. "To tell the truth, it used to bother me."

My use of the past tense with Ruby was a giveaway that I wasn't being totally honest. Whatever internal defenses I had developed or guardians that watched over me from another realm must have kicked into gear, because as much as I wanted to, I stopped myself from opening up more than I already had. "Most of the time I just ignore them."

"I want an ice cream bar; a milk nickel," she said, changing the subject.

"No problem. I think they sell ice cream over near the parrots." I led the way.

"You actors must make a lot of mazuma," Ruby commented as I put my billfold back in my rear pocket after paying for her ice cream.

"I do okay," I said proudly. I wanted to tell her that I sent most of my money home to my folks in Texas, but something told me to button my lip. That time I took note and didn't say a word.

XXXX

When I dropped her off at home a few hours later, I wasn't altogether sure how things had gone on our date, but I decided to risk it anyway.

"I had a nice time," I said in a half-truth tone of voice. "I hope you did too. Can I see you again, Ruby?"

She hesitated for a few excruciating seconds. "What did you have in mind?"

I had hoped for a simple yes, but clenched my jaw, steeling myself for a dreaded no. Her answer threw me off. I had no chance to think or seek counsel from Jack, Marian, or Kitty. "How about a walk on the beach?" I suggested impulsively.

"I go to the beach all the time. How about someplace different; someplace exiting . . . maybe a place with movie actors."

"Then we'll have to dine somewhere that s hopping," I said with a counterfeit certainty born of desperation. My instinct told me that might well be my last chance with her.

"That's the ticket. Just let me know when and where." She spun around, ran up the steps of her boarding house, and slammed the door behind her.

I was so keyed up all I could think about was spending more time with Ruby. If I knew then what I know now, I would have hightailed it and never called her back. They say hindsight is twenty-twenty. But back then, when it came to reading women, I was as blind as a bat.

I had no idea about dinner joints that were jumping, but I knew who did. The next day I called my buddy Meyers for some suggestions.

"If you really want to impress the dame, take her to the Brown Derby for a Cobb salad. It's the latest rage."

At my mid-morning break on the lot I went to The Napoli to find Ruby and tell her about the plans for our next date. When I got there, I looked in the picture window in front of the place. Toward the back of the restaurant, amidst the early lunchtime crowd, I spotted Ruby. She was waiting on two bellbottoms. Not wanting to interrupt her work, I waited. After ten minutes, she was still talking and laughing with them, so I left. That night I called her.

"Hey, Jake. I was thinking that we should go to Chasen's. My girlfriends say that's the place for the hoi-polloi," she said, diving into the conversation without hesitation.

"That's a possibility. But I . . . I have another suggestion for a real in-place."

"And that is . . . ?"

"Well, I hope it's okay with you. My friends at the studio say the place to see and be seen is the Brown Derby."

"Swell. I like that idea. Gotta go. See you Thursday night or sooner at The Napoli." She seemed genuinely happy with my choice.

I could hardly wait. It wasn't the typical butterflies any kid gets before seeing his girl. Again, for me, that date had more significance. It was a chance to feel regular, like I fit in with other young people my age. During that week I got some advice.

"You need to put your best foot forward," Jack had counseled me. "Women like a well-dressed cowboy." With Marian's help I picked out a new tie at Bullock's Wilshire. If they didn't need to be custom made, I would even have gone into hock and sprung for a new suit and shirt. I even got a haircut for the occasion. Lucky for me, my barber didn't charge more to cut hair off of extra big heads.

When I picked up Ruby that Thursday night, she looked dreamy.

"You're awfully pretty tonight," I said when she opened the door to her apartment. Even if Jack hadn't advised me to be complimentary, I would have said it anyway. That night, at least, Ruby's good looks untied my tongue.

The Brown Derby was packed.

"Right this way, Mr. Earle," the *maître d'* said. "We have a special table picked out for you."

"Wow, you're a big to-do here." Ruby smiled. I could tell she was impressed that I was getting the celebrity treatment. I was sure glad Meyers had called ahead and pulled in a few markers for me.

With the benefit of the experience that's come from all this time, I can say that I was trying so hard to impress that girl that I had not the slightest clue just how uncomfortable she was with herself and how out of place she must have felt in those surroundings. That night I overlooked how much time Ruby spent celebrity watching and wondering what everybody else was eating. The inexperienced, shy west Texas boy that I was even ignored how she flirted with our waiter and how she didn't really ask about me much. Oh yes, I almost forgot: Ruby never mentioned my new tie or even my haircut.

XXXX

A few days later Jack and I had lunch at The Napoli.

"How's things with you and Ruby?" he asked.

"First it was Kitty, then Marian and Meyers, and now you. Everybody wants to know about my personal life," I said in polite exasperation. "I really don't want to talk about it."

As I spoke I looked over Jack's shoulder and saw that Ruby was working the counter. I thought I recognized one of the sailors sitting there as the same guy she waited on earlier in the week. She seemed to be spending an awful lot of time with him. And I seemed to have had a thing for women who were interested in other men. I started to feel jealous.

"How are things going with Ruby?" Jack asked again. I ignored his question. "Jake, what's got into you boy? You seem all balled up."

"I don't know what you're talking about," I said, trying to put him off. But like a shark that smells blood in the water, he kept coming at me.

"Come on, Jake, cough it up. What's been happening with you two?"

"I'm not sure. I guess I'm confused. Sometimes she seems interested in me and sometimes she doesn't. And I'm still not very comfortable with her. She makes me feel like a kid. I bet you're sorry you asked."

He took a sip of coffee, smiled at me, shook his head, and waited for more details.

"Jack, wherever I go people stare. I don't think she's altogether pleased with the attention I get." I looked down at the table, a bit embarrassed by what I was about to say. "Maybe I'm just imagining things, but I think she's interested in other guys . . . at least more than in me. I think that sailor sitting at the counter over there might even be dating her." I lowered my voice. "Maybe I'm just not enough of a man. Maybe I'm not big enough of a star for her."

Jack pushed himself back from the table and turned his head to glance toward the young seaman sitting at the counter. "Jake, that's a load of bushwa. Now hobble your lip and listen. You just haven't gotten used to the saddle. Boy, you lack confidence."

In my embarrassment, I kept looking down, nodding my head in agreement.

"What are you good at?" Jack asked. "I mean, when I first dated Peggy's mother, I was a champion roper. Some weeks I even lived off the money I won in those rodeos. When my future missus saw me riding in the arena, why, she didn't have a chance. I swept her off her feet."

"I think I get your drift, Jack. You want to know what skills I have." He nodded. "You mean besides acting?" I asked.

"That's right."

"Well, I'm certainly not a cowboy,"

"That's for sure."

We both laughed. I hesitated for a minute. "I can . . . I can dance."

"You can what?"

"I can dance."

Jack's jaw dropped open. He looked dumfounded. I knew he must be thinking that it was astounding for somebody with Gargantua's proportions to be a good dancer. Sensing I owed him more of an explanation, I told Jack about my teacher in El Paso and how I learned to dance.

"When I was about fifteen, to try and get me out of my melancholy, my folks enrolled me in Karma Dean's dancing school. Back home, Karma Dean was the cat's meow. She was an exotic, black-haired, ebony-eyed beauty who taught El Pasoans all the finer points of ballroom dancing. I'll never forget what she said after she saw me dance in that first class: 'You're such a big fella. I can't believe you can move that body with such grace. It's a bequest young man, a genuine gift from the goddess Terpsichore. You must not waste it. You must develop and share it!'"

Jack pulled a pouch of tobacco, a pack of rolling papers, and a small blue box of wooden matches out of the pocket of his dungarees. His yellowed fingers expertly rolled a fag. Then, in a phosphorescent whoosh, he ignited a match by scraping it on the bottom of the table, lit the cigarette, and inhaled deeply. He exhaled a ring of smoke like a corral for some imaginary mustangs. Then he spit out a couple of pieces of loose brown tobacco.

"Well, don't stop now, Jake. What happened?"

"It was unforgettable. Karma met with my folks. She wore red flowing scarves and when she came into our parlor I thought she walked on air. Karma talked about my talent, insisted I train rigorously, become a professional hoofer and tour with her across the country. Can you imagine Mama's and Papa's reactions? It was Old World meets Isadora Duncan, west Texas style."

"Who is Isadora Duncan?" Jack asked.

"She's a famous jazz dancer; the one that just moved to Russia."

Jack nodded. "I think I saw her picture in the papers."

"Well, my folks were not about to let their teenage son go on the road with a female *artiste*, let alone a gentile." Years later on the vaudeville circuit, what Karma had taught me came in handy when I hoofed it professionally.

It's ironic to think back on how Mama and Papa reacted to Karma's offer. Just one year later my parents pushed me to go to Hollywood and become another type of professional entertainer.

"Jack, I'm not much of a talker."

"I dunno that I'd agree, Jake."

"But when it comes to dancing, I can hold my own."

"That's settled then." Jack put his lit cigarette out on the bottom of his boot and dropped the butt into the white ceramic ashtray that sat in the middle of our table. "You have to take the little lass dancing. You've got to go to a fandango."

XXXX

On our last date, Ruby and I danced to the Rhythmaires at the Palladium. I should say she stood on my shoes while I danced. The crowd gave us a wide berth and eventually made a circle around us. That night we were the center of attention. I felt like we were carved dancers on a giant music box. Everyone else in that auditorium became our audience. They actually applauded for us. I felt freer than I could ever remember. I wanted the music to never stop.

Sadly, the orchestra finally took a break. We were both out of breath and parched. As we walked to the punch bowl, I felt myself stand taller. That deep purple punch was the best tasting I'd ever had. When we finished we went outside on the balcony with a few other couples.

"Hey buddy, great job," someone said, patting my forearm. "You sure can move it."

Two laughing, twin brunettes in matching frilly, lilac dresses stepped in front of us. "We wish we had a big swing in our backyard," they said in unison as if reciting a poem. Then they giggled and walked away.

It was a perfect night with a full harvest moon, blue against Los Angeles's adolescent skyscape.

"Jake, you amaze me. Who would have ever thought . . . I mean, you can really cut a rug." Ruby shook her head.

I was genuinely happy, on cloud nine, in love, or whatever I assumed that to be. Baby Peggy's father was right: All I needed was a little confidence.

The few couples standing closest to us moved away. Ruby and I were now alone along the balcony's ornate Spanish railing. I reached for Ruby's hand, looked down at her, and struggled to express myself.

"I think . . . I think I have deep feel—"

"We better get back inside," she said pulling her hand away abruptly.

"I'm sorry . . . I . . . "

Ruby walked quickly back into the crowded ballroom. For what seemed like forever, I stood there, all alone and mortified. After a while, I went back inside. We must have made quite a picture slouched against the ballroom's far wall; me, with my hands in my pockets and Ruby, with her arms folded, tapping her foot, looking like she just missed the last train. After a few more songs, Ruby started to rub her right temple.

"I'm getting a headache," she said. "If you don't mind, I want to call it a night."

On the taxi ride back to her place we didn't say much. I thought maybe I had been too forward. I mean, Ruby wasn't one of those types of girls if you know what I mean. And then again, maybe I wasn't forward enough. After all, in *The Young Rajah* Valentino didn't wait for Fanny Midgley to kiss him. He just grabbed her. Maybe I wasn't clear enough with Ruby about my intentions. I mean, I was in love. I even fantasized about marrying the girl.

The next two times I asked Ruby out she was busy; she was so busy she didn't have time to talk. Finally I decided to take the bull by the horns. As Jack and I walked toward The Napoli for lunch, I bought some flowers. That time all they had left were a dozen tired, canary-yellow roses. We sat in Ruby's station. She didn't seem at all friendly, like something was bothering her. By the time she set our blue plate specials down on the table, I couldn't hold myself back. I had to ask her.

"You want me to do what? Go steady!" She recoiled. Her voice was cool and her tone bordered on ridicule. "Listen, I thought you would have gotten the message. What do I have to do, Jake, send you a telegram?" She drove the knife in deeper. "I have a fella!"

I was hurt but not totally surprised. *Why had she even gone out with me in the first place?* I thought. I felt like I'd been kicked in the stomach and taken for a ride. Looking back on it, I can't believe how naive I was. I felt like a fool. Then she added insult to injury.

"And even if I didn't, my mama raised me better than to get involved with show people. You think I want to be a part of a freak show? No way! No how!" Her voice was loud enough for everyone in the restaurant to hear.

I don't know what came over me, but it was like a black cloud of hornets. Without even thinking, I stood up. Towering over her, I threw the roses down on the table, knocked over my water glass, and ran out into the street.

When Jack found me, I was sitting on a bench in my dressing room with my head in my hands. He sat down next to me. "Well that's one horse's ass of a woman; a real ignoramus. Ruby is dumber than a dumb Dora. She's dumb as a cow. Can you believe someone like that trying to give you the mitten?" He was doing his best to comfort me. "You deserve better, much better. Don't let that hash slinger get you down. You know, Jake, women are like streetcars: you miss one and in five minutes another one will be along." Jack backhanded the air as if he were shooing away a horsefly.

My friend had the best of intentions but no idea of the tailspin I was in. He had no way of knowing that Ruby's rejection had stirred all the memories of all the rejections I'd experienced over the years. Like the debris at Santa Monica beach after a storm, all my garbage had washed up. I didn't fit in. There was no way that being a regular guy with a regular girlfriend was in the cards for me. Over the years, I would in fact learn more painful lessons at the hands of unavailable women, but I would also find comfort in the arms of a special someone who really did recognize and appreciate me.

I never ate at The Napoli again. After a few days, it came to me that Ruby was taking me for a ride to see what she could get. That whole episode showed me I was lonely; so lonely that I was in love with the idea of being in love.

Now I understand that I was both less and more fragile than I thought. I had come a long way since the pain of my early years in El Paso. I had begun a new life performing as a tall comic in silent pictures but just under the surface I was a tender, scared little boy. Old doubts resurfaced. *I'm a fool to think that a normal woman would ever have feelings for someone like me*, I thought.

Like a river flowing fast under thin ice after an early thaw, my sadness threatened to flood me. At any time, I could easily fall through the cracks, dragged into its dark depths, unable to get back to the light.

CHAPTER 13

Cotton Candy and Cacahuates

"Night Watch," Jake Erlich

I don't remember how I got home from Val's party but I must have been feeling no pain because early the next morning I had one hell of a hangover. I sat in the pie car and did my best to fend off a splitting headache by washing down several aspirin with a cup of particularly strong joe.

Over the years I've noticed that when you're feeling down all your troubles and doubts deviously unite and come at you at once. That morning I obsessed about whether to leave or stay in the circus, about Val and over what, if anything besides genuine kindness, was behind her offer of the scholarship to art school.

"*Guten Tag*, Jake."

It was Daisy Doll and Lya Graf standing in front of my table. I forced a smile. At that point, I had no issue whatsoever with Daisy but seeing Lya made me uncomfortable. I'd kept my distance since our unpleasant parting outside of the Western Union office the day before.

"Good morning, ladies," I replied perfunctorily.

"You and Frank Buck put on the Ritz last night," Daisy said. "I saw you get into a cab just outside the Garden after the show. Where were you two Don Juans off to?"

"Maybe you can call Buck a Don Juan, but I'm certainly no lothario," I replied.

"Come on, Jake, no false modesty if you please. Spill the beans to old Aunt Daisy and the lovely Lya. What were you two dandies up to last night?"

Not so much her question, but Daisy's tone was detective-like, pushy, bordering on being intrusive. It made me think there was more behind her words than idle curiosity. I was suspicious, but I knew once Daisy was on the scent of something she was as tenacious as Lya. I was in no shape to fend them off, so I humored them with candor. After all, as my mother often said, "the best lie is the truth."

"A pretty young artist whose been hanging around in the menagerie threw a party and invited us."

"You actually think she's attractive, Jake?" Lya asked in a tenor that was almost challenging. I hadn't realized that Lya had ever even laid eyes on Val. Evidently she had, and didn't like what she saw. Lya and I had had hundreds of conversations about everything from baseball to Roosevelt. But up until the day before at the Western Union office when I told her of my dilemma over whether to stay or leave Ringling Bros, I'd never seen her angry. Experiencing that side of her had confused me. Once again, in less than twenty-four hours, I was surprised by what Lya said and how she said it. It even crossed my mind that she might be jealous.

Within a few minutes I told the two little women all about Val's party, including my encounter with Diego Rivera and Frida Kahlo and the talk about art school.

"Artists . . . art school; they're a bunch of libertines and queers. A word to the wise, Jake Erlich: Those types and the high society snobs they hang out with are no damn good . . . they're as phony as a three-dollar bill." Daisy pointed her index finger at me as if it were a weapon.

I was shocked at how angry, judgmental, and downright bigoted she sounded. Her words did not at all fit with how I had experienced Val, Frida, and Diego. I wondered what kind of wound Daisy must have suffered from someone like them to be so hostile. Later, I even asked her about it, but she would never say. Whatever was behind her tirade that morning in the pie car, it pissed me off.

"Mark my words, those rubes don't like show people. You can trust those mud show ticket-takers as far as you can throw them! Count your change my friend! Count your change!" Daisy admonished.

"Daisy's right. They'll turn on you at the drop of a hat, Jake!" Lya added, giving me the one-two punch.

I hesitated, unprepared for their intensity and unable to think of a response. Then without thinking, I slammed my hand down hard on the table. It made a loud sound, like the crack of a rifle shot on a cold December morning. The force of my huge hand on the pie car table knocked my cup off its saucer, splattering black drops of coffee everywhere.

"You don't even know Val."

Daisy and Lya looked startled and frightened. To be honest, my uncharacteristically hostile response frightened me too.

"Whoa, whoa! We must have touched a nerve. Why are you so touchy?" Lya asked.

"Maybe we don't know this dame, Jake, but you don't either. Judging from your nasty reaction, she must have really gotten under your skin, like some fungus that infects the monkeys in the menagerie." Daisy spoke in a tone that was at once scolding and protective.

At that moment I felt she was acting more like my mother than my friend and I didn't like it. What's more I didn't like her offensive metaphor. I was not accustomed to being so unhappy and angry with my friends. It was upsetting and made me anxious.

I held my breath for a few seconds, trying to compose myself. "Thanks for your concern, ladies," I said, exhaling. "But I'm a big boy. Now if you'll excuse me, I've got to get to the Garden for the matinee."

Before I could stand up, they both spun around and waddled away. *Don't you worry! I can take care of myself*, I thought. Boy, was I ever wrong.

XXXX

Later that afternoon, I sat on my sideshow platform in the basement of Madison Square Garden waiting for the first show to begin. In those days I did a lot of waiting in that chair. The effects of my hangover and my dustup with Daisy and Lya that morning were still with me. I felt awful. While I sat there, I replayed what had happened in my mind's eye. Though I was still upset, I had second thoughts about how I'd reacted. Maybe I had been too defensive about Val.

"Hiya, Jake. A penny for your thoughts." It was Lya, standing at the base of my platform. She took a cautious step closer. I looked down at her and smiled, happy at her apparent effort to make amends.

"I was just thinking . . . " I said, reflexively.

Lya looked at me sympathetically. "Not another word; you need to cut yourself a little slack," Lya said as she struggled up the steps to my platform. She wore a light blue, ruffled ball gown that made a swishing sound as she moved. For that show she wore her dark brown hair in a Marcel Wave. Lya looked great. "Maybe Daisy and I were a little pushy." Lya picked her way carefully up the stairs, holding up the hem of her dress. "You know we only mean the best for you. We're like a family in here. I think Daisy and I were trying to protect you," Lya explained, a bit out of breath from her climb.

I can take care of myself, I thought for the second time that day, but again I didn't say it. I was confused. On the one hand I was relieved to patch things up with her; on the other, I was still angry. You have to know, I wasn't proud of my hostile reaction to her offer of an olive branch. In those days it was completely out of character for me to do something like that. Lya smiled warmly and moved still closer. She smelled like gardenias. It was strange but her perfume reminded me of Val's.

Three women, two tiny and one normal sized, had me bewildered.

"Doors!" the blower bellowed, signaling the start of the show and the approach of the crowd.

You know, in all the years I was with the circus, I never got used to that sound. It always gave me gooseflesh, and not the kind that's exciting or holy. Lya ran down the steps and quickly moved to mount her platform, which was situated about twenty feet away. Then about two hundred faceless sideshow fans stormed into the space we shared with the menagerie.

Usually I would say hello, wave, or smile as the throng approached. Sometimes my reaction was authentic, often it was forced. But that day, I just sat there in silence. My mind drifted to the party the night before and to Val's green eyes.

"Ouch, shit!" I said as the pain of the assault shot from my lower leg, up my spine, to the top of my twenty-gallon-Stetson-covered head. Before I could say another word, I saw a young mother grab a nasty ten-year-old brat, swat his behind, and drag him by the arm off my platform and across the menagerie to the exit. It was amazing that someone so small and innocent looking could cause such agony to someone my size. He, like many other little bastards over the years, had kicked me in the shins to make sure I wasn't on stilts. My lower leg throbbed. Instinctively I rubbed it for some relief.

"*¡Qué maldito* (What an evil little boy)!" I looked out to see Frida Kahlo at the foot of my stage. "*Pobrecito* (you poor thing), that must really hurt," she said with the self-assurance and dignity of a woman who was no stranger to agony herself.

"You can say that again. It's a hazard that goes with the job." I forced a smile to free me from her gravity. "What are you doing here?" I leaned forward to hear her above the roar of the crowd.

"I am doing research, studying the artist in his natural habitat," she said with a smirk. "Maybe I'll find a model for a painting."

I wondered at the real purpose for her visit.

Frida wore a red sundress with yellow and brown embroidered sunflowers over layers of petticoats. The hems of her petticoats were also embroidered, but with some words or a design I couldn't make out. She also sported a navy blue mantilla. The colors accentuated her darkly exotic features. I came to understand that her clothing was a costume that reflected roles she had chosen to portray.

Some artist, I said to myself. I stood up and stepped off my platform. "Can I buy you a Tastee-Freeze?"

"No," she said sternly. "But you absolutely can buy me some cotton candy and *cacahuates* (peanuts)." She laughed impishly.

At that very instant, Lya Graf sashayed by the front of my platform. The way she stared at me made me think of my parents' police dog, Doogan, guarding the old chicken coop we kept in the backyard of our house on Fewel Street. If I didn't know better I would have said Lya was checking up on me. As I looked at her, it came to me that she resembled a miniature version of Frida Kahlo, albeit in a blue ball gown. If you can picture it, she was every bit as attractive and exotic, but more conservative.

"Lya, this is my friend Frida. She's one of the people I met at the party last night."

The two women nodded with chilly politeness. They examined one another with a razor's edge vision of dueling *pistoleros* (gunmen). The intensity was so thick you could cut it with a bowie knife. It made me even more edgy than I'd been all day.

"If anyone asks, would you please cover for me? We want to step out for a minute and have a soda," I said to Lya.

Lya stepped closer, extended her little arm, put her tiny hand on my knee, looked up, and batted her eyelashes. "Sure, doll," Lya said with a wink and a smile.

"Maybe your friend would like to join us," Frida suggested.

"No, thank you," Lya said curtly. "Someone's got to work for a living around here."

Frida smiled uncomfortably. When we walked away, I turned around to say thank you and saw something strange. Lya was no longer smiling. She stared at me intensely like she had in the telegraph office the day before. I have this indelible image of Lya that afternoon as an immovable force, standing there with her hands on her hips and her high heels firmly planted in the sawdust.

XXXX

My new Mexican friend and I leaned against a wall behind one of the concessions. Frida balanced a bag of roasted peanuts under her right arm while she devoured fists full of the sticky, pink cotton candy like a famished school girl. I munched on a Tastee- Freeze.

"We were all so impressed with you, *Jacobo*," she said. The way she looked at me didn't fit with someone who loved cotton candy. "Is it true you never had any formal art training?"

"That's *verdad* (true)," I said, stuffing the remnants of the ice cream cone in my mouth. "But I don't want to talk about art."

"*¿Te gusta todo esto* (Do you like all of this)?"

"What do you mean *all of this*?" I asked.

"You know, *el circo* (the circus), the sideshow, *todo* (all of it)."

I was taken aback by this woman's directness. After all, I had only just met her the night before. It seemed I was suddenly surrounded by strong, outspoken dames. But there was something about Frida that was also disarming, even alluring. I tried to avert her inquiry with a platitude and a question of my own. "Well, it's a living, and in this day and age any living is a good living. Tell me about Val."

Normally I would have beaten around the bush and never been so open, but something about Frida Kahlo sparked a recklessness that scared the living daylights out of me. I couldn't help myself. I was drawn to her like summertime moths are lured to a circus gaslight.

"Oh, I see," she said in a tone that implied she understood the question behind my question. "We met her and her husband last year, when Diego and I made a trip to Manhattan." She pitched the white paper cone that had served as the cotton candy's spine into a nearby trash can. Then Frida opened the bag of peanuts, put one in her mouth, and crunched into it, devouring the crisp kernel inside. She spit the shell onto the floor and continued. "Val is not really a *cuate* (best friend), but we are *conocidos*, (acquaintances). She doesn't share her secrets so I don't share mine. Like so many of you *gringos*, she's *cerrada*, how you say it . . . closed."

I realized that Val and Frida were not as intimate as I'd imagined. I nodded.

"As you can tell from how they live, her *marido es un millionario* (her husband is a millionaire). He's the president of Humboldt Oil."

I took my pocket watch out of my pants and checked the time to make sure I didn't lose track of how long I'd been away from the sideshow. Since the fiasco with the rube a few days before, I didn't want to draw any unnecessary attention to myself.

"I don't know what to make of it," I said. "There was a lot of expensive art in her home, but I didn't see any of her sculptures."

"You're very observant," Frida replied.

"I know she must have a lot of her own pieces. Where does she keep them?"

"She keeps them in the closet or she throws them away." For some reason her answer made me sad. "*Eres un sabio*; you're a wise man." Frida shook her head and her dangling, turquoise ceramic earrings bounced against her cheeks.

"Why do you say that?" I asked.

"*Pegaste en el clavo* (You hit the nail on the head). That pretty lady fancies herself an artist but *no cree en sí misma*. She doesn't believe in herself; she doesn't think she's any good. That's why you never see her art displayed at her house or any place else. Val and her husband are patrons of the arts and surround themselves with artists. *Pero a esa niña le hace falta fuego*—in English, that girl lacks fire."

Something didn't fit. From what I had observed, Val seemed vivacious and full of life. Only later would I understand that something was, in fact, absent in her.

"It's no wonder when you think of that cold *viejo* (old man) she sleeps with," Frida explained. "He would stir a woman's passion like old socks would season a *caldillo* (spicy stew)." Frida rolled her eyes and put her hand in mine.

I felt uncomfortable. If I knew then what I know now, I would just have enjoyed the experience. But at that time it was a bit overwhelming. You see, that was the second time in less than half an hour that a woman had touched me. Back then, I could easily remember months that went by without being touched like that, even once.

"Val tries to make art. She buys art, she even wears it, *pero nunca lo vive*; she doesn't live it. She doesn't breathe it. She doesn't die for it. You know, when I or my frog of a husband don't paint we feel constipated, *que nos estamos muriendo* . . . like we're dying inside."

I looked away uneasily. I just wanted to know a little about the woman I had a crush on, not to psychoanalyze her. "Frida, I think it's time I get back to the show," I said.

"¡*Ay Dios mío* (Oh my God)! I hope I haven't offended you. Sometimes people tell me I'm too honest."

"No problem. Don't worry. It's just that I can't be gone too long."

As Frida and I walked back to the sideshow through the menagerie, I noticed peanut shells falling gracefully from the folds of her billowy, red *Tehuana* skirt. They looked like miniature coffee-and-cream-colored pigeons taking flight from a crimson belfry.

"My toad of a husband is having a showing of his art in a few weeks. You know, since that awful fiasco at Rockefeller Center, he hasn't worked in your country. When will that poor *pendejo* ever learn? But he does have exhibitions. I'd like to invite you to attend," she said.

"I'd love that," I replied. The idea intrigued me. You see, I had never attended an art show opening before, much less one for a big-time artist like Diego Rivera.

"One more thing," Frida said.

"What's that?"

"You know that *Alemana* (German) . . . *la enana* . . . the midget?" She asked as we approached the entrance to the sideshow.

"You mean Lya?"

"*Sí*. She likes you."

"I know. We're friends," I replied.

"No, I mean she likes you."

"I don't think so."

"You men are such *pendejos* (idiots) . . . Dense like adobe bricks. You're usually the last to know."

That's absurd, I thought, brushing aside her insight.

XXXX

A few seconds later I stepped back onto my sideshow platform and had a seat.

"I'm going to wander around *por un ratito* (for a little while)," Frida called to me as she stepped toward the crowd gathered in front of Kookoo the Bird Girl.

"Have a good time," I called back to her.

I looked to my right to the small wooden table where I kept a stack of enameled, silver-painted lead replicas of my ring that I sold to the rubes for a quarter. Selling those rings was one among many attempts I made in those days to not just sit in that sideshow tent and be an exhibit. Each ring was inscribed with my stage name and height: *Jack Earle, 8 feet 6 inches.* I picked up one of the rings and held it in the palm of my hand. It was not light and it was certainly not heavy, but still it had weight and substance. I rolled it back and forth in my fingers.

Its circular shape made me think back to one of the first real conversations I had with Clyde Ingalls when things were still good between us. It was 1926 and we were playing a four-day run in Cincinnati. It was the first time I'd ever visited that city. I recall it was a key hub in the Underground Railroad that helped southern black slaves make their way to freedom in the north. Ingalls and I were walking together under the Big Top near the center ring shortly before the opening spec. He stopped and looked around in awe, as if he were a tourist in some Italian basilica.

"Look at that, Jake," he said. "Isn't it magnificent? Do you realize you are working in an ancient institution with roots that go very deep?"

As gruff as he was, Ingalls was also a walking encyclopedia about everything that had to do with the circus. In short order he taught me that the word "circus" originally came from the Latin word for circle and the ancient Roman structure where chariot races were held and bloodthirsty crowds watched Christians torn to bits by wild animals. He said that Ringling Bros traced its more contemporary form to an English showman. In the 1760s, audiences paid to see him gallop his horses in circles. In the 1780s they first named that type of show a circus. Ingalls also shared how the first three-ring circus was originally presented by none other than that hustler *par excellence*, P.T. Barnum himself. I would have never guessed that my kindly circus professor and boss and I would have ended up crossing swords the way we did.

After that initial lesson in Cincinnati, I became a student of circus history and lore myself. I amassed quite a library of circus books that I stored at my folks' place in Texas. Sitting on my sideshow platform that afternoon in Madison Square Garden and looking down at the lead ring in my hand, I recalled reading something strange in one of those books that I've never forgotten; the connection between the circus and another ancient round structure: the cemetery. It seems that cemeteries were originally called *Kirshe* after their circular shape. Just like the circus. The bodies buried in those ancient round cemeteries were often decapitated. The severed head would be placed alongside the rest of the corpse, symbolizing the spirit's triumph over the body.

Eventually *Kirshe* came to mean "a church." Sitting on my sideshow platform and holding that ring in my hand, I laughed to myself as I thought of Ringling Bros circus as the church where a Jewish giant would struggle to free his spirit from the shortcomings of his massive frame.

XXXX

The warm sound of Yiddish drew my attention from the ring in the palm of my hand back to the sideshow. I looked down from my platform perch for the source of that familiar, sweet sound, and saw a middle-aged couple and two young children. They all had the hollow-eyed look and wary walk of the refugees that I saw from time to time at the circus. I imagined they'd fled the mess that was brewing in Europe. Their Yiddish banter was music to my ears. I hadn't heard any *mamloshen* (mother's language) since my last visit to El Paso. Unable to restrain myself, I stepped off the platform to get closer to them. I just had to join in.

"*Vos hert zich* (What's happening)?" I said in a jovial voice. The family of four abruptly froze. With the same alarmed look, each one of them stared up at me. They didn't have to say a word. I knew what they were thinking: *Impossible! How can it be? He's the world's tallest man; a giant who speaks Yiddish.*

"*Zind sie a landsman* (Are you a countryman . . . a member of the tribes of Israel)?" The father asked in an amazed, albeit quiet tone.

"*Vos clares die* (What do you think)?" I responded with a laugh.

I love how Jews like to answer questions with questions. It turns out they were from Warsaw, fresh off the boat, in New York less than a month.

I told the newcomers about my family's Polish connection and about the relatives we still had living there. Then I reached up to the table next to my chair and grabbed another ring. I now held two of them. I tried to hand the rings to the little ones. Not knowing what to do and looking frightened, they took a step back. Their parents nodded, letting them know it was okay. They both took a step forward. Ever so slightly, they smiled as they examined and then clutched their new treasures. Somehow I knew this encounter would become a tale that would be written in letters sent back to the Old Country and repeated for generations to come in the family lore of the ones who survived. As they walked away, the family turned back twice to wave. I wondered about my Polish relatives and what trouble might lie ahead for them.

XXXX

Frida, who had been eavesdropping on our conversation, stepped out of the crowd. She motioned with her fingers for me to come closer. I leaned forward. As she whispered, I felt stirred by her warm breath on the side of my face. "*¿Eres judío* (Are you Jewish)?" she asked.

I felt all the muscles in my jaw and gut tense. "Why do you ask?" I fired back reflexively. I had learned to be cautious of those kinds of questions. Jew-haters were everywhere in those days, from Henry Ford's maniacal tirades to Father Coughlin's hate-filled weekly radiobroadcasts.

"I'm part Jewish, too. *Mi Papi, que descanse en paz, era judío* (My daddy, he should rest in peace, was a Jew)," Frida whispered back. "But I was raised as a Catholic. Diego's half Portuguese Jew and half *Indio*. Some combination, huh?"

Then she began to fire questions at me. She wanted to know everything about what it was like to grow up as a Jew in west Texas. She took a long breath. "Maybe we'll come visit you there someday," she said. Then she paused for an instant and began her investigation anew. "Maybe you're the descendent of some long lost tribe of Jewish giants," she said with a laugh. "Did you have that ceremony they do for boys? What's it called; a *Bar Mitzvah*?" Her curiosity seemed genuine as the menagerie's musty animal odors that from time to time wafted into the sideshow.

"I did," I said, looking over her shoulder as if I could see the past there.

CHAPTER 14

Cuco and the Four Horsemen

"The Jungle," Jake Erlich

It was the first time I'd been home from California in seven months, and I could hardly wait. I never told anyone, but there were many nights in Hollywood I was so homesick for my family and friends that all I could think about was coming back to El Paso. But I know now that homesickness can be a drug that washes away distressing memories.

When I came home that first time, there was no avoiding them. The old hurts were front and center in my mind. Those memories and the engrained habits they triggered to protect me, like keeping to myself, seemed impossible to erase. For me, hurtful recollections and the rituals I used to avoid them were like the deep ruts carved in dried mud that scarred the dirt roads in the Upper Valley. Try as I might, when I traveled down those paths it was too easy to slip into the furrows in my mind.

Despite starring in several pictures and all the accolades it brought me, being in my hometown again made me fall into old, depressing routines. For the first few days of my vacation I stayed at home, sleeping and spending more time than I should have alone in my room. My only outing was to help my dad in the store.

"Jake, you need to get out and enjoy yourself," Papa insisted one night after dinner.

"Maybe you should drop by the high school and visit your friends," Mama suggested.

I knew my parents well enough to tell they were worried. "No, that's okay. I don't want to bother them. I'm fine just being home," I resisted. Truth be told, I was anxious and concerned, not about seeing my friends but about how the others I might run into would react.

Then as Ben and Myer cleared the dinner plates from the table they joined in. "Just go for a while," Ben suggested. "What could it hurt?"

"Your friends are always asking about you," Myer said. "Ever since *A Corn-Fed Sleuth* played in town, kids I don't even know have approached me to ask about you."

"They did, huh?" I was surprised. "Okay, okay, *genug*. I'll drop by the school tomorrow, but just for an hour and no more."

Back then, I thought I had agreed just to get them all off my back. But in retrospect I believe I agreed to visit that school because I had some unfinished business there and some of my own demons to face.

The next afternoon I found myself outside the closed door to Mrs. Kelly's sixth-period geometry class. I picked that class because I knew my pals, Bobby Goldoff and Abbie Kahn, would be in it. There I was with my ear pressed against the door, unsure of what to do next. In my life I've often felt like I was on the other side of the door, on the outside wanting to come in, frustrated, struggling with just how to do it. I started to knock, but hesitated. I felt anxious again, almost sick to my stomach.

Maybe I should just turn around and forget this whole damned business, I thought. But if I left, my family would find out. You see, I knew they would ask and there was no way I could lie to them. If I left, they would be so disappointed in me. So I was on the horns of what, to me, was an awful dilemma.

"This is how you sketch a 135-degree angle." Through the door, I heard Mrs. Kelly's high-pitched, squeaky voice punctuated by the sound of chalk scratching across a blackboard. I imagined the scene inside the classroom. Only half of the students would focus on the blackboard and the teacher's mathematical hieroglyphics. My friend Bobby would probably be dozing off, Abbie would be staring out of the window and daydreaming, while the others wrote love letters, talked about the upcoming district championship game, or worked on their homework.

That's when, in a flash, the idea came to me. *Why not make a grand entrance?*

Once I was committed, I pushed away any jitters as to whether they would approve, and readied myself for the mysterious pantomime I was about to perform. At first my hand, then my arm went through the open lintel above the door. Snake-like, I made my oversized appendage saunter from side to side, gradually descending, creeping and pausing along the way for a Mata Hari effect. When I heard laughter and whispers coming from the other side of the door, I imagined Mrs. Kelly spinning around, angry and anxious to catch the culprits in the act. I visualized her reaching for her yardstick to smack someone, but she was soon captivated as well. By then my fingers had reached the door knob. I felt a chill from the brass. Ever so slowly I turned the knob and opened the door. I paused again for maximum theatrical affect. Then with the flare of Houdini emerging from nowhere, I materialized in the doorway.

"Ta-daaa!" I exclaimed.

Everyone in that room, including Mrs. Kelly, applauded. The first ones out of their seats were Bobby and Abbie. Then they and the rest of the class dashed to greet me. Their friend and classmate, Jake the movie star, had returned home.

My surprise visit to El Paso High a few days after I arrived in town for my brother's *Bar Mitzvah* was a big success. My gamble paid off. In the past, some in that class had mocked, humiliated, and even thrown rocks at me. But in my triumphant return, if just for a few minutes, I almost forgot all about that—but not quite. I wish it wasn't so, that I was a bigger man, but truth be told, under my semi-polished actor's veneer I was still resentful. For a little while, though, being on stage, the center of attention and all, helped me push past the painful memories.

The students' enthusiasm was intense and intoxicating. Like a blizzard in a forest it was easy to get lost there, to lose your bearings, to lie down, seduced by false promises of warmth. But sometimes, as I've learned, sham warmth is better than no warmth at all. Being on stage at El Paso High that afternoon in Mrs. Kelly's geometry class temporarily numbed my recent Ruby-inflicted wounds and helped me to forget. Despite the reality of my situation, you have to remember I was still very young and, like most young people, I took everything so seriously. Well, whatever my circumstances, I was grateful for the amnesia.

After the three-thirty bell rang, most of the class hung around. It seemed they all wanted to talk with me. I knew it was childish, but I wished Ruby could have been there to get a glimpse of my newfound status.

"You're a sight for sore eyes," Bobby said.

"Your mom said you were coming. We've been counting the days," Abbie added as he grabbed my hand and pumped it.

Tom Lee, who in later years became one of the most famous artists in the Southwest, stepped forward with a copy of the new *Spur*, El Paso High's yearbook. Tom and I had been in school together since the first grade. I wouldn't say we were best buddies, but he'd always been nice to me and we were friends. He opened the yearbook to a cartoon he'd drawn entitled "The View from Mount Erlich," and handed it to me. It was an image of several students peering through a telescope positioned on my head. From the look on his face I could tell he was proud of his caricature and wanted to share it with me.

"They let me have a full page, Jake; as a matter of fact, in the first ten pages of the book. Isn't that the berries!" he exclaimed.

"That's really nice, Tom." I forced a smile. I glanced at the *Spur*, quickly handed it back to him, and turned to face Bobby and Abbie.

The look of disappointment on Tom's face as I turned away let me know that hadn't been the reaction he was expecting. I was ambivalent about that cartoon. Behind my initial polite, reflexive grin, I also cringed. I know some might have viewed that drawing as a means to connect with my peers, a symbol of the stature I had attained in the world and the respect and recognition I longed for. On the other hand, that yearbook drawing was a stark reminder that my physicality was, and continued to be, my classmates' primary focus. As much as my stature elevated me, it also served to exile me to my own lonely island, much like Napoleon on Elba. But unlike Napoleon, I would never break free.

My plan was to only stay at El Paso High for an hour, but Bobby, Abbie, Sally Doherty, Buddy Rogers, and several others begged me to stay.

"Why, I'd be happy to stay," I said, surprising myself. After a few minutes we all walked out to Tiger Field together. The crowd grew as word spread I was back at El Paso High. Several kids approached me for my autograph.

"Have you met Ruben Navarro?" Abigail Rosen asked. "He's so dreamy!"

"Do you ever run into Tom Mix?" inquired Jack Hardin. "You know, he also went to El Paso High."

I ignored his question, scanning the faces in the crowd. Some of them I recognized, and some I'd never seen. *Do they even know who I am?* I thought. I wondered if any of them, even my friends, ever really knew me. *Last summer, before I went to Los Angeles and was discovered, when I spent so much time in my room alone, I don't remember any of them coming to the house, I thought. I doubt if any of them had even one iota of understanding about what I'd been through.*

I got a glimmer of the pain and anger behind my masquerade. It was intense and unflattering. I felt myself stuck in one of those damned ruts in my mind yet again. For a minute I regretted ever coming back to El Paso

High. I felt detached from my body, almost hollow. That vacuum filled with negativity and I sensed myself as weightless, floating above the crowd of students, looking down on everything. Then something strange occurred.

I imagined that it was a scene in a movie I was directing. The first shots were from the point of view of the tragic, young giant who returns to his school; *but what about their perspective?* I asked myself. Did I really know any of them, how they saw things, the sadness in their lives, what made each of them feel different and less than perfect? When I changed the position of my camera and shot the scene from their perspective, my sadness shifted a bit. Things didn't feel as intense. I didn't really understand what was happening, but in a flash I was back in my body with the throng of students next to the athletic field.

Even though they were still drawn to me like metal filings to a magnet, I felt more comfortable. Rosy Pedrosa, who I'd known since third grade at Vilas School, pushed her way through the crowd.

"*¿Te has enamorado?* Have you fallen in love yet, Jake?" I flinched. Rosy always was a little clairvoyant.

"*Solo diez veces*; only ten times, Rosy." We all laughed.

The time disappeared, but when the sun started to go down and the temperature began to drop, I knew I had to get home. Several of us walked together down Shuster towards Sunset Heights. As we passed their respective streets, the group got smaller and smaller. Finally, at Prospect, I was alone.

I turned up the collar on my custom-tailored Pendleton against the cold and thought how different I'd felt than when I left El Paso High just the year before. I wondered what was different. Clearly some of my classmates had changed how they felt about me. I can say that it wasn't only the others who altered their attitudes toward me. There was something different about me, too. When I bounced up the steps of our front porch and walked into the house, I felt happy and hopeful.

"Jakey, you're late! Wash up and come help me with dinner," Mama commanded.

I'm late? I thought. *That's strange*. I looked at my Elgin wristwatch. It was later than I thought. My walk home took longer than usual—a lot longer. For the first time I could remember, I had walked home on the sidewalks and not by way of back alleys.

XXXX

During that two-week trip home, I frequently helped out at Geneva Loan. It was the holiday season and Papa needed my assistance. My family's pawnshop was a special place full of great stories; a banquet of fantasies.

During that trip, I guess because he thought I was old enough or because I'd passed through some unspoken initiation rite, early one morning Papa invited me back to his office to show me something he never had even mentioned. While I sat at his rolltop, he retrieved a dusty old strongbox from its resting place in the black safe in the wall behind his desk. When he set it down it made loud clank. Then Papa slowly opened the creaky strongbox, sifted through several dusty documents, and finally took out two yellowed pieces of parchment. I scooted closer to him so I could see.

"I got these in 1919 when I bought the building. It is a bill of sale and the original land grant from the king of Spain awarded to the previous owner's grandfather," Papa said.

I imagined that the person who received the land grant had accompanied Francisco Vasquez de Coronado, his troop of conquistadores, the priests and the Indian slaves that made up the first European expedition to lay claim to that place.

"This land and this building belong to our family. It's part of our family's roots. Never give it up." Papa banged on the desk with his fist for emphasis. "In the old country *unzara mensionen* (our people) couldn't ever own land, and you know what's happened there," he said, looking past me.

I didn't understand the full depth of what my father was saying, the importance of roots and a sense of place and all, but I do now.

At my family's store, when there were no customers around, I easily got lost in the hodgepodge of new and used jewelry, watches, firearms, and tools. I recall how that day I explored the contents of one of the showcases near the front of the store. Under a pair of German harmonicas, a set of rancher's wire-cutters, and a tray of *Arbolito* pocketknives, I discovered a real treasure. With an archeologist's care, I brushed off the cobwebs on an artifact that was originally used to hold up some cowboy's britches. Little by little, I was able to distinguish a hand-etched image of a stagecoach robbery from El Paso's not too distant wild-west past. The commemorative brass belt buckle was framed with the engraved words: "Wells Fargo & Company EX—El Paso 745 T." It was heavy in my hand. When I turned it over I found more surprises. The words read, "Wells Fargo and Company 1883, Express Award—Drink is Evil—Be Ever Alert and Faithful" and "Tiffany—Broadway, New York." I thought about the stickup this belt buckle commemorated. I imagined ducking down in that coach as the stage driver risked his life in a shootout with Billy the Kid and his gang. Then came the ceremony when the company muckety-mucks came to town and awarded the driver that piece of expensive, hand-forged brass. Afterwards, over a shot of red-eye in the saloon, Lil, the pretty dance hall girl, gave the scrawny hero a peck on the cheek and then took him upstairs for a poke.

If you haven't already guessed, fantasy has always come easy to me. Sometimes I didn't even realize I was fantasizing. I always liked to try on others' normal-sized lives. I was like a vampire sucking the lifeblood of strangers to feed some deep hunger, filling a dark empty place in this huge, cavernous body of mine. My sojourn in pictures did nothing to dampen that pastime. If anything, it intensified it.

I daydreamed over the buckle for a while longer.

"Oh *monsieur, monsieur*, what have you there?" It was Rene Gillis, or "Frenchie," as we called him. I was so lost in my fantasy I hadn't even heard him walk up beside me.

"Hello, Frenchie." I quickly put the buckle back in the showcase.

Besides my family, the most memorable of the treasures at Geneva Loan were the people who worked there and the customers. Frenchie was one of my favorites. As an orphaned, sickly eight-year-old, he had come from Paris, France, to stay with his uncle on a small ranch near Raton, New Mexico. Living the rough life of a sheepherder, he grew strong with forearms the size of cottonwood trunks. I often wished I had that kind of strength. To become a citizen, Frenchie fought with the Yanks in the Great War. He won a Silver Star for gallantry, but Jerry's mustard gas stole the sight in his right eye and the hearing in his right ear. When he returned, he married the daughter of that famous outlaw, Belle Starr. I loved to watch him work with customers. When one annoyed him, Frenchie would cock his chin. They never saw it coming. He'd pick a language he was sure the unsuspecting customer didn't speak, and with a charming smile, pummel them with insults in English, French, or Spanish. Inevitably the satisfied patron would thank him for his courtesy and service before leaving the store.

"I was just daydreaming," I replied, not a little embarrassed at being caught.

"Careful, my boy," Frenchie said, winking. "Sometimes it's easier to tumble into a dream than to claw your way out of it. *Comprenez-vous?*"

Many years later when I met Val, I should have recalled Frenchie's admonition about fantasies.

XXXX

Myer's *Bar Mitzvah* was a week away. At about three on Thursday afternoon I was back helping out at Geneva Loan. Business was at a lull. Ignoring Frenchie's warning, I was daydreaming again, staring out of the glass-and-wood front door and feeling a million miles away.

I felt a chill in the air and noticed bone dry tumbleweeds flying down the street. Premature darkness had replaced the late-afternoon sun. A powerful west Texas norther was brewing. I loved those kinds of storms; the dramatic interchange between wind and earth in the high desert as nature's uncontrollable might was concentrated and then released. The air, charged with static electricity, promised that the storm would wail through town by nightfall.

The heavy front door flew open. Cuco, draped in a ragged army surplus coat and a gray woolen serape, stomped in out of the cold. He was an old Mexican, part Yaqui Indian and a mountain of a man. Cuco took two worn leather saddlebags off his shoulders, slung them down on the counter, and smiled at me.

"*Hola, amigo*," he said, giving me a bear hug. Several times a year, Cuco would come to Geneva Loan and buy tools, guns, and jewelry that he would resell south of the border. Each time Papa and he would sit for a few hours in the back office and haggle over price. Papa would always say: "*Cuco, eres un coyote*. You're a *ganiff*. (You're a coyote. You're a thief.)"

And Cuco would always laugh and respond: "*Me estás robando . . . vendiéndome chafa, que no vale pinches papas*. (This is highway robbery. You are trying to sell me junk, not worth as much as fucking potatoes.)"

Sometimes Cuco came to the store with a *zoftick* twenty-year-old, who he called Gordita. She was pretty, but looked as disheveled as he did. When asked about her, he'd wink, rest his bear-claw size mitts on your shoulder, and say: "*¿Qué crees, diablo indecente? Es mi sobrinita.* (What do you think you damned indecent fellow? She's my niece.)" But I never believed him.

Papa told me Cuco used to wrestle bears in one of the small *carpas* or circuses that frequented little towns in Mexico. Come to think of it, before I joined Ringling Bros, he was the first circus performer I'd ever met. Refugio, our watchmaker, who Papa said was a *shiker* (drunk), had a different story about Cuco's background and it had nothing to do with any circus. I noticed that when Cuco came into the store, Refugio would always go to the toilet or leave in a hurry for some last-minute errand.

"Why do you always leave when Cuco comes into the store?" I asked once.

"*Ese maldito es un brujo. Cuidado, mi hijito*. How you say . . . be careful. That son of a beech; he's a witch."

But despite Refugio's admonition, I liked Cuco. There was something different and special about him. I loved his stories and the jailbreak intensity with which he told them. Sometimes he wouldn't say anything to me. He and I would just stand there in silence. It was almost as if we didn't need to speak. On that particular pilgrimage to Geneva Loan, after he finished his business with Papa, I asked him about his past.

"You really want to know about Cuco?" He laughed and shook his head.

"Yes, yes I do."

"*¿De veras* (Really)?"

"*Sí*."

"I don't like to talk about myself, but for you my friend, of course. I was born *en un pueblito cerca de Culiacan en el día de los muertos* (in a little village near Culiacan on the Day of the Dead). My parents were poor *peones*. They tell me my grandmother was sold as a slave."

I listened intensely, as if his words contained some secret meant especially for me. I wondered if perhaps in his story I would find some wisdom about where I belonged, some clue about how to avoid those awful ruts in my mind.

"*El patrón mató mi papa*. The master killed my father. Then he came looking for my mother and tried to attack her. Lucky for us he was drunk. She hit him on the head with a *metate* (a stone bowl used for grinding corn)."

"Then what happened?"

"We ran away to stay with my *tía* (aunt) who lived on the outskirts of *El D.F., La Capital* (Mexico City). We stayed there until *el terremoto* hit. There was a *fuego* (fire). *Fué horrible, un desastre* (It was horrible, a disaster)."

Up until that point I understood everything he had said. But he had used a Spanish word I'd never heard before."Cuco, what is a *terremoto*?"

"*Hay*, Jake, that's an earthquake."

"I thought a *temblor* was an earthquake."

"You see, Jake, *en español* we have many ways to paint pictures with our words; more than I think you do *en ingles* (in English.) A *temblor* is a little shaking. *Un terremoto*, is a quake that shakes you to your core, *hasta las nalgas* (to your buttocks). It feels like a giant picked up your house and smashed it into the ground. If *un terremoto* doesn't stop, it shakes so hard all your bones shatter, the world crumbles, and God has to begin building all over again. I guess that's why my *mama siempre me dijo* (mother always said) that a *terremoto* means big changes are coming."

His words gave me the chills. I wondered if there was some *terremoto*, some big changes in my future.

"Then what happened, I mean after the *terremoto*?" I asked.

Cuco took a step toward me and stared intensely into my eyes as if he lost something there. "We moved to *el norte* (the north) with the clothes on our backs. A few years later my mother was killed." Cuco looked at the floor and shook his head. He paused for a moment and continued. "She was a *soldadera* (soldier) fighting with Villa *en la batalla de Juarez* (Battle of Juarez). They sent me to live *con las monjas*, with the nuns. In the orphanage, the Brothers taught me to wrestle." Cuco moved his arms as if he were grappling with an invisible opponent. "You know the rest." He flicked the back of both of his hands at me as if shaking off water.

"*Ya*, enough *witty witty* (talking). I have to go," he continued. "If there isn't a *tormenta* (storm), no blizzard, my train leaves for Saltillo *a las siete* (at seven)." He grabbed his raggedy coat from where he had left it on the counter and put it on.

I felt confused, even a little exasperated. I forgot how abrupt and strange he could be. I didn't even have a chance to tell him about me, my adventures in Hollywood and the doubts and struggles I was having. At that moment I had no idea how perceptive Cuco really was.

Cuco had hurriedly packed his saddlebags full with his purchases, put on his serape, and stomped toward the door. About halfway there he froze in his tracks, spun around, came back to where I was standing, and stared up at me. Now is my chance, I thought.

"Cuco can you help me—"

"Jake, for a long time, I've been meaning to ask you," he said, interrupting me. "Do you know the meaning of the word *yanki*?"

I was dumbfounded. Why in the blazes, out of the blue, would he ask that? I sensed that Cuco didn't have time or patience for me to talk about my troubles or even to ask him about the reasoning that led to his question, so I answered him.

"Isn't Yankee a word used to describe Americans and especially soldiers who fought for the North in the Civil War?" I must have sounded like a horse's ass of a professor.

"No, no" the orphaned, ex-bear wrestler, seller of jewelry and tools, and witch, said definitively. Cuco stepped toward me and pointed his index finger upward at the middle of my chest, as if he were fixing the location of my heart.

"*Escúcheme*, listen closely," he ordered. Then he stepped even closer and dropped his voice to a whisper, conveying something cloak and dagger. "*Mis antedecentes* (my ancestors), the ancient *Yaquis* who first lived in this place before the *gachupines* (wearers of spurs—refers to Spanish colonists), used that word to mean 'star man.' *Es una palabra*, a word to describe those who can look down from the heavens and see what others cannot," he said.

Then he abruptly turned and began to walk way. Cuco paused and glanced up at me before he stomped out of the door. "*Hasta luego*, my *yanki* friend," he said as he disappeared into the frosty afternoon air.

XXXX

That night as I lay in bed thinking about Cuco's visit and how he said I was a *yanki*, I wondered if when he spoke about being a man who looks down from above, he was talking about the sensation I had earlier that week at El Paso High when I felt myself uncontrollably floating above the crowd. Or was he describing something entirely different?

While I was mulling that over, the blizzard hit, dumping a foot of snow on El Paso. Howling winds knocked out our power and sculpted tree-high snow drifts. The next morning, my brothers and I stood on our porch, speechless, amazed at the vista. The Franklin Mountains pierced through gray-black cloud banks, transforming them into mythic Appaloosas majestically enveloped in flecks of white and brown.

Seeing all the snow, I thanked God Myer's *Bar Mitzvah* was still a week away. But by twelve noon, true to form, the west Texas sunshine came out. By late afternoon, much of the snow had melted. With the snow mostly gone, that night, as we did every Friday, the family would attend *Shabbat* services at the old B'nai Zion Synagogue on North Oregon Street.

XXXX

As I've said, I love football, but my baby brother was a fanatic. His favorite team was Notre Dame. In his billfold he carried a prized possession: a crumpled cut-out article from an old edition of the *Los Angeles Times* that I had sent him. The piece described Notre Dame's October victory over Army and immortalized Stuhldreher, Miller, Crowley, and Layden as the famed Four Horsemen. All season long Myer had read and listened to every account of every game. He talked to anyone who would listen about Notre Dame's upcoming appearance in the Rose Bowl. I loved my brothers so much. It made me melancholy to be away from them. When I look back, I miss all of those mundane things, like talking about football; all the things you take for granted when you think you will always be living together.

At that very moment Coach Knute Rockne, the Four Horsemen, and the rest of the Notre Dame football team were traveling across country to Pasadena to play in that game. A few days before, Myer had learned that their train had scheduled an 8:15 p.m. whistle-stop at Union Depot in El Paso. He thanked his lucky stars that the snow had melted and wouldn't interfere with his plans to see his idols. But even before the blizzard, there was another fly in the ointment. Notre Dame's train was due in El Paso at the same time the family was supposed to be at the synagogue.

"I'll never have this chance again. There's absolutely no way I can miss seeing them!" Myer confided to me.

"I don't know, Butch." That was my baby brother's nickname. "If Papa finds out, there will be hell to pay."

"Jake, you're always worrying. I've got it all under control. You see, I have a plan."

Myer described how he, Buddy Goodman, and Sidney Stern, also big football fans, would ask to sit together during the service in the pew closest to the back door. I was to help by assuring Mama and Papa it was okay for Myer to sit with his friends. Our family, the Goodmans, and the Sterns typically sat toward the front of the sanctuary. The wily conspirators counted on being able to slip out, unnoticed.

"We'll skip out, run to the depot, see the Four Horsemen, and be back before anyone's the wiser," my brother assured me. I was so fond of Butch and his escapades. I knew I had to do my part in that caper to help him out.

Friday night everything unfolded as planned. Mama, Papa, Ben, and I, the Goodmans, and the Sterns sat at the front of the crowed *shul*. When Myer asked to sit with his friends I assured my folks it was fine. The three boys sat together in the back of the place. I turned around and saw Myer looking to where Mama and Papa were sitting. I knew he was anxious to pick just the right time to sneak out and not get caught. But it was already 8:05 and getting late. Myer must have been thinking if he didn't act soon he'd miss a once-in-a-lifetime chance to see his heroes. It was now or never.

Two minutes later, I closed my eyes while enjoying Lester Farber's sweet voice *dovening* (praying). Mr. Farber sat in the pew in front of us. When he *dovened*, the sound of his tenor voice made me feel connected; that things were orderly and right in the world.

I so yearned for that feeling of belonging. It was a rare commodity; something I had not found in Los Angeles. To be honest, I've traveled all over the world and that feeling of belonging, of community and connection I'd grown up with in that small synagogue, is something I've rarely felt anywhere else. It is something I truly miss. It's too bad that when you're young and all you can think about is getting away from home, you don't appreciate what's there.

When Mr. Farber stopped singing, I opened my eyes and turned around to see the boys executing their escape. Myer, Buddy, and Sidney got up, stepped into the aisle, and began creeping toward the back door. They were almost there when Rabbi Roth stood up.

"As is our tradition, please rise, turn to face the rear door, and join me in singing *L'Cha Dodi* to welcome the Sabbath Bride."

Myer, Buddy, and Sidney froze in their tracks. The congregation was now standing and facing the rear door and the three culprits. The jig was up. The boys made a break for it. Papa saw them dart for the door.

"Myer! Myer!" he yelled impulsively. His voice echoed off the walls of that tiny sanctuary.

Myer and his friends froze in their tracks just outside. At Papa's shout there was pandemonium in our synagogue. Everybody in the place made a run for the door, dashed out, swept around the astonished boys, down the front steps, and into the street. You see, when Papa screamed, "Myer! Myer!" a few congregants heard, "Fire! Fire!". That's all it took to empty the place.

All these years later, I still remember standing on the synagogue's steps on that chilly December night. I was a co-conspirator in what might have been Myer's great escape. I wanted to laugh, but I thought twice about it. The hangdog look on my little brother's face telegraphed his disappointment over missing his heroes and his fear of awful, inevitable consequences he would soon face.

But I couldn't hold myself back. I bent down and whispered in Myer's ear: "You've got a plan, huh? Oh boy, when we get home, you're gonna get it."

He looked up at me, scowled, and said something under his breath. All I could make out was that he told me to take a flying something-or-other on a rolling donut.

CHAPTER 15

The Blue Book

Jake at the Tucson Rodeo, circa 1926

Myer's fears of doom and gloom didn't materialize. Mama and Papa just bawled him out. I figured they didn't take it as a capital offense because of Myer's coming *Bar Mitzvah*, and maybe because I was home and they were happy.

Oddly, that made me sad. There in that modest house in a poor family of European immigrants, I mattered. There I had an impact; I belonged. I didn't feel that anywhere else. Despite my burgeoning success in silent pictures, it didn't seem like I really counted there. It's strange, but even as a celebrity in Hollywood, I didn't feel I was significant. After all, who really cared if I lived or died there?

The next week flew by as we eagerly awaited Myer's *Bar Mitzvah*, which, by the way, fell on New Year's Eve and came off without a hitch. My little brother did a great job. I was so happy to be with my family. A few weeks before, when I had broken up with Ruby, I was sure I'd never feel happy again. But the celebration was also bittersweet for me because it marked the end of my vacation and reminded me that in a just two days I'd leave the love and support I had at home and have to return and face my new life in Hollywood.

Los Angeles still didn't feel like home. At the very least, when I was in my parents' home, I could be myself. For a brief instant, I even wistfully fantasized about staying in El Paso and working with my father at Geneva. Truth be told, times were tough and the store could not support all of us. But beyond that, from a place beyond knowing, perhaps the place where the *yankis* reside, I understood that although I had once belonged in El Paso, I no longer did.

The Sunday afternoon following Myer's *Bar Mitzvah*, we indulged in a lunch of Mama's special holiday delicacies: chicken *tamales* and *mole poblano*. The flavors of her *tamales* and *mole* were so good that eating them was otherworldly. As I look back on it now, her intermingling of yellow, green, and scarlet-maroon sauces on the plate makes me think of Kandinsky's palette. Opening the delicate corn husks that encased her *tamales* freed an intoxicating aroma of late autumn, Indian corn, and Hatch jalapeños. Her *masa* was so golden light and the chicken so deliciously tender that eating that pre-Colombian version of dumplings was like dining on air. Biting into the *mole*, your taste buds were embraced by a sultry, hand-ground essence of dark chocolate, peanuts, and smoky red chile.

"If you can pry yourself away from the table, it's time for the Rose Bowl," Myer said.

For the next few hours my brothers and I hovered around the Motorola and listened intensely as Notre Dame's Fighting Irish beat the Stanford Indians, twenty-seven to ten.

XXXX

"Come on, Jake, you'll miss your train!" Papa screamed. I was running late, really late. Monday morning, January 2, 1925, had gone anything but smoothly. First I lingered too long at the breakfast table. Then I didn't remember where I had stashed my shoes the night before. For someone like me that's a major problem—it's not like I can stop at any shoe store and buy a pair off the shelf. Then the buckle on my valise broke. We ended up using one of Papa's old belts to rope the damned thing closed. All in all, I almost missed the early train back to Los Angeles.

Leaving my family was never easy. After that visit, which was my first trip home since I started working in movies, parting was particularly painful. Although I knew I had to leave, I didn't really want to.

I had to make a mad dash for the train. Once aboard, I stood panting on the platform between the cars. As we crawled out of Union Station, I waved goodbye to my family and watched them dissolve into my memory. Inhaling deeply, I felt tightness in my belly. It was as if a cold steel door in some gaping place slammed shut, trapping me inside with ancient ghosts.

Then I entered the train, creeping along, almost doubled-over at the waist, careful to not bang my head on the railway car's ceiling.

"How you doin', Mr. Earle?"

I looked several paces down the car and saw the broad, gold-toothed smile of that car's porter. He was dressed in a crisp white tunic and a shiny black cap, with spit-shined shoes to match. I had met him when I traveled on the same train to El Paso a few weeks before. Over all my vagabonding years, I met many porters and conductors, bartenders, and waitresses.

Usually they remembered my name even if I didn't recall theirs, giving me a strange, false sense of being at home on the road.

"Did you have a nice Christmas with your folks?" he asked.

"I sure did." I didn't know him well enough to explain we didn't celebrate Christmas.

"Anything special you be needin' for your trip to the coast? If there is, you just let old Frank know."

"Thank you very much, Frank. I may take you up on that." I turned into the entrance of my compartment, stooped, and contorted myself even more to enter it. Although I had traveled to El Paso on the Golden State fourteen days before with the same type of accommodations, today the space felt cluttered, confining, and almost claustrophobic. I sat in the crowded compartment's uncomfortable chair and closed my eyes.

Images of Myer trying to sneak out of synagogue made me smile. Then I pictured my parents at the dining room table laden with Mexican food. A craving for closeness, and the sense of connectedness and belonging it afforded, tore at me. There was something profound, primal, and freeing about the power of *we* and *us* that I felt in El Paso that I hadn't attained in Hollywood with my all struggles and quests for *me* and *I*.

The smallness of the room started to get to me. I wanted to be around people, even strangers. I grabbed my black satchel, stood up, left the compartment, and walked two cars down to the club car. It always took special effort to walk and keep my balance the first time I tried to walk inside a moving train. With all the train travel I've done, I never tired of walking between the cars and feeling the cool air perfumed with the fragrance of digested coal belched out by grimy locomotives.

By the time the train passed the crossroads at Mesa and Doniphan it began to pick up speed and so did I. Within a few minutes I sat at a table in the club car, or what in pre-Prohibition days had been called the bar car. My long legs precariously extended into the aisle. I sipped on a ginger ale and observed the other passengers. My overactive imagination helped to ease my tension. In my fantasy we were on the Orient Express. The young couple sitting directly across from me was on the lam running from her ruthless father, a notorious colonel in an army of Ottoman mercenaries. Now I envisioned the old man sitting at the bar as a one-time gunslinger, trying to forget his past by constantly riding the rails. The middle-aged woman knitting a coffee-colored sweater with the young boy next to her was a lookout for a notorious train robber who would attack us just outside Lordsburg. Ah, thank God for my imagination. In those days, it really helped to distract me from my melancholy. I locked westward out one of the club car's rectangular windows at barren cotton fields, harvested just two months before.

"Can I offer you another soda pop?" asked the old waiter as he stepped over my legs.

"No, thanks," I grunted. I wondered if I would ever overcome my shyness and feel at ease talking to people besides waiters and porters.

More often than you might imagine I did think of quitting the picture business. But when I'd contemplate doing that, I'd imagine the disappointed look on my folks' faces. You see, it wasn't so much that Mama and Papa were secure that I was earning a living in Hollywood but, more than that, I knew they'd found some peace of mind believing that I'd found my place in this world.

I stared out at the cactus and scrub brush growing alongside the rails. *I'm solitary and always alone, like some huge exotic plant in an arid west Texas garden*, I mused. Then I dozed for a while.

When I woke up, we were just outside of Las Cruces. A few more people had come into the club car. I looked around. The middle-aged woman knitting the sweater smiled at me. By the time I made myself smile back she had looked away. I hated my shyness. Since I'd moved to Hollywood, despite my run-in with Ruby, I did feel a bit more confident, but I was still too shy to strike up a conversation with a stranger. I looked out of the window again. In the distance I saw the majestic Organ Pipe Mountains and imagined the miles of gypsum white sand dunes beyond.

Leaving El Paso was like trudging through those desert dunes—with each step forward, the sand shifts and pulls you back, I thought. It made it easy to forget where you were and where you're going, but not where you've been. It gave you a false sense of stillness.

I sat up, startled when I got a glimpse of my reflection gazing back at me in the window. That felt too intimate, almost frightening. By then, I was accustomed to seeing my costumed image on the movie screen, but in the train window's reflection I looked like an apparition, almost gossamer. I turned away from the club car window, reached under my seat, and opened the black satchel I had stashed there. As the Golden State headed westward toward my new home and an uncertain future, I removed the rough draft of the scenario for my next movie, *Obey the Law*, and started to review my new role.

Tuesday afternoon I arrived in Los Angeles at about one o'clock. It was late, but I decided to drop by the studio anyway and check in.

"Happy New Year, Jake. Welcome back," Kitty said. "Tomorrow is a busy day, fella. You have a seven a.m. call on Stage A where you will be shooting most of the day. You have a fitting in wardrobe at three p.m. Then there's a premiere tomorrow night in Silver Lake. Laemmle's people expect you to attend. But first thing tomorrow in the a.m. Stern wants to see you, outside Stage B where he'll be working. He said it's important."

Suddenly I felt nauseous. The slight sense of homesickness I still carried was immediately extinguished by a more powerful emotion: fear. *What do I do now?* Although I was feeling more secure with my work, every time the old man called me in, I still worried I might get shit-canned.

I looked at Kitty for some kind of a clue as to why Stern needed to talk to me. As if she could read my mind, Kitty shook her head to let me know she had no idea what he was up to.

"Why can't I see him now?" I wanted to put this worry behind me.

"Sorry, kid. He's gone for the day. You'll just have to wait until morning."

By the time I got to my place it was dark. I tried to exorcise my restlessness and worry by unpacking and cleaning my apartment. No such luck. The demons stayed with me until midnight when I finally turned out the lights. Then I had a hell of a time falling asleep.

He must not have liked what he saw in my last movie. Maybe the ticket sales for my pictures have gone south. In an incessant, futile attempt to explain the trouble I was in, image followed image; frames of film projected in the darkened movie house of my mind.

The next morning, I got up before dawn, fumbled for my clothes, dressed quickly, and made my way to one of the many trails I occasionally hiked in the Hollywood Hills. I wanted to get a walk in before work to see if maybe exercise might calm my jitters, if just for a bit.

The trail was steep. My knees and hips usually hurt when I hiked. That morning, maybe because of the early hour or the bone chilling ocean breeze, the pain was piercing. But I kept moving, as if I were trying to get away from something. After about fifty yards, I took a deep breath. The scent of eucalyptus and pine stirred me from my sleepiness but the anxiety stayed with me. Within thirty minutes, now wide awake and high up in the hills above Crescent Heights, the exercise finally started to pay off. I had stopped focusing on the discomfort in my joints and I felt a bit less fearful. Purple light began to spread in the bruised morning sky. I looked back down on Hollywood and saw the red, orange, and blue tiled roofs on the Mediterranean style houses and apartments. Among them, I recognized large wooden studios on Poverty Row.

Those barns house the industry that pays for my bread and butter, I thought. But that might not be for long. I was just starting to feel comfortable in that city, and now it was probably going to end. I couldn't make a living in El Paso. What would I do if Stern fired me?

I walked another hundred feet. The trail got steeper. I rested for a minute and admired an oak tree. It was so old and huge that some of its gnarly, confused roots grew above ground, spreading across my path. Things, wild or tame, that were taller than me were always a source of comfort and distraction.

Suddenly, two blue jays lurched from a high branch in the oak tree, disappearing into the new morning sky. I heard a threatening sound. Involuntarily, I jerked my head downward. I intensely focused on the primeval noise coming from the thicket growing on either side of the trail. Something small slithered into the brush. My heart pounded. It was odd how a creature so tiny could cause palpitations in somebody of my Titanic size. I looked up the trail. Then I took my watch out of my pocket. There was no time to make it to the top. As it was, I was late for my meeting with Stern. Even so, on my way back, I moved more cautiously, unsure if the snake I thought I saw was an illusion, something harmless, or deadly.

It's a sign; some kind of an evil omen that your good fortune in Hollywood is about to end, I thought.

XXXX

Once I got to the studio I hurried across the lot, almost breaking into a run, oblivious to all the activity swirling around me. I was good and late.

"Hi, Jack, how was Texas?" Mel Tomlison asked. He was the cameraman on the last picture I shot before my trip. I walked right by him as if he wasn't there. All I could think about was how I would tell my parents I'd been fired.

Stern was standing just outside of Stage B signing forms on a clipboard for Mortimer Chaslow, Century's round-shouldered, green-visor-wearing bookkeeper. "I don't want excuses! Just get it done!" Stern bellowed.

Mortimer walked away, muttering to himself. Stern slowly turned to look at me. I imagined he was a warship and I was about to be blown out of the water.

"Erliiish," he said, articulating the German pronunciation of my name as he did on serious occasions.

I was growing more anxious by the second. Whenever he began a communication with someone's last name you knew it was very bad news. His tone was inscrutable. I braced for the worst. As I'd seen him do so often in the past with others who displeased him, Stern put his left hand in his pocket and pointed at me with his gnarly right index finger.

"Well, they finally decided. The list came out early this *morgan*." A word of German slipped through his English, lubricated by some powerful emotion that I was certain foretold that I would soon be unemployed. "Your name was on the list."

Involuntarily I shook my head, trying to make sense out of what he was saying. What was he talking about? What list? The list of people to be cut from the payroll?

"What are you talking . . . ?"

"Sha." Stern raised his right hand as if he were a running back stiff-arming a tackler. "I won't pay you another dime, not a nickel more. Just because they give you some *furcacta* (crappy) award. *Vershtaste* (Do you understand)?

"What award, Mr. Stern? What are you talking about?" My anxiety, a combination of waiting for the sword to decapitate my movie career and not understanding what my boss was saying, was too much for me. I began to pace back and forth in front of him.

"What's with the walking? Do you have *schpilkis* (an attack of nerves) or something?"

"It's just . . . it's just that I thought you were going to fire me," I whispered.

"What are you, *mishuga* (crazy)?"

I stopped and stared at him. "You mean I'm not losing my job?"

"Of course not!" Stern began to laugh. "I thought everybody in the company knew. You've been selected for the new *Blue Book*."

It wasn't that I was relieved. At first I didn't understand what he was saying. Then I flat out didn't believe him.

Over the brief time I had been working in Hollywood, my reputation as a dependable, hardworking actor with good mugging had grown. I was learning the importance of expressing emotions with my eyes and not my words, a talent Fred Fishbach, my first director, said was essential for making it in that town. Of course some of the people in comedies were hacks and the roles I got were not exactly *The Shiek*, but since I first arrived in Los Angeles, I think my acting had improved. Like my father had found his gift with watchmaking, I wondered if just maybe acting would eventually become my trade. But I knew I was green, a novice, if there ever was one. That's why I was so shocked and skeptical when Stern told me the news. I mean, being included in the *Blue Book* was a big deal.

Sensing my doubt, Stern moved closer to me and reached into his breast pocket. Then he removed and unfolded an official looking document. "See for yourself," he said, handing it to me.

I held the expensive linen stationary in my fingertips and felt it had more weight and importance than any other piece of paper I'd held before. Below the embossed, sapphire logo the Blue Book, handwritten in elegant calligraphy were the words: "The Board of Directors is pleased to announce our *Blue Book* honorees for 1925." I scanned the list of twenty names and among them saw: Cecil B. DeMille; Charlie Chaplin; Mary Pickford; Theda Bara; Rudolph Valentino; Douglas Fairbanks, Sr.; and Harold Lloyd. And about halfway down the page I saw my stage name: Jack Earle.

"Now do you believe me? No more *narishkeit* (foolishness). This is important for Century. There will be a ceremony and a party at the Cocoanut Grove, the first Saturday night in March. No excuses. You'll be there. If you don't own a monkey suit, buy, borrow, or steal one."

I felt like I had swilled too much of Papa's schnapps. "Don't you worry, Mr. Stern! I will be there with bells on!"

That would turn out to be one hell of an unforgettable party.

CHAPTER 16

Cocoanut Grove

Jake in another silent picture, Century Studios

Since Frida had first mentioned it, I had eagerly been anticipating Diego's art show. The two weeks since Val's party and Frida's visit to the circus had gone by quickly, and before I knew it, I found myself in a Manhattan gallery where the opening party for Diego's exhibit was being held. However, at that moment I was not admiring any art but troubled by the disapproving glances of a very snooty-looking couple. The two of them seemed appalled that I was wrestling with the stiff collar of my tuxedo shirt. When I noticed them staring at me, I dropped my hands to my sides and did my best at acting nonchalant. But it was too late. I hated that getup. If Val hadn't insisted it was a Black Tie event I never would have worn the damned thing.

So there I was at that fancy Fifth Avenue art opening with a lot of fancy people, a bit embarrassed and certain that my gyrations with that damned collar made me look like a crazy man. It had been quite some time, actually several years, since I last wore that costly, custom-made torture chamber, and I'd forgotten how God-awful uncomfortable it could be. If it wasn't for getting to spend a little time with Val, I certainly would never have put up with that kind of torment.

To take my mind off my discomfort I walked around the place. Soon I passed a full-length mirror on one of the gallery's few bare walls. An out-of-date tuxedo that glistened from having been pressed once too often gazed back, reminding me of the 1924 Hollywood *Blue Book* Awards, when I first wore that getup.

XXXX

Being nominated for Hollywood's prestigious *Blue Book* gave me a new sense of confidence. It was around that time that I intensified my study of the work of other actors I admired, like Charlie Chaplin. With the goal of making the audience laugh, I worked hard to perfect my on-screen timing and movements. That led to a good reputation and more work. Like my body, my poise grew, albeit more slowly. I even started to write a movie myself: *Stop, Look, and Listen*. What I wrote wasn't exactly what you would call a script. In those days we called them *scenarios*. Scenarios told a story in visual terms to help the actors and director get the idea you were trying to convey.

My new found self-confidence helped me to make a new friend that worked at the studio. He was an assistant cameraman named Tom Rosen. One night shortly before the *Blue Book* Awards, Tom and I decided to go to the movies.

"I'm going to invite Vernon Dent, another camera operator. He works with Mack Sennett," he informed me. I was hesitant, but Tom convinced me that Vernon was a nice fellow and that I would like him.

For our outing, the three of us went to see the premiere at the Embassy Theater of a new flicker, *Old San Francisco*. When the movie ended, I was uneasy and irritated. As the three of us walked to Brown's on Hollywood Boulevard for coffee, that discomfort was a pebble in my shoe that became more and more difficult to ignore. When we finally got to the restaurant the place was packed, but we managed to snag a booth near the back.

Dent, a skinny man no more than five feet tall with a pocked face, took a long drag on his cigarette. He shook his head and exhaled the smoke with a powerful sigh, as if he were pushing something away with his breath. Then he laughed. "If you didn't already dislike Chinamen before that picture, you sure would afterward." He raised his voice either because he felt we couldn't hear him above the din of the crowd or because he wanted to emphasize his words. "Personally, I can't stand those slanty-eyed bastards."

I felt the muscles in my stomach tighten. In that innocent era when I heard someone say something like that it still shocked me. *Bite your tongue. Just keep quiet. After all, you just met this guy*, I said to myself. As if I would have actually spoken up. The Jake I knew in those days might have thought about it, but when it came down to brass tacks, he would have never spoken up, particularly to a stranger.

"Just like in the picture, you don't wanna get caught in Chinatown after dark. It's a bad place, full of dope-dealers and whores. Once I had one of those China girls."

Did he just say what I thought he said? I wondered. *This guy's a jerk*. My throat tightened. The discomfort I felt during the movie and our walk to the eatery was displaced by another, more distinct feeling: I didn't like Dent. I wanted to challenge him, but I just couldn't. So I sat there listening, doing my damndest to conceal my displeasure, masking it behind polite conversation. I wondered if anyone could tell that on the inside I was fuming. But after a few more minutes, I just couldn't hold back anymore.

"Are you trying to say that . . . ?" All I had the balls to do was ask that inane question. I knew exactly what he was saying.

"Do you disagree?" Dent's question put me on the spot. I felt heat between my ears. I wanted to say something more but I was afraid of what would come out of my mouth.

"I . . . I . . . " I stuttered.

"That picture reminded me of *The Birth of a Nation*," Rosen spoke right over me. He was a thirtyish six-footer with a big beer belly, black curly hair, and a little boy's impulsivity.

"Why?" I asked, annoyed at the interruption, but relieved to avoid a confrontation with Dent.

"You know how Griffith made things black and white . . . you know all good or all evil." He shook his head as if agreeing with himself. Then he took a large bite of the seven-layered chocolate cake that put Brown's on the map.

"Come on!" Dent fired back. "*The Birth of a Nation* is a fine picture, possibly one of the best ever made. Maybe Griffith took some poetic license. But after the war the darkies were corrupt. I think a lot of the do-gooders who are pissed at Griffith's ingenious portrayal of Negros are probably high-yellow themselves!" I felt Dent could read my mind. I knew he was baiting me.

Then a *dibuk* took possession of my body. I visualized myself slamming my fist on the table. In my fantasy all the words I had tried to swallow shot out of me like an eruption at Mount Etna.

Poetic license, my ass! You're a racist, I barked to myself. The forceful reply I longed to make echoed across vast empty prairies in my mind and disappeared. With one hand I removed my glasses. With the fingers of the other I rubbed my eyes. I think I must have been trying to cage some newfound, untamed emotions that were halfway out of the corral. I worried what I would do next. My head started to ache. I visualized a recent newspaper photo I saw of a young black man who was lynched somewhere in Alabama. *Do you know what pogroms are?* I imagined asking Dent. I saw myself not waiting for a response but answering my own question. I would tell him about those deadly race riots and my mother's nephew who was beaten to death in Poland by poor peasants drunk on lies and vodka provided by the Czar's secret police. I would hammer this idiot with images of people being raped, murdered, or burned to death. In my fantasy I would tell Dent and Rosen about the German film I'd seen last week at the Hampton Arts, called *Der Golem*. I would astutely point out how, just as Griffith did with blacks, that movie portrayed all Jews as evil and dirty. Rosen and Dent would sit there solemnly, taking in what I said, embarrassed and remorseful for their ignorance. I would finish my indictment by pointing out that poetic license in movies could be dangerous. If we're not careful, our films could be like vodka for peasants, I would add. I stared at Dent as he ate the last piece of apple pie on his plate. *Those goddamned Jew-haters!* I thought. The anti-Semites are not just in Germany. But I never uttered a word to either of them. Instead I clenched my jaw and sat there.

"Jake, are you all right?" Rosen asked. "You haven't said a thing since we sat down and started talking about the movie."

"No, I'm okay. I've just got a bad headache." I was amazed at all that had just gone on between my ears and that neither Rosen nor Dent had the slightest idea about any of it. The waiter brought our check. Once we had paid and walked out I made some excuse and got away from them as quickly as I could.

XXXX

That night walking home I thought about the Negroes in *The Birth of a Nation*, the Chinese in *Old San Francisco*, and the Jews in *Der Golem*. I thought about how angry I felt and why.

When I got back to my apartment a half hour later, I was still upset. I felt confined and anxious. The walls of the place started to close in. Even my clothes felt tight, as if I was trapped in them. I was furious but uncertain about what caused me to feel so bad. Was I angry at Rosen and Dent, or at myself for not speaking up? Sure, I was Jewish, but something else about that conversation had riled me up. Then from some dark vault deep in my memory, images of Dr. Epstein's exam room came flooding back to me. I could hear the doctor's raspy voice. Each of the words I remembered robbed me of a little bit more of my happiness, as if what he had said grew more powerful and pernicious in its recollection:

"I've never had a patient like this . . . monstrous growth, consistent with that of giants." I felt a metal belt wrap tightly around my lungs, squeezing the life out of me. *"Jake's certainly not going to have a normal life."* It felt like I couldn't breathe; like I was dying. I ran across the living room, opened the big picture window, stuck my head out into the cold night air, and took a deep breath. And then another and another and another. I finally calmed down. Then it hit me.

The people I portray in my movies are always the same, I thought. Just like the Jews in *Der Golem*, the Chinese in *Old San Francisco*, and the Negroes in *The Birth of a Nation*, my roles are limited. They're never normal. My size confines me to what others think I am and am not capable of doing. It's not just that the audience's expectations hold me back but it's Stern and the other studio bosses who pick my parts as well.

Although I was really beginning to like making movies, it was clear to me that my acting could only go so far. Stern would never stop typecasting me as a cruel, raving giant; a furious idiot who had been cuckolded; or bumbling hayseed detective.

I closed the window. The lethal band around my lungs loosened, and the life-crushing tightness in my chest finally disappeared, as did my headache. My clothes were magically no longer two sizes too small. Exhausted, I crawled into bed.

"Poetic license, my ass," I said out loud, clicking off the lamp on my night table. *I probably won't be sleeping much tonight,* I thought.

XXXX

A week had passed since my awful evening with Dent and Rosen. It was one of those in-between California afternoons, too cool for spring and too warm for winter. Jack Montgomery and I happened to be walking on the sidewalk across from The Napoli when Ruby came charging out of the restaurant toward me. After she crossed Sunset, she buttonholed us.

"Jake, I haven't seen you in a cat's age. How have you been?" she asked in a flirty voice once she'd caught her breath. "Hi, Jack. How's tricks?" she added. "Listen, I read about the *Blue Book*. That's a big deal. Congratulations! If you don't have a date for that affair, I'd love to go with you."

Does this dame have amnesia? I asked myself. The pain in my belly reminded me that I didn't. For an awful few seconds I stood in a paralytic silence as the band I had felt around my chest after the discussion with Dent and Rosen started to tighten again. I looked around and wished I could melt into the sidewalk. Ruby didn't take the hint.

"How about it?" she asked in a demanding tone.

Finally I looked down at her. "Why . . . " I took a deep breath. My face felt hot. "Ruby, I'm flattered. You know . . . you know . . . I don't have a date," I said, looking up and off to my left as if that was where I stored my social calendar. I had absolutely no idea what I would say next. Where were Marian and Kitty when I needed them?

"Jake . . . " Jack impulsively tried to interrupt and protect me from inviting this she-viper close yet again.

"Just a minute, Jack." I held up my hand, cutting him off. Ruby looked up at me and batted her eyelashes. "Ruby, I . . . I don't have a date for the party, but to tell you the truth, I'd . . . I'd . . . I'd really rather go by myself than with you."

Ruby looked flabbergasted. The tightness in my chest and the fire under my face miraculously disappeared. An astonished Ruby stood there, frozen and staring down at one of the many cracks in the sidewalk. I found myself walking faster and faster, almost breaking into a run to get away from her and the consequences of what I had just done. I had never talked like that to anyone besides my brothers, let alone a woman. In that moment I felt heady, alive, and particularly light. But I'd be a liar if I didn't admit I also felt guilty.

"Wait up; where's the fire?" Jack said, trying to catch me. "Jake, what's got into you? You were not very nice to that girl. Pardner, that was downright mean."

I kept walking. *I don't know what's got into me either,* I thought. That was the first time I realized that maybe I wasn't as nice as everyone thought I was.

XXXX

"Jake, can you help me with this tie?" Myer asked, standing in front of the cut-glass mirror that hung over my dresser. Ben elbowed his way in front of my little brother to brush his hair. I had sensed there would be a last-minute run on the limited hot water and mirror space, so I finished dressing well before my brothers. Since that was the first time I would wear my new tux, I wanted to be sure I had plenty of time to get it right.

In a little over an hour the cocktail party, dinner, and dance honoring me and the nineteen other actors and directors selected for the *Blue Book* would begin. I had anxiously been waiting for that night since Stern told me I'd been selected back in January. Mama and Papa had to stay in Texas and tend to the store, but the date of the party coincided with both my brothers' spring vacations from school. So Ben and Myer came to town to celebrate with me.

The days leading up to the award ceremony had passed in a blur of activity. I started out the week by taking the boys on a tour of Hollywood—or Gower Gulch as we used to call it—originally the site of a small ditch that carried run-off water from the Hollywood Hills.

As I'd walked with my brothers through town I thought how fitting it was that I was making my home in a place where ditches became gulches. After all, my tallness seemed made to order for use in an industry known for hyperbole. I thought about all the smoke and mirrors and trick photography and stunts directors used to accentuate and embellish my height. I wondered if people in the movie industry would ever comprehend that there was more to me than that.

On our tour I pointed out some of the small studios with names like Sterling, Quality, and Waldorf. Then we walked up to the gates of United Artists, a huge studio, the largest of them all. I explained how it was started by Douglas Fairbanks and Mary Pickford, and how later Charlie Chaplin and D.W. Griffith joined them. While we walked through Hollywood, Ben had whistled at a group of young flappers. One of the girls had pointed at me and whispered something to her friends. Then they all laughed and walked away. I did my best to ignore it and not let my brothers see that under my new Hollywood identity I was still awfully self-conscious.

The next day my brothers accompanied me to the Century lot. There they saw me shooting *Hit 'Em Hard*. At one point, I walked off the set with tears in my eyes. My brothers were concerned, so I explained that the klieg lights that shined down on every other actor shined directly into my baby blues. I told them how those lights spit out a lot of carbon dust that got in everybody's eyes, sometime resulting in a sunburn of the eyeball, or what people in the business called "klieg eyes."

I pointed out that for some actors it got so bad they had to quit making pictures. I remember thinking, *I sure hope that doesn't happen to me*. Little did I know that before long, "klieg eyes" would be the least of my worries.

Later that week I took the boys on a long walk around my neighborhood. In those days I lived in a cozy apartment in Whitley Heights with an arched doorway, large picture windows, a roof and mantel made of blue terra-cotta tile, and intricate ebony iron work on the gates, railings, and balconies. My place also had a small interior courtyard with miniature mandarin orange and grapefruit trees. As I recall, there was a little gray granite fountain in the middle of the courtyard with a rusted love seat next to it. At dawn and sunset on spring and summer days when I had the chance, I'd sit there, listen to the water flowing in the fountain, the robins and mockingbirds and, for a while, forget my worries.

Whitley Heights had large pepper trees everywhere. It was a jewel-toned mosaic of green grass and yellow roses, lavender jacaranda blossoms, scarlet and coral bougainvillea. I loved it when the palm trees swayed in warm Santa Ana winds. I told Ben and Myer that moviestars like Charlie Chaplin, Harold Lloyd, Richard Barthelmess, Francis X. Bushman, and Wallace Reid all lived in my neighborhood. That morning we spotted the original Latin lover himself, Rudolph Valentino, dressed in riding clothes walking two huge mastiffs and a rather large Doberman pinscher. I shared that the rumor was that women in the neighborhood would feign working on their lawns to steal a peek at him. Later I learned he wasn't too interested in women. But I didn't have the heart to tell my starstruck brothers.

XXXX

My big night had finally arrived, and somehow we made it to site of the party on time. The Cocoanut Grove was situated at the swanky Ambassador Hotel, one of the newest hotels in town. When we moved through the lobby, for an instant all eyes seemed to turn to me. Continuing to walk, I heard the telltale percussive *pop* and saw the flashlight bursts from several cameras light up the room. Though I still wasn't comfortable with that kind of attention, like it or not, I was becoming a celebrity. One of the things that accompanied my new, albeit unwanted, fame was interest from the fledgling Hollywood press corps. And that night, they were out in force. Photographers and writers covering the awards banquet for *Variety*, *The Hollywood Reporter*, and *Photoplay* hovered around an elegant Clara Bow dressed all in red.

"Isn't that the 'It Girl?'" Ben asked.

"That's right, Benny. It's Clara Bow," I answered.

"Who's the *alta cakcer* she has for an escort?" Myer inquired. "The old fart looks like he could be her father."

"That's Charlie Murray. He's a comedian who works with Mack Sennett. Murray's got to be at least thirty years her senior," I said.

"Maybe she likes her meat well aged," Myer quipped.

I laughed under my breath to not egg him on. "What kind of talk is that for a *Bar Mitzvah* boy?" I quipped.

"Hey, Jake, can we get a picture?" It was Enrico Fatalli, a reporter with *Variety*. The three of us turned to face him. I tried my best to smile, but all I could think about was how damned uncomfortable I felt in that new tux.

There was no way any of the men's stores in Los Angeles had carried formal attire that would fit me. When I told Papa I was having a terrible time finding a monkey suit, he called his friend Nandor Schwartz at the Popular Dry Goods. Schwartz had me go to a tailor he knew in L.A.'s garment district for a fitting. Then I mailed Schwartz my measurements. He had one of the tailors who worked for him in El Paso sew me a custom-made tuxedo. Yeah, it was custom fit all right . . . the jacket was tight. It was so tight I worried that if I took a deep breath I would tear it to pieces. The pants were too big. Since I couldn't find any suspenders to fit my frame, and my belt wasn't doing the trick, I had to almost constantly pull up my pants. I agonized that if I had to stand there with those photographers much longer my trousers would fall down next to my ankles. Now that would have made quite a picture. I could visualize the headline in the next day's paper: "Boy Giant Loses Pants at Awards Dinner."

"C'mon, guys," I said. "Let's get away from this zoo." You know, to this day crowds still make me anxious. We then made our way to the entrance of the Cocoanut Grove. When we approached the doorway, everyone in the line to be seated turned and stared at me.

"Do they always stare?" Ben asked.

"Folks here are just like they were in El Paso. Wherever I go, people gawk," I answered. "Maybe someday I'll get used to it."

I noticed Lionel Barrymore further up in the queue. He was elegantly dressed in a top hat, white tie, and tails. Besides the fact that he was already six sheets to the wind and swaying back and forth like a sailor in a typhoon, something else made me curious about him. He carefully clutched a large box covered with black cloth. From the way he held it the box must have been heavy.

"*Ers a shicker.* He's already loaded," I whispered to the boys. Knowing his reputation for theatrics and practical jokes, I was sure the box he carried contained some kind of a surprise, but I didn't say a word about it.

By then we had reached the front of the line of smartly dressed people. "We're the Earle party," I said to Johnny Manos, the club's host.

"Right this way, gentlemen. We have special table for you up near the front with the other honorees."

If it wasn't for my poorly fitting outfit, all the stares from strangers, and that I wished my parents were there to share this experience, I would have felt like a million bucks. Manos guided us through a space as big as an airplane hangar that was full of fake palm trees to where we would be seated. Ben and Myer's heads were taking in the sights like a couple of hungry hummingbirds at a bug rally. We passed about a hundred circular tables with white linen tablecloths, silver dinner settings, and center pieces made of purple and red tulips. At just about every table we passed someone was pouring a drink out of a hip flask. Some of the flasks were silver. Some were gold. Some were covered with leather. It was Prohibition, but that wasn't going to stop that crowd from celebrating.

When we approached our table, I saw that Jack and Marian had already been seated. They jumped up and gave me a hug. "Jake, were so excited for you." Marian beamed.

"You can say that again," Jack added. "Hiya, Ben. Hiya, Myer," Jack greeted my brothers, whom he had met at the studio earlier that week.

"Gentlemen, I would like to present you to Carl Laemmle's nieces. He's asked us to look out for them tonight." Jack began to introduce three luscious-looking girls dressed in matching sapphire, sequined gowns. "This is Sarah Beth," he said pointing to a blonde who looked to be about nineteen sitting on the opposite side of the table.

"Charmed, I'm sure," she answered in a flirty voice.

"This is her sister, Annabelle." he pointed to the brunette who sat to her left. She nodded as if to give her approval to a knight who had asked to bear her colors in a joust.

"This is our baby sister, Lena," Sara Beth added, tapping the exotic red-head who sat to her right. Lena smiled.

"It's a . . . it's a . . . pleasure to meet you," I said awkwardly.

"I hope I can get a taste of that pleasure, too," Myer whispered. Even though he was barely thirteen my little brother wasn't at all shy with girls. On the contrary, Butch was very precocious. I could just envision it: the president and founder of Universal Studios stalking my bird-dog of a baby brother with a shotgun.

"Keep it in your pants, junior," I whispered. "These three are the big boss's *mishpacha* (family)."

Once we were introduced to the girls, Ben leaned close so he could be heard above the orchestra and the noise of the crowd. "Judging from those three dames, I think I'm gonna really like this party."

"You too, Benny?" I asked, shaking my head in mock disapproval.

"Say, isn't that Rudolph Valentino sitting two tables to our right?" Ben asked.

I looked over Ben's shoulder to be sure. From my bird's eye view I good easily see him. "That's right," I said.

I explained to my brothers that Valentino was responsible for naming the Cocoanut Grove. One of his good friends was the club's host, the man who had seated us. I told them how after Valentino finished shooting *The Sheik* he had called Manos and said there were a bunch of fake palm trees at the studio to be had for less than five hundred *samolians*. Manos bought them all, placed them there and *voila*, the Cocoanut Grove was born.

XXXX

"I think the brunette likes you, Jake," Jack whispered. "She keeps staring at you."

I forced a smile. "I have to watch out for your matchmaking, Jack. I haven't forgotten what happened the last time you tried to fix me up."

"Jake, do you think Babe Ruth would ever get a home run if he didn't even swing the bat?" Jack asked.

I looked down at the table and shook my head. A loud drumroll drew everyone's attention. It was ten o'clock. The dinner plates had been cleared, dessert and coffee had been served, and it was time for the honorees to be recognized. Ronald Cochran, the publisher of the *Blue Book* took his place on the bandstand behind the large round microphone the crooner used. I looked around the room and saw people adding hooch to their after-dinner coffee. *This crowd is getting tanked*, I thought. When Cochran called the first honoree, Cecil B. DeMille, the director literally dashed up to the bandstand.

"I bet the studios wish he finished his pictures with that same speed," Cochran commented. The room roared.

"What's so funny?" Ben asked

"It's an industry joke. The guy makes spectacles like the *The Ten Commandments*." They take forever and a day to shoot. DeMille had a cast of 25,000 for that picture. Can you imagine what that budget must have been?" I asked, looking down at my empty dessert plate and shaking my head. *I'll never have the chance to work with a serious director like that*, I thought. Any other time, that conclusion would have made me melancholy but not that night. My sadness was dissolved by the excitement in the room.

"No I can't," said Ben.

"Where'd he find so many extras?" Myer inquired.

"He used soldiers from the Eleventh Cavalry as the Egyptian Army and Orthodox Jews for the Hebrews."

I couldn't believe what happened next. Sarah Beth opened her evening bag, removed a shiny silver flask, unscrewed the top, and took a swig. Then she handed it to Annabelle, who took a drink and passed it to Myer. Annabelle winked. I couldn't tell if she was winking at me or Ben. But I would bet dollars to doughnuts she was winking at my big brother.As a rule, cute girls didn't flirt with me. Myer started to take a drink from the flask. I saw Marian and Jack's eyes get wide.

"Girls, does your Uncle Carl know about the flask?" Marian asked.

"Well, not really. But I figure what he doesn't know won't hurt him," Sara Beth replied.

"Best put it away, ladies," Marian said.

I reached over and grabbed the flask out of Myer's hands. "Come on, Jakey. You're such a killjoy. Mama and Papa wouldn't mind."

"Oh, they wouldn't, huh? Well I do. I'm not going to spend this special Saturday night holding your head while you vomit up bathtub gin." I passed the flask back to Sara Beth, who shot me a disapproving stare as she stashed the flask in her purse.

"How long until you get called up?" Myer asked, adroitly changing the subject.

"I'm not sure. I hope it's soon. I'm starting to get a little anxious."

"Sara Beth, on second thought, could I borrow that flask for a second?" Jack asked. Sara Beth retrieved the flask and passed it to my friend, who handed it to me. "Take a snort of the rotgut, Jake. It's strictly for medicinal purposes."

I took a drink and felt a shivering and then a deep burn in my belly, but my nerves quieted. It seemed like an hour went by as other actors were called to the dais.

"Well, folks, next it's my privilege to call up one of Hollywood's newest stars and the *Blue Book's* tallest honoree ever. He's a walking Woolworth Tower and a talented one at that," Cochran said.

Now it was finally my turn. I walked slowly to the bandstand, careful not to trip and make a fool of myself. As he had done with the others, Cochran presented me with a copy of the new *Blue Book* and shook my hand. Even though I was proud, I felt sad that my parents couldn't be there. When I returned to the table, my brothers, Jack, and Marian were all on their feet, patting me on my back and hugging me.

"*Mazel tov,* Jake! *Mazel tov!* Ben and Myer said in unison. Then Laemmle's nieces gave me some scrumptious hugs that felt particularly good. The brunette squeezed me extra tight. I don't know if it was the thrill of getting the award, the strong coffee I had after dinner, or getting hugs from three cuties, but my heart was racing.

Ten minutes later, after Cochran presented the last *Blue Book*, the Lopez Orchestra started a swinging rendition of "The Varsity Drag." Before you knew it, Ben asked the blonde to dance. For him that was par for the course. But I couldn't believe Myer's *chutzpa*: He jumped up and whispered something to the redhead. Soon they were on the dance floor next to Ben and his partner doing the Charleston. I shot a glance across the table at Annabelle. I wanted to look down at the tablecloth but she held me with her gaze. Then she winked at me. There was no mistaking it that time; she was flirting with me. Her wink ignited a bolt of electricity that shot up and down my spine, awakening a hunger I had done my best to ignore since the Ruby ordeal. An agonizing debate between opposing counsel in the courthouse of my mind was in full swing.

Do I ask her to dance? No way! She'll probably say no! For God's sake, she's Laemmle's niece. Not so fast, Jake. What's the worst that can happen? The dame winked at you. Come on; find your cojones. *That's it. If my little brother can do it, so can I,* I thought.

"Would you like to—"

I felt a tap on my shoulder. "Hey, buddy, can you help a guy out?" a slightly intoxicated bald man in a disheveled tuxedo asked. "I'm trying to get my sweetie one of those monkeys," he explained, pointing to one of the nearby phony palm trees. I thought it was the booze talking.

"I beg your pardon . . . monkeys?" I was confused by his request.

"You don't know?" He looked surprised. "At big to-dos like this, Manos stashes toy monkeys in the trees. They're a real hot ticket. My honey wants one and I can't reach it." I scanned the room and saw several men standing on chairs, trying to stretch up to the fronds of the Cocoanut Grove's signature royals. Some even had their legs wrapped around the trunks trying to climb them. "Come on, be a sport. I'd really appreciate it," he pleaded. I looked across the table.

"Annabelle, when I . . . when I come back we're gonna dance, okay?" I said.

She smiled. "You betcha!"

I stood up and followed the fellow who had pled for my assistance. As we walked, I felt something small—larger than a rat but smaller than a dog—scamper across my feet. I thought I was having a hallucination. Then I clearly saw it: Two monkeys ran across the floor, leaped onto a nearby empty table, and devoured scraps of uneaten *marjolaine* cake that had been served for dessert. *I thought this guy was talking about toy monkeys,* I said to myself. As this scene repeated itself around the room, women and men screamed, laughed, and fled their tables.

"Hurry it up! That son of a bitch freed a cage of live monkeys in here," I heard a waiter say to a busboy as they ran by me. "If we don't catch them soon, this place is going to be a disaster zone."

In the next day's *Variety* I would read that Barrymore's cloth-covered case had, in-fact, contained a surprise: three spider moneys and three howler monkeys. All of them were hungry and set to wreak havoc when Barrymore let them loose.

The fellow who had asked for my help was undaunted by the chaos. He grabbed my forearm and led me to a palm tree situated in the middle of the night club. Three other drunks, a chubby one with red jowls, a tall, skinny one with a droopy moustache, and one that looked like he was a linebacker for the Chicago Cardinals were all standing on tiptoes on chairs trying to reach the same prize. They were jumping, reaching, and contorting themselves, competing like island boys for a coconut. I effortlessly reached up through the throng, grabbed the stuffed animal, and presented it to the bald man.

"Hey, thanks, buddy," he said gratefully.

By now the other *toy* monkey hunters had stepped down from their chairs and accosted my new friend.

"Hey, what's the big idea?" the chubby one said belligerently.

"We were here first!" bellowed the one with the droopy moustache.

"Now fork it over!" the drunk linebacker demanded.

Things got more heated. A small crowd began to gather. I stepped back. *This is going to get ugly,* I thought.

"What's up, Jake?" It was Ben and Myer. They saw me from across the room in the middle of what appeared to be a donnybrook and charged to the rescue.

"It's just children fighting over toys," I explained.

The fat one grabbed the prize. A tug-of-war began. Then the shoving started. Fists started to fly. I heard the sound of smashing glass. It happened so fast, I couldn't see who hit who first, but people started flying across tables.

"*Vámonos*, boys. Let's get out of here before they call the paddy wagons." Pushing through the mob that had gathered to watch the brawl, I saw monkeys on two more tables enjoying a midnight snack.

XXXX

"Wow, what a night! I attended a Hollywood party, danced the Charleston with a gorgeous doll, and saw movie stars doing battle," Myer said as he undid his tie and sank back into the comfortable leather armchair in my living room.

"It certainly was a night to remember," Ben added, pulling off his shoes and lying back on my flowered sofa.

I was disappointed that I never got to dance with Annabelle, but as I looked at Myer and Ben, more than anything I felt a deep gratitude for them and the peace that comes from sharing important moments with those you love.

Then, as if it was possessed, a glass-framed photo of the cast from my first movie skidded across the coffee table and smashed onto the ground. I looked at Ben and Myer, wondering how that could have happened.

Then the ground started to shake.

CHAPTER 17

The Subway

Jake and Major Mite, Circus World Museum, Baraboo, Wisconsin

"I've been looking all over for you." The sound of Val's voice and her reflection in the mirror next to mine brought me back from my reminiscence to the art gallery and Diego's opening.

"Are you okay? You look like something's wrong," she said.

Seeing how lovely she looked in her gold evening gown made me forget any distress I was feeling. "I'm right as rain; just not accustomed to sporting a monkey suit."

"I'm glad you made it. Let me say you do look handsome in your tuxedo," she said coquettishly. I felt my face flush. "Have you been here long? Have you seen much of the exhibit?" She voiced her questions quickly. Val's demeanor was bubbly, like the champagne she sipped.

"I haven't seen much of the show yet. I . . . I just got . . . I just got to the gallery." Compared to how animated she was, I spoke slowly, with scrutiny and great effort. It felt like each word I struggled to utter wore its own uncomfortable tuxedo shirt.

"I can't wait to see how they've displayed Diego's work," Val said casually, looking around the space as if she were searching for a special someone. Thinking back on it now, I was attracted to her at least in part because I envied her freedom and weightlessness.

"Is your husband here?" I asked, more out of politeness than genuine interest. As soon as I asked that question, I regretted it. Maybe inquiring about her husband made her think I was a cad, up to no good, or ham-handedly telegraphing that I wasn't interested in her. My mind started to race with a million scenarios of how I screwed up and why she was unhappy with me.

"No, he's up at Saratoga for the races until the first of next week." Val put her glass down on the tray of a passing waiter. "Come, let's explore."

Then, as if I was a blind man and she was a child, Val took me by the forearm and escorted me to where one of Diego's murals had been hung. It was a huge colorful piece done in lush reds, greens, oranges, and grays that depicted some kind of workers' rebellion. I loved how he told stories visually.

"He is so gifted," Val said. Along with the genuineness of her compliment, somewhere between the bright blues and yellows that highlighted her words, I thought I detected a longing in her voice and a dark shade of envy.

"He . . . he sure is," I answered, uncomfortable with my own dark thoughts. What did Val think of me? Why would someone so elegant and lovely, someone who could have her pick of Manhattan dandies, spend this special evening with me? "I think that the woman handing out the guns in that piece looks like Frida," I said, pushing away my doubts.

"You're right," Val answered. "Sometime we will have to talk about their politics."

As we walked on, the crowd parted for us. Val ignored the attention, but from my perspective, high above the throng, I sensed that she enjoyed it. "Have you seen Diego or Frida yet?" I asked.

"You can just forget about talking to either of them tonight. At this shindig, those two are the cat's meow. When I came in, I saw them for an instant, but they were surrounded. If you want to chat with them you'll need a machete to cut your way through the jungle of fans, sycophants, critics, and collectors." Val chuckled as if she found music in her own words. Then she opened her handbag, took out a cigarette case, and removed a smoke. "Would you like one?" she asked.

"No, thanks," I said.

Val gently tapped her cigarette on her monogrammed silver case and placed it between her lips. Her heart shaped lips were seductive. I envied that cigarette. Without thinking about it, I reached for the lighter in my pocket and lit it. For an instant the flame made everyone else in the room disappear.

"You know, this art scene can be so exciting. I try to never miss a major opening. But it can also be trying." I wondered what she meant by *trying*, but I didn't ask. Val removed the cigarette with one hand and pulled me to a smaller painting of a big-eyed Indian child with a basket of white and gold flowers. It was displayed in a corner of the room next to a window. She motioned for me to come closer. I bent down and her lips brushed my ear. "Someday you will have your own art opening. I'm sure of it." Her warm, whispered words caressed my face. I'd never met anyone like her.

"What about your sculpture?" I asked impulsively. "Judging by what I saw last week in the menagerie you're really good, Val. Maybe we'll share an opening."

Val abruptly took a step back. *Did I offend her?* I wondered.

"Jake, I have some special news I'd like to share with you, but it's altogether too noisy in this gallery." Val smiled and winked at me. "Let's get out of here and live like real New Yorkers." She had ignored my question and changed the subject. But at that moment I didn't care.

XXXX

"Hey, wait up!" I shouted. Val was almost a flight of stairs ahead of me on our decent into the bowels of the subway. I imagined I was Orpheus climbing down into the nether world to rescue Eurydice.

"Come on, slow poke!" she yelled back to me. With my size and bulk, I was moving as fast as I could. When we finally reached the shiny white-tiled room where we would board a train headed uptown, I was out of breath and amazed. New York had everything you could imagine. All the latest and the greatest, including an underground train that traveled almost as fast as my imagination.

About a minute later the train arrived. After the mechanical doors opened, in order to board, I had to bend at the waist. Luckily the car wasn't crowded. We immediately found seats where I could stretch my legs.

"We'll stay on for only a few stops. Then we'll get off near Central Park. How does that sound?" she asked, clearly happy to be giving me a tour of her city by night. "Are you hungry? I know a great diner at Seventy-Ninth and Park."

"No, I'm really not hungry. I ate at the circus before I came tonight. But I am anxious to hear the news you mentioned back at the gallery."

"Well, that's going to have to wait a while. I want to build up the suspense."

I didn't know what to say. A few seconds into a painful silence, I turned my head and gazed out of the window to Val's left. As we rambled through a tunnel, I felt hypnotized by the subway's movement and the pitch-black darkness that embraced it.

"What were you thinking just now, Jake?" Val asked as we approached the first stop. Her tone was unexpectedly serious.

"It was really nothing," I said, looking back at her.

"Come on, Jake, what were you thinking?" she pleaded. As the subway train pulled away from that stop, I remember feeling that Val sounded like a little girl.

"I was just thinking that it would be nice if life was like a subway."

"Whatever do you mean?"

"Well, it would be nice to choose when you get on and when you get off."

Val looked down at her sequined lap. "That would be nice," she said sadly, turning to look out into the darkness herself. There was a squeaking, screeching, squealing sound as our train began to stop. "Hurry, Jake, this is where we get off."

I stood up and stepped into the aisle.

Ka-thump. I hit something or something hit me in the head. The collision knocked me to my knees.

"Oh my God! Are you okay?" Val shrieked.

I raised my hand to my head. When I removed it, it was covered in blood. Val opened her purse and handed me her handkerchief.

"What happened?" I asked, sitting on my keister and still seeing stars.

"You hit your head on the car's ceiling fan," a young mother with a toddler said as she handed me a clean diaper to use as a bandage. I was mortified. I hated that kind of attention. My head started to ache.

"I'm so sorry. We must have missed our stop," I apologized.

"Why are you sorry? Don't worry about it," Val reassured me. I tried to stand up and couldn't. As we approached the next stop, two male passengers helped me to my feet and Val and I exited the train. For a few minutes we sat on a bench in the station.

"Does this happen to you very often? I mean, crashes with low-hanging objects like airplanes?" I could tell she was trying to lighten my mood.

"Well, I would have thought that run-in with a chandelier at a Chicago speakeasy and my awful night in the Cook County Hospital would have taught me a lesson. But I guess I'll never learn," I said, trying to mirror back her levity and make the best of the situation. Underneath my clowning I was embarrassed and disappointed. My fantasies were dashed. I genuinely liked that woman and I wanted her to like me. After the incident on the train I worried she thought I was a klutz and a freak, not capable of going out with her on an ordinary date. But thanks to my experience as an actor, I knew how to keep up a false front.

By the time we finally climbed out the subway I was not only dejected but also feeling pretty tired and woozy. All I wanted to do was catch a cab back to the freight yards and climb into my bed on the circus train. But Val insisted we go to her place. I wasn't comfortable going to a married woman's home when her husband was out of town. I also felt like a hypocrite. I mean, I was comfortable enough to go out with and have romantic fantasies about a married woman, but I felt bad about going to her place. I wondered what my parents would say if they ever found out.

"I think it's best if I just go home," I said.

"I will have none of that," Val demanded. "We're going back to my place until I'm sure you didn't do any serious damage. That's the least I can do."

After the cab dropped us at her home, the snooty butler opened the door. He took one look at me and immediately charged to the rescue. It turns out Scotty was a good sort who had been a medic in her majesty's service in the war. He did his best to patch me up. As he worked on me, Val poured the three of us snifters full of brandy.

"Did you get that nasty scar from a collision with another ceiling fan?" he asked as he finished bandaging my scalp wound and noticed the star-shaped scar above my right eyebrow.

"No, that one came from a *terremoto*."

"A terre . . . what?" he asked.

XXXX

My brothers and I had been back from the *Blue Book* awards ceremony for a couple of hours when it started. It began with a rumble. My apartment house in Hollywood trembled and yawned. Then the rumble turned to a freight train's roar. The building shuddered, shivered, and shook. Like a drunk's dancing, there was no rhythm in the movement. It was chaotic. In a scene that in other circumstances would have made for good slapstick, Ben and Myer dove under the coffee table. I tried to do the same, but in that cramped space there was no room for my torso, let alone the rest of my giant body. Like a sailor on deck in a typhoon, I staggered across the room and tumbled through the doorway to my bedroom. As if some mythic god was having a tantrum, glasses, plates, and bottles of milk were hurled to the ground where they shattered into a thousand jagged pieces. Furniture bounced across the room. Transformed into a deadly projectile, my new Sears and Roebuck icebox soared through the air. The roaring sound and spine-snapping shaking seemed to last for an hour. Before or since that awful sixty seconds, one minute never lasted so long.

That earthquake was not a *temblor*. In every sense of the word it was like the *terremoto* Cuco told me he had lived through in Mexico City; powerful and destructive. When it finally stopped, I struggled to shake off the shock's paradoxical aftermath. I felt both the overpowering need to find refuge in sleep and a panic-triggered reflex to run from the danger and vomit along the way. I came out of hiding first; then Ben did and finally Myer.

"Are you okay?" I asked.

"I'm fine," Ben fired back calmly. "But you don't look so good." By now blood dripped down my forehead, into my eyes and onto my face. Ben grabbed a dish towel from the sink and handed the makeshift bandage to me.

"What the hell was that?" Myer asked in a trembling voice. Unlike Ben, he was not able to mask his distress. "Are you sure you're okay, Jake?"

I almost passed out at the sight of my baby brother's face as he watched the crimson blood dripping down my cheek. I learned afterward that I had a two-inch gash on my forehead just above my right eyebrow, gouged by a flying piece of broken glass. After the shaking stopped, a wall of dread had made me shut down. It took seeing Myer's reaction to my injury to get me going again.

"You have a gash, Jake. Let me clean that up," Ben said.

I was totally disoriented and felt like I was in someone else's apartment. My normally neat and tidy place was now upside down. Nothing was where it was supposed to be. Searching for the first aid kit, I had to walk through thick, gooey syrup made of Ajax, milk, honey, and powdered detergent that had spilled onto my hardwood floor. Everywhere I looked the ground was covered with books, shattered glass, and a rescue mission's inventory of things that I didn't even know I had. After what seemed like twenty minutes of excavation, I finally found a tin of bandages and a bottle of antiseptic that had somehow survived the destruction.

"You look shell-shocked," I said to Myer while Ben tended to my wound.

"You don't look so good yourself," Myer quipped.

Then the ground started to shake again.

We looked at each other in terror. The three of us instinctively started to dive for the refuge we'd found a few minutes before. But that time the shaking was only an aftershock that lasted a few seconds. Nonetheless, it startled us and made us even more jumpy. Once Ben had bandaged my cut, we went out into the street where half the neighborhood had fled.

It was a strange community of the dispossessed. I saw bathrobe-clad families huddling under trees, making makeshift beds for children. In a communal healing from the trauma they had just experienced, some of the refugees were talking. I imagined they were sharing their unique stories of the earthquake; a new mythology that would be handed down for generations. A few people sat alone, gazing off into the cloudless night sky. Something told me those were the ones whose foundations had fractured, their mooring cut. For them, the shaking had not stopped and would not stop for some time to come, if ever. I felt an affinity and connection with my neighbors from the trauma we had shared.

I also noticed something very strange: For the first time I could remember, people weren't staring at me.

Even in the darkness, the degree of devastation on our block was clear. I imagined this destruction multiplied by a thousand for all the other blocks that must have been hit.

"Look at that!" Ben said, pointing to a pile of rubble that had served to decorate the front of my building. "That's all that's left of those sconces."

I felt the chill from a cool breeze that must have started during the *terremoto* high up in the nearby snow-capped San Bernardino Mountains that surrounded the City of the Angels. Later, mapmakers would claim that in just one minute, the earthquake had caused those mountains to grow a foot taller. I would laugh and think that I'd finally heard about something that grew faster than I did.

A siren and clanging bells added to the tumult. We looked farther down the street to a surrealistic dreamscape as two houses exploded in red, gold, and yellow flames fed by a ruptured gas main. Both homes burned to the ground that night. It was a miracle that the families escaped with only a few scratches.

After about an hour of aimless wandering, we made our way back inside to see if we could sleep. Around four in morning I began to doze. The awful sound of the *terremoto* crashed back into my consciousness. I sat up. Then I forced myself to lie down again. As I tried to sleep, I remembered Cuco's admonition: *Terremotos* mean big changes are coming. I felt vulnerable and small. Unlike other times when I found those feelings to be comforting, that time I just felt scared. I tried to will my fear away with images of a different kind of chaos. It worked. Finally, I drifted off to sleep with a smile on my face as I recalled monkeys eating cake at the Cocoanut Grove.

XXXX

Within a few days the frequency of the nerve-shattering aftershocks gradually decreased. Then, as if God replaced them in his secret bag of magic tricks, they disappeared. Other than the omnipresent piles of gray and brown rubble that lined the streets, my only reminders of the *terremoto* were a nagging headache, difficulty falling asleep, and the star-shaped scar on my forehead.

The next week my brothers left. Ben went back to the University of Arizona in Tucson and Myer returned to high school classes in El Paso.

Soon I would start working on my next picture, *Taxi! Taxi!*. It was my forty-ninth movie. Kitty, Jack, Marion, and Zion were going to hold a big bash after my fiftieth flicker, which I was to begin shooting in two weeks. We'd talked about going to the horse races in Agua Caliente and had even had put down a deposit on several rooms at the Casino Hotel for the celebration.

When I think back on my life, so many of the challenges I confronted were created by external things: a low-hanging chandelier, a subway fan, a small chair, a dashboard that left no room for my knees, a stranger's unwanted stares, insults and rocks hurled by cruel people. Those awful things were pretty much expected and strangely familiar. Some of the trials I faced came from internal things: demons like depression and self-doubt. Over the years those challenges also became predictable. But some of the dragons on my path were neither familiar nor expected. They ambushed me.

XXXX

"Would you like another drink? I'm already two snifters ahead of you," Val said with a hiccup. She ran her finger around the rim of her crystal snifter and looked at me alluringly.

"No, thanks, Val," I said. Even though I knew I should leave, that it was an inappropriate situation, somehow I couldn't make myself get up. So I sat there longer. Scotty had retired for the night, taking his first aid kit with him. We were now all alone in the fashionably cozy walnut-paneled den. It felt like Val was flirting with me and was sitting a little too close for my comfort. I wondered what her husband would think about all this.

"I best be getting back to the circus train," I said half-heartedly on the oversized couch where we were sitting. To be honest, I really wanted to stay. I was curious about what Val might do next. That said, I kept thinking that curiosity killed the cat. Hell, I wasn't sure what I'd do next. Then Val put her hand on my knee. I scooted away from her.

"Just hold on a minute," she said. I found the slight slur in her words to be disarming. Abruptly, she stood up and left the room. I noticed a slight wobble in her step. I smiled when I heard her singing to as she climbed the steps to her bedroom. Given her behavior and half-baked state I worried that she would return wearing a negligee. To calm my nerves, I slowly stood up from the sofa and began to walk around. My pacing reminded me of one of Buck's big cats. I even briefly considered leaving while she was upstairs.

Several framed photos on the mantle above the flagstone fireplace caught my eye. I walked across the room to study them more closely. In one, two young girls who looked like identical twins and a middle-aged couple were on horseback in front of a corral somewhere in the mountains. In another, the same little girls and adults sat on the bow of a speedboat docked at a marina. Another photo captured Val and her husband walking down the gangway of the steamship *Lorelei*. They both wore flower leis. I kept listening for Val's return. Like a Peeping Tom, I would have been mortified if caught stealing a glimpse at her secrets. In yet another photograph her husband and two other men, all dressed in suits and wearing fedoras, were standing with a jockey and racehorse bedecked in flowers in the winner's circle at some racetrack.

Thinking I heard Val approach, I shot a glance at the den's doorway. There was no one there. I was alone, feeling like an intruder whose trespass would be severely punished when discovered. Sort of like Jack in the giant's lair. But I couldn't help it. Just then Val burst into the room. I was an interloper, caught in the act. As she walked across the room toward me she tripped and fell on the scarlet Ottoman rug. I quickly moved to help her up.

"Are you okay?" I asked. Even lying on the ground in her semi-inebriated state she looked adorable.

"I'm fine, I'm fine," she said in an irritated voice waving me off. As she stood up the look of irritation on her face was soon replaced by a half smile. I imagined that after her fall she was embarrassed and now doing her best to mask the effects of the brandy. She straightened her dress and I noticed that in her right hand she held what looked to be some kind of brochure. "This is for you, my friend. It's the catalogue for the Ringling School of Art," she said eagerly. I was relieved to have not been caught snooping. "They have a great sculpture program. My friend Gustav Peters—you met him at my party. Remember he's the director of the New Museum of Modern Art? Well, he thinks that school would be perfect for you," she continued.

I had heard rumors about an art school that John Ringling had founded in Sarasota. That was back in 1931, before the board's decision to replace him with his nephew, John Ringling North, in the management of the circus.

"I can't afford that," I blurted out.

"Please, money should not be a concern. As I said at the party, my husband, James, and John Ringling are prepared to offer you a full scholarship. You can start early next year, when the circus winters in Sarasota."

She's on the level about this, I thought. Val looked at me, waiting for a response. I couldn't focus on any art program. All I could think about was how beautiful Val was and how attracted to her I felt. I realized I needed to do something to not appear rude, so I just sat down on the sofa and quickly thumbed through the publication.

I had had a really hard night. My head hurt and I was exhausted and confused. What was I doing in the apartment of a married socialite at midnight? If I did accept the damned scholarship, would I be doing it just to please this pretty lady? Would I be doing that for some fantasy of happiness; for a one-in-a million long-shot chance of not being alone? Art school? I had never thought of myself as an artist. Who was I kidding? That's all I needed; to start over somewhere else and yet again not fit in. I hated new beginnings and all the anxiety that went with them. *What if I go there and the students and teachers don't like me?* I worried. I recalled having the same anxieties before I started working in silent pictures. I sighed.

At that moment all I knew for certain was that I needed to get to know Val better. If it took going to art school then maybe that's what I should do. Hell, at that moment I probably would have signed up to paint the Sistine Chapel.

Val looked at me expectantly. I felt pressured. Maybe it would be best to think about this before I made any foolish commitments that I wouldn't or couldn't live up to. So I used my injury as a way to deflect the conversation, buy some time, and avoid saying something I would later regret. "Val, I'm not feeling very well. I have a royal headache. I need to be going. Can we talk about this at some other time?"

Val didn't react as I expected; she persisted. She walked over and sat down next to me on the sofa. She had her left hand awfully close to my thigh. I kept looking at her wedding ring. It was platinum with a huge blue-white solitaire diamond surrounded by small sapphires. "Well, Jake, this weekend I'm going to our country place upstate for the rest of the month."

I felt like the floor had just been pulled out from under me. I know this may seem really strange because I hardly knew that woman, but my disappointment at not getting another chance to see her before the circus left New York made my head reel. I had no idea of who she really was or what she wanted with me. But sometimes I wonder what would have happened if I had just grabbed her and kissed that night.

Even though I had grown up in a border town, lived in Hollywood, and traveled with the circus, as I've said, when it came to the ways of love I was still innocent and I was no match for her. However, I wasn't totally naive. Over the years I had had women try to seduce me, as if sleeping with a freak would be some kind of a feather in their bonnets or magic amulet. But I sensed there was something more to Val than that. There was something special about her. She was always respectful. Though she could be haughty with others, she wasn't that way with me. She always looked in my eyes and listened deeply when I spoke and she always smelled great, like flowers. I just couldn't figure out where I stood with her. And I didn't yet understand why she was so hot on me going to art school.

Val looked at me intently. "Listen, Jake. I don't want you to get the wrong idea. I do get lonely." She paused and ran her fingers through her hair, and smiled. "But I'm not trying to have my way with you or anything."

I couldn't say anything. I was shocked at her honesty. Then she took the brochure from my hand and thumbed through it. "One of the things I like best in the world and that is most important to me is recognizing talent and helping artists."

"Val—" I started to object.

"I know, I know. You don't think you are an artist." She appeared to be genuinely interested in me. I liked how that felt. "I have an absolutely wonderful idea. Early Sunday morning Scotty will take me to our summer place upstate. It is a gorgeous drive. Why don't you come for the ride? We can stop for a picnic lunch along the way and hash this art school thing out. I know you have concerns. I can even take my sketchbook and paints." Val didn't wait for my response. "Scotty will have you back by nine p.m. How about it? Is it a date?" she asked forcefully.

"I have to work. If I can . . . I . . . Why . . . why sure, Val." I answered impulsively.

"Scotty and I will swing by for you at around eight Sunday morning. Now I'm going to have him drive you home."

"No, I'm okay to take a cab."

She stood there and looked at me, frowning. "Jake, one thing you will learn about me is that I usually get my way. Scotty is out front waiting for you now."

I laughed. In part I laughed because I appreciated how strong willed she was. In part I laughed because I recognized how I would need to carefully pick my battles with her. I was also relieved to be leaving her apartment before anything I truly regretted had occurred. As I left, two thoughts ran through my mind: I still wasn't sure what to do about art school and I couldn't wait to see Val again.

On the twenty-minute drive back to the circus train, I sat in the rear of her Pierce-Arrow limo in silence. The cool evening air coming through the open window made me feel better. It smelled like rain. The back seat, unlike most other cars I rode in, was roomy enough for me to stretch out. When we arrived, I didn't wait for Scotty to open the door. I got out of the limo, thanked him, and started to walk away. A gentle rain began to fall.

"Sir, may I have a word?" Scotty called out to me. I turned around and walked back. In the dark I could barely make out his face. The only thing I could see was his one gold front tooth illuminated by a ray of light from a gas lamp in the rail yard. "Mr. Erlich, it is not my way to intrude on others' personal business, but you seem like a nice sort."

"Thanks," I said quietly. I put my hand on the roof of the car and waited for him to continue.

He cleared his throat. "A word to the wise; Ms. Val is a kind, captivating woman but in the years I've been in her service I've seen her break many hearts."

I didn't know what to say. *It sounds like he's warning me. No, that couldn't be right*, I thought. I just nodded and walked away through the dimly lit freight yard. At that hour, the yard was abandoned but for a couple of drunk roustabouts returning from a night on the town. I felt a strange combination of exhaustion and exhilaration.

As I approached Car 96 where all of us freaks slept, I noticed that the only light still on came from Lya's sleeper. I wondered why she was up so late. I wondered if she had a date. She was such a pretty girl, but I had never seen her with a boyfriend. I had always thought of her as someone I could turn to, a pal. But lately there was something strange about her, the way she looked at me, her tone of voice. Why had she been so upset with me at the telegraph office? Why had she been so rude to Frida when she came to visit me at the circus? I couldn't figure her out. Nothing against females of the species but, even now, I can't say I've ever been able to figure any of them out.

CHAPTER 18

Major General George Moseley, U.S. Army, Retired

"Seven Come Eleven," Jake Erlich

I have always been somewhat of a worrier. That Sunday morning waiting for Val and Scotty to show up in the parking lot was no different. I worried about what might and what might not happen. I worried about my parents, about morals, about being alone again with Val, or never seeing her again. I even worried that I had gotten confused about the day and time she said she would pick me up. I had walked back and forth so many times I must have worn a path in the freight yard's cracked asphalt.

But there were so many other things on my mind. Not the least of which was having asked Ingalls if I could skip the matinee that Sunday. Getting the time off was actually easier than I thought. You see, despite how demanding he was about me signing my contract, I think he really wanted and needed me back in the show for next season. So he let it pass as a sign of goodwill. After all that had happened, I still can't believe I had the balls to ask him.

As I paced, I worried. What if that day I stole a kiss or what if Val slapped my face? What if we argued about art school? What if I told her I had decided to leave the sideshow, and in her anger she took back her offer and said she never wanted to see me again? I imagined one scenario after the other, wrestling with the unknown and trying to control it. None of my what-ifs brought me any peace. My head felt like it was ready to explode.

Honestly, I'd been fretting for hours. I was so uneasy that I got dressed and ready to go before dawn, hours before Val asked me to be ready. I was so nervous I changed my clothes three times until I decided on the denim pants, powder-blue linen shirt, and navy cardigan I wore. I'm sure you understand; I wanted to look my best for the occasion. At eight a.m., when Scotty finally pulled the shiny black Pierce-Arrow into the lot, I thought I would be relieved. But that scene created its own distress. As I approached the car, Harry, Daisy, and Lya strolled by, coming back from their morning constitutional.

"Pretty swanky, Mr. Erlich," Harry said as he moved toward me. "I will have your bath drawn at quarter past three, my lord," he added, mimicking a Boston Brahmin's butler. His thin yet powerful voice, loud enough to be heard all the way to Westchester, drew attention from anybody in earshot and embarrassed the hell out of me.

Daisy and Lya just stared disdainfully. That was unpleasantness I hadn't planned on and I didn't need. The two little women's silence spoke volumes. To tell the truth, it got to me more than Harry's sarcasm. I couldn't stop thinking about the mean comments they both had recently made about Val. So I didn't even wait for Scotty to get out of the car and open my door. I opened it myself and climbed into the back of the limo so quickly that I banged my knee. I took a deep, exasperated breath and shot a glance at Val. That encounter with my friends was very awkward for me. I wanted to ignore the three of them, but I just couldn't. So I rolled down my window.

"Harry, Daisy, Lya, this is my new friend, Val," I forced myself to say. Val scooted across the seat so she could see them. Now she was looking down at the three little people through the open window and sitting very close to me. I don't know what made me more uncomfortable; Daisy and Lya's disapproval or the feel of Val's thigh pressed up against mine.

"Hello," Harry said politely as he tipped his hat. Daisy and Lya just stood there alongside the limo in stony silence.

"Charmed, I'm sure," Val said, ignoring their rudeness. Val was fashionable as always, dressed for the season in pastel-purple pants, a matching blouse, a plum-colored beret, and light-gray leather gloves. Her gorgeous green eyes and the way she smelled were intoxicating. That really helped to distract me from Daisy and Lya's evident displeasure and the throbbing from my bruised knee.

Scotty put the Pierce-Arrow in gear and began to pull away from the curb. *Bang!* It sounded like something had crashed into the rear of the limo. *Bang! Bang!* Twice that disturbing sound repeated, reverberating violently.

Scotty slammed on the brakes as if he had hit someone. His head jerked forward so violently that his chauffer's cap flew onto the dashboard. I spun my head around so fast that I wrenched my neck. I saw Frank Buck slamming his fist into the rear fender of the car. *Bang! Bang!* Then he aggressively marched up to Val's side of the limo. Her gloved hand timidly cranked open the window. Buck bent down and stared at me scornfully. He didn't say a word but his hard, searching look made me feel guilty. I wasn't sure why. After all, I hadn't done anything wrong. Buck wasn't even her husband. Then he stared at Val.

"What gives, Guinevere?" His cocky words and thin smile did a poor job of disguising his displeasure.

"We're just out for a Sunday drive, Frank," Val answered nonchalantly.

"And I wasn't even invited. *Boo-hoo.*" He stood there glaring as if he were waiting for an invitation to join us or some kind of an apology. A long minute passed in very uncomfortable silence. Val looked troubled.

"We've got to go or we'll get caught in traffic. Ta-ta. We'll talk soon, I promise." She spoke in a casual tone, but when she rolled up her window I saw that her hand was trembling. I turned around, gazed through the rear window, and saw Harry, Daisy, Lya, and Frank Buck frozen there like cigar store Indians watching us slowly drive away.

"What was that about?" I asked.

"Oh, it's nothing. Frank's just having one of his moods."

A few nights earlier, when I'd seen them walk off together at Val's dinner party onto the terrace, I had begun to wonder if anything was going on between them. Val's answer didn't do a thing to diminish my suspicion. It made me think there was more to their connection than just friendship. Even though I told you that I was still somewhat naive, I hadn't just fallen off the turnip truck. It made me really uncomfortable to realize I most likely had a rival besides her husband.

The prospect of having to go up against Buck didn't make me any too happy. He was a casual friend. In my time with Ringling Bros, I'd known him to dominate tigers and men. He was a man's man, if you know what I mean. He knew how to use a whip, a chair, a gun, and his will to get his way. *That's just what I need*, I thought, *something else to worry about.* I tried to calm myself. *Val is unavailable anyway. After all, she's married*, I thought. But if she were in the market for a man, how would she ever pick someone from the sideshow like me over that dashing, great white hunter with nerves of steel who performed in the center ring?

The Sunday morning cross-town traffic was very light so we made excellent time driving out of the city. I did my best to put my worries about Harry, Daisy, Lya, and now Frank Buck out of my mind. Within an hour we were in the rolling, green hills of the majestic Hudson River Valley. Billowy storm clouds to the east reflected in the flowing river framed the spectacular scenery. As we drove past, I took in an explosion of scarlet and lavender tulips, gray granite stone bridges, and stately farmhouses with ancient, crimson barns.

Despite the gorgeous landscape, I had a hard time staying awake. You see, the night before I had tossed and turned until four in the morning, worried about the significance of the time I would spend with Val, wondering about Scotty's admonition, and going over and over in my mind what I would, could, or should say to her on our drive.

"How is your head after that nasty wound you got on the subway?" Val inquired. "Let me see," she ordered, moving closer to me. The touch of her warm fingers on my forehead stirred me more than coffee.

"It's fine," I said, yawning. "Thank you for asking."

Val went on to speak about Diego's showing, the circus, even the Yankees' upcoming season. As she spoke I mostly listened. I fantasized about kissing her passionately and her kissing me back. I tried to push the thought of that forbidden pleasure out of my mind, but I couldn't.

Then Val leaned over and pinched my arm. I was mortified. For an instant I believed she knew what I was thinking.

"Tell me it's this restful scenery and not my boring conversation that is putting you to sleep," Val said, chuckling. I wondered what she would have thought if she knew what was really distracting me.

"Oh, no. It's not you; far from it. Please excuse me," I said. "I just didn't sleep very well last night."

"How about a cup of joe and some breakfast?" she asked, squeezing my knee.

"That sounds like a plan." I yawned again and tried to take a cat stretch but my arms inadvertently hit the limo's ceiling.

"I think next time we'd best take a convertible," Scotty chimed in, noticing my mishap in the rearview mirror.

"If you're adventurous, I know a dive just ahead where they have wonderful blueberry pie," Val added.

Blueberry pie for breakfast; that does sound adventurous. Just like something this daring woman would dream up, I thought.

A few minutes later we entered a small town and Scotty pulled the Pierce-Arrow over at a seedy-looking diner. We parked in front. When I got out of the car I noticed that it was getting overcast and that the temperature had dropped. I buttoned my sweater and hoped rain wouldn't ruin our picnic.

As Val and I walked into the crowded restaurant, all eyes turned to us. I tried to avoid the attention by looking away. Val gazed right back at the staring patrons, challenging them with her eyes. I wasn't used to having someone from outside of the circus look out for me like that. I liked how it felt. When I crumpled up my body to sit in that tiny booth, adults and children, some in their Sunday best who looked like they'd just come from church, and some in coveralls who looked like they were right off of the farm, kept on staring.

"Mornin', folks," the gray-haired waitress said with a casual but brisk manner. "What'll it be?" She took hold of the pencil stashed above her right ear.

"Coffee and cream and a slice of that heavenly berry concoction for me," Val said, removing the beret she'd been wearing. Then she shook her head and freed a treasure trove of beautiful auburn curls hidden underneath until they rested gingerly on her shoulders. I imagined touching that hair. That forbidden fantasy gave me chills of pleasure and guilt. Again, I worried I might lose control and do something I'd regret. Then another delicious fantasy came to mind: I visualized Val posing in the nude for me as I painted her portrait. In my fantasy her auburn hair gently hung down over her chest, almost, but not quite, concealing her breasts. I wondered what she would look like unclothed. *I bet her body's voluptuous*, I thought. *"Jake, she's a married woman!"* I heard my father's stern voice admonishing me. My conscience quickly threw black paint all over that dangerous image.

"And you, hon? Would you care for any breakfast?" the waitress asked.

"Me? I . . . I'll have," I stammered, flustered, as if she had also seen my illicit portrait of Val. My face felt warm. I hoped I wasn't blushing "I . . . I'd like two eggs, sunny-side up; hash browns; toast; and black coffee," I said, finally getting my wits back.

"You are a big one, mister. You sure that's gonna be enough food?"

"That will be plenty for me," I said as Val and I handed her our menus.

"Your mama must have slaved in her kitchen day and night just to feed you," she laughed, shaking her head from side to side and walking away before I could respond.

"Jake, your parents brought you up right. You are always so polite," Val said.

"Thank you," I replied, semi-smiling.

"Does the attention ever get to you?" she inquired, lifting her chin to indicate she was referring to all those in the restaurant who were currently staring at us.

"Yes, sometimes it does, Val. Sometimes it really does get to me," I said, more forcefully than I had intended. My straightforward answer and the unambiguous tone that delivered it surprised me. This was the first time I had ever honestly confided in a woman besides Mama, Daisy, and Lya. I mean, I had said pretty much the same thing to my brothers, my parents, and a friend or two back in El Paso, but never to a woman outside the family or the circus.

Then Val reached across the booth. Her hands looked tiny. She took hold of my massive right hand and squeezed. The little bit of pressure she exerted released a tsunami of pent-up longing. I wanted to grab her hands like she'd grabbed mine. I wanted to tell her more. It wasn't only that strangers' stares got to me. Truth be told, I hated them; the stares and sometimes the strangers, too. I wanted to run away and meet a wizard who could cast a spell and make me a normal-size man with normal dreams and fears; to fit in a normal-size suit; to wear normal-size shoes and sleep in a normal bed; to have a normal job. I longed to share all of this with Val but I didn't say a word. I just gazed out the plate-glass window to my right at the sidewalk outside.

"That's enough about me," I said, changing the subject. "I don't know much about you. You're a fantasy to me."

"I think fantasy is good. I like being mysterious, like Queen Norma. It's romantic," she said in a teasing voice. "Fantasy is color and hope; a circus." Val laughed, took a sip of her coffee, and looked out of the window, mirroring what I had done a few seconds earlier.

"You speak like a poet," I said.

She paused. Her mood changed as quickly as mountain weather. "I'm no poet. I know there's no fantasy in the real world. It's black, white, and gray, with too many bad dreams."

Her voice was full of sadness. Suddenly she seemed older, much older. Val let go of my hand and sat back in the booth. There was a real melancholy about her and that was the first time I'd seen it. But it didn't make her any less appealing.

Just then the waitress brought our breakfast. Val looked relieved. After a few bites of blueberry pie she smiled at me. "Sorry, I didn't mean to rain on this beautiful Sunday."

"That's okay," I said, looking into her eyes. "Sometimes I get sad, too."

She brushed her hair out of her face and glanced away. When Val finally turned back, I noticed that she looked tired. She had dark circles and crow's-feet around her eyes that bled them of their sparkle. I wondered about her sadness. I knew that I felt guilty about being with her, and I wondered if guilt was affecting her as well. I wondered if she was worried about Frank Buck.

A minute of silence passed. I started to ask her what was troubling her. Then I bit my tongue. *It's none of your business, Jake*, I thought. Looking back on it now, I know the distress I sensed in Val and my need to rescue her must have been overwhelming for me; more overwhelming than my fear of any negative reaction she might have.

"Val, what's wrong?" I couldn't believe I had actually asked that question.

"I don't want to talk about it," she said dismissively.

"Why?" I insisted.

"It's personal." I felt her pushing me away. I didn't know what to say. Then there was an awkward silence. I toyed with my napkin. Val fidgeted, shifted slightly, and looked at me. "Look, Jake, I don't mean to be rude, but I'm a very private person and I don't really know you."

So it's okay for me to tell her about myself. But she won't open up to me. That's a bum deal if I ever heard one, I thought.

Val looked up and to the right as if that was where she kept a cabinet in her mind stocked with things to talk about when she was confronted by her own demons. Then she gazed down at the table and methodically added two teaspoons of sugar to her coffee and began to carefully stir her cup. The ritual seemed to help her gather her thoughts, decide what to say, and dissolve whatever was bothering her.

"Jake, I had a call from the director of the museum. He asked if he could go ahead and send his recommendation letter for you to the art school. I told him I would see you today and get back to him on Monday," Val said in an annoyed tone. "I need to know what you plan to do."

"I know, but . . . ." I replied, looking down at my eggs, not even aware of how she had changed the subject. I would come to learn how masterful she was at getting off the hot seat.

"What are you afraid of?" she asked, almost angry at my hesitation.

"More coffee?" It was our waitress. After she topped off our cups, she walked away.

I wondered why Val sounded upset. "Listen, I appreciate what you've done for me. I really do. But why is this so important to you?"

"Listen, Jake, real talent doesn't come along every day. I should know. I have been around enough phonies and wannabe artists." She paused and looked across the restaurant before continuing. "So when we see somebody who—"

"What do you mean, *we*?" I blurted out. I felt myself getting hot. I felt half-exposed and vulnerable, and I didn't like it

"Frida, Diego, my husband, Gustav Peters, and I are all convinced that you have natural, artistic ability," Val answered.

I imagined myself asking her a myriad of questions. *What about your husband? How does he feel about me? Did he go along with this just because you wanted him to? What does he think about us spending time alone? Does he even know?* I began to tense up with worry. In those days I was a slave to worries about what Val might think or do. I thought of a thousand things I could or should say, but I didn't utter a word. I just sat there like a lox.

"Does your husband really think I'm talented?" I have no idea why when I finally spoke up I asked that stupid question. Whereas the sun and the moon set on Val's impressions of me, I couldn't have cared less what that old fart thought. I imagined that if Val were my wife I'd never let her go on a picnic alone with another man, and I'd certainly never let her anywhere near a swashbuckling lion tamer.

"He respects my opinions in these matters but he recognizes ability like yours when he sees it," Val said. "Are you just going to waste a once-in-a-lifetime opportunity like this, Jake?"

Her challenge made me feel fidgety. Val wanted to talk about art school and I wanted to talk about us. But I couldn't, so I just sat there listening to her, feeling like a coward.

"Do you know how many young men would kill to have a chance like this, especially with a depression going on?" She was resolute. My heart beat faster. "I need you to decide, or at least tell me why you won't go." I felt cornered. My ears started to ring. Then Val lifted her spoon out of her cup and threw it down hard on the table. Her ferocity startled me. "I just hate it when people do things that don't make any sense," she said irately.

Maybe she was trying to provoke me. Well, whatever her intent, I couldn't stand how I was pussyfooting around. I don't know what came over me. I just blurted it out.

"What am I to you, anyway? Some kind of an art experiment?" I was shocked by what had just come out of my mouth. My heart pounded so fiercely it felt like it would split in half.

"What do you mean, 'an art experiment'?" Val sat forward. I sat back in the booth. She was paying attention to me in a way she never had before. There was something about the way she looked at me. It was deeper and more intense and made me feel as if we'd stepped into a different dimension. Val was more here-and-now present. You have to believe me, there was absolutely nothing I wanted more in my life then her undivided attention. But I was terrified of what I was going to do with her when I actually had it. And I was truly frightened of what other unpredictable things I might say or secrets I might reveal. I struggled to put the brakes on my impulses, to gather my thoughts, and to explain logically what I had just asked. Then I clammed up again.

"Check, please," I heard a man in the booth behind us say.

"Check," I heard a woman at a table across the room call.

"Can we get our bill, sweetie?" someone else asked.

The sound of three people requesting their bills simultaneously in a small diner like that was distracting. I was thankful for the diversion from our intense conversation. I noticed that, in unison, a few customers had gotten up from their tables and booths. They moved in the excited fashion of people who have someplace to be and are late. I also noted a small line gathering at the cash register that had not been there a few minutes before. Someone opened the door, a cool rush of morning air flowed into the place, and some customers exited. I looked out of the plate glass window and observed that the half-dozen or so people who had just left the diner crossed the street and turned right, walking down the sidewalk in the same direction. In the distance, I saw them join a group of about twenty more men, women, children, and old people. Some in that crowd carried placards that I couldn't quite make out.

"It looks like there is something going on out there," I said to Val, pointing toward the window and the street beyond.

She turned to look at the hubbub outside. For some reason the animation and excitement in the hoard reminded me of the throngs of people I'd observed over the years scrambling to get a glimpse of a circus parade that was about to start.

"Nice try, Jake, but no cigar. I'm not that easily distracted. Were you even listening to me?" Val asked in an exasperated tone, looking back at me. "Am I having this conversation with myself?"

Ignoring Val's question, I turned and saw our waitress laying a rotund man's bill down on the counter. "You take care, Charlie," I heard her say. "Give my regards to the missus." I waved my hand to get her attention, motioning for her to come to our table.

"Is there a carnival in town? Is there going to be an election or something?" I asked, pointing outside to the people on the sidewalk. "That's a lot of foot traffic for a Sunday."

"Aw, it's those goldarn crackpots. Every Sunday they have those damned rallies in front of the school and steal our customers. Just a second," she said, stepping away.

"I'm sorry, Val. I was sidetracked by all the commotion." It was a lame effort to apologize. Before I could say anything else, the waitress returned with a flyer that she set on our table.

It read: *For the good of the race, only healthy seed must be sown:*
Stamp out hereditary disease and unfitness!
Join our cause: Eugenics is the modern answer
Rally this Sunday: 10 a.m. in front of the Ulysses S. Grant Grammar School
Featured speakers: Major General George Moseley, U.S. Army, Retired
State Senator Elroy Mandeville
Professor Stockwell Gibbs, PhD, Ithaca University

We looked up at the waitress who was still standing there watching us. "Yeah, they're like tent preachers in these parts; moaning and groaning about the future of mankind, science, and the betterment of the white race. If you ask me, it's a load of horse puckey!" As she spoke, the hair on the back of my neck started to stand up and I felt an ominous dread in the pit of my stomach. I tried to stand up.

"I've heard about these guys. Have you, Jake?" Val asked. I sat back down.

"Come to think of it, last week I did see a piece about eugenics in the *Times*," I said. This whole subject gave me the creeps. In my nervousness, I began to tap the table with my fingertips. I really didn't want to be having that conversation.

"What did the article say?" Val asked, evidently not at all in tune with my anxiety. Looking back on it, I really felt uncomfortable and that I wanted to get out of that diner and that little town as soon as possible. Val was oblivious and I was too embarrassed to talk about my uneasiness.

"I remember reading that eugenicists were people committed to stamping out what they felt were racial impurities." As I spoke, I nervously turned my head away from Val and the waitress to watch the crowd outside on the sidewalk. There was something foreboding in the air that made me feel even more concerned, but I wasn't sure why. Large groups of people anywhere besides under the big top gave me the willies. My gut reaction to the eugenicists turned out to be right on the money. I would soon learn that my friends and I and other less fortunate souls were the impure and imperfect ones whose seed those sons of bitches didn't want sown.

If I only knew then what I know now I would have understood that the words the eugenicists spouted were not harmless philosophical and scientific speculations. Sooner than I could have imagined possible, their hairbrained ideas would be used to justify incarceration, forced sterilization, and murder, even of people I knew and loved.

"Eugenics seems like it's really popular," Val said, looking out at the crowd on the sidewalk.

"Around these parts, it sure is," the waitress added. "It's a genuine grassroots movement; a political phenom."

"It's something we should see firsthand." As she spoke, Val's voice sounded more and more energized. Then she whirled away from the window and gazed at me, an excited blush on her face. Just like a mare at a dead run back to the barn at feeding time, there would be no stopping her. "I have an idea. As long as we're here, let's go to the rally, Jake." Val's tone was that of spoiled child demanding to go to the circus.

"I don't think so. This isn't exactly a concert. I'm not interested." Something inside warned me that going to that meeting was a very bad idea. "Can't we just get back in the car and drive out of this burg?" I pleaded in a whisper.

"Oh, don't be a killjoy. My husband told me about these rallies and Moseley. He heard him speak and described Moseley as the William Jennings Bryan of this generation. I absolutely must see him," she demanded, ignoring what I had just said. "I promise we won't stay long. We'll have plenty of time for our picnic." She gave me a flirtatious smile. "Check, please."

XXXX

From where I stood under a huge elm tree across the street from the grammar school, I could see about a hundred people hovering together in front of a portable wooden platform decorated with red, white, and blue bunting. The left side of the stage was bordered by the Stars and Stripes and a sign that read "Save Our Race." On the right side stood a large "Eugenics" placard and the blue, green, yellow, and red New York state flag. If they were magically granted the power to speak, I wondered what the mute goddesses of liberty and justice emblazoned on that standard would have said about the ordinary folks assembled there and the travesties they advocated.

By the time we arrived, Moseley had already begun to harangue the crowd. They were a mixed multitude, dressed like the folks we'd seen in the diner. I imagined the audience was comprised of good people—you know, salt of the earth types; a kind, God-fearing lot. The skilled speaker mesmerized the crowd with eloquence, emphasizing his words carefully, bobbing and swaying like Billy Sunday. His costume, the dress blues of an army officer, complete with brass buttons, medals, epaulets, and a gold sword, added to his authority and impact.

Val demanded that we cross the street and squeeze to the front of the crowd for a better look. With a premonition that comes from too many close calls and the need for self-preservation, that time I overrode my desire to please her and insisted, with the same fervor, on staying right where I was. As stragglers passed me they turned to stare, only drawn onward by another, more compelling show across the street.

"'To arms, to arms,' the patriot Paul Revere cried. Today the danger is just as great but more insidious." As Moseley started to speak I got the chills, stirred by his words and aroused by his charisma. Then I listened more closely to what he was saying. That's when I got truly frightened.

"It's not the British we should fear, my friends and countrymen, but crossbreeding of the races and the homosexuals. I tell you today that the degenerates, the dope fiends, and the Jews, all financed by well-heeled foreigners, are threatening the home of the brave and the land of the free."

The crowd broke into applause. At once I felt like he was talking about me. I took a step back and tried to camouflage myself behind the elm tree, as if someone of my proportions could ever hide in plain sight.

"For their own good and ours, the deviants, the feeble minded, the idiots, and the imbeciles, should be institutionalized. Let us use the wonders of modern surgery that the good Lord has blessed us with to stop the menace. If you don't take a stand, those morons will grow up to be criminals and prostitutes. If you talk to any doctor—and believe me, I have studied with the most esteemed practitioners of the Hippocratic arts in the land—our nation is threatened by a plague of sexually transmitted infections. Lock up the unfit! Don't wait until next week or next year. Do it today! Keep them away from our children!"

The more he stirred himself and the crowd into a crescendo of emotion, the more frightened I became.

"As my esteemed colleague, the good Professor Gibbs, who is to follow me on the dais will point out, there is no doubt of the correlation between dependency, delinquency, and mental defect."

"Amen, brother!" an old woman yelled from the horde. I scanned the crowd nervously for Val. For an instant I thought I saw her head.

"The blacks and Jews, southern Europeans—in short, any group of deviants without the superior pedigree of us Nordic and Anglo Europeans threatens our children's future."

"Yes! Yes! Yes!" The audience chanted in one unified voice. They were like a starving fire and his words were the oxygen that made it blaze. It looked as if only a few in the crowd weren't swept away.

I became more and more alarmed, like a trapped animal. Again I searched the throng and couldn't see Val anywhere. It was as if the crowd had swallowed her up. I wanted to run away, but I couldn't just abandon her. As I frantically searched the crowd, I noticed that some of the spectators standing at the rear had turned around and were staring at me. Some were even pointing. I felt like a Christian captive in the underbelly of the Colosseum, sure I would soon be devoured by wild beasts. I took another step back behind the tree. Then I took another. My breathing was rapid and shallow and my heart was beating hard as terror at what would happen next grew. I had heard stories of angry crowds turning their wrath on innocent bystanders. Images of blacks and Jews who had been lynched, easy targets for the rage of the dispossessed, passed through my mind. The Depression was a dangerous time to be different. I almost panicked. I flashed back to how I'd felt all those years ago on the banks of the

Rio Grande. I saw myself running away from Eisenbeis and his henchmen and the rocks they threw. But that time there was no river in which to swim away. There was no escaping the danger, at least, not until Val returned.

"We must ensure every child's right to be well born by containing and stopping cold the contamination of the races. Join with me, brothers and sisters. Commit to the eugenics crusade. Give whatever you can, two bits or a dollar, and once and for all stop the degenerate practices going on in every city in this land that contaminate the young, debauch the innocent, and curse the state."

The crowd broke into frenzied applause. I broke into a sweat. Here I was, a Jewish giant, an aberration of nature in the midst of an army bent on stamping out racial impurities.

I have to leave and leave now, I thought as I anxiously scanned the crowd two or three more times. *Where the hell is Val?* There was no trace of her. I wanted to run away. I really did. But like a cowboy holding back a mustang who stepped on a cottonmouth, despite my panic I pulled back on the reins and made myself stand there. I thought I was going to be sick.

At that instant, Val finally pushed her way through the crowd of eugenic lunatics and ran across the street to where I was hiding. *Thank God! I thought she'd never get here*, I said to myself.

As she approached, she looked furious. Gone was the countenance of a bratty child demanding to see the show. She was absolutely purple with rage and looked like she had been holding her breath.

"I want to get the hell out of this place," I said before Val could utter a word.

"Can you believe these idiots?" she screamed in an exasperated tone, ignoring my demand. I wished she would quiet down. All Val needed to do was be overheard by one of the true believers who had already spotted me. After Moseley's rant, if one of them heard her words it would be like lighting striking bone-dry kindling. "They want to put everybody who is not like them in jail and sterilize them." She put both of her hands on her head as she spoke, for emphasis or to signal disbelief. I envied her courage. But truth be told, at that instant, I felt more dread at what would happen if the crowd across the street got wind of what she was saying than envy.

That's exactly what happened. A group of four large young men who looked like linemen on the local football team and a pregnant woman peeled off from the back of the pack and walked across the street toward us.

Now we're in for it, I thought. I grabbed Val's arm and started pulling her along the sidewalk, back to the limo.

"What about that hogwash about the Jews?" She wouldn't let up. "Don't you want to do anything about this?" Val demanded.

"Shhh!" I tried to quiet her. At that instant, in my mind, I heard an age-old Jewish admonition: *Don't make a* shanda *for the* goyim; don't make a scandal. Don't draw attention from the gentiles by stirring things up.

The five people from the crowd, like sentries who had discovered infiltrators in their camp were now pointing at us.

"Val, it's time to go. This is going to get ugly. This isn't our fight."

"This isn't our fight?" She looked at me with a puzzled look. Then some primitive instinct made her turn to look at the four gorillas and the pregnant woman who were making a beeline toward us. I saw her clench her fists and take a step toward them.

"Come on, you idiots!" she yelled.

I started moving and hauled her along with me. "Please, Val. Think about it," I pleaded.

She turned around and glared at me. "Jake, maybe you think too much," she said, storming off toward the limo.

As I followed her, I kept looking back over my shoulder. The pregnant one had stopped her pursuit, but the four other hooligans were still tailing us. Val and I walked faster, hoping to lose them. Then I heard the kettle-drum sound of rolling thunder. After another block or two it began to drizzle. I glanced over my shoulder again and saw that our pursuers had stopped and returned to the circus taking place in front of the grammar school. By the time we reached the car, it had begun to pour.

CHAPTER 19

Carol Marie

"The End of the Magic," Jake Erlich

Tic-tic, tic-tic, tic-tic.

I was mesmerized by the syncopated, monotonous sound of the windshield wipers battling the downpour. The rhythm of the two giant metronomes was only occasionally interrupted by the swish of an enormous puddle of gray rainwater baptizing the entire limo.

Val gazed out her window and acted as if I wasn't even there. We had been driving for three-quarters of an hour in silence. It was cold in the limo so I buttoned my sweater. Then again, maybe it was just Val's frosty manner that caused the chill.

Boy, I really blew it this time. I knew this was too good to last, I thought, making a small doodle with my index finger in the canvas of moisture that was covering the inside of my window. The critical voice that was always present in my mind began its indictment. *You should have made a stand, argued with those eugenics bastards or at least done something,* I said to myself. *But what did she expect me to do, take on the whole crowd? She doesn't know what it's like. I've been fighting this battle since I was seven.* Silently, I tried to mount a defense, but I was no match for the wily prosecutor that lived in my head. I was frustrated and angry. Then, as if I were destroying evidence, I rubbed the palm of my right hand aggressively into the window, erasing my doodle and making a loud squeaking sound. *I bet she thinks I don't have any balls. What was I thinking anyway? Val and I would have never worked out.* Now my critic became more ferocious. *What would she have possibly wanted with a freak like me?*

We drove through a lake of a puddle. That time the limo fishtailed. I felt a surge of nauseating adrenaline. Within a couple of seconds, Scotty had things back under control, but the violent movement made me revisit something I wished I could forget. Suddenly I was standing on the ledge of that hotel room again, twelve floors above the Manhattan sidewalk, daring myself to step into space and end it all.

"Scotty, as soon as we get to the farm and you drop me off, please take Mr. Erlich back to the city," Val instructed. Though I was expecting her rejection, its guillotine swiftness was still shocking.

You should have jumped, I silently berated myself.

About twenty minutes later Scotty drove through a gate in a five-foot-tall, white split-rail fence that appeared to stretch from here to tomorrow. Val picked up her pocketbook, which was resting on the floor next to her feet. She reached into it, removed a gold compact, opened it, and eyed her reflection in the mirror as if she had lost something there. Then she reached into the purse and pulled out a lipstick. She applied the waxy crimson color to her full lips and finished off the job by powdering her cheeks. She did that expertly, like actors I'd known. I wondered what kind of performance she was preparing for.

Val seemed detached. In stony silence she continued to ignore me. My throat tightened. I thought about the fiasco with Ruby. Once again a woman had rejected me. With Ruby, the warnings—though I chose to ignore them—were more evident. Despite Scotty's admonition, Val's unexpected coldness towards me was a surprise.

The gate we entered looked like an inverted horseshoe. It consisted of three huge, rough-hewn oak posts, two of them parallel and the third balanced above the others. A large rectangular sign hung from the middle post, high enough that a horse trailer could easily pass beneath it. The words on that varnished cedar sign had been skillfully burned into the wood. They read, FOUR OAKS FARM—HOME TO NEW YORK'S FINEST THOROUGHBREDS. The rain had let up enough for me to make out a bit of the scenery. I wished nature's beauty could have taken my mind off the awkwardness in the car.

Once inside the gate, we continued to drive for at least a mile. *This must be a huge place,* I thought. The magnificent grounds attested to the wealth of Val and her husband. A fence ran along either side of the road, bordered by finely trimmed emerald-green pastures, outlined by massive oak trees that must have been planted before the Revolutionary War. Here and there under the trees I spotted small groups of black, chestnut, and dapple-gray horses, and some colts seeking shelter from the storm.

We finally pulled up in front of what looked like my image of a grand old southern mansion, complete with a portico, four Corinthian columns, and a veranda with three large rocking chairs. All that was lacking to complete this picture were slaves picking cotton and someone playing the banjo, singing a Stephen Foster tune. *Here is where I get the axe*, I thought.

Two people, each carrying a black umbrella, ran to the Pierce-Arrow. One of them opened Val's door. It was her husband, James. His kind, caring gesture surprised me. I started to feel uncomfortable, like a thief caught in broad daylight trying to break into somebody's house. Maybe James wasn't as bad a husband as I had imagined and their relationship was not as awful as I'd been told. The other person who had run out to the car was a red-haired, portly woman with a ruddy complexion in a maid's uniform.

"Welcome to the ark," James said, sticking his head in the car. Val looked up at him. I could have sworn I saw her bat her eyelashes. Then she threw her arms around his neck and kissed him on the lips. I felt confused.

"I thought you'd be at the races, Jimmy," Val said.

"The track was just too muddy, so we called it a day after the third race." He looked across at me with a puzzled expression on his face.

"You remember Mr. Erlich from the party at our house," Val said nonchalantly. "He rode up to keep me company. But he won't be able to stay. He's got to get back to the city." She got out of the car.

James looked relieved. I wondered why. Based on Scotty's warning and my surmising about Frank and Val's liaison, maybe James was painfully aware of his wife's peccadilloes. Maybe he was worried about me, as well.

"Good-bye, Jake," Val said as she walked away with the maid holding the umbrella over her head. Her husband paused and shut the door to the limousine, touching his hand briefly to his hat, before turning and following her. My heart sank like the *Lusitania*. I felt brushed off, confused, and bruised. I looked out my window, wishing I could find refuge under an oak tree, like one of Val's horses.

The sound of the limo's passenger door swinging open surprised me. It was Val. She slid across the back seat until she was sitting close enough for me to hear her whisper. Her hair was wet. I remember the smell; there was something animal about it.

"Jake, you're not an art experiment to me. You are much, much more. Thanks for spending the day with me. Sorry I've been such a pill." Then she reached over, grabbed my arm, and kissed me on the cheek. Before I could say a word, she dashed back into the rain.

As we started to drive back to the city I felt tortured by self-doubt and taunted by forbidden possibilities. After the rally I had assumed that Val's cold attitude was a rejection. Then her kiss gave me hope that made me dizzy. Little did I know that Val's mercurial response had nothing whatsoever to do with me.

On our long drive back to the city, Scotty volunteered that he had been with Val and James for many years. I felt I could trust Scotty, so I asked him about Val's background. He told me things that let me know she was a lot more complicated than I could have ever imagined.

Val Marie and her identical twin sister, Carol Marie, the only children of a wealthy furniture magnate and the pretty factory worker with whom he'd fallen in love, were born in High Point, North Carolina. Val was the first of the twins to be delivered. Her birth came off without a hitch. But when Carol was delivered, there were serious complications. When she came into this world she was blue. Her umbilical cord was wrapped around her neck, starving her of needed breath. The result was some minor brain damage.

Val was a vivacious child. You would never know it to look at her, but her identical twin sister, Carol, was slow—or what they used to call *simple*. The parents doted on their daughters, raising them in the lap of luxury. Travel, servants, private teachers, and special help for Carol Marie; nothing was too good for the twins. But when the girls were twelve, tragedy struck.

The family was summering at their place in Kennebunkport. In mid-August, on a moonless midnight cruise in the family's new Garwood speedboat, there was a terrible accident. Val's father and another couple they were entertaining were killed instantly. Her mother died in the hospital two days later. No one ever knew exactly what happened, but high speed, alcohol, and an unlit rock outcropping on Maine's treacherous coastline all played a role in that misfortune.

At first the orphaned girls went to live with their uncle and aunt in Atlanta. The uncle and aunt were childless socialites who felt an obligation to help their kin. Things went fine for about a year but when the uncle—I think his name was Joe-Joe—died of a coronary, things fell apart. The aunt, Rita, was left penniless with a mansion and a mountain of debts from her deceased husband's gambling and land speculations. To survive, she had to sell the place. Soon afterward, Rita decided to move her new family to New York to live with a spinster sister who taught school in Manhattan. But she worried about taking Carol to the big city. Rita knew that to make ends meet she would have to go back to work and there would be no one to look out for her niece. She didn't want to, but she felt she had no choice. Just before she and Val moved north, the aunt packed Carol off to the Georgia State Asylum for the Feeble and the Insane in Menken.

"For two months Miss Val was disconsolate," Scotty said. "She wouldn't eat and she cried herself to sleep every night, pining for Carol Marie."

He told me that Val even ran away to Menken twice. Once she grew up, she made it her business to spend at least every Christmas and Carol Marie's birthday with her at the asylum. She vowed that when she had the money she would take her twin out of that snake pit. But once she did get married and had the means, James had other ideas that torpedoed her plan. Though he spoiled Val in every way possible and provided the security she had been robbed of as a child, there was no room in his high-on-the-hog lifestyle for a misfit like Carol Marie. "After all," he assured her, "keeping her in that place is for Carol's own good. How would we educate her? How could we travel abroad? Can you see her with our friends at the club?"

I learned that Carol had never left the asylum and died there of influenza two years back. As Scotty recounted the story, Val's melancholy and her violent reaction to the thugs at the eugenics rally made more sense.

Even though Scotty filled me in on Val's background and I had a much clearer picture of who she was, when it came to Val and me and what I meant to her, I was still befuddled; I had no clearer idea of where I stood with her than I did the night I first visited her Manhattan apartment. I wondered about the meaning of the kiss she'd given me earlier that afternoon. More than that, I could still feel her lips on my cheek. And I liked it.

I tried to get more information from Scotty. I hoped that he would disclose something else about Val, some tidbit that would provide a key to what I should or shouldn't do next. I needed to know whether or not I had a chance with her.

"I've already said too much, sir," he replied.

XXXX

"If you look over there, through those fir trees, just off the highway, you can see Camp Siegfried, the home of the Kraut-loving German-American Bund," Scotty said.

I don't know if he meant to or not, but his comment distracted me. I looked to my right and saw a group of rough-hewn log cabins and a large white building that looked like a meeting hall.

"What is that place?" I asked.

"It's a resort for American Nazis run by that son-of-a-bitch traitor, Fritz Kuhn."

I sat forward in my seat. "How is it you know about Kuhn and that place?" I asked.

"Ever since Jerry has started to rearm, I've made it my business to keep up with all things Teutonic. Mark my words; we didn't finish the job in the war to end all wars. I'm sorry to say it, sir, but in my estimation we'll be fighting with the Germans again sooner than later and too many more good lads will be lost." As we drove by Camp Siegfried through the late afternoon shadows, I felt a chill in the car. After that we both got quiet.

As we continued to drive, I sat back and gazed out at the countryside. The rain had stopped and the sun was breaking through the clouds. I rolled down my window. The air smelled fresh and clean. I noted the sundry shades of green; the shadows now warm on the hills and just how different the same landscape looked depending on the hour of the day and the position of the sun. Though exhausted, I fought the weariness and kept watching the scenery, as if I knew what waited for me in slumber. But I couldn't stay awake. I fell into a very deep sleep and had a bad dream.

When I woke up, I couldn't get my bearings. It was dusk; not fully dark, yet not light. I was in an in-between place as well; not fully alert, yet no longer asleep. I rubbed my eyes hard trying to rouse myself and get some sense of where I was. Usually I would awaken from nightmares relieved they had passed, with the comfort that they were just dreams. That time, though I seemed awake, I was disoriented and found no such solace. Vividly the images kept replaying: hiding behind the crate, escaped tigers, fangs so close I could almost feel them puncture my skin, my reflection in those savage feline eyes, the ice, the blood, the windswept emptiness. Usually I like to dream; it's like going to the movies. But that one was just too real.

"Are you okay?" I heard Scotty ask. "You've been sleeping for about an hour and a half. You were moaning. I think you had a nightmare."

"I'm fine, thank you," I said.

"We'll be back in the city soon. In the meantime, do you want me to stop?"

"No, thank you, Scotty. I'm okay," I answered. "What time is it?"

"It's about six o'clock, sir."

I can still make the seven o'clock show, I thought. "Instead of dropping me at the circus train, would you mind taking me directly to Madison Square Garden?"

"As you wish," Scotty said.

XXXX

Because there was no traffic, we made it back to the Garden in plenty of time for me to don my giant genie costume for the opening spec. I was still upset by that awful dream as I rushed to get myself dressed. I knew what I had to do. Before I took my place in the backyard lineup, I searched for Lya. I found her near the entrance to the arena, smoking a Camel and talking to Daisy Doll. They were both dressed as miniature Ottoman dancers. Daisy wore a pink silk midriff blouse, matching puffy pants that gathered at her ankles, and shiny gold, pointy shoes. Lya was dressed exactly the same, but her belly dancer outfit was cobalt blue.

"Hello, ladies," I said. "Lya, I was wondering if—"

"Not now, Jake!" Lya said sternly as she dropped her cigarette butt on the floor, crushed it, abruptly turned around, and stomped off to find her place in the line.

Why was Lya so rude? Was she still angry at me? Was she really jealous of Val? I was truly puzzled by her behavior. I looked to Daisy for some kind of an explanation. "What gives?" I asked.

"Jake, Lya's got a lot on her plate right now. Cut her some slack."

"What do you mean, Daisy? What's going on?" I nodded and bent down on one knee to listen more closely.

"Last night she received a cable from her folks in Dresden." Daisy put her hand on my shoulder and continued, "With the political troubles in Germany, her parents are having a tough time. You know her mother and father both lost brothers in the last war. Since Herr Hitler sent his troops into the Rhineland in March and Eden vowed to defend France, you can wipe your nose with the Treaty of Versailles. They're sure it's just a matter of time until there's another war."

As Daisy spoke, I had shuddered thinking about Lya's family and my family in Poland and what they might soon be facing. Then I thought about the eugenics rally and Camp Siegfried. At that instant the world seemed very small. Europe wasn't so far away and the Atlantic wasn't as big and protective as it once had been. I had an eerie realization: It wasn't only friends and relatives in distant lands that were threatened.

"Her folks want to leave Germany, but they don't have the means," Daisy continued as she took a step back. "Lya wants to go home to Dresden to help, but she can't for at least six months. She's trapped until our season ends."

Lya and I have a lot in common, I thought. *We both know what it feels like to be trapped.* As if to clear some space where my heart should be, Daisy touched the middle of my chest with her red polished index finger. "So if you need to talk to her about something, I'd give it a couple of days, okay, sweetheart?"

"Sure, Daisy, whatever you say." I stood up and moved toward my place in the line. Though I understood why Lya couldn't help me out, I was still disappointed. I guess the interpretation of my nightmare would just have to wait. I'd have to deal with my discomfort on my own. As I walked away from her I remember being surprised that Daisy hadn't given me the fifth degree or even asked anything about my day trip with Val. Harry wasn't so diplomatic.

"So, you've decided to come back and slum with us commoners," Harry said as he saw me approach the lineup. "How was your picnic with the fair Miss Val?" His sarcasm didn't faze me. I was focusing on Lya and the tough time her family was having. Harry walked over to me and began to knock on my right leg as if he were knocking on a door. "Hello! Hello, is there anybody home in that skyscraper of a body?" he asked with a laugh.

"Sorry, my friend, I was distracted. Oh, yes . . . our picnic got rained out. It was a strange day; even disturbing."

Harry took a step back and shook his head. "You took a Sunday drive in the country with a beautiful, rich broad in her chauffeur-driven Pierce-Arrow. What's this strange or disturbing business?" Harry asked with a chuckle.

"Well, to start with I had a run-in with a mob of fanatics who think eugenics is the answer to everything that ails the world." I proceeded to tell Harry about the rally and Moseley's speech. "They were like Darwin on absinthe," I said. "You know, survival of the fittest gone mad."

"What's so crazy about survival of the fittest?"

The hair on the back of my neck stood up as the gruff voice posing that question made it sound more like a declaration. I smelled danger, the kind you face when you confront a wounded animal. I turned around to see Frank Buck grinning at me. He was dressed for the show, wearing his pith helmet, khakis, and holstered .38 long nose revolver.

"I was just telling Harry about what I heard at a eugenics rally," I tried to explain. "Those guys have some pretty nutty ideas, Frank." I involuntarily looked down at his gun.

"I know about eugenics and Moseley. I think what they say makes a lot of sense. When you've been around big cats as much as I have, you know there's something to culling out the weak, the deformed, and the sick and only letting the fittest breed." As he spoke he pointed at me. I couldn't tell if his gesture was meant as an exclamation or to use me as an example of the idea he was trying to get across.

I took a step toward the lion tamer, pointed down at him and spoke in a centered voice that I didn't know I had. "Maybe that's true for your cats Frank, but we're not talking about animals. We're talking about human beings."

Buck took a step toward me. Harry moved between us. There was an instant of very uncomfortable silence. Our dispute was more primitive than a disagreement about science, philosophy, or values. It had to do with Val. I clenched my fists. I was about to go into battle with someone who had been my friend over a woman I barely knew.

"For the love of God, would you look at that?" Harry said in utter astonishment. Buck and I looked down at the little man standing between us. He was gazing through my legs at the amazing scene taking place behind us. Then Buck and I followed Harry's gaze.

What I saw took my breath away.

There stood the tallest soul I'd ever laid eyes on. He and an older fellow were talking to Clyde Ingalls. I immediately knew who the tall one was. I had heard stories about that young giant and had even read a piece about him in *Time* magazine, but I'd never actually come face to face with him. At just shy of nine feet in height, he was truly a sight to behold. I couldn't help myself; I had to get a closer look.

I don't know if I was magnetically drawn to him because we had something in common. After all, I had always complained that I never fit in and that no one truly understood me and what I was going through. Of course, there were other giants: Big Jim Tarver and the like. But I was always, by far, the tallest. Now there was a fellow giant, a *compadre*, someone taller than me with whom I could form a community, a gargantuan fellowship of two.

Impulsively I walked over to introduce myself to the only person I would ever meet who was actually taller than me. Harry and Buck followed. Maybe my attraction to the young giant was because, like most other people, I was fascinated with the freakish. Maybe I was no better than every other rubberneck who gawked at me in the sideshow. For the first time in my life, I wanted to ask someone else that obnoxious question I'd probably heard more than ten thousand times: "Hey you, how's the weather up there?"

As we got closer, for some reason I slowed down, almost stopping. Harry and Buck passed me by. Maybe I was feeling threatened and I needed to evaluate the danger. It was clear, unless there were some smoke and mirrors at play, that this huge, young fellow would take my title as world's tallest man. As much as I complained about my life in the circus, I was frightened to lose what made me special and unique and, in those awful times, to give up the meal ticket that went along with it. But at that instant, I did my best to hide those fears.

I could see that the young colossus looked to be about twenty. The older gray-hair with him looked sixtyish. They were each dressed in matching charcoal-gray three-piece suits. The younger man had a protruding jaw like mine. But unlike me, he stooped severely to the right and supported himself on a dark-brown, wooden cane with a silver handle. He didn't smile, but looked like someone who was either in a bad mood or in pain, or both. The gigantic young man was engaged in intense conversation, so he didn't notice me spying on him. He was bigger than any man I'd ever seen, but under his wire-rimmed glasses, his face was boyish and there was something fragile about him. I imagined that behind the suit, glasses, stern demeanor, and immense body, he was vulnerable and hiding from a world that might pounce.

His name was Robert Wadlow, the man history would label as the tallest person ever. I had heard rumors about him for months. In magazines and newspapers I had learned that Wadlow had the same condition as I did. But, whereas I started my abnormal growth when I was seven, his gigantism began when he was a baby. He was born just over the Missouri state line in Alton, Illinois. Later, I would visit Alton. I recall it had a sleepy, river-town feel, neat tree-lined streets and quaint old houses that made me think Mark Twain could have lived there. When Wadlow entered kindergarten at Alton Elementary School, he wore the clothes of an eighteen year old. In 1925, when he was just seven, the *New York Times* did a spread that labeled him the "World's Tallest Boy Scout." When I first saw him face to face in 1936, at age eighteen, he was eight feet, eleven and a half inches tall.

As we approached, the older man noticed us first. Then Robert Wadlow swung around to look at me. I immediately sensed his sadness; it was palpable. It clung to and exuded from him like the atmosphere and gravity of some immense, dark planet. Though he stared at me he seemed lost in his thoughts.

I was the first one to speak. "Hello, I'm Jake Erlich," I said, extending my hand. As I spoke, I could sense that several circus performers stepped out of line to get a glimpse of this momentous meeting. "And these are my friends, Harry Doll and Frank Buck," I added, pointing to them.

"Jake is our current giant, at least for the time being." I felt Ingalls toying with me. "Jake, this is Robert Wadlow and his father," Ingalls said. Then the elder Wadlow extended his hand and shook mine.

"It is a pleasure, sir." Wadlow's father spoke in the staid and formal Lutheran tone of others I'd met from the Midwest.

Robert cautiously extended his hand, but he looked away and not into my eyes. When he shook my hand, I looked to the ground and noticed that his massive feet were at least several sizes larger than mine. As he continued to shake my hand I noted his firm businessman's grip and that this was the first time I shook hands with someone with a bigger hand than mine. As if Wadlow had awakened from a dream, he stared intently at Harry, Buck, and me. I could have sworn I saw disdain in his unsmiling eyes.

"Robert will begin performing with us starting tomorrow," Ingalls said.

"Have you decided where you will place his platform in the sideshow?" Harry asked.

"That won't be necessary. Our boy prefers to not appear in the sideshow," the elder Wadlow said. His voice sounded protective, albeit polite.

Any semblance of being judgmental of the circus and those who perform in it was hidden under a diplomat's smile, camouflaged by layers of small town sensibility and a highly evolved skill of avoiding confrontation. "In everyone's best interest, Robert will only be with the circus in Madison Square Garden and in Boston. Then he'll only be seen in the opening and closing acts of the program." He nodded as he finished speaking, indicating that he had nothing more to say on the matter.

The young giant turned to Ingalls. "Please refer to what I do as *appearing* and not *performing*," he said softly, correcting him. Though Robert Wadlow was polite, it appeared to me that the young giant wasn't as skilled as his father at avoiding provocation.

"I don't see the difference," Buck commented in a matter-of-fact tone.

"You see, sir, show people and freaks perform, and that is not what I am. My work with Ringling Bros circus will be strictly a matter of public relations and promotion. I hope that is clear." He may have tried, but at that instant he could not mask his contempt for who we were and what we did for a living. Wadlow wasn't as fragile and vulnerable as I had originally thought.

Harry, Buck, Ingalls, and I stood there, astonished and silent. I was to learn later that, at that instant, Harry and Buck, who didn't normally agree on many things, wrote Wadlow off. But for some strange reason my instinct was still to reach out, try to smooth over this rough beginning and welcome the newcomer.

"If I can be of any assistance—" Before I could even finish my sentence, without uttering another word, the two Wadlows and Ingalls abruptly turned around and walked away. I felt slighted and did my best to paper over my hurt feelings. As they walked away I remember noting that young Wadlow had a lot of trouble moving. He looked like he was about to topple over; as if he were a giant walking tree damaged in a tornado. Then Bradna, the ringmaster, blew his shiny silver whistle with a piercing, shrill sound and Buck, Harry, and I, like well-trained animals, found our places in the lineup.

As I waited for the spec to begin, I wondered what Ingalls had up his sleeve with Robert Wadlow. *Is he trying to push me into signing that damned contract? Is he trying to convince me I'd be easy to replace? Is he just trying to cover his bets and be sure he's not left without a giant for next season?*

XXXX

Later that night tormenting questions played over and over in my mind, not allowing me to sleep. *Should I stay or leave the circus? In bleak times like those how else could I support myself? If I stayed what would become of me? How much longer could I keep up the arduous travel? Was I wasting what little time I had left? Would I even have a choice?* Up until then, though I had wrestled with it for years, whether or not I stayed or left Ringling Bros was a decision that had always been up to me. I thought about it constantly.

Now, if Wadlow replaced me, I might not have any say in the matter. They might really let me go. I think in part, I devoted so much time and energy to that worry because that choice was one of the few things in my life that I could control. Giving up that precious bit of control frightened the hell out of me. It meant stepping out into the empty unknown in more ways than I could possibly have understood. Talk about a lack of control . . . that sleepless night I also was bothered by thoughts about Val and art school. *Was there really any possibility for us? Was art school an utter waste of time? If I did go, would that get me any closer to her? How long would it take my teachers to see that I was a phony?* Maybe all that drama about Val and art school was also a diversion. Maybe dillydallying in my head like that was safer than facing my demons in the real world.

I had finally dozed off when there was a loud knock on my door. I wondered if it was Frank Buck, ready to challenge me to mortal combat for Val's affections. I jumped up, put on my bathrobe, and cautiously opened the door. Buck was nowhere to be found. It was Silvio, a retired clown who did odd-jobs with the circus including selling tickets and delivering the mail.

"Excuse the interruption, my friend," the gray-mustached funny man said in his Italian accent. "This special-delivery letter came late Saturday afternoon, but George, the weekend mailman, just missed you. He was going to wait until mail call on Monday. I thought it might be urgent so I said to myself, 'Silvio, you better deliver it yourself after the show.'" Then he handed me the letter. My heart started to pound. All I could think was, *Who died?*

"Thanks," I said, and slammed the door. I ripped open the envelope. It turns out that no one had died, but the message was ominous:

Dear Jake,

Please don't worry! Your mama and brothers are fine. But I need your help. I have had a letter from the family in Lodz. Things are very bad there. Since Pilsudski's death, Dmowski and the rest of the anti-Semites are coming out of the woodwork. Hating Jews is now the official policy of the Polish government. Between that and Hitler's threats, I need to travel to Poland as soon as I can to convince our mispacha *to get out while the getting is good. I have written, but letters don't do any good. They don't seem to think there is any danger. I know they are wrong.*

The trip itself and maybe getting one or two of them out to start will take $2,000. But since the bankruptcy I can't get my hands on any extra geld. *Can you loan it to me? Please let me know your answer as soon as possible.*

Your mama and I would do anything to avoid putting this kind of pressure on you, but we don't have anywhere else to turn. I hate to write like this but if the Nazis and the Polaks have their way, it's a matter of life and death. I hope you are well.

Love,

Papa

I got back into bed and read and re-read the letter several more times until I finally turned out the light. Lying there in the darkness I thought about Lya and her letter from home.

I woke up tired but strangely peaceful. Then I understood why I felt that way. I was no longer worried about whether I should stay with the circus, or even troubled by whether Wadlow would displace me next year. For the present, the die had been cast. My decision was apparent. I had no choice. I needed to help my family. The only way I could lay my hands on that kind of cash was to get an advance on my salary. The only way Ringling Bros would even contemplate such an arrangement was if I signed my contract and borrowed the rest.

I sighed and gazed in the mirror that hung in my tiny compartment. I looked tired. *Get used to it, champ. You're gonna to be staying with the circus for quite some time to come.*

CHAPTER 20

Sightless

"Swanee River Mood," Jake Erlich

Circus Arrival

By Jake Erlich
(from *The Long Shadows*)

Through the chill of dawn
Comes the long shrill hoot,
A magic echoing
Along the sleepy sidewalks,
Promising the spangled
Calliope and clown . . .
Sleepy-eyed men emerge
Slowly, hitching
Their reluctant trousers.
The horses neigh,
Elephants trumpet,
From cautious cages
Comes the muffled roar
Of the lions. Wagons
Rumble off the flat cars.
Horses are harnessed,
And then begins
The trek to show ground!

From warm beds leap
The wide-eyed youngsters,
Rushing to watch
Each wagon passing,
Over and over exclaiming
"The circus has arrived!
The circus has arrived!"

I have often wondered why Wadlow grew taller than I did; after all, both of us suffered from the same disease. Was it just a fluke of nature, like one tree growing taller than another? That kid being taller than me wasn't just a coincidence. It was a combination of things: mostly science and fate.

To really explain what I mean we have to revisit my days in Hollywood. You know I've faced my share of expected obstacles, like the unwanted scrutiny of strangers who only saw me as an oddity. Then there were all the familiar, internal demons, like depression and self-doubt. But some of my worst trials were unexpected and unfamiliar. They ambushed me.

Like many of my peers in silent pictures, I did my own stunts. I already mentioned that I'd been hurt making movies before, but not very badly. While filming my forty-ninth movie, my luck ran out. It was 1926 and I think we were shooting in Silver Lake. That morning I was precariously balanced fourteen feet above the asphalt on scaffolding that was attached to a speeding automobile. In those days we called them *funny* cars. Well that funny car was doing about forty miles an hour when it plowed over a pot hole. I lost my balance and crashed to the street. A wooden camera boom attached to the same contraption splintered and a two-by-four-sized chunk of it smashed into the back of my head.

When I came to I had a fractured nose and blurred vision. At the Kaspare Cohn Hospital they insisted I stay the night. By the next day, my vision had gotten much worse. Everything appeared blurry as if I was peering through murky ocean water, but I could still see large shapes and silhouettes. My doctors told me not to worry, I had "klieg eyes"; you know, they thought my eyesight had been hammered by those nasty klieg lights that we used on movie sets. They had promised, by the next morning, my sight would return to normal. It didn't. When I opened my eyes from a dreamless sleep, all I could see was pitch-black darkness. I was totally blind and terrified.

Specialists were called in to treat me. After a few more days the new physicians finally got a handle on what was happening to me. They said I most likely had a brain tumor that had swollen to the size of a walnut and was squeezing my optic nerve, robbing me of my sight. The words "brain tumor" took my breath away. Many years later I would learn that that same tumor had been growing on my pituitary gland since I was seven and causing my abnormal height.

Those doctors told me my prognosis was bleak. "Most likely, you'll never see again," they said. Having my body controlled by hostile forces was hauntingly familiar. At that moment I felt the same panic I did when I was a kid and first realized that my growth had a mind of its own. Besides all of the challenges I had to deal with because of my size, now I would also have to cope with being sightless. Once again, I had no choice in the matter. I've lived through enough to know that one way or another, at some time, everybody faces changes that are unpredictable. But since I was a boy, for me, sudden, unwelcomed changes didn't come once in a while. They were my constant companions.

There was no way I could keep working at the studio, so I took an immediate leave of absence. When Kitty came to visit me at my apartment a few days after my accident she brought my last paycheck and assured me things would all work out. "Don't worry, sweetheart," she said. "Your sight will return." But I knew she was wrong. I knew I'd never work in pictures again. I was despondent.

The next three days waiting for Papa to arrive from El Paso to take me home were torturous. I needed help with everything—even going to the toilet. It was humiliating. I couldn't even cook for myself so my landlady had to bring me every meal. I did make some valiant efforts. But after I almost started a fire in the kitchen and burned my hand cooking some eggs, I just gave up. Though I'd lived in that cozy apartment for two years, now it was a foreign, dangerous place. At times I felt like a tiny infant in a huge, nightmare world waiting for some boogeyman to leap out of the darkness and grab me. At other times I felt so big that the walls were closing in on me. I'm not proud to admit it, but for those three days I did absolutely nothing. I just sat there, feeling sorry for myself.

Along with my vision, all of the distractions I had become so adept at using to wall off my worries disappeared. Since I couldn't work, read, write, or people watch, I tortured myself with obsessive worries about my past and my future. I thought about what a burden I'd been to my poor parents and how that burden would now increase a thousand times over. I couldn't see any way out. That's when I began to wonder if everybody might be better off if I just ended it all. But how could I do that? In order to kill myself, I needed to be able to see.

That train trip home was awful. It stood in stark contrast to all my previous travels. I could no longer gaze out of the train's windows at the passing scenery, watch people in the club car, or read as I loved to do in the past. It had always been a challenge for me to navigate on a moving train, which was cramped even for normal-sized, sighted people. But now, even with Papa's help, that trip was daunting. Unaccustomed to my new, dark world my movements were tentative and timid. "It's okay, Jakey. I'm here to help," Papa assured me as we walked through the train and I clung to his arm. I was so banged up and bruised from bumping into doors, ceilings, and people that when we arrived in El Paso, I was thankful; so thankful I wanted to get down on my hands and knees and kiss the ground. *I'll never set foot out of this house again,* I promised myself when I finally walked through the front door into the safety of my parents' home.

During those sightless days I became grateful for parts of myself I hadn't fully recognized or appreciated for a long time, if ever. The smells and sounds of my folks' home came into sharp focus, as did the feelings of the objects I could touch but not see.

I thought I knew my parents' place like the back of my hand, but I didn't really know it at all. I had no choice but to draw a mental blueprint to safely get around. I recall memorizing how many steps led up to the porch that draped around the front and left side of our simple, white, stucco home. My mental map of the inside included the living room that stretched across the entire front of the house. On the right wall, a fireplace was centrally nestled beneath a stone mantle. The hearth was bordered on both sides by bookshelves with etched-glass doors. I mourned the fact that I'd never read those books again.

Although I had visited our new home on Kansas Street many times, I began to experience it in a different way. I remember wondering what other things in my life— places, people, parts of myself—I had thought I knew, yet I'd really been blind to. My blindness got me thinking about how I saw myself. I wondered how long I would carry in my mind's eye the portrait others had painted of me and if I'd ever paint a new self-portrait. The thought of being a blind painter made me laugh. It was a new kind of laughter for me: bitter and sardonic.

I believe that losing my vision helped me as an artist. I think I had to go blind to really see. But believe me, in those days things weren't all sweetness, light, and self-discovery. I don't know how my poor parents put up with me. I was a royal pain in the ass. I was irritable and would fly into a rage at the drop of a hat. I remember one afternoon, sitting on the porch shaded from the sun by the house's overhang. I was enjoying the the scent of the tea roses Mama had planted in our front yard.

"Hello, Jakey," Mama said as she stepped from the house onto the veranda. "I brought you a nice cup of tea and some sweets."

"Thank you," I said as she guided my hand to a cup and saucer.

"Would you like a *schtikel* (piece) of sponge cake?" she asked.

When I reached up to where I thought the plate of cake was, I clumsily bumped it out of Mama's hands and it came crashing down, knocking the cup and saucer out of my hands and sending the scalding tea splashing onto my lap. I jumped up, knocking the chair over.

"Goddamnit!" I shouted. "I hate this!"

"It's okay. It's okay," Mama said, trying to dry me off with what I imagined was a dish towel.

"No, it's not all right; nothing's all right!" I screamed. "Just leave me alone!"

Then I heard Mama walk away. I was miserable: wet, burned, and feeling guilty as hell for yelling at her. I stood there feeling helpless, clumsy as an ox, and sullen. A few minutes later while thinking thoughts of which I'm not very proud, I heard someone else's footsteps approach.

"What's the matter, Jake?" Papa asked. I heard him lift my chair back into place and I sat down.

"I can't stand this." I felt his hand on my shoulder. Though I was already a grown man, when I felt Papa's touch that afternoon, I began to sob. I told him how I felt trapped in my body. I told him how I hated God for the awful hand I'd been dealt; how unfair it all was. I told him about the constant, tormenting voices in my head. I shared how those voices had quieted for a while during my time working in Hollywood, but recently, after I'd gone blind, they'd come roaring back with a vengeance; voices that screamed cruel things like: "You're a burden on your family!" "You'll never amount to anything." "You're a freak." Papa just listened. After I finished unburdening myself, I was exhausted. I started to get up to go to my room to rest.

"Can I have just a minute more of your time, son?" Papa asked. I nodded and sat back down. "Jake, I agree; life has not been very fair to you. I know a lot of what hurts comes from what's happened and from how others see you. You can't control any of that. But I think your pain also comes from how you think. You know, about many things that happen to us in this life we have no choice, but about a precious few things we do have a choice. I want to tell you a *misa* (story)."

As I was growing up, just about every other lesson Papa wanted to teach me was couched in a story. But that afternoon I had no patience for his allegories. He didn't seem to notice or care that I was bothered. Papa went on to tell me an old Hasidic tale I had never heard before.

"A *Rebe* was once asked how to tell if another teacher was truly one of the wise ones."

I wondered why he was sharing this odd story with me at that particular time. At other times I was patient with Papa and his stories, but then I was so tired and angry, it took all my effort to just sit there and listen.

"'Ask this teacher if a person can ever be free of dark thoughts,' replied the master. 'If he answers *yes*, you know he's a charlatan.' It's not a question of having or not having bad thoughts. Jake, you're just like everyone else. We all have to battle with the darkness. The heart of the matter is not whether or not you have ugly thoughts, but whether you accept them. You see, it's not the cards you're dealt, son. It's how you play them."

Then without saying another word, Papa got up and walked away. I sat there on the porch, struggling to make sense of what he had said. How could Papa, Mama, or anyone else for that matter, ever understand what I was going through?

Despite my father's words of wisdom, the next several months were a struggle. It was all I could do to just keep hanging on to some shred of hope. When my friends Bobby and Abbie came by to visit I didn't want to talk to them. Kitty and all the other sighted, well-wishers who promised I'd see again were wrong. My vision didn't return. Regardless of the new acuity of my senses, I still constantly bumped into things, often tripping and injuring myself and destroying whatever object I collided with.

"What's the use of going to see those damned quacks? They don't have any miracles for me," I had said before one of my doctor visits. But Mama and Papa wouldn't let me give up. They kept pushing me to not throw in the towel and the doctors to tell us what more could be done to make me see again.

After another few weeks, we were all at our wit's end when the doctors decided to try an experimental treatment to shrink my tumor: X-ray therapy.

I didn't want to subject myself to any more disappointments, but to please my parents I went along with the plan. Week after week, as my therapy wore on with no apparent effect, we all finally began to accept that I would never see again. I would lay awake at night struggling with the reality that I would spend the rest of my life being blind and dependent on my family. The new, exciting world I had only recently discovered in Hollywood became a distant memory that faded away with my sight.

After another three weeks of X-ray treatments, I woke up one morning and something was different. I thought that maybe, just maybe, the blackness I saw was not so black; maybe the dark was growing a bit lighter. The change was subtle; so subtle that at first, I didn't tell anyone. I think I was afraid I might be imagining the whole thing and that the slight improvement in my vision was nothing more than wishful thinking.

A week later, when I awakened, I knew it wasn't my imagination. I kicked the covers off, swung my feet out of bed without thinking, and launched myself in the direction of my parents' room. Along the way I banged into the small table we kept in the hallway, knocking the china vase it supported to the ground with a loud crashing sound.

"Mama, Papa, come quick!" I shouted. My parents and younger brother came charging into the hallway from their bedrooms. "It's just like what happened when I went blind, but in reverse," I said breathlessly.

"Reverse? What are you talking about?" Myer asked with what must have been an incredulous look on his face. "Ouch!" he shrieked, hopping and holding his foot. He must have stepped on a piece of the broken vase.

"It's like I'm looking through murky water; but I can make out shapes and forms," I explained.

"What do you mean?" Papa asked.

"I can't see any of you in detail but I see each of you as a silhouettes standing around me," I explained with a cautious smile. "There you are, Papa. There's Mama," I said, stepping forward and putting my right hand first on Papa's shoulder and then on Mama's. "There's Myer," I said, pointing to my brother. I knew they were all looking at one another in disbelief.

I'll never forget the meeting with Dr. Ziltzer the next afternoon. He was the family's doctor in those days. I was sitting on a Foley table. Papa and Mama sat in chairs to my right and my brother stood to my left. I couldn't remember Myer ever attending a doctor's appointment with me, but that visit was a big deal, so he came.

"I've conferred with the specialists. It's good news, young man! It will take a while, Jake, but the X-ray therapy is working. Your vision will return to normal. That's to say, twenty-twenty. It might even be better than it was before." Though the doctor stood right in front of me, his words seemed unreal. I had had my hopes dashed so many times before. Then as what he said sunk in, I jumped to my feet.

"Are you sure? Do you promise?" I asked, almost challenging Dr. Ziltzer.

"I promise and I'm sure," he said without any hesitation. We all stood there in the silence that houses news that's too good or too bad to be true. Then I threw my arms around Dr. Ziltzer, swept him off his feet, and for the first time in my life hugged my doctor. Mama hugged Papa and Myer.

When I finally put Dr. Ziltzer down, something very strange happened. We all began to laugh. We laughed and laughed. It was the type of laughter that is deep, contagious and full of healing. Even Dr. Ziltzer laughed. I'd never had an experience like that before or since. You see, starting with that awful consultation in Epstein's office when I was seven, doctor's visits were always dreadful events, full of fear and hopelessness. But that visit was like a reprieve from a death sentence. From that day until now, I have been truly grateful for my sight. But I'm also always afraid that I will go blind again. In a kind of an unending, terrible dream, I dread what other losses I'll be forced to confront or face again. If I allow myself to dwell on those scary thoughts, my fears can easily gallop away with me.

My recovery was very gradual; like the passing of an awful winter. Though for a time the X-ray treatments left me feeling very weak, slowly but surely, just as Dr. Ziltzer had promised, my sight returned. What's more, I was left with some unanticipated, positive aftereffects. One of them was that I never had to shave again. The other was that I stopped growing. If you can believe it, since I was seven years old I'd never, ever, stopped growing. A dead giveaway was my constant need to buy new shoes. Whereas other people bought new shoes because they wore the old ones out or wanted a new style, I bought new shoes because the ones I wore no longer fit. Though, by then, I didn't need a new pair every two weeks like I did when I was a kid, up until the X-ray treatments, I needed new shoes several times a year. The last pair I ordered was a size twenty-six-and-a-half. It took several years for me to put it all together. If not for those

X-rays after I went blind, I would have kept growing, and within a couple of years, if not sooner, that would have killed me. So you see, if not for the fall from the funny car, the ensuing blindness, and the X-ray treatments, I might have been as tall as Wadlow, and I most certainly would not have been here boring you with this story.

My vision came back and with it an indescribable sense of relief. Then I began to truly enjoy my time at home. Even though a letter had come from the Stern Brothers asking when I would be coming back to Century Comedies, at least for the time being, I pushed any worry about returning to Hollywood and what I would do with the rest of my life out of my mind. I felt a new strength and energy. I loved catching up with friends and being indulged by my parents.

It was late springtime in El Paso. Those mild days were inevitably transformed by dramatic dust storms. They turned the sky black, made the temperature drop, and everyone experienced the gritty feel of sandy real estate in their eyes, ears, and mouths. After the storms passed, the ever-present aroma of honeysuckle was even stronger. Besides the dust storms and flowers, late spring heralded the coming of a very important event in El Paso; a special occasion eagerly awaited by young and old alike. In springtime, the circus came to town.

Almost everybody loved the circus. It was the mid-1920s and throughout most of the United States, there were still only two major types of entertainment: the county fair and the circus. The circus coming to town is still a big deal, but in those days it was really something. At one time or another everybody fantasized about running away to join one of the traveling shows that came through town. In west Texas, nothing, and I mean nothing—rodeos, football games, itinerant theater and ballet companies, or even bullfights—matched the circus for thrills and chills, color, and pageantry. For the locals, the circus was a place to not only watch a performance, but also smell it, breathe it, touch it, taste it, and walk all over it. It was a unique way to escape the humdrum of daily life for other, more electrifying times and exotic places. In those days, in bigger cities, the audience for a major circus like Ringling Bros, Barnum and Bailey could sometimes be as large as fifteen thousand. "The Big One," or "Big Bertha," as we affectionately called Ringling Bros, was a place where folks would watch eight hundred artists performing a two-and-a-half-hour spectacle that included twenty-two acts. Believe you me, in those days shows like that were rarer than rain.

Although my family would always go to the circus when it came to town, I had generally refused to go along. You might be surprised, but going to the circus wasn't one of my favorite things to do. As a matter of fact, unlike just about everybody else, I didn't particularly like it. Remember, I hated crowds.

When Ringling Bros came to town that spring, I had been lounging around the house for several weeks. Once I felt strong enough, I began taking morning walks with Papa up on Crazy Cat Mountain. Although I never understood how Crazy Cat got its name, I imagined that it might have come from a cougar who dined on loco weed. About five thirty every morning but *Shabbas* (the Sabbath), Papa and I would face east toward Crazy Cat and Jerusalem—the site of the Holy Temple—pick up our black *siddurim* (prayer books), and recite the morning prayers. Then we'd tiptoe out of the house and continue east. First we walked up Kansas to Shuster Street, past El Paso High. We'd continue on to North Brown, turn off the pavement there, and start climbing the steep switchbacks through the desert up to Rim Road and the base of Crazy Cat. The smells and sounds of the desert at that time of morning were exquisite. As we climbed, I watched Papa on the trail ahead of me. He always brought his typical strength and grace to his hiking. You know, you can tell a lot about a person by watching how they move. As Papa walked ahead, I remember how he'd glance back at me. After all he'd been through with me I couldn't help but think he was worried about what misfortune would next cross my path. After another thirty minutes of climbing over rocks, past mesquite trees and the squatty cactus that live in that high desert, we would pause.

From the top of Crazy Cat we could see El Paso, the Rio Grande, and just past it, *Ciudad Juarez*. One Sunday during one of those hikes with Papa, I looked down at the river and recalled a late afternoon stroll I'd taken down there the week before. It was a special time of year on the border; the air was so sweet and still, you could almost see it. The sunset that night was crimson purple. By the river, the shadows created a deep green sheen on the cottonwood's leaves. Sheer, silvery dragonflies hovered over the water like fairies. At the Rio Grande's edge, close to the spot where I'd almost drowned, a family of three—two adults and a little boy—emerged.

They weren't bathers. They hardly noticed the sunset's beauty. They were not headed south, with the water, but north. Like immigrants everywhere, they swam against the tide, bridging the invisible boundary between nations. In those days, no sheriff, posse, or army with repeating rifles was there to stop or even protest the event. The only witnesses to that passage were me, two Swainson's Hawks swooping overhead, and a lone Great Blue Heron strutting quietly through the mud near the shore on a hunt for his dinner. I watched the three pilgrims slowly emerge from the river. Once on dry land, they lowered the rolled cuffs of their pants and made their way through the long weeds. As they passed, the trampled green sprang back, erasing the only evidence that they had ever been there. I wondered where they were headed next. I paused, blessing their journey with a smile. I've always felt a special kinship with immigrants. Like me, they travel to their own distinctive beat and though they try, they never quite seem to fit in.

That Sunday morning up on Crazy Cat with Papa, I recall thinking about the artificiality of borders and how much blood and treasure had been lost for something not visible to the naked eye.

The electric lights, mostly on the El Paso side, shimmered like red, blue, green, and orange jewels in the morning haze. The Mexican side of the Rio Grande, or *Rio Bravo* as they call it there, had many more dirt roads that led to neighborhoods with row after row of shacks. Many of them were built out of scavenged wood and even cardboard. Most of those shacks had no running water or electricity. As you know, they still don't. Looking back at the border from the mountainside, I thought about how you can't know what's on the other side of a boundary until you cross it yourself and experience, firsthand, what's on the other side. When Papa I began to hike back down the mountain, I noticed my movements were heron-like, at once grand and awkward, the very image of the majestic blue river bird I just recollected.

That morning by the time Papa and I had returned home, we were particularly hungry. The rest of the family was waiting at the breakfast table for my Mama's special German pancakes, a treat she only made on Sundays. I remember these golden hotcakes. They filled the whole plate and were so light that if it weren't for her fabulous, deep red strawberry jam, those flapjacks would have floated right up to the kitchen ceiling.

As we finished breakfast, there was a loud knock at the back door. It was my two friends, Bobby Goldoff and Abbie Kahn. We'd been classmates since our days at Vilas Elementary School. Bobby was short and overweight when he was a kid, but he would grow into a slender young man. Abbie was tall and thin. Years later, Bobby would become a successful insurance broker. Abbie would be killed fighting in the Battle of the Bulge during the war.

The minute my two friends walked into our kitchen they seemed more antsy than normal. Bobby and Abbie sat down at the table and Mama promptly served them the remaining pancakes in the skillet. As they ate, they explained the purpose of their visit.

"The circus has been in town for a few days," Bobby said. Bobby was a born salesman. I knew the circus was in town and I wondered what he had up his sleeve.

"So?" I said. "When you mentioned it the first time I told you I didn't want to go."

"Tonight's the last chance to see the Ringling Bros show in El Paso until next year. We've already seen it once but it's so good we're going a second time," Abbie added.

Good for you, I thought.

Both of my friends begged me to accompany them that evening, but I had no interest whatsoever. They were up to something. I just knew it. For the next twenty minutes they *knudged* and pleaded. Finally, just to get them to stop pestering me, I reluctantly agreed to go.

But that night, by the time my friends came by for me in Bobby's Model T Ford, I had changed my mind. Thinking about the crowds and the noise was the first thing to put me off the idea. Then, during the afternoon, I also started to feel tired. At first I thought it was the effects of my morning hike with Papa. Then I figured I was still dealing with the aftereffects of my X-ray treatments. In either event, I didn't want to push things, particularly to do something I didn't want to do in the first place. So I decided to not go. All I wanted was to stay home and enjoy a good book, a treat that not too long before I was sure I'd never have again.

To tell you the truth, I've always been a bit superstitious. After my bout with blindness I was even more irrational. I know it doesn't make any sense, but I also didn't want to go because I thought if I went to the circus that night I might catch something that would make me sick and take my sight again. When you've had so many things go wrong with your body as I have, you don't want to tempt fate.

Bobby and Abbie stood in our family room looking like they'd lost their dog. Mama and Papa sat at the nearby dining room table playing gin rummy, trying to act like they weren't paying attention to the drama unfolding between my friends and me. Myer hovered nearby.

"Come on, Jake. It'll be fun. Don't ruin the party," Abbie implored.

"It's Ringling's best show yet!" Bobby added. It turns out I was about to ruin my friends' carefully hatched scheme. "You just want to stay home? We never get to see you!" Bobby sounded frantic as he tried to use guilt to sell me. That didn't work either.

"Just go on without me," I said emphatically, putting my book down in my lap. I could be really stubborn when I wanted to be. You know that trait has helped me more than its hurt.

"Jake, Papa and I think you should go," Mama interjected in a forceful tone she rarely used as she put her cards down on the table. We all looked over at her.

"Listen to your mama, Jake!" Papa added forcefully as he put his cards down as well.

I didn't know why going to the circus that night was such a big deal for my parents. But after all they'd been through with me recently, despite my discomfort and fears, I really didn't want to go against their wishes.

"All right! All right! I'll go, but just for a couple of hours. Agreed?" I asked, standing up and leaving my book on the easy chair where I had been sitting. My two friends looked at one another and smiled.

"Agreed!" Bobby said, shaking my hand as if he were closing a deal.

It turns out Bobby, Abbie, and some of my other friends—I think it was Dave Price and the Powell boys—had gone to see the circus parade that announced Ringling Bros arrival in El Paso the week before. They stood at the corner of Mesa and Mills Streets and watched the one-and-a-quarter-mile-long procession. Though I wasn't always a circus fan, I loved the parades, especially the hand-carved wagons that carried the caged animals. But to be honest, my favorite part of the circus parade was the band. If I close my eyes now, I can easily visualize those forty musicians astride matching white horses, festooned with blankets made of red velvet sewn with gold piping.

I hope I'm not boring you with all this circus nostalgia. Where was I? Oh yes . . . to cut to the chase, earlier that week my friends had been flabbergasted when they saw the giant in the circus parade marching along with the other performers. Later they told me that after several seconds of standing there in total astonished silence they all began chattering at once. The boys were certain I was a foot taller than the professional giant. They agreed something had to be done to introduce me to the powers that be at the circus. Thus, they began to hatch a plot to prove that I was bigger than Ringling Bros, Barnum and Bailey's big man. Their scheme would result in one of the most embarrassing moments in circus history.

CHAPTER 21

Big Jim Tarver

"The Midway," Jake Erlich

To fit in Bobby's automobile, I had to sit with my head crammed against one of the windows in the backseat, my torso uncomfortably scrunched across the two Powell boys, and my legs sticking out of the other window. Dave Price and Abbie sat in the front seat with Bobby. Thank goodness the circus grounds were located at the intersection of Paisano and Copia, only fifteen minutes away. The closer we got, the more I felt the energy in the car change. I didn't understand why at the time, but the air in that automobile absolutely crackled with excitement. They didn't dare to divulge their plan to me. They already knew I didn't particularly want to go to the circus anyway and I would never agree to participate in a plot that might embarrass someone else, particularly someone with whom I could identify.

After we parked the car on a vacant lot off to the left of the show grounds, my friends strolled and I trudged towards the circus midway. The gentle evening breeze carried the aroma of popcorn, hot dogs, and, occasionally the pungent odor of the damp straw they used in the animal cages. It also brought the sound of what must have been several hundred people and hundreds of fluttering flags.

As we got close enough to see the torches that lit the perimeter of the midway wagons, you could easily make out the buzzing of the crowd. The headache I felt coming on did not mix well with the racket.

"Bobby, I don't feel very well. I'm going to go back to the car and wait for you." I really didn't want to be there.

"What did you say?" Bobby shouted above the noise. But it was no use. He couldn't hear a word I was saying.

Then we entered the midway, pushed onward by the crowd—or as circus people call it, "the tip." I was carried along against my will, as though I'd suddenly been injected into the bloodstream of some rare creature. The five of us glanced back and forth to ensure we didn't lose touch with one another. I felt I'd crossed a boundary into a mysterious, scary place. I was too stressed to notice all the people in the crowd who were staring at me.

Opposite the sideshow tent, three large wagons painted in bright hues of red, blue, yellow, and white sat along the midway. Old men were selling tickets through the windows in two of the wagons. Looking at their craggy faces, I imagined that if anyone would take the time to listen to those old-timers, they'd have great stories to tell.

I hung back and watched as the crowd funneled through five gates where their tickets were collected. Most of the ticket holders headed for the huge menagerie where the animals were kept. Many would get their first glimpse of elephants and scores of other exotic creatures, including hippos, giraffes, lions, zebras, polar bears, orangutans, macaws, and kangaroos; not to mention the herds of draft and show horses.

Maybe it was because of my months of blindness or my relative isolation while I recuperated at my folks' house, but that night at the circus I was overwhelmed. I felt like I was one of the small-fry I saw who were clutching balloons or cotton candy in one hand and using the other to hold on, as if for dear life, to their parents. I thought that from those kids' perspectives, their parents appeared to know where they were going. Actually, as most children sadly learn, sooner or later, their parents are just as lost as everyone else.

All along the midway, we passed concession stands selling peanuts, dolls, and lizards. Bobby was hungry. He was always hungry. So we stopped at a wagon with dazzling decorations called the Circus Diner, where he bought a hot dog and a soda. His parents, who kept kosher, would have killed him if they found out.

I wanted to make our first and only stop the Big Top. That way I figured we'd leave as soon as possible and I could get back home. I imagined we'd see the main show first: the lion tamer and his big cats; the high flyers on the trapeze; the trained elephants, bears, and horses; and, of course, the clowns. Then maybe we'd spend a little time in the menagerie after the show. The freak show was not high on my list of priorities. But my friends had another agenda. They insisted on dragging me to the sideshow tent first.

In those days the sideshow was a major part of the institution of the circus, and Big Bertha had the best-known and most respected sideshow in the business. Early arrivals like my friends and I, who bought separate tickets for the sideshow, provided the circus with a big source of income.

Walking down the midway—the area between the sideshow tent and the main circus entrance—the six of us boys looked to our right and saw "the banner line," the rows of huge, colorful canvas paintings that hung down the wall of the sideshow tent and presented the attractions to be found inside. Bobby took the lead, the others followed, and I, very reluctantly, brought up the rear. We saw a portly man with a bowler wearing a red plaid coat and black tie, parading back and forth on a small stage. I would soon learn he was called the "talker" or "blower." The talker's job was to get passersby like us to lay down two bits for a ticket.

I can still hear that loud, clear voice reverberating through my memory as it did through the crowd that night so long ago: "*Hurry, hurry, step right up folks . . . the most amazing gathering of oddities ever seen in one place. Just a measly quarter, twenty-five pennies, the price of a shave, or ribbon, will give you access to the eighth wonder of the world. Folks, we've scoured the globe to bring you these marvels and monstrosities, looted from the ends of the earth . . . From the rainforests of Brazil to the depths of the jungles in deadly, darkest Africa; we almost drowned in the mystic headwaters of the Yangtze Kiang River, fought for our lives against cannibals in the Antipodes, braved frostbite on the slopes of the Himalayas, and battled Tartars in the Caucasus, looting these treasures to provide this exhibition to feast your refined eye and mind. Buy now! Avoid the rush and long lines later. Hurry! Hurry! Hurry! Step right up, ladies and gentleman. No waiting, no delays. Tickets are now selling in the doorway.*"

As if on cue, the crowd squeezed us nearer to the blower. We had no idea, but at the appointed time in the pitch, circus workers planted in the crowd worked like dogs to herd us and the rest of the unsuspecting throng closer to the stage.

"Okay, guys, whose gonna be the ballyhoo?" Abbie asked as we were driven forward by the surge. "The last time they were in town it was a snake charmer. Remember that huge boa constrictor coiled around that pretty young thing?"

"How can I forget?" Dave Price answered. "I fell in love that night. I even applied for the snake's job."

Then the talker cleared his throat, signaling the ballyhoo to enter and tempt us towners. Our attention zeroed in on three young black women who stepped on stage.

"*Ladies and gentlemen, from the deepest depths of darkest Africa we present the world's most astounding Aborigines—the crocodile-lipped women from the Congo—the Ubangis. If you like what you see here, wait until you get inside!*" the blower promised.

Mesmerized, we gazed at these attractive, barefoot African women costumed in green, gold, and black raffia and feathers. But what drew our attention was not their good looks or exotic costumes. Each one of them had terribly misshapen lips. They were really from the Congo, but they weren't Ubangis and they weren't crocodile-lipped. It's a really sad story.

It turns out that their mothers, as their mothers before them, had secured large disks inside their lower lips. I later learned that that awful custom began as an attempt to disfigure young women and, in so doing, make them ugly and undesirable to marauding slave traders.

As with the blower's hype, advertising and exaggeration were key mechanisms of the circus experience. With the precision of an exactly executed military campaign, advance men had arrived in El Paso days before the circus and placed posters on every available surface in town, including walls, fences, and barns. Circus advertising literally blanketed El Paso, as it did everywhere else they performed.

That night in 1926, as I stood with the rest of the crowd, all of us hypnotized by the excitement, I couldn't help but notice that many people were staring at me instead of the ballyhoos on stage. Some of the circus employees, including the talker, were intently watching and pointing at me as well. As I've already said, though I hated it, I was used to that type of attention. I watched as people ahead of me approached the ticket sellers behind their high red podiums, reaching up above their heads to the counter to pay.

When it was my turn, the astonished old-timer who sold me my ticket opened his eyes wide. Ticket sellers in other circuses were known for pocketing the change of unsuspecting customers who did not have the advantage of my height and couldn't see the shenanigans that were going on. I would soon learn this was not the case at Ringling Bros, Barnum and Bailey—nicknamed "The Sunday School Show" by competitors because their management would not tolerate that kind of scam. Three months later, I met that same ticket taker. He told me that after work the night he first saw me, he swore to his friends who thought he was drunk or touched in the head, that while sitting at the high podium he'd looked up to a rube.

As I entered the sideshow tent with my friends and we walked past the calliope perched in the doorway, I had no idea what was about to take place. I looked around the circumference of the eighty-by-one-hundred-and-twenty, oval-shaped space and couldn't wait to get out of there. By the time we were all in the tent, the talker had moved inside with us. He greeted the crowd with a boisterous, "Hello, folks!" and directed our attention to Kookoo the Bird Girl, all the while moving us along like sheep in a pen, trying to make way for the next group of customers. At the back of the tent there was a big sign that said "This way to the Egress." Soon I'd learn that many an excited sideshow fan would hurry his family along to make sure they had time to see the exotic egress.

My friends pushed forward. I moved hesitantly, more focused on the exit than the people on display. When I walked by the talker, he looked me up and down. Like some Amazonian snake about to eat his dinner, his jaw just about came unhinged.

Once the astonished blower got his wits about him, he tried to speak to me. "Hey, high pockets! You, kid, come here."

Not on your life, I thought. I scooted away from him as fast as I could while acting like I didn't hear what he said. That blower gave me the creeps.

We moved methodically; too methodically for me. Evidently my friends didn't want to miss any of the human oddities on display. All I could think of was getting the hell out of that claustrophobic tent as soon as I could. Some of the sideshow performers just posed, but most interacted with the crowd. Despite the freaks' efforts to be entertaining, my tentativeness soon became real discomfort. The longer I stayed inside the sideshow tent, the more I felt that any anonymity afforded me as a face in the crowd had disappeared. Even though I wasn't up on a freak show platform, I felt like I was on display.

Finally, we boys approached the exhibit for the giant, Big Jim Tarver, who Ringling Bros had billed as the world's tallest man. Circus folks who recount what happened next describe it as the meeting of two mammoths. It was truly one of the most amazing and embarrassing moments in the annals of the circus. Big Jim Tarver, barrel-chested and heavyset, was by no means a small man. When I approached the colossus in his large, white cowboy hat and Western attire, he glared at me, looking confident and imposing. Then, as if he became suddenly aware of something dangerous, he glanced from side to side and took a self-conscious step backward. The audience gasped and began to audibly whisper. Tarver dropped his gaze down. He looked embarrassed.

Later Big Jim would tell me that, like an old gunslinger worried about a younger and faster rival coming to town, he knew someday he'd meet a taller man, and he dreaded that prospect and all the awful things that encounter would portend. I wouldn't really understand what he was talking about for several years until I met Wadlow.

The crowd's murmur grew louder. Then it finally dawned on me what the hubbub was about. You see, the El Pasoans grasped that their own native son—that's me—was a foot taller than the professional giant. I abruptly spun around and tried to press through the crowd but there were too many people. I was trapped. Some in the audience began to point, first at me and then at Big Jim. I was so mortified, I just wanted to melt into the sawdust that covered the dirt floor.

"How tall are you, mister?" someone asked.

"Look at the size of his hands!" another shouted.

Then other angrier voices rang out. "What a gyp! He's taller than the tallest man in the world."

"I want my money back."

I realized too late that I was embarrassing the poor man. I spun around again and just pushed people out of my way. Then I got out of there as fast as I could.

I saw the talker, who had apparently observed what had happened, power his way through the crowd to get close enough to talk to me. Before he had a chance to do that, I slipped out of the exit and disappeared into the throng. Later I learned that the talker did accost my friends. With the lightning speed of a puma, he swooped down on Bobby and peppered him with questions:

"That tall kid that came into the sideshow tent with you; who is he? I know my boss is gonna need to talk with him. How can we get in touch with that boy?" The talker removed a pad and pencil from his coat pocket.

"He's a giant, too; from right here in El Paso," Bobby spoke the lines he memorized for that occasion, confident and pleased that the plot was unfolding as planned. "His name's Jake Erlich and for a few weeks he's staying with his folks. His mom and dad have a store here in town."

The talker nodded, licked the tip of his pencil just like a cub reporter on his first big story, and scribbled down every detail of information Bobby fed him.

XXXX

"That was really something. I mean, you were bigger than the big man," Dave Price said on the ride home.

"Look guys, I don't want to talk about any of that. It was really embarrassing. I feel bad enough that I humiliated that poor bastard." Gazing out the open window in the back of Bobby's Model T Ford at the dusty west Texas night, I smelled something foul in the air.

"They must be butchering steers over at Peyton's Slaughterhouse tonight," Abbie said. I held my nose and wished I'd never let them talk me into going to the circus in the first place. We drove the rest of the way home in silence.

The next morning, I went to Geneva Loan with Papa. Trying to put the whole unpleasant experience behind me, I didn't say a thing about what happened at the circus to anyone in my family. It must have been about nine a.m. when a stranger walked in the door.

"I'm looking for Jake Erlich," he said, chomping on the stub of an unlit cigar, looking right at me. I was standing back behind the cashier's cage, but because of my height it was easy to spot me there. You see, I was head and shoulders above the bars. That fellow turned out to be Clyde Ingalls. The first time I laid eyes on him, I thought he looked like a traveling salesman with straw hat, seersucker suit, striped tie, and diamond stickpin.

"And just who are you?" Papa, who was standing in front of the cage, asked.

"Ingalls is the name; Clyde Ingalls. I'm the manager of Ringling Bros, Barnum and Bailey's sideshow," the stranger said.

Frenchie took a step forward from behind a showcase where he'd been polishing some jewelry. "What do you want with Jake?" he asked protectively.

The well-dressed stranger took a step back, looked up at me, and tipped his hat. "Why, gentlemen, please don't be concerned. I have no mal intent. It's just that after our fans nearly rioted when they realized your boy was taller than our giant, I decided to come see him and discuss a business opportunity," he explained. "Now that I've seen him with my own eyes I'm glad I took the trouble to come down here."

I stepped out from behind the cage so I that I was standing between Papa and Frenchie. At that point, I felt embarrassed that I hadn't told my family about what had happened at the circus the evening before. Then

Ingalls took a neatly folded piece of paper from the inside pocket of his expensive suit. With a snap of his wrist the paper unfolded like some kind of royal decree. Then he dramatically pointed his index finger up at me. "Young man, I have a golden opportunity for you. How'd you like to be a giant in our circus?" he asked.

The cadence and tone of his voice reminded me of the talker I'd heard the night before on the midway. What I remember most about that first meeting with Ingalls wasn't his fancy getup but the words he used. He didn't ask if I wanted to "play a giant" or "act out the role of a giant." He asked me if he wanted to *be* a giant. Back then I had no way of knowing what those seductive words meant, but before long I'd find out. When I heard his proposal the first thing I did was to sigh and worry, not about myself, but about someone else.

"What's going to happen to that other guy, the giant that works for you?"

"Don't you fret about it, son. If you join up, there is plenty of room at the Big One for more than one giant!" Ingalls assured me. It turns out, Big Jim stayed with the circus for another two seasons. Looking back on it now I think Ingalls read my question about Big Jim as an indication that I was taking the bait. For what seemed like forever, we all stood there in silence. Papa seemed pensive. I remember glancing at Frenchie and thinking he still looked protective, but also like he had *shpilkes* (nerves) and couldn't wait to tell his wife that his boss's son might be joining the Ringling Bros Circus.

"Well, I've got to be getting back to the show grounds," Ingalls said, sensing the mood in the air and the need to leave us alone to mull over what he'd said. "Just read the proposal I've drafted and think about it, will you?"

Papa eyed Ingalls suspiciously, stepped forward, and carefully took hold of the piece of paper that laid out one extraordinary possibility for my future.

"Thank you for your interest in my son," Papa said politely as he extended his arm and shook hands with Ingalls. I was amazed at how much my father had changed since that afternoon four years before on the Santa Monica Pier when the two talent scouts had tried to convince him to give me a shot in silent pictures. As for me, suffice it to say my head was spinning. "You'll have our answer before the circus leaves town tomorrow," Papa said.

Then Ingalls spun around and strode out of the store with a spring in his step and lightness about him that wasn't there when he walked in. Papa put on his spectacles and began to read the contract. Frenchie tried to peruse the offer over Dad's shoulder.

"I've got to get some air," I said as I left them. Walking out into the morning sunshine, I felt the heat that was just beginning to rise from the sidewalk in front of our store. By the time I reached the plaza, I calmed myself enough to begin thinking in earnest about Ingalls proposition. I continued to consider the offer for the rest of the day and early that evening as I sat on my bed at home waiting for dinner. On the one hand, joining up with the circus might be an alternative to going back to Hollywood. As I learned firsthand, that work was physically challenging and plenty dangerous, too. I wondered about my future in pictures and the limitations of my typecast roles at Century Comedies. I wouldn't get rich, but at least Ringling Bros would offer room and board, a steady paycheck with a little more in it than I earned in the flickers, and I wouldn't have to do any more of those damned stunts. I smiled when I thought about all my friends who had, at one time or another, talked about running away to join the circus. In my case, I didn't have to run away to join up, they'd come looking for me.

It took a while, but I had adjusted to life in California and had developed some good friendships and a pretty comfortable working relationship with the cast and crew on my pictures. But circus people, freaks . . . they were an unknown commodity. I wondered what it would be like living and working with them. If I joined the circus I'd be constantly on the move. That would be a tough life. I worried about spending most of the year on the road, living on a train, using outhouses, and staying no more than a few days in any one place. And for someone my size that was not a pretty picture. After all, living at home was challenging enough. What kind of creature comforts, if any, would be available for me on the road? When I worked in Hollywood, it calmed me to know that it took only the better part of a day on the train to get home to my family. In Los Angeles I also had a steady stream of visitors from El Paso that helped take the sting out of my loneliness. If I did take the job with Ringling Bros, most of the time, I'd be a hell of a lot farther away from my family and friends. What if I got homesick? Joining up with Ringling Bros was going to be a big, fat step into the unknown, a step I was afraid to take.

A loud knock on my bedroom door brought me out of the debate raging in my head.

"Jake, Mama's *broigas* (angry). She said to tell you to get your behind to the table before your soup gets cold. Everybody's already sitting down and waiting for you," Myer warned. I had totally forgotten that my folks scheduled a big powwow at the house that night to discuss Ingall's offer. Besides my parents and brothers, Dr. Ziltzer was invited as well.

"I'll be right there," I assured him. As I ran into the dining room everyone stopped talking and looked up at me from where they sat. From the looks on their faces, I couldn't decide if they saw me as the guest of honor or a defendant in a murder trial. Mama had prepared one of my favorite dishes: corned beef and cabbage. But that night I moved the food around on my plate, doing the best I could to hide the fact that I couldn't eat a morsel of it. Despite my efforts at subterfuge, I knew Mama noticed. But she didn't say a thing. I think she didn't want to embarrass me in front of our guest.

After the dinner dishes were cleared, we all sat around the table and everyone voiced their opinions about me joining the circus. I mostly listened. Their words actually echoed what I'd been struggling with all day long.

"Jakey, I'm concerned if you stay home you will get depressed again," Mama said.

"You've got to work. And there's not much, if anything, for you to do in this town," Papa added.

"Going back to silent pictures would mean you'd have to do your own stunts again and that would be altogether too dangerous," Dr. Ziltzer warned.

Though everything they said made sense, I felt they were all trying to sell me on the circus. "I agree with every point you're making. I've even thought about most of them myself, but something just doesn't feel right about it," I argued.

"What doesn't feel right?" Myer asked.

"I don't know, it just doesn't," I said, pushing away from the table in frustration. I didn't realize I was so irritated. "Why can't you understand? I don't want to join a sideshow and be called a *freak*. I don't want to degrade myself like that. Would you?" I said without thinking. It seemed that I roared the words *freak* and *degrade*.

Papa, who had been sitting quietly at the opposite end of the table, jumped to his feet. "Being a freak is in your head. It's a state of mind!" he roared with equal force. "Do you want to hide at home, eat cookies and drink warm milk with your Mama, detach yourself and avoid the rest of the world and everybody in it, like you're incapable, like there's something terribly wrong with you?" Papa's question stung worse than a slap across the face.

I think that in some cavern in my psyche, where my most profound insecurities live, I was petrified that joining the circus meant I was incapable of doing anything else; that there was something truly lacking in me, that the only asset I had or would ever have in this life was my height. So I rejected all those well-intentioned arguments that pushed me to take advantage of a golden opportunity while I could.

I was too upset to make any decisions that night. Early the next morning, after little or no sleep, I woke up before anyone else, snuck out of the house, and went for a walk by myself. That time my hike didn't take me to Crazy Cat but in the opposite direction toward the college, the Texas State School of Mines and Metallurgy. We locals called it the Texas School of Mines. I liked the buildings on that small campus. Their Asian architecture, with its red roofs and thick walls was like me, out of place in this west Texas landscape. As the story goes, after a terrible fire devastated the school, Kathleen Worrell, the wife of the dean, convinced her husband to construct several new structures in the Bhutanese, *Dzong* style. She had seen photos of Bhutan, the Land of the Thunder Dragon, in an article in *National Geographic* magazine written by a Brit who traveled there at the turn of the century.

About six thirty a.m. I walked through the campus, all but abandoned at that early hour. Just beyond it, I hiked up to a high bluff that overlooked Mexico. There I leaned on a huge red boulder and began to think and pray on my choices. I reviewed much that had happened in my three and a half years in Hollywood and what my prospects were for a future there. I carefully considered what everyone had said the night before, particularly Papa.

I was in deep contemplation when a distant steam whistle drew my attention down the rock face in front of me to Donaphan Street, and beyond to two sets of railroad tracks, the old ice house, the Phelps Dodge Smelter and, just behind it, a familiar stretch of the Rio Grande. I heaved a sigh, recalling that it was pretty much in that same spot, that if not for a Good Samaritan saving me by my hair, I would have drowned in an undertow. Then my focus was abruptly yanked from the river and its memories to a speeding freight train barreling along the tracks below, heading eastward. The behemoth had two locomotives, at least fifty cars, and a caboose. *At the speed that monster's traveling, he'll be in Dallas by sunset*, I thought.

Maybe it was the huge freight train, my recollections, or something else, but at that instant my thoughts swung back to the circus. I thought about how popular the circus was; how when Ringling Bros came to El Paso, schools would close, factories like the Smelter below would shut down and just about everybody in town would attend. For many families like mine, circus day was a sacrosanct, yearly tradition. I recalled the crowd I'd seen on the midway two nights before. The grown-ups seemed to magically become young again, like their kids. Maybe the circus was a place for new beginnings. Despite my misgivings about the sideshow, maybe Ringling Bros would be a place for me to get a fresh start. Maybe I could use the circus as a bridge out of the labyrinth of my sadness and as a new chance to connect to the world. Up to that point in my young life, when it came to the church of the circus, I'd been an agnostic. Though I still had many concerns, at that moment I started to feel a bit of the passion of a convert.

A surge of excitement started in my feet, shot to my solar plexus, and then to the top of my head. I ran all the way home to wake my family and tell them about my decision. That very afternoon, I borrowed Papa's fountain pen, the one he only used for very special occasions, and signed a one-year contract with Ringling Bros, Barnum and Bailey Circus. Two weeks later, full of equal parts trepidation and eagerness, I left El Paso to meet up with the show in New York and begin my career in the circus. I had no way of knowing that I would never live at home again.

CHAPTER 22

Robert Wadlow

Sideshow Banner Line, Hertzberg Circus Collection, Witte Museum, San Antonio, Texas

Ten years later, in the spring of 1936 when we closed that eventful month-long season opener in New York City and made the jump to Boston, I remember being amazed that so much time had gone by since I began my career with Ringling Bros. I continued to be preoccupied by time; how I'd spent it, squandered it, and how much I had left, when we began our five-day run in Beantown.

Boston and New York were the only places in the country where we appeared in arenas, and I didn't like it. Compared to performing under canvas, particularly at the Boston Garden, arenas felt artificial and confining. And in those places the sideshow was always set up in the basement near the menagerie, making it even more claustrophobic. It might have been that in cities with the indoor venues, like New York and Boston, there wasn't as much to distract me as everywhere else.

Where we performed under the Big Top it was easier to get caught up in the hustle and bustle of circus life. Imagine what it was like moving 1,608 troopers, hundreds of animals, and tons of equipment on a hundred-car circus train that was almost a mile long. All that commotion made it easy, at least for a while, to forget your problems and lose yourself; even a self as big as mine. After all, what with only twenty of all the stops we made in a season being in big cities where we stayed for more than one night, there was an unbelievable amount of coming and going in circus life. Our schedule was grueling. In an average season, I must have appeared in more than four hundred performances, traveled for 218 days, and covered more than sixteen thousand miles.

At each new stop the curtain went up on the drama again and again. On too many mornings to count I'd be mesmerized watching Ringling's wagons skillfully unloaded off flatcars and pulled by teams of magnificent draft horses to the ten-acre show grounds.

I wasn't the only one who was transfixed. In each city an army of kids and adults would come out to watch the show. In less than four hours, art and science were woven together to craft seventy-five thousand yards of canvas and seventy-five miles of rope into our mobile playhouse. The logistics were amazing; man, oh, man, what a complicated affair that was.

For most of the time I was with The Big One, our Boss Canvas Man was named Billy Barnes. In each new city Billy and his crew went to work on the white leviathan we called the Big Top. Its skeleton consisted of more than one hundred and fifty poles, ranging from the thick, sixty-two-foot center poles to thinner seventeen-foot side polls. It took twenty poles, forty-seven feet in length for the inner circle, and thirty-four poles, thirty-seven feet in length for the outer circle. Guy wires, the sinews of the beast, held most of the poles to five-foot stakes, driven three feet into the ground to secure the damned thing.

When I first started with Ringling Bros back in '26, the stakes were driven manually by sweaty roustabouts slinging heavy black sledgehammers. Later the bosses bought fancy steam-driven machines for that job. The clanging, smacking sound of those pile-drivers was deafening. You know, it was also almost musical; a cacophonous symphony of the Industrial Revolution come to the midway. Once I imagined raising the Big Top as an ancient Ionian epic featuring rough-edged roustabouts as mariners, each with his own tattered stories of broken dreams, scars, and criminality. In unison, Ulysses' crew strained to hoist forty thousand pounds of sail and struggled to take up the slack in six hundred guy wires, making the ancient vessel fast for yet another storm, securing the sailors from the sea monsters that lived beneath the waves. *"Heave it—weave it—shake it—take it—break it—make it,"* cried the crew boss, who took the role of the Greek chorus.

Without that intoxicating distraction, it wasn't so easy for me. So after the closing spec on our third day in Boston, I wasn't at all surprised that all I could think about was escaping from the claustrophobic arena out into the fresh air for a smoke. When I did, even though it was early June, I shivered from a bone-chilling breeze. You see, the Garden was built nearby to the rail yard in North Station, very close to a network of canals at the mouth of the Charles River where it empties into Boston Harbor. In that spot, it was common for nasty winds to whip across all the icy water and send chills up and down the spine of whatever poor creature was in their way.

In a futile attempt to get warm, I fastened the collar button on the flimsy cowboy shirt that served as the top of my costume. An assistant animal trainer exited from the arena via the same door I had. He was leading one of the show's Arabians, evidently going to school her or have her walk something off. The trainer and I nodded, acknowledging each other. I didn't feel much like talking. You see, throughout that evening, and every other day that week in Boston, all I could think about was getting back to the train to see if I had a letter from Val. I was obsessed.

The last time I spoke to her was on the telephone two weeks before, just as we pulled up stakes to leave New York. That was when I told her I would accept the scholarship to art school. I still wasn't convinced about my artistic abilities or the talent Val, Frida, and Diego swore I had. I think I agreed to attend art school because I thought it was my only way to stay close to Val. In those days that pipe dream was probably one of the only things I had to hold on to. I mean, for a while, I held out hope that things would get better for me when I'd leave the sideshow for good. Then I got Dad's letter asking for money for his trip to Europe and to get the family out of harm's way. Those obligations brought me crashing back to the real world. I needed my circus salary, and because of it, I signed on again. Before the ink from my signature on that damned contract had even dried I had made up my mind up that, in this lifetime, I'd never leave the sideshow.

Back in New York, when I shared my decision about art school with Val, she told me how happy that made her feel. I remember that she promised to write soon with details, but she didn't. It wasn't that I gave a wooden nickel about going to art school. I just wanted the contact with her. I was so disappointed when the only letters I got were from my mother and Frida.

When I read Mama's letter about her and Papa's upcoming trip to Poland, I couldn't help but worry. From everything I had read, heard on the radio, or seen in newsreels, war in Europe was inevitable. I fretted about my parents getting caught up in that mess and hurt because of some half-baked scheme to help relatives I'd never even met. As for Frida's note, well, suffice it to say that woman confused me. I couldn't tell if she was genuinely interested in me as a friend, if she thought of me as a freakish oddity—a sort of exotic pet that would add to her notoriety—or if she had some other unmentionable plans.

When no letter came from Val, a severe voice in my head snarled that when it came to ever getting her affections I was like Peter Pan, living in fantasyland. But I couldn't shake the memory of how gorgeous she looked the last time I saw her, sitting in the back of her Pierce-Arrow, soaking wet from that rainstorm. "You're not an art experiment to me. You're much,

much more." I could still feel her breath on my ear as she whispered those words. Thinking about it made me feel warm all over. There had to be something between us. I just knew it. I wondered if, perhaps, the letter she had promised to send had been lost in the mail. I pictured Val in a hospital bed unconscious. Maybe she was sick or she'd been injured. The feeling of someone or something scampering across my feet brought me abruptly back from my visions of Val to where I stood in the cold outside the Boston Garden. It was a similar sensation to what I had experienced many years before after the *Blue Book* awards when one of Barrymore's monkeys ran across my feet. Instinctively I looked down. There I saw a whirl of white as Major Mite in tie and tails stormed by me in a huff. He looked livid.

"God damnit!" The little man fumed as he swatted the rump of the black Arabian that stood in his path, spooking it sideways.

The trainer jerked the reins and the horse's red-feather-clad head snapped back. Then the trainer gave Major Mite a menacing look, made a fist, and swore at him under his breath.

"Whoa there, big fella," I said, sensing things were getting out of control and stepping between the little and normal sized men. Up until that episode outside the Boston Garden, the most outlandish thing I had observed about Clarence Chesterfield Howerton—Mite's real name—besides his height was his mischievous nature. He was what you call a *pistol*, a real prankster. But that night something had evidently infuriated Clarence and I saw a different, more threatening, volatile side of him. I debated whether to just let it go.

Typically I avoided out-of-control, unpredictable people like the plague. When I encountered one, I'd head for the hills. Maybe that's because much of my life has been so damned out of control and unpredictable. But since I'd tackled that jerk in front of Gargantua's cage a few weeks before back in New York and met Val, all bets were off. My old rules of order seemed to have fallen by the wayside. I missed that order and the sense of calm and stability that came with them. Since then my stomach constantly churned. I could feel knots the size of golf balls in the back of my neck. Frequent thunderbolts of pain shot down my lower back and legs. I imagined my body was a massive hand trying to grasp and hold onto something that was slipping through my fingers like sand. Still, for a few seconds I debated whether, as I would have in the past, to let sleeping dogs lie. But that dog wasn't sleeping. The way he looked, he might bite and some big dog might bite him back. Clarence was my friend and I couldn't let that happen.

"What's got into you?" I asked as the animal trainer led the Arabian back inside.

"Wadlow!" said Clarence. He kicked the ground, spraying pieces of gravel everywhere. "Who does he think he is?" The little man looked up and spoke as if he were addressing some invisible audience behind me. I glanced back to see Lady Olga, the Bearded Wonder, standing there, smoking a cigarette, and listening. Olga was the second of the sideshow's bearded women. Unlike Adrienne, the other bearded lady, I liked Olga. Please understand—Adrienne was a Nazi-loving, son of a bitch, who had, more than once, called me a dirty Jew.

That night, Olga was dressed in a strapless, ruby-red ball gown. I remember thinking she must have been freezing. Her costume was meant not only to accentuate her freakishness, but also her femininity. At least with me and Clarence, they just tried to dramatize our height, not compare and contrast it with our masculinity. They didn't care what we wore as long as it matched the theme of the spec and it made me look gigantic and Clarence look tiny. Maybe what the powers that be at Ringling Bros considered feminine was so engraved in our circus fans' minds that a beard and a ball gown were too juicy a contrast to overlook. *The circus sure loves hyperbole,* I thought. Would Olga's carefully combed and curled beard have looked as long and gnarly if she just wore a sun dress or the plaids of a lumberjack? It's no wonder that so many freaks are ladies.

Clarence didn't wait for my or Olga's response but continued on his own. "Wadlow doesn't say two words to any of us." I nodded. Clarence was off on a tirade and I decided to just listen. "He sits by himself and only talks to his dad."

I had observed Wadlow's standoffishness with my own eyes. As a matter of fact, though he had been asked to join me and the other freaks for a meal at Delmonico's in New York he never showed up. At the time, none of us spoke about it, but I knew we all felt odd. After all, in my ten years with the circus, no newcomer had ever rejected an invitation for a welcoming dinner from the other freaks. I just wrote it off. At worst, it was a kid being rude and, at best, Wadlow just didn't know any better.

"Does he think he's better than we are? He always appears in a coat and tie and not in costumes like the rest of us. He's made it clear he'll never

ever set foot in the sideshow. Does he have some kind of a superiority complex? Does he think there's something shameful about being a freak?" With every question, Clarence picked up steam. Even in the torchlight I noticed that he had a throbbing vein in his forehead, just like my father. As he got more intense it throbbed more. I wondered about the immense anger in that little man.

"Come on, he's just a kid," I added. Olga stepped to my right side and nodded in agreement. Looking back on it, I think underneath my calm veneer I disliked the boy giant myself. But that made me really uneasy. I asked myself why.

"Yeah, some kid. Are you sticking up for him?" Clarence asked. "He's no better than a rube."

"What happened that you're so hot?" I asked. I think that Clarence's emotions were hard for me to stomach. In the past, that kind of feeling was a treacherous jungle where only men like Frank Buck ventured to trap ferocious man-eaters.

"I said hello and he acted like I wasn't there; didn't even say a word."

I recalled the night at Madison Square Garden, a few weeks before when I first met Wadlow, and then in Boston when we first appeared in the circus together. I had greeted him on both occasions and both times he hadn't given me the time of day. Maybe what I had written off to youthful rudeness was something else altogether.

"What's your take on Wadlow, Jake?" Olga asked.

I, as many of the other freaks, had noticed that Wadlow's contract with Ringling Bros gave him special privileges that weren't afforded to anyone else. None of us liked prima donnas and, whether or not Ingalls and the Wadlows had intended it to occur, that's how we saw him.

Those of us in the sideshow: Major Mite; the Dolls; our other giants, Bill Madsen and Miss Lundy; Siamese twins like the Gibbs Sisters; Burkhart "The Boneless Anatomical Wonder"; Kookoo the Bird Girl; Hubel the Human Bellows; the Makeana South Seas Dancers; contortionists like Twisto the Human Knot; Miss Suzanne the Snake Charmer; Amok the Head Hunter; Miss Pictoria the Tattooed Woman; Susie the Elephant-Skinned Girl; Haig the Man with Elastic Skin; Adrienne and Olga, our bearded ladies; HoJo the Bear Boy; the Giraffe-Necked Beauties from Borneo; Irene the Fat Woman and Tom Ton the Fat Man; the Ubangis; Habu the Man with the Iron Tongue; Peter Robinson the Skeleton Doll; the Robed Hindu Fakir; Cliko the Wild, Dancing, African Bushman; Whirling Dervishes and Negroid Albinos; armless and legless wonders; and all the sword swallowers, fire eaters, magicians, and knife throwers; we were a close-knit group, a family. Equality was our code, the essence of the sideshow culture, the foundation that bound our strange community. It was a given that we didn't have the status or earn the big bucks of top-billed performers. But we freaks had something else: camaraderie. Wadlow did not blend in with the rest of us freaks. He was an outsider, a freak among freaks. For us, the kind of dissention he introduced could be poisonous.

I smelled trouble. But I chose to ignore it. *This isn't my fight,* I thought. *I am going to stay out of it. Keep quiet,* I said to myself.

I recalled one of Papa's favorite sayings: "The spoken word is worth a *kopeck*. The unspoken word is worth ten." To buy some time, I reached for the chipped, cherry wood Danish pipe and worn black leather pouch I kept in my back pocket. When I scraped a match across the door to the arena to light my pipe, the little flash of phosphorous lit up Clarence and Olga's faces, giving them the look of trolls. I took a few puffs and noticed the glow from the orange embers and the feel of the sweet smoke in my lungs. I closed my eyes. When I opened them the nightmare image had passed. I was calmed enough to respond to Olga.

"I don't really dislike Wadlow. I think we need to give him a chance." I felt torn. It's true that I was developing a genuine dislike for him, and there were not too many people on the list of those I disliked. I now understand that it was hard to admit I felt negative about another freak, particularly a giant who was more a boy than a man. After all I'd been through I prided myself on being tolerant. But I couldn't overlook how Wadlow and his dad had a hardscrabble Victorian sternness about them. They never hung around after our performances, always making a swift exit to a waiting hired car. His mother never came to any of our shows. She apparently didn't want anything to do with the circus. They were very different from my folks. Rain or shine, whenever the circus came to El Paso, my family always attended the show. I couldn't imagine ever being invited to the Wadlow house for a meal. When the Ringling Bros came to town, my parents always invited the freaks over for Sunday dinner. Watching Wadlow during our performances that week in Boston, I felt he didn't connect with the audience. It was like he didn't care about the fans. He would wave as he walked around the Big Top, but it seemed very mechanical, like a giant machine. I thought Wadlow was just there for the paycheck. It troubled me to think that since Papa's letter, maybe I was doing the same thing. But we were different. Whereas I enjoyed the Circus Lover's Banquets we'd attend from time to time, I could visualize him there as much as I could picture Okies being welcomed in California.

"Let's get to know him a little better before we make any final judgments," I said, at once counseling my friends and hiding my darker feelings. Olga nodded and Clarence shook his head and looked away in disgust. Underneath it all, if Olga and Clarence knew how I really felt, they would have thought I was a hypocrite.

My suggestion to take our time and get better acquainted with Robert Wadlow would never happen. We didn't have a chance. After we finished our run in Boston, he never returned to the show. Some said it was a contract dispute with the suits. Others said he just plain hated circus life. I have my suspicions, but none of us freaks were ever told why he actually quit. Strangely, I felt sad about him leaving and, at the same time, relieved. Reflecting on it now, I know I had unfinished business with him that I worried would never be resolved.

"Good riddance! I'm glad we're done with him," Clarence said when we talked about it as we set up in Pittsburgh.

I've got to say, back then, the whole damned Wadlow episode made me edgy. Little did I know, I would run into him again and that encounter would change my life.

XXXX

As happened with so many of the years I was with Ringling Bros, the rest of the 1936 season went by in a blur. One of the things that I do recall with crystal clarity during that summer was the stifling heat. It was firecracker hot. The heat came early and it just got worse. I wondered when, if ever, the day would come when they'd air condition the circus train like they'd learned to air condition the Big Top. Maybe someday they'd even air condition automobiles. It was so hot that many a night we'd sleep out in the open on the flatcars, drifting off to a summertime symphony: crickets, cicadas, and the circus train's *clickety-clack*. The sleepy scene was lit by silvery summer moons shining through pine forests, twinkling fireflies, and the occasional oranges and blues of a hobo campfire.

That scorching summer, as I fell into deep open-air sleep, the peacefulness masked a phantasmagoric world of struggle where billy clubs of well-fed railroad bulls cracked skulls on too many a poor man and boy who tried to ride the rails; where flat-headed, soulless eyes ripped black men and women from their beds and lynched them from ancient oaks, who, if given the power to speak like men, would wail with the shame of what they saw. A half a world away in Germany, jackbooted thugs were already playing their part. That wasn't the kind of nightmare you could erase by opening your eyes.

Once, sleeping on one of those flatcars somewhere in Tennessee, I woke in a pool of sweat, forgetting where and who I was; the awful noise that roused me the crashing coupling of clumsy, giant iron-lovers in a freight yard. A few minutes later, careening into the unknown, my terror passed as the mass of that circus train with its dark sense of purpose hurled, once again, through the night. A fierce centrifugal force held me down, pinning me on that flatcar, preventing me from being flung into the emptiness; paralysis the price of my calm and safety.

As I lay awake on the flatcar, unable to sleep, I recalled what had happened the night before. We were playing in Chattanooga. Lou Adler, one of Ringling's most famous clowns, and I were walking together down the midway. Lou was fifty, bald, and stoop shouldered. Once he removed the greasepaint and the prosthetic nose he looked to be a lot smaller and older than when he appeared under the lights. Lou was an intelligent, quiet sort of fellow who was the most well-read person on current affairs I'd ever met. Maybe that's why I took a liking to him. We'd talk about what was going on in the world. But I never pushed him to talk about his past. Maybe that's why we got along so well. Someone told me he'd been a drunk. Someone else swore he had a run-in with the law. Another one said that before he joined Ringling Bros he had lost a child. Whatever secrets haunted him, I didn't care. Besides his other attributes, Adler was a walking encyclopedia and master of the craft of clowning. He was the first guy I'd ever seen who used the spotlight to get laughs, playing hide and seek with it. Adler spoke like a clown poet about the devoted fans who came back season after season for the escape afforded by the drug of laughter. He was the Homer of clown cosmology, recounting tales of white-faced, scary clowns; of lowly crowd-energizing anarchists, intent on stealing control from the ringmaster; and the ones he called *contre-august*, the diplomats who struggled to make peace under the Big Top. I now comprehend that the world of clowns Adler described for me mirrored the larger world at that time. Besides his vast knowledge of the history of clowning, Adler had a special way with children. He was the one who offered some important advice early in my circus career that I took to heart.

"Jake, learn from us clowns. Many are the times I've scared a kid. I'm sure you must scare the bejesus out of them, too."

"It's those damned fairytales about evil giants. We need better PR for big guys like me." Even though I tried to make light of it, Adler had hit a nerve. You see, as I aged, one of the saddest things to me was the way I often frightened little ones. I'd always secretly wished some author would write a fairytale with castles and treasure and a giant who would never, ever harm a child.

"When I deal with kids I make sure to always kneel down so as not to tower over them, and I always let them touch me first," Adler continued. I was grateful for his guidance and have never forgotten it. It was shortly after that conversation that the whole nasty affair went down in Chattanooga.

That night Lou and I strolled down the midway chatting about the Berlin Games that had just closed. "That son of a bitch Herr Hitler is sure getting good press," I said. "But I'm confused. I thought the Americans were going to boycott the Olympics because the Nazis weren't allowing any Jews who qualified to participate."

"Well, that mustached weasel pulled a fast one on us."

"What do you mean?" I asked as we passed the Tastee-Freeze wagon.

"Do you know who Gretel Bergmann is?"

"Yeah, sure; she's that gifted high jumper, broken all kinds of world records. Wasn't she supposed to be a favorite for a gold medal?"

"That's right. She's Jewish, too, and she was on the Nazi's Olympic team."

"I don't understand." I said, barely avoiding a slow-moving family in front of us.

"Well, the whole Bergmann business was a goddamned manipulation, a sham. The Nazis used Bergmann as a decoy," Adler said. "Would you please slow down, Jake?" he begged, evidently out of breath. "I can't walk as fast as you do and talk at the same time." I slowed down. "It turned out that after our athletes set sail for the games, the Germans booted Bergmann off the team. But Hitler got his comeuppance."

"How's that?" I asked.

"Those damned Huns must have been fit to be tied. You see, Ibolya Csak, a Hungarian Jew, actually took the gold medal in Bergmann's event. That's not to mention how Jesse Owens made them eat crow in the track events when he smashed Hitler's Aryan supermen for more gold medals." I shook my head and laughed as we kept moving through the throng. "Later, I found out that the story of Bergmann didn't end there. Get this: The Nazis replaced Bergmann with a woman named Dora. Well shortly after the games, reporters uncovered that Dora was really a fellow named Heinrich. Here's mud in your eye. Heil Hitler," Lou quipped. As if on cue, we both raised our thumbs to our noses in a salute.

Just then I spotted Harry Doll strolling down the midway ahead of us, close by to the entrance to the menagerie.

"That little man sure can move!" Adler said. "I bet he walks faster than you do, Jake."

"I need to talk with Harry before the evening show. See you later." I left Adler behind and sped up to catch Harry. He was only a few paces ahead of me when it happened. A wiry rube who looked to be about twenty, dressed in coveralls and a green flannel shirt reached out and tried to grab Harry by the neck. Without thinking, I stretched out my right arm to stop him. I didn't mean to, but somehow my hand caught him on the chin and he went down.

Because of Ingall's rage and how he threatened me after I clobbered that drunk who tried to hurt Gargantua at the start of the season in New York, I was sure that what happened spelled the end of my circus career. Sometimes, I wonder if when I tackled that rube in the menagerie in Madison Square Garden, I was really trying to force Ingalls to fire me; to make a decision that I wasn't brave enough to make myself. But by the time we played Chattanooga I honestly wanted to stay with the circus. I needed the money and I wanted to have an excuse to see Val again. So when we met with Ingalls the next morning in the small tent he used for an office on the show grounds, I was plenty worried. I was more than grateful that Harry went to bat for me.

"Clyde, that damned redneck grabbed for my throat," Harry had reported. "If not for Jake that rube might have killed me."

"All I did was spin him around," I told Ingalls meekly.

"Well, whatever you did you sent that jackass to the hospital with a fractured jaw. Now our lawyers will have to settle with his claims. You've got two strikes, Erlich!" an exasperated Ingalls screamed. "One more incident of fisticuffs, whether there is a good explanation for it or not, and you're finished. Now, both of you get the hell out of my sight."

After I calmed down I concluded that Ingalls decision wasn't based on Harry speaking up for me. I was certain if Wadlow hadn't quit the show, Ingalls would have given me my walking papers right then and there.

"Thanks again, Jake," Harry said as we strolled through the backyard after our meeting. "Big fella, last night you might have just saved this little man's life."

"It was nothing," I said. "I just gave him a tap." I was quick to answer. I don't know why, but it's always been hard for me to stomach it when others were grateful to me.

"I hear you sucker-punched another one, Jake."

I knew that sarcastic voice. I looked up from Harry to see Frank Buck standing right in front of us, just outside the bull yard. I had been doing my best to avoid him.

Harry stepped in front of me. "That's not what happened," Harry said in a challenging tone. It was strange to see someone not even a quarter of my size defending me.

"Ya, ya!" Buck said, discounting Harry derisively. Without saying a word, Harry and I both understood that Frank knew the real skivvy on what had happened with the rube the night before. In Ringling Bros that kind of gossip spread faster than dysentery. "Next maybe you'll go after Max Baer. But you wouldn't do that. He might fight back and, oh yeah—he's one of your kind, right?" Then Buck stomped away.

I didn't miss his anti-Semitic jab. Buck wasn't your typical Jew-hater. I don't think he hated Jews at all. He was just sore and jealous because of Val. Watching him move across the midway, I wondered if perhaps, just perhaps, the night before, that unlucky rube got more than he bargained for because I hadn't received a letter from Val.

CHAPTER 23

Artemus

Hertzberg Circus Collection, Witte Museum, San Antonio, Texas

I used to wonder why I stayed in the circus so long. Maybe it was the numbing predictability of circus life, a massive production line that even that damn anti-Semite Henry Ford would have envied. The discipline of life in Ringling Bros was like opium and coffee. At once it would rouse or tranquilize you, making time pass quickly or obliterating it altogether. Circus trains transported thousands of folks, hundreds of animals, and tons of equipment; leaving one location at an appointed hour and almost always—barring unforeseen troubles like weather, wrecks, or a drunken star thrown in the hoosegow—arriving at another town precisely on time. The whole thing worked like fine Swiss clockwork. Day in and day out, the early morning rumble of razorbacks unloading wagons off flatcars and the neighing of draft horses harnessed for the trek to the show ground; thousands of stakes rhythmically pounded into the earth and hundreds of poles adroitly raised by roustabouts and beasts; canvasmen hoisting the white fabric that served as the massive banner and refuge of our mobile community, a canvas where the gods painted portraits of modernity come to the heartland; blacksmiths, barbers, and tailors busy at circus chores; bleachers set, midway eateries stored, stocked, and opened; ostriches, giraffes, anteaters, lions, tigers, cheetahs, bears, seals, gorillas, parrots, and ponies, their cages set in place by performing Indian elephants; a mystical totem granting a glimpse into an exotic world that many had never seen before and might never see again; wonders fit for the King of Siam. Then we would take it all down, do it all over again in the next town.

Whether in the freight yard at dawn or midnight, at barren fairgrounds where the enchantment would soon occur, or in melancholy empty lots where all that was left of the magic were a few pieces of discarded trash and the blurred site of the last circus wagon leaving town, there always were the crowds. At times I must admit I was very lonely, but solitude was always a rare commodity. Maybe that's why I stayed so long. For us in the circus, or for any huckster, politician, or priest—be it Billy Sunday, even for FDR—it was the same. After all those years with Ringling Bros, Barnum and Bailey, I learned that the key ingredient for entertainment's addicting elixir wasn't mystery, costumes, music, super-human feats, dancing girls, animals, or freaks, but an audience. It was an unspoken contract, a covenant, a communion of sorts. The fans needed us and we needed them. In those days, I don't think I fully comprehended that I was part of the audience as well, a witness to a spectacle that would not come this way again. Strangely, the same thing, being a witness to a grand, passing parade, had happened to me once before when I worked in silent pictures.

XXXX

Late in the season of 1936, we did a three-day run in Macon, Georgia. After that oven of a summer, I was grateful that fall came early. A pleasant east wind cooled things down enough so the worst of the awful southern heat and humidity seemed to have passed.

But I couldn't really enjoy the weather or anything else. All I could think about was how one of Frank Buck's young Bengals had been badly burned in Atlanta the week before. Frank had brought Artemus to the circus three seasons before. When I had laid eyes on that malnourished cub, it was love at first sight.

"Where'd you get the baby tiger?" I had asked.

"His mama died birthing him," the lion tamer had explained. He went on to tell me how Artie—that was what we nicknamed him—had been abandoned in some dirt-water town in eastern Alabama by a mud show that was about to go bust. A veterinarian friend in nearby Mobile heard about it and called Buck. As luck would have it, at the time the circus was playing only a day's drive away. Buck went up there, purchased Artie from the county sheriff, who was taking care of him, and trucked him back.

"He'll never make it," Doc Jameson, Ringling's vet, had said. But with bottle feeding and a lot of care and affection, Artie beat the odds. Whenever possible, I'd play with the cub, feed and bathe him, and even clean his cage.

Come to think of it, that's how Buck and I first became friends. Before that, Frank Buck didn't interact much with me or any of the other freaks. Like most others in the circus, he adhered to our unspoken caste system. Whether you were a Big Top performer, a freak, or a roustabout, you were expected to eat, play, and sleep with your own kind. We were our own miniature, traveling civilization complete with history, traditions, and social classes. But the more I hung around and volunteered to help with Artie, the more the barriers between us came down and the more our friendship grew. It was amazing how that young Bengal brought us together. That's when I first got a glimpse of how complicated a man Buck was. Besides how he treated his few, close friends, Frank Buck was much more patient with animals than he was with people. He had a way of seeing things about critters others missed. Buck was the one who really got me to appreciate how we underestimate them. Tammy, one of our bulls, had a calf that was a runt. I mean, that baby elephant was so small she couldn't reach her mama's teat. Buck suggested that her handlers put a small stepping stool in the pen with Tammy and her baby. I remember standing there with Buck as Tammy used her trunk to position the stool beneath her and to nudge the calf onto it so he could nurse.

"Dumb animals? Dumb animals, my foot!" he said as we stood there watching that amazing scene unfold.

What a shame that all that mess with Val had to come between us. I wished things could be like they were. But the chances of that ever happening again were slim to none. Before all of that crap came down the pike, whenever I had free time, I would hang around to observe Artie. I noticed that as he grew, as if they were threatened by him, the other tigers gave him a really bad time. They beat the hell out of the adolescent cat every chance they could. I remember thinking that he was an outsider, like me. Maybe that's why I was so fond of Artie. You know, I've always been drawn to outsiders.

Over the years I watched him grow from a scrawny kitty into a majestic cat. Lying there in my bunk, I thought of how much I missed wrestling with Artie and rolling with him in the straw inside the large, steel tiger cage under the Big Top. I didn't get to be physical too often. As a matter of fact, the only people I'd ever really horsed around with were my brothers. Wrestling with that young tiger was a treat. It made me feel alive in a different way than anything else did. I loved Artie's musty smell, the rough feel of his hide, and how he could easily overpower me. Once while we were wrestling, I saw my reflection in his yellow and ebony eyes. They were huge. I wondered what the young tiger must be thinking. Did he see me as a freak? When we played like that he almost seemed to purr. That was when Artie was younger, before he got so big and strong; before he gashed my right arm and that kind of play became too dangerous. Those were the halcyon days when Buck and I were still buddies. Although in later years reporters wrote that I had a lot of friends, I didn't feel that way. Like a man who has known starvation cherishes even crumbs, my friends were precious to me. I valued them all and hated losing one, even Frank Buck.

Let me tell you how Artie got burned. Don't worry about having a strong stomach; I won't go into the awful details. That night in Atlanta we played to a packed house. Everything had gone like clockwork. Buck's Bengals were a big draw. They were the center ring act just before the closing spec. In the finale, as he always did, Artie led the other cats in a lunge through a flaming tunnel. Then all seven of those majestic beasts lined up behind Buck and stood up on their hind legs. They towered over him. The roar of the crowd during the standing ovation that followed was deafening.

The fire started in tinderbox-dry bales of hay stored under the tiger cages. Some say it was a drunken roustabout or a disgruntled cage boy or a careless fan's discarded cigarette that was to blame. One cat died on the spot. If not for Buck's valiant effort, which cost him two badly burned hands, more tigers would have burned to death right there and then.

In the circus, just like on a ship at sea, fire is predator, never to be trifled with. Before that night, I had always thought of fire as a risk to human life. After Atlanta, my definition of life would never be so limited again.

"It's that damned burn. I give him no better than a fifty-fifty chance," Doc Jameson had said later that night when he examined Artie. I tried to comfort myself by thinking that he was a fighter; that he would be all right. After all, I had heard the same vet say Artie wouldn't make it when he was just a cub, and he did.

Ever since Artie was burned in Atlanta I hadn't been able to sleep. That night in Macon was no different. As if I could turn my back on what I knew happened and thereby make it all disappear, I rolled over and faced the wall in my tiny compartment on the circus train. I thrashed about, trying to erase the awful images that flooded my mind, but I couldn't. I forced myself to focus on the shooting exhibition I had put on in the Big Top earlier that day and struggled to come up with some new tricks.

Five years before, at the start of the 1931 season, struggling to be more than a passive exhibit just sitting in the sideshow tent and to keep things fresh, I had approached Clyde Ingalls with the idea.

"Isn't selling those damned lead rings enough for you?" Ingalls sounded irritated. I told him about the special 410 Winchester skeet gun, which my friend, Bob Phillips, a master gunsmith back home, had made for me and how I had been practicing at Sheriff Orndorff's Shooting Range. When I visited El Paso, Bob loved it when I'd come into Allen Arms on San Antonio Street where he worked and *kibbitzed* with his customers about the woes and wonders of circus life.

"You're so down to earth for a celebrity," Bob had once said.

"Some celebrity!" I was always good at batting away nice things people said about me.

I remember the day Bob presented me with that skeet gun. "That thing looks more like a cannon on the Battleship *Arizona* than a shotgun," I said.

Bob laughed along with the other six El Pasoans present in his shop that day. One of those fellows was Colonel Charlie Askins of the U.S. Border Patrol. At the time he was the World Champion Pistol Shot. Charlie later had said that if I'd wanted to, I could have been a world champion myself. But I never quite believed him.

At first, Ingalls had scoffed at my idea of doing a shooting exhibition under the Big Top. "Come on, come on, Clyde, let me show you what I can do," I begged. "I'm not asking for any extra pay. I just want to do more than sit on my keister in the sideshow tent."

He hemmed and he hawed but I finally convinced him. When he actually saw how good I was with my skeet gun and my matched set of ivory-handled, .44 Caliber Peacemakers that Colt Firearms had presented to me as a public relations ploy, he changed his tune. Other than for marching in the parade of freaks and in the specs, it was a big deal for a sideshow act to perform under the big top. I guess management didn't think we were good for much else. So someone higher up than Ingalls had to give my act the stamp of approval. I think part of the reason Ingalls was fit to be tied when I had delayed and resisted signing my contract was because he'd gone out on a limb for me like that.

When I learned that two days later I would be auditioning for none other than John Ringling North, I was petrified. "Don't let me down, Jake," Ingalls had warned.

The day of my audition I was so nervous that I couldn't eat. I perspired plumb through my shirt. My hands were so sweaty I worried I'd lose my grip on my guns and that sweat would drip in my eyes and foul up my sight. John Ringling North had always been courteous to me, but we weren't exactly friends. Talk about a class system; he was my boss's boss's boss.

What if I miss every single shot? I worried. Well, I didn't miss one. When I had finished firing my last round, John Ringling North just stood there. He didn't say a word to me. It was so quiet and I was so anxious. The only thing I remember hearing was the sound of my heart beating. *He must have hated it,* I thought. Then my boss's boss's boss chuckled.

"Why, Jake, you don't have to shoot out the center of the target. Your arms are so long all you have to do is stretch them out and poke out the bullseye," he said. It turns out that he was very impressed with what he saw and approved giving me a try doing a trick shooting routine in the third ring while the clowns were performing, just before the Flying Codonas went on.

That night in Macon, my recollection of how I started my shooting act didn't help me put Artie's accident out of my mind. Well I tossed and turned for hours until I finally drifted off.

I woke up struggling to breathe. I couldn't tell if it was day or night. It was still quiet outside, but I heard an owl crying. I tried to breathe deeply, to calm myself, but my chest felt like it had an anvil on it. I was terrified and certain I was dying. I needed to run, but I didn't know what I was running from or where I was running to. I sensed a ravenous presence lurking nearby. But I wasn't sure if the predator was in my compartment or in my gut. Finally, I caught my breath. Struggling to orient myself, a stream of questions came to mind: *Where am I? What time is it? What day is it? Calm down, Jake,* I told myself. I remembered pulling into the station in Macon the night before. Then I recalled Artie's accident in Atlanta.

It all came back: the fire, the horrible smell of burned hide, the yelping animals, and Doc Jameson's warning that the big cat might not make it. I reached over and found the tiny switch for the light in my compartment and turned it on. The darkness seemed too much for the little lamp as it struggled to illuminate the space. Then I lifted the blinds on the window and saw that we were in a rail yard somewhere. I tried to stand up, but my head swirled. I felt drugged and lay back down. That time I fell into the sleep of a drunken sailor.

I woke to the sun streaming through my window. But even that deep sleep couldn't erase the confusion and fear I felt from the nightmare I had just had. It clung to me. If it had hands, they would have been wrapped around my neck. Though my room was cool my nightshirt was soaked with sweat like it had been just before Papa and I had made our first trek to Hollywood.

Something must be really bothering me, I thought. I had seen horses break their legs because of those damn trip wires they used in pictures. I'd also seen animals injured and die in the circus. But nothing had ever upset me like Artie's accident. Not fully conscious or asleep but in some strange in-between state, I finally propped myself up on my elbows, threw back the covers, and labored to swing my feet onto the floor. I rubbed my eyes as if that could make the fear and confusion pass. But it didn't. There are bad dreams and then there are bad dreams. Some bad dreams you wake up from, with the thankful realization that they were just dreams. This was a nightmare that didn't pass. The images replaying in my mind were so vivid: hiding behind the crate; the escaped tiger; his fangs so close to my flesh, I could almost feel them puncturing my skin; my reflection in his eyes.

That's when it hit me. I had the same dream driving back from Val's horse farm to Manhattan at the beginning of the season. Now, the dream was repeating itself, with more intensity, demanding to not be ignored again.

XXXX

That morning I felt lousy. It was a real struggle to just get myself dressed when all I wanted to do was lie back down in my bunk and go back to sleep. The dream, like Delilah's shears, had sapped me of my strength. Splashing water on my face didn't help. I was still woozy. The only thing that kept me moving was the overwhelming need to find the one person in the circus who I knew might bring me some relief. I had to find out what, if anything, that nightmare meant and more importantly what it was trying to tell me.

XXXX

I found Lya in the hallway, outside the pie car coming back from her breakfast. After I had the nightmare the first time I had wanted her to interpret it but she brushed me off. Daisy had said it wasn't a good time, that she had just received bad news from her family in Germany. Her negative reaction to Val caused me to not pursue the matter. But that morning I was too upset to let any concerns stop me. I didn't waste time with niceties.

"I had a night—"

Lya took one look at me and without me even finishing what I was saying she knew what I needed: "Meet me at my tent at one p.m. before today's matinee."

For the next three hours I did my best to keep busy. I didn't feel like eating. I was too antsy to read, and in that state I certainly didn't want to talk to anyone but Lya. Finally one o'clock rolled around.

Madame Lya did her soothsaying in a small tent off the midway nearby to the sideshow. When I anxiously ducked inside, I was enveloped by the subtle, musty smell of her perfume. The aroma blended easily with the faint scent of sandalwood, given off by the two flickering candles on the small wooden table at the center of the tent. On either side of the table there were two ancient and battered folding chairs. Red glass beads hung from the ceiling. A brass statue of the Hindu elephant god, Lord Ganesh, the remover of obstacles, sat between the candles. The walls, draped with a fabric done in a saffron and ginger-colored Indian motif, gave off a strange warmth. Lya stood by the table. She barely came up to my knees.

She wore a bright purple, cotton robe over her costume, which was a gold, formal evening gown. Lya also wore black fishnet hose and black, patent leather high heels. Her hair hung in neatly ordered black ringlets. The little woman's makeup, particularly around her obsidian eyes, was thick. The rumor was that many a rubberneck had lost his balance during one of her readings and fallen into those dark pools, never to be seen again. I could envision that myself. I knew she was attractive, but I never sensed her womanliness so strongly before. Strangely, it grounded me. For the first time that day, I thought about something besides Artie and my nightmare.

Pointing to one of the chairs, she signaled for me to be seated. I scrunched my body down into a chair never meant for someone my size, and worried for an instant if, as had happened so often in the past, the chair would shatter under my weight. But my concerns about that chair dissolved, replaced by anxiety from my nightmare, which had momentarily disappeared and then came flooding back. Lya sat beside me and took my massive hand in her tiny ones: "Tell me the dream."

I shifted uncomfortably and began. "Since Atlanta and that awful mess with Artie, I've had a hell of a time sleeping. When I got into my bunk last night it was no different. I tossed and turned recalling all the particulars of the accident. Lya, last night was the second time I had the nightmare."

"When was the first time?" she asked in a matter-of-fact tone.

I hesitated for a second not wanting to bring Val's name into the conversation. I wasn't sure if I was trying to protect Val, Lya's feelings, or to ensure that I wouldn't be denied my peace of mind because of Lya's jealousy. I decided to be honest with her. That was a first for me. In the past I always placed everyone else's well-being above my own. I told Lya how I had the nightmare on my way back to the city from Val's farm.

"A-huh," a poker-faced Lya said as she looked beyond me. She nodded. "What about the dream?"

I cleared my throat. Though I felt pressure to hurry through it, I forced myself to speak slowly. "Razorbacks loaded one of many circus wagons onto the train. Simultaneously, a group of rowdy elephants were loaded into one of our elephant cars. That's a scene I have witnessed hundreds of times. But that train was different. The locomotive was futuristic, like something from *Flash Gordon*. It was made of shiny metal that had a chrome-like finish. In my nightmare, as opposed to standing around and chatting or boarding the train, like I typically would do, I hid in the freight yard and watched the whole process from a safe distance." I began to speak more rapidly as if time was running out. "The razorbacks, the noisy elephants, the ultra-modern locomotives, the whole business . . . "

"Slow down, Jake," Lya said. "I've been so rude. Would you like a cup of tea?"

"No, thank you." I exhaled blowing my breath out of my mouth. The candles flickered as I continued to recount my dream. I told her how suddenly there was big trouble. Cage boys frantically began to run around, shouting the alarm. Three of the tigers had escaped. Then I smelled an odor that only those of us who work in circuses or zoos recognize; the piss of big cats. I sensed that close to me, too close to me, something was terribly wrong. I paused for a few seconds to catch my breath, sighed, and continued. "I looked down and spotted the same orange and black striped fugitives crouching behind the discarded crate that I used for cover. Lya, they were half a foot away. I could taste the danger. I knew beyond knowing, that if I looked into the ice-blue eyes of one of those Bengals, they would devour me."

"They had blue eyes?" Lya asked.

"That's right." I wondered if the blue eyes had some significance.

I stopped my story and looked out across the room, indicating that I had finished. Lya sat back and sighed. "What a wonderful dream, Jake," she said, squeezing my hand. "It's all you: the locomotive, the big, blue-eyed Bengals . . . all of it."

I looked at her, puzzled. *How can she describe the nightmare as wonderful when it scared the hell out of me?* I wondered.

"You've been hiding, my friend, trying to stay invisible, comfortable in the past. Now it's time to move forward. It's not safe for you to hide anymore. Do you think you can stay static? Do you think there is security in the same-old, same-old? It's all illusion. We're all planets plummeting through space seeking some kind of an orbit."

I had trouble listening to her. I was bothered by her words, not sure if they made me feel better or worse. Something had changed with Lya. Was this the same woman who had given me hell about wanting to quit the circus?

"What about the tigers? They were really scary. They were going to eat me."

Without hesitating, Lya fired back, "They are guarding the gates at the temple of change. There are three tigers because they're what is earthy, emotional, and sacred in you." She leaned in closer. "It's natural to be terrified of the unknown. Nobody likes to tumble turn and plunge into emptiness."

I had no idea what she was getting at. Yet her words were like a stone thrown into a clear and calm pond of water. They enter with a splash but leave no trace other than a few ripples as they sink and disappear.

It took me years to understand what Lya meant but at that moment, all I felt was frustration. I had a world of more questions troubling me that hadn't crossed my mind before I sat down in her tent. Lya abruptly stopped speaking and looked down at her tiny wristwatch. "We'll have to continue this another time," she said, "but before we do, there is something I need to tell you."

I sat forward, responding to the gravity in her tone and gritted my teeth. I hoped she would give me a clue, some idea, a shred of something I could grasp on to so I could understand my nightmare and unravel my restlessness. Then, out of the blue it came to me. *I bet she's going to tell me she has feelings for me,* I thought.

"I have told you that things are bad for my family in Dresden." I nodded. "Jake, I have a very strong intuition that I need to go home."

Her words hit me like I hit that rube in Madison Square Garden. "Lya, that's a mistake!" I said adamantly. "With the Nazis and their craziness and what looks to be an inevitable war in Europe, why in the hell would you want to put yourself in danger like that?"

"Jake, this isn't up for discussion," Lya snapped. As she spoke I felt myself very protective of her and, for the first time, very attracted to her. "My mind is made up. I've already bought my steamship tickets. After the season ends in Tampa, I take the train to New York and board the *Queen Mary* for my voyage to Hamburg."

Not knowing what else to do, I just sat there looking at Lord Ganesh and shaking my head. Lya stood up. "If you'll excuse me, I'm expecting a paying customer."

I stood up and forced myself to thank her. Besides my concern for Lya, at that moment I also felt unfinished and disappointed that I hadn't found the solace I was seeking. Slowly, as if I was unsure of my footing, I moved away from Lya, awkwardly stooped over, and carefully pulled the flap back so I could exit the soothsayer's tent.

A few weeks later we closed the show in Tampa and Lya left for Germany as she said she would. I would never see her again.

XXXX

When I walked out into the light from Lya's tent, I was momentarily blinded by the sun. As soon as I got acclimated and started to make my way down the midway toward the sideshow tent, several roustabouts darted by.

"He's dying," I heard one of them say. "Doc Jameson said it could be any time now."

My stomach tightened. I followed the roustabouts to the veterinarian's tent. With every step I dreaded what I knew was about to happen. Several other roustabouts and troopers huddled around the outside, murmuring. I pushed by them and made my way inside where it was eerily quiet. The circus was always such a noisy place, so that silence was strange, out of place, almost holy. There were a half-dozen more people inside the vet's tent standing in a semi-circle, staring down at something or someone on the ground. Doc Jameson stood in front of them. He was also looking downward.

I peered over everyone to see what they were staring at. It was Frank Buck sitting on the sawdust, cradling Artie's head in his lap. The Bengal's eyes were closed as if he were sleeping. Artie's breathing was very shallow and raspy. Then he gasped for air. I stepped forward so I was now standing next to Doc. For an instant, Frank looked up at me and then back to Artie. There was something indescribable going on in the tent; something that occurs just before dawn and just after sunset; something from the mysterious in-between world where forms take shape and shadows dissolve. I imagined that outside Doc Jameson's tent there was a jungle where every big cat in the world waited to see what would happen next.

After a few more minutes, Artie's breath became even more labored. It was painful to listen. I sighed and felt that all the muscles in my body wanted to cramp in protest of the inevitable. Then in an instant that beautiful tiger lifted his massive head, opened his eyes, and gazed at Frank Buck. It wasn't a look of fear. I swear that tiger was trying to comfort him. Then Artie sighed peacefully, laid his head back down, and died. I stepped forward, kneeled down and rested my hand on Frank's shoulder.

For the next five minutes the only sound in that tent was the lion tamer weeping.

No one ever mentioned what they saw in Doc Jameson's tent; the tiger's death or Frank Buck's tears. I still fondly remember that big cat and sometimes I can swear I see him out of the corner of my eye. One more thing: after Artie's death, things got better between Frank and me. Our friendship would never be what it had been before Val, but he seemed to forget that he was angry at me. After Macon I never had that nightmare again. I wondered why. But though I was nightmare-free, there was a sadness that settled on me like a thick fog. Whenever I wasn't busy I would think about Artie. You know, I mourned for that cat more than then I ever did for most of the people I know who had died. Was I upset because he was so young? Did Artie remind me of friends who had passed through my life without me ever really knowing them? I wondered if besides noticing my massive frame, would anyone ever really know me?

XXXX

On a cloudy December morning after the 1936 season ended, Frank and I buried Artie's ashes at Ringling's winter headquarters in Sarasota, Florida. That afternoon, when I got back to the modest bungalow I was renting in Gibsonton, there was special-delivery letter waiting for me. It was from Val.

CHAPTER 24

The Ringling School of Art

"Self Portrait," Jake Erlich

As soon as I saw the return address on the fancy parchment envelope, I tore into it and rapaciously read the letter. It must sound crazy; after all, I was barely acquainted with the woman who wrote it. But in those days what I still longed for most was a few more minutes alone with her.

What Val had written only stoked my appetite. I read and re-read how she and her husband would spend Christmas, New Years, and the month of January in Miami. Then in early February, they would visit their friends the Ringlings at their Sarasota estate. She promised that would give us a chance to spend some private time together. I wondered what she meant by private time. I couldn't restrain myself from filling up the empty canvas of her ambiguity with my romantic assumptions. Val confused me. Although she was a married woman, I was sure she had lovers; I mean there was no damned way that her connection with Frank Buck was platonic. And she was so flirtatious. The woman was an enigma.

In her letter she wrote of how proud she was of me. She went on to say that if she had only been blessed with the talent I had, she would have loved to have attended art school. I wondered about that. Based on Val's sculpture that I saw back in the basement of Madison Square Garden when we first had met, there was no doubt in my mind that she was gifted. It seemed to me that with her ability and her husband's money, art school should have been easily within her grasp. Yet strangely she made it sound like an impossibility. I was to learn that in art, as in love, Val preferred to dabble.

XXXX

I moved to Gibsonton, where many Ringling Bros freaks lived during the winter months, and counted the days until Val would arrive. In the past, for the brief time I needed to be close to Sarasota and Ringling Bros winter quarters during the off season, I always resided in a stately, old hotel in nearby Tampa.

Tampa was a jewel of a city. It had a university with blue tiled roofs and golden domed Moorish architecture. I loved gazing out of my hotel room's balcony at the Hillsborough River and the graffiti on its stone banks left by all the college crews that had raced in its waters. I imagined the athletes who painted those words as celebrated warriors battling the ravages of time and its cruel agenda to erase them and wash away their heroic feats from memory. I wondered who would paint my name on stone after I was gone. How would I be remembered; as a comedian in silent flickers, as a circus freak?

I loved my time in that tropical city with cigar factories in the vibrant Ybor section of town where, legend had it, sweet, young maidens rolled rich tobacco leaves on their thighs. Ybor also housed one of my favorite restaurants, the Colombia. There, circus friends and I frequently treated ourselves to *paella* flavored with black cardamom and saffron while fiery, castanet-snapping *señoritas* danced flamenco.

During those days, when I had to go to Ringling Bros' offices in Sarasota for a new costume fitting or for some other circus business, I would take a trolley for the two-hour trip along the beach. The whole way there I'd lose myself, gazing at indigo and turquoise ocean. I loved those outings.

Someday I envisioned an engineering genius would build a massive skyway between Tampa and Sarasota. It would magically climb almost as high as the billowy, animal-shaped clouds that drifted over the bay, hovering as if they were hung from strings by some divine puppet master. That futuristic bridge would cut the travel time to Sarasota in half. Until then, if I stayed in Tampa, I had to be satisfied with a lengthy commute. But that winter, due to my commitment to attend art school, I rented a place in Gibsonton.

To get from my small bungalow to class and for the frequent trips to Tampa I decided that I needed to buy an automobile. Buying cars was more costly for me than for the average Joe. After I purchased my brand-new 1936 Buick Series 80 Town Car with a nailhead engine at the dealership in Tampa, as always, I hired a mechanic to remove the front bench. He then extended the steering wheel nineteen inches so I could drive from the back seat. It took two parking attendants to handle that jalopy. One would pull himself up on the steering column, grab the wheel, and peer out over the dashboard. The other one would sit on the floor operating the gas pedal, clutch, and brakes with his hands. They looked like little boys trying to drive their father's car. Those automobiles were expensive to buy, customize, and maintain. But you know, I did save on theft insurance. You see, I didn't need any. I was the only one who could drive the damn things. Within a few months of buying that Buick, it would save my life.

The first Monday after New Year's, I would start my classes. I had no idea what I was in for. My schedule would be very busy and afford little idle time to pine for Val, but I would still find myself daydreaming a lot about her. I would imagine that by day we would attend the Ringling School of Art together. On breaks we would critique each other's work. At night there would be chichi art openings, candlelight dinners at Siesta Key serenaded by a Jamaican steel drum band, and barefoot moonlit strolls under swaying royal palms on Lido Beach. But those lovely fantasies were a far cry from the real demands of my classes, which would consist of seminars on photography, life drawing, sculpture, and oil painting. Although I was sure that the students and the teachers would each have their invisible club foot, their secret sources of shame and inferiority that made them feel different and unacceptable, no one in that school would end up appearing to be out of the ordinary but me.

The Dolls helped me set up housekeeping in Florida. I thank my lucky stars I had such wonderful friends. Ever since I began working at Ringling Bros they had looked out for me. Few people in this world knew me as well as Harry and Daisy. Besides being my closest friend in the show, Harry had also become a role model for me. Even though I was so big and he was so small, what with all the taunts and teasing and cruel tricks, we'd had similar experiences growing up. Harry told me that when he was a young man in Germany, he and some friends went to a beer hall in Bavaria. When he went to the W.C., four drunks grabbed him. Harry fought back valiantly, bloodying one bully's nose and giving another a fat lip. But if his friends had not come looking for him, he would have ended up in the urinal. But besides the fact that he was courageous, what impressed me most about him was how he always carried himself with dignity, and how kind, caring, and considerate he was to his family and friends. Harry was practical, resolute, and wise. Once, when I was bemoaning my life, I remember asking him how he felt about having such a small body:

"To be honest, at times, I have been bitter about my destiny; but at this point in my life I can't do anything about it. So I try to make the best of the situation. I've concluded that you're either a king or a knave; it isn't what I say or do or how big or small you are. I try to give the world the best I can and hope that the best will come back to me."

During the winter break I was almost a permanent fixture at the Doll's place. At their house in Gibsonton, the size of the furniture was a problem for me. So when I visited their home, I would usually sit in their garden on a huge, heavily reinforced rattan patio chair they had made especially for me. Sometimes for meals or in inclement weather, they would move it inside.

The Sunday night before my first week of classes, the Dolls invited me to their home. I loved Daisy's cooking. She had prepared one of her specialties, Pompano in the Bag. But their custom built table was so small I had to balance my plate on my lap. After dinner, Daisy began to clear the dishes. I started to stand up and insisted that I help.

"You just relax, Jake. You're a prized student now. You need to save your energy for school," she demanded. "I can't believe the whole thing that society dame and Ringling concocted for you is actually happening. You know, I still don't trust that broad as far as I can throw her." Then she walked over to the carved maple cupboard that rested against their dining room wall, stepped on a stool, removed a crystal ashtray, and set it down in front of her brother. "I can't put my finger on it, but there's something off about her," Daisy continued. I looked at Harry. He didn't say a word and just stared down at the table avoiding my gaze. Then Daisy picked a cup and a saucer from the table and turned to look up at me. "Jake, I sure hope your interest in that wench is—as they say—purely academic."

"Don't worry, Daisy. Val's just been very kind to me." I tried to head Daisy off at the pass and avoid any more discussion about her character, my romantic intentions, and the argument I knew would follow.

"Kind, my ass," Daisy was baiting me. I didn't bite and just sat there quietly. "In her last letter from Dresden, Lya asked about you, your highfalutin female friend, and your art classes." It appeared that Daisy sensed the tension and shifted topics. I was relieved. "I'll be sure to bring her up to date the next time I write to her," she added.

"How is she?" Hearing Lya's name made me miss her. I was surprised how much.

"She says that things are tough." Daisy went on to say Lya felt there was evil lurking around every corner in Germany. "Although others chose to deny what was happening, she and her family could not turn a blind eye on it," Daisy said. "Even though she's only half Jewish and convent-schooled, Lya is disturbed by the Jew-hating, which is becoming more violent every day. She is also deeply troubled by newly passed euthanasia laws."

"What are those?" I asked.

"The Nazis made a law that allows them to execute people who are crippled or retarded, like a veterinarian would destroy a rabid dog." I shook my head and looked away, recalling the frightening eugenicist rally that Val and I fled in upstate New York. "Lya wants to get her folks out of Germany as soon as she is able, but it's not easy." I nodded in agreement. "Lately she's been particularly alarmed."

"Why's that?" What Daisy said worried me.

"A few days after she got home, police detectives came to her parents' house. Then they came back again. Each time their behavior was more threatening. They interrogated her about a newspaper photo of Lya and J.P. Morgan from the front page of the *Washington Post*."

"That's the PR shot Clyde Ingalls had taken after Morgan testified at Senate hearings last year," Harry explained.

"That's right," Daisy continued.

"The press loved that photo with Lya posed sitting on Morgan's lap and all. But it seems Hitler hated it," Harry said. "That lunatic has an axe to grind with J.P. Morgan and anyone associated with him."

"Why?" I asked.

"Around the same time that that photo appeared in the papers, Morgan's bank turned the Nazis down for a loan. I sure hope no harm comes to our friend because of it," Harry added.

Daisy looked agitated. "Enough about that; would anyone like an after-dinner drink?"

"Not for me," I said.

A moment later Daisy had cleared the last of the dinner dishes and left us alone.

"I like having you over, Jake. It's not only your scintillating conversation, but when you come to the house my sister gives me a pass from doing the dishes," Harry said. I kept thinking about Lya and worrying she was in danger.

Harry pushed his chair back from the table, pulled a Pall Mall from the package in his breast pocket, took out a cigarette, tapped it on the table, lit it, and blew a couple of smoke rings in the air. "How do you feel about going back to school?" he asked.

I shrugged and told him how ambivalent I felt. Harry shifted his tiny body in the wooden captain's chair that seemed to swallow him up. I explained that on the one hand, I was actually looking forward to studying art and, for the first time since my sophomore year in high school, being back in a classroom.

"High school? Jake, we always thought you were a college man," Harry replied, snuffing out his cigarette in the ashtray.

I reminded him that I had started making pictures when I was just sixteen. I told him how my schedule in Hollywood was so demanding that there was no time for school. "College, you say?" I folded my napkin and put it down on the table. "I never even graduated from high school." I went on to confide in Harry that my knowledge came from what Lya Graff had called the *University of the Universe*. "I also read a lot," I added. I have always loved to read. My library consisted of books on everything from horses and botany to mythology and psychoanalysis.

I shared with Harry how excited I was to experience an environment that cherished knowledge and imparted wisdom. It would turn out that the Ringling School of Art did, at a cost, dispense knowledge, but certainly not wisdom. But I also confided that I felt that I was wasting time. "After all, there's a depression going on. The world is going to hell in a handbasket and I'll be spending my time painting, sculpting, and taking pictures. Can you think of anything less productive?" I asked.

"Look, Jake, it depends how you define *productive*," Harry answered. "It doesn't have to mean working with a pick and shovel all day or dying the richest man on the planet. Listen, buddy, not everybody is blessed with the talent you have and the opportunity to develop it. All season long you break your balls. But I think this is about something besides being productive." Harry paused. "It seems to me there's something else bothering you about going back to school."

"Harry, you've got my number." I went on to admit that though I was excited about school, I was also very anxious about not fitting in.

"You think you're the only Jew?" he joked.

We both laughed. "Well, Harry, here I go again," I said, looking him in the eyes. "I'm afraid I'm going to feel like Gulliver in the Land of Lilliput."

At thirty, I knew myself well enough to predict that in a new situation like art school I would agonize about being different. That would precipitate a storm of painful self-consciousness, which would surely prevent me from taking full advantage of the experience and drinking it in for all it was worth. New beginnings were always so exhausting for me. They usually released the part of my personality that I'd jokingly given a name: Pharaoh, the all-powerful, evil one who lived between my ears and constantly tried to enslave me.

Looking forward to Val's visit the way I did helped me to not worry so much about that new beginning. It was like a narcotic that blocks out the pain of a broken arm. I wondered what would have happened if Val hadn't been planning to visit me in Florida. Would the gunnysack full of feelings I carried around have made me crazier than I already was? Would it have been too much for me? Would those nasty feelings have pushed me to step out onto the ledge of another building for a swan dive onto concrete, but that time in Florida?

"My friend, don't you worry about it. Even though your pants are a lot bigger, remember the other students and the professors at that place all put their trousers on just like you do; one leg at a time."

As Harry spoke, I sighed and determined that that time I would not let Pharaoh take charge and ruin things. It would turn out that all of my concerns about not fitting in at that school would be the least of my worries.

Later that night, on the drive home from Harry and Daisy's place, my head buzzed with equal parts excitement and worry. I was so preoccupied about my classes the next day that I missed the turnoff toward my bungalow. When I realized what I'd done, I decided to just keep driving.

Five miles down the highway I took the cut off to Nokomis Beach. After I parked my car by the side of the road, I removed my shoes and socks and rolled up my pants for a late-night walk on the shore. At that hour I had the beach to myself and didn't have to worry about any unwanted stares. Gazing out at the Gulf of Mexico, I heard seabirds in the distance, but on that moonless night it was too dark to see beyond the phosphorescent breakers. After about ten minutes of walking, my mind cleared. As I walked I thought of myself as a *yanki*. You remember Cuco told me *yankis* are star men who look down from above. But that night on the beach in Florida, I looked down not so much on everyone and everything else, but on myself.

What in the hell are you doing, Jake? I asked from my perch in the clouds. *Why are you even here? Is it because of some infatuation with a married dame or some need for the validation of an art school diploma?* At that instant a large wave broke, rushed to shore, soaked me from the knees down and brought me down to earth. The water felt good. I just kept walking.

After a few minutes, I sat down, lay back in the sand, and looked up at the stars. *I want a canvas that stretches from Hollywood to Manhattan, as vast as the Milky Way*, I thought; *an epic canvas where I can splash vivid colors and paint what I've seen and felt and what I fear: a giant child drowning in the Rio Grande; Hollywood marquees with my name in neon lights; blizzards in the desert; blindness, bullies, banner lines and blowers; crowded midways and circus parades; breadlines and hobo camps; fortune tellers; married women and menageries with pachyderms; gorillas and tigers who growl in the night. I want to paint some kind of meaning and order out of it all.*

The next thing I knew I was in a deep sleep. Soon I was dreaming of a summer storm somewhere on the plains. Rain was coming down in buckets. It was a real blowdown. The wind was God-awful bad. Roustabouts cried for help. An orange and red lightning bolt illuminated the night just enough for me to see Val in a ragged scarlet gown and the sideshow tent that was torn in two. With its guy wires and stakes ripped free from the ground, the tent was about to blow away. I ran to help but fell in the mud and couldn't get up.

Rain pounding on my face from a midnight squall that had blown in from the gulf roused me from where I'd fallen asleep on the beach. Running back to my car, I felt disoriented. By the time I got to my Buick, I was sopping wet.

XXXX

For somebody who was ambivalent about art school, I was sure taking the whole business seriously. Two days before school started, to get my bearings and be sure I would be on time, I had even walked the campus and carefully studied the map of the place. That's when I understood why the brochure had stated that the Ringling School of Art was the largest institution of its type in the southeast.

Monday morning my first course was to be held in a small white stucco building on the east side of campus. I recall the excitement I felt when I read the quote painted above the entrance: *Life is short. Art is long.* As I walked through the place, everything sparkled as if it was new and had recently been waxed; the walls, the floors, the windows, even the other students. *This is what it must be like in college,* I thought proudly.

The room for my photography class was empty and dark. *Something's not right.* I ran into the hall, fighting the panicked feeling that I was lost. I walked as quickly as I could to the administration building across the quad. Hopefully they could straighten me out. With each step I grew more and more anxious. *I'm going to be late for my first class. What a great way to start my art education.* When I walked into the administration office all of the students in that packed space turned around and stared at me. The sole secretary on duty was overwhelmed. I needed to take matters into my own hands. I reached into my pocket and took out my class roster again. Then it hit me. I realized I had been so nervous that I somehow had been looking at the location of my first class on Tuesday. I walked faster. I must have entered three other buildings looking for that photography class. In each one the hallways were crowded and noisy. I tried my best to dodge and wind my way through the crowd without smacking into anyone or drawing too much attention to myself.

That's when I bumped into a short, middle-aged man dressed in tweed with a bushy head of sandy-brown hair. I whacked the stack of books and battered black briefcase he was clutching out of his hands and onto the floor, almost knocking him over as well.

"Watch where you're going, you jack in apes," the little man said angrily.

"I'm so sorry, sir. I didn't mean to," I replied obsequiously, trying to help him pick up his books. It seemed that each and every one of the students in that hallway had stopped what they were doing and stared at us. The little man appeared as self-conscious and embarrassed as I was.

"Just leave them be," he shouted as he grabbed the books I held in my hands. "Be careful before you end up hurting someone." That tweedy, overwrought man would turn out to be Dr. DeWitt, the teacher for my oil painting class. Very soon I would wish that I hadn't started out on the wrong foot with him.

Breathless and sweating profusely, I finally arrived at my photography class just as it was about to begin. There was only one seat left. Wouldn't you know it; it was situated in the center of the front row. I had no choice. Klutz that I was, I clumsily made my way over and around the other students who were already seated. Then I tried to force my body to fit into an awful desk that seemed to not want any part of me. That institutional piece of wooden furniture was more like an apparatus from a medieval torture chamber. Snickers and laughter from some of the other students added to how mortified I felt. I thought I must have looked like I was trying to squeeze into a baby's chair. My face flushed with embarrassment. If I could have, I would have run out of that room, but that wasn't an option. Slowly I stood up and made my way to the back wall, doing my damndest to not to step on anyone's feet. It was evident that no one had made any special arrangements for someone of my size to sit in class. Eventually and grudgingly the school provided some furniture that fit me. But for the two weeks it took to make that happen, I just stood at the back of each class, sticking out from everyone else like a giant, sore thumb.

Unlike my other classes, photography was a delight. Our first assignment that week was to have a classmate shoot a portrait of us. We were then to critique it for the class. Ever since my friend Ewing Waterhouse introduced me to the art of taking pictures when I was fourteen back in El Paso, I had been captivated by cameras and photography. That fascination only grew during my time in Hollywood.

Later that week, when I examined the photo that had been taken of me I saw more and more gray hair in my temples. *Look at those* canas (*white hairs*), I said to myself. I wondered why it was that I had survived to my thirties, when most of the giants I knew had not made it out of their twenties. The portrait somehow made me recall my last encounter with young Wadlow. *Growing as fast as he was, how long could that boy survive?* I asked myself. *I don't know how much time I have left either*, I thought with a shudder. I recollected the graffiti on the banks of the Hillsborough River in nearby Tampa and felt a new urgency to not waste any time. I visualized the phrase from a psalm my father had printed and framed on the wall behind his desk at Geneva Loan: "Give me a heart of wisdom, oh Lord, that I may number my days." Though I didn't like to think about it, I felt certain some blind force of nature had already numbered them for me.

I think that helps to explain my attitude about my classes. You see, all my courses weren't as exciting as photography. I think that maybe the reason

I detested my life drawing, sketching, sculpting, and oil painting classes so much was because it felt like they were a waste of my time. I felt crazed, like a mystic compelled to directly experience the divine and not fritter away the little time I had studying religion. If it wasn't for Val and not wanting to disappoint her, I would have left after the second week.

While my photography professor, Mr. Gillcrest, taught us about light and shadow and urged us to take license to explore and experiment and to express ourselves in the medium of film, the other professors did just the opposite. They were narrow-minded priests who required exact, unquestioning adherence to the catechism of how to hold a brush and pencil and place charcoal on paper and oil paint on canvas.

I should have known there would be trouble after the welcoming lecture the headmaster, Dr. Crane, gave to an assembly of all the students at the end of the second week of classes. Something that he said—or maybe it was his condescending tone—made me remember a conversation with Frida Kahlo the last time I saw her, when I told her I'd accepted the scholarship to attend art school. At that time she shared an experience she had at the National Preparatory School in Mexico City before her crippling accident. I hadn't realized it then, but her story was a not-so-veiled warning.

"It was a heady time back then. We students weren't just artists, but irreverent revolutionaries," Frida explained, going on to tell me that once she and a group of her closest friends, I think she called them *Las Cachuchas*, even tried to take over the campus in protest over some repressive rules the administration put into place. Imagine that.

What infuriated me came after his lecture. When Dr. Crane asked if anyone had questions, a young female student shyly inquired whether we would be exposed to the techniques of the modern artists who had exhibited their work at the Armory Show. I wondered what the Armory Show was as the pasty-faced headmaster peered over his monocle at the young girl.

"The impressionists, the expressionists, the abstract painters; they're not artists. What they do is profane anarchy; garbage, a Bolshevik bastardization of classic representation. If you want to learn that trash you should go elsewhere, young lady."

Even though I knew little about modern art, what I heard him say enraged me. I had reluctantly decided to attend the Ringling School of

Art primarily to please Val. Though I didn't want to admit it, I wanted to try my hand as an artist. Even though getting a formal education in art wasn't that important to me, Dr. Crane's arrogance made me wonder if I had made an awful mistake. At that time I wondered if my emotional response was because Crane seemed like a bully. Since I turned seven bullies had set me off. But after all these years, I think it was something else entirely.

Back then I was just beginning to accept my differences and find a way to express them. That was a time in the world when despots were trying to crush, stamp out, and destroy differences. I'm sorry to say that that is still going on. I believe I was offended that the place I was to study art—a place sponsored by a showman who had founded the circus where I earned my livelihood—appeared to be run by tyrants who were threatened by art that was different from what they thought it should be. It seems that Dr. Crane and Major General Moseley were cut from the same cloth. It was fitting that Crane was the headmaster of a repressive school.

Sitting there in that auditorium, I imagined what Diego Rivera would have said had he been present at that lecture. Despite the concerns I would come to have over how he treated his wife, I did admire his courage. At that moment I was certain Diego would have jumped to his feet and shouted, "You are an emotionally constipated lackey of the ruling class, a petty bourgeois slave of fashion, blind to artistic truth, and frightened of freedom. If you want exact representation use a goddamned camera!"

I wanted to defend that young woman and say something, to challenge the haughty headmaster like Diego would have, but I didn't. I just sat there imagining Diego doing it, and feeling my heart hammer.

XXXX

As day followed day in art school, I did my best to repress any revolutionary inclinations I might have had enough so I could tolerate the place and learn from my professors. To be honest, I did appreciate their knowledge, skill, and technique. But as time went by, I also found it increasingly difficult to stomach their stifling rigidity; a rigidity that was suffocating any sparks of creativity I had. Despite my experience at that school, not because of it, I would come to love the god of art and the importance of expressing myself.

I'm not proud to admit it: I think I mostly tolerated my discomfort at that school because I knew Val would be visiting soon. I rationalized that the aggravation I experienced was just a steep staircase I needed to climb up to get to her. She was the reward, the medicine, and the purpose for the pain. To me, studying art was still secondary; a lark. My eyes were on the prize. That was Val.

XXXX

After a month of school, she and her husband finally arrived in Sarasota. Val called me as soon as she got to town and we planned to meet three days later, at seven o'clock on Friday evening. You can imagine, all week long that's all I could think about.

By eight p.m. on the appointed Friday, I was dejected and anxious. I sat alone at the bar in Dean's Diner, a seafood dive near the beach, nursing a Ramos Gin Fizz and wondering where Val was. *Something must have happened,* I thought. But after another half hour of waiting and another drink, I knew she was not going to show up. I started to stand up to leave. That's when I felt a tap on my back and turned around. When I saw her smiling face, my anxiety and dejection dissolved.

"How's tricks?" she said, climbing onto her knees on top of the bar stool next to mine. Then Val threw her arms around me and gave me a warm hug and a kiss on the cheek. "Will you ever forgive me for being so late?" she asked coyly. "My husband didn't leave for his business dinner in Tampa when he said he would. I just couldn't get away," she explained. Then Val reached up to me and tenderly put her hand on my cheek. "My dear, sweet Jake, we have so much catching up to do."

During the next two hours, over stone crab dinner and a bottle of Bordeaux, we did just that. Val told me about their trip abroad and what she described as the inevitability of another war. I told her about my run-in with Wadlow and Artie's death. After dinner, we sipped our coffee and shared a slab of Key Lime Pie.

"Tell me about your first month of art school Jake," Val insisted. "I'm absolutely green with envy."

"School is fine," I said, wishing I was a better liar or that I could have been more blunt with her and owned up to how unhappy I really was. But I just couldn't.

"What do you mean 'school is fine,' Jake?" Val asked, as if she could read my mind.

"Well, I'm learning a lot," I said.

"'I'm learning a lot!' Is that all you can say? My good man, where's your passion?" I wondered where her's was. Val's smile faded into a frown. "You are not that happy there, are you?" Her question felt more like an indictment and put me on the spot.

"Well, I . . . I . . . " I stuttered, unable to bring myself to tell her the truth. My hesitation spoke volumes. She looked genuinely disappointed. I felt I had let her down. I had dreaded that.

"Now, Jake, this is a once-in-a-lifetime chance." Her tone became sterner. "The Ringling School doesn't admit just anyone. It's hard as hell to get in there. Unlike all the other students, you have no formal art background, so it took us a lot of work. Even though you're a performer in Ringling Bros we still had to pull a million strings for you. I don't want to hear that you are even thinking of quitting. You need to buck up and make the most of this opportunity."

As Val lectured me, I noted the coldness in her that I had first observed after the eugenics rally. I felt I'd been banished. That made me panicky. She stopped, took a breath and, without giving me a chance to respond, continued. "Dr. Crane and his staff have impeccable credentials. People come to study with them from all over the world. Anybody who is anybody in the art scene knows them and the school." She reached across the table and put her hand on my forearm. She appeared to soften. I felt relieved. "Jake, promise me you will see this through. Don't let me down."

I wanted to tell her about the headmaster's arrogance and how I felt stifled, but I just looked down at my half-empty wine glass. After a minute, I looked into those beautiful doe eyes. "Don't worry, Val. I promise. I'll see it through." I was grateful to have been reprieved from my exile.

She took hold of my right hand and squeezed it. "That's my big guy. Well, it's getting late, Jake, and I need to be getting back to my husband and the Ringlings."

"It's early," I said, looking down at my wristwatch. "We got to spend so little time together. Do you really have to go?"

"Yes, I do. My husband will worry."

I'm ashamed to admit it, but I didn't care how her husband felt. It put me in mind of King David and how he'd sent Bathsheba's mate to die in battle, so he could have her for himself. For the first time, I understood why King David did what he did. I knew that if I had that power I'd have done the same thing to have Val. I paid the check and asked the hostess to call Val a cab.

At that moment, I felt genuinely disheartened, maybe like Val felt when she accurately intuited that I was unhappy. As we made our way through the bar I was too upset to even notice or care if anyone was staring at us. Then we walked in silence to the parking lot and into the soft Florida night. The only light on the rickety front steps at Dean's came from the flashing neon restaurant sign next to the highway and an old light fixture powered by a single bulb that hung over the door. Val sat down on the top step leading to the doorway and I sat on the bottom step. When we turned toward one another I saw that we were face to face.

For the next painful minute we sat there in silence.

"Val, you confuse me," I finally said, emboldened by the fact that I didn't know when I would see her again. "Do you remember the last time I saw you?" I didn't give her a chance to respond. "I do. It was in the back of your limo at your horse farm. You were drenched by a downpour." Val stared intensely at me. "Do you remember what you said? 'You're special to me, Jake.' Well I don't feel special right now." I was surprised by my candor. "I have missed you and I was looking forward to tonight but I don't get that feeling from you." My right leg stared to cramp and I stretched it out to its full length. Then I continued. "Besides your interest in my art education is there even an *us* to talk about? Are we just friends?"

Val brushed the hair out of her eyes and scooted across the rough wooden stair, closer to me. "Us?" she said, laughing and looking away. "It's complicated, Jake."

It was almost impossible to take anything in but her intoxicating fragrance. She smelled like a bouquet of lilacs after light rain. Without uttering another word, Val moved even closer to me. I found it hard to concentrate and even harder to stay angry. She reached across and put her hands on either side of my face and kissed me on the lips. I drew her to me and kissed her back, hard, like I'd never kissed anyone before. I felt the blood rush from my brain; whatever was happening, it left me light-headed. After all these years, I can honestly say I can still feel her hands on my face and taste that kiss.

If it hadn't been for the harsh glare of the cab's headlights and the grinding sound of tires turning onto the gravel in front of Dean's, I think that kiss might have gone on forever. Val quickly stood up and straightened her skirt. I stood up as well and followed her to the taxi. I closed the door and the cab pulled away.

That night I had a hell of a time sleeping. I imagined all kinds of scenarios that might play out between us. Some had happy endings; some were tragic; all of them were unreal. The one that upset me the most was that things wouldn't get worse or better. They would stay exactly the same.

Around three a.m., I started to doze off. Just before I fell asleep I thought that despite the fact that I didn't really like the Ringling School of Art, I would have to make it work.

XXXX

I honestly did think I could make it all work out, but several things happened to prove me wrong. As my Mama always said: "*Mensch tracht und Gott lacht* (Men talk and God laughs)." It didn't help matters any that for the next week, though I tried and tried, I could never reach Val. I called her several times and even sent her a card. Needless to say, our midnight walk on Lido Beach never happened. We didn't even meet for another meal. I was going crazy thinking about her, but there wasn't much I could do about it. After all, I couldn't exactly sneak around Sarasota spying on Val and not expect to be noticed. I guess I would have made a piss-poor private detective.

Then, I finally received another letter from her. In it she explained that she would be unable to see me for the rest of her time in Sarasota. She and her husband had been invited to take a cruise with the Ringlings on the *Symphonia*, their two-hundred-and-twenty-foot yacht, down to Cuba. Oh, the life of the rich during the Depression. I can make jokes about it now, but then . . . then . . . especially after that good-night kiss, I expected more; at least the courtesy of a phone call. It was excruciating. The only ones I had any contact with outside of school were Harry and Daisy. Truth be told, I was lonely and livid.

Despite my disappointment and the awful experience I was to have a few days later in my oil painting class, I did try to make the best of my time at the school.

XXXX

"Erlich, I see you are having trouble holding the brush as I have said an artist should." DeWitt snarled, circling behind my easel and me like a little pesky mutt nipping at my heels. I couldn't help but think that ever since our harsh introduction he had it in for me.

"Yes, I am having trouble professor. But if I can paint holding the brush the way I do, what difference does it make?" I answered. I heard the other students murmuring in the background.

In my two months at the institute I found that the people I encountered were no different than those I'd come in contact with everywhere else. Any idealized illusions I had about artists being less neurotic and more principled, a kindly, utopian, accepting brotherhood of the creative, were soon dashed. Don't get me wrong—there were several who were genuinely friendly; an interesting, intelligent and principled lot that I would be proud to call friends. And there were also those who couldn't have cared less who I was. Those two groups of people didn't bother me. Among those who did bother me were the ones who were drawn to me because I was a celebrity or because they were fascinated by my freakishness. Then, as in every group I ever dealt with, from Hollywood to Hanover, there were those who were threatened by me. As a new student, I thought it would be different. I mean, they couldn't have been intimidated by my artistic ability. At that point, nobody, let alone me, knew a thing about what I could or couldn't accomplish as an artist. I have always thought that I threaten some people in a primal place that makes them want to use me as the model for cave drawings and hunt me down and kill me. I felt as if some of the ones I intimidated were another brand of predator. They were jackals, stalking me, waiting for me to make a mistake. I used to think I was paranoid. As a matter of fact, I sometimes still do. But that feeling wasn't paranoia. I had experienced it many times before. "You're not crazy my friend," Lya once said after a performance in Pittsburgh when I described how I felt. "In German, we even have a name for it. We call it *schadenfreude*. It's the elves laughing when the giant stumbles."

But what really blindsided me at the Ringling School of Art was how many of the jackals were my teachers; especially DeWitt.

"Are you questioning me, Erlich?" Dr. DeWitt admonished. I could feel the eyes of the other nine students focused on me and the humiliation that was about to take place. The murmurs disappeared, replaced by a deafening buzz in my ears. I stared down at the little middle-aged man. "If you can't even hold the brush the way the rest of us do, maybe you ought to think twice about being here. Maybe it's time for you to go back to the freak show?"

I was so embarrassed and angry. If class hadn't ended at that moment, I feared I would hurl that pip-squeak of a professor and all of his *should*s and *must*s out of the window.

A few seconds later I was standing all alone in the empty classroom, my only company ten easels arrayed in two large semicircles and the pungent odor of turpentine. I tried and tried to hold the brush the way my teacher had commanded but I just couldn't. My massive hand and fingers would not allow it. I recalled Val's look of chilly disappointment when she concluded how I felt about that place. I remember how she warmed up when I'd promised her that I would stay at the school. I snapped the brush I was holding in half and hurled it across the classroom.

I don't exactly understand it, but after Val let me down and DeWitt humiliated me, something snapped besides that brush. I started to take my classes more seriously. It came to me that it wasn't so much that the courses at the school were a waste of time, as I was wasting time by not being fully awake. I guess I had been off in some fantasy land in my head, imagining a make-believe castle where Val and I would live the day after tomorrow; a castle with haunted closets full of dusty costumes made of linen, feathers, and lace for actors that would never be born and plays that would never know the thrill of an overture on opening night. Val's voyage to Cuba and the DeWitt's put-down slapped me back to the here and now. Strangely, I started to make some new friends in my classes and to appreciate just how talented some of the other students were.

XXXX

I don't want you to get the wrong idea. Art school wasn't all about the high drama of revolution, rejection, and rebirth. A good part of it, like any education, consisted of tedium, triviality, and the struggle to learn new things. Sometimes I even had fun. That usually occurred when my professors weren't around. Then I felt free to experiment and express myself with camera, clay, paint, and charcoal. It's weird and somehow fitting that it wasn't my anger at the headmaster or how Dr. DeWitt had humiliated me that made me break my promise to Val and finally quit art school. Rather it was a quiet conversation with a girl from South Carolina that took place about a month before my program was scheduled to end.

On an absolutely gorgeous Tuesday afternoon that demanded to be celebrated outdoors, I saw the young woman who had asked Dr. Crane the provocative question after his speech. She was sitting alone on a mound of grass on the quad, eating a sandwich under a palm tree. Her white linen dress and big, white sun hat stood in stark contrast to the orange, red, and purple bird of paradise flowers just behind her. Although there was a relatively small student body, that was the first time I had seen her since the beginning of school. Something she said that day in her controversial query to Crane had stuck with me, and I wanted to ask her about it. *Carpe diem*, I said to myself.

I strolled over to the mound where she was eating, looked down at her, and smiled. "Hello, my name is Jake," I said, softly introducing myself.

She looked up at me, raised her eyebrows and smiled. "I know who you are. Everybody does," she replied, brushing a wave of her unruly blond hair out of her face with her right hand. "You're really good. Just last week I admired a painting of yours that I saw displayed in Dr. DeWitt's studio.

"After how DeWitt has treated me I'm surprised he didn't put that thing in the trash."

"He can sure be a crotchety so-and-so. And with him, it's his way or the highway. You don't want to cross DeWitt," she added.

"You can say that again." I laughed, comforted to speak to someone who agreed with me about that place, or at least about DeWitt.

"Jake, I love your colors; they're bold yet romantic like Lautrec. I've never seen a perspective like yours; always looking down on things. And your subject matter . . . well, I've never seen anyone paint about the circus."

"Thanks for the kind words."

"I mean it . . . it's not malarkey," she said.

"Well, I love color. I paint the world as I see it and from up here it seems I look down on just about everyone and everything. I paint what I know and one of the few things I do know about, firsthand, is the circus." I lowered myself to my left knee. "What's your name?" I asked.

"I'm Carolyn. Carolyn Lynch," she said, drawing her knees to her chest.

"Tell me about you, Carolyn." I was surprised by how easy it was to talk to her.

"Well, I, too, am a painter. I'm from Charleston, South Carolina."

"What do you like to paint?" I inquired

"What I really love is watercolors. I love painting pictures of the dilapidated plantation houses near where I live," she explained.

"Carolyn Lynch, do you mind if I sit down?" I wondered at my new confidence and how my words, like water after a snow melt, flowed without hesitation. Usually when I spoke with a woman for the first time the experience was fraught with anxiety and stuttering, but not that afternoon talking to Carolyn. Maybe I wasn't anxious because Carolyn was so complimentary or maybe it was because we had something in common.

"Be my guest, Jake," she said with a huge welcoming smile.

I slowly lowered myself down to the grass where she sat. Because of my massive size, doing something like that, so easy and taken for granted by others, was a major production requiring focus and attention. As I gradually sat down, my body moved in increments. I imagined my movement resembled that of an ancient castle's drawbridge slowly being lowered, with creeks and clanks over a moat.

"Carolyn, since the beginning of school I have wanted to tell you I was bothered by how rudely Dr. Crane responded to your question. I was very disappointed in him."

"Well, I half knew how he was going to answer me before I even asked. But the troublemaker in me couldn't let it be." She raised her shoulders as if to punctuate her words. "You see, like so many schools in the country this place is about realism, not emotional expression." As she continued I began to feel that I liked her. "The powers that be want us to paint things as they are and not as we feel them," she continued.

"Did you know that before you signed up to come here?" I asked.

"Yes, I did."

"I didn't. I didn't know or care enough about art school or art to understand the difference."

"Hum," she said thoughtfully.

"If you don't mind me asking, why the hell did you come here?" I said.

"My parents are both classically trained art teachers. Ever since the Armory Show in 1913—"

"That's what I wanted to ask you about—" I blurted out impulsively; then quickly apologized. "I'm sorry I interrupted you. Please continue."

"Since the Armory Show both of my parents have been wringing their hands about the future of art. The only place they would let me go was a conservative, regional school like this. So my choices were pretty clear; get married even though I wasn't in love or go to the Ringling School of Art. What were you going to ask me? It seemed pretty important."

"It's just that you mentioned the Armory Show. I have no idea what that is."

Carolyn nodded and went on to tell me that the Armory Show was the first major exhibit of modern art in the United States. It took place in 1913 in New York City at the Armory. As she spoke, she got more and more animated. "Scores of artists, like Monet, Cézanne, Picasso, Munch, and my spiritual mentor, Kandinsky showed their work in this country for the first time. I was actually there, Jake," she said.

"How is that?" I asked.

"I was a just little girl about three and we were visiting my aunt in New Haven at the time the show took place. My parents dragged me to it, not really knowing what it was. They were so disgusted that halfway through they demanded we leave. But as they told me later, I didn't want to go. I put up quite a fuss. My mom called it a hissy fit. "

"Wow that show must have been the cat's pajamas," I said. "You mentioned your spiritual mentor, Kandi . . . Kandowitz . . . ?" I mirrored the posture of my new friend.

"Well, I've never actually met the man, but I've seen some of his work and read everything I can get my hands on about him," she said, holding up the book she had been reading. There was something about that girl that moved me. When she spoke you couldn't miss how alive she was. Her passion was contagious.

"You have really pretty eyes," I said. I could feel myself blush. She had big, beautiful, cat-shaped brown eyes.

"So do you." Carolyn opened the art book she had been reading and scooted closer so I could see it. Then she showed me several color plates of Kandinsky's paintings. My jaw came unhinged. His work was amazing, inspiring. It was like nothing I'd ever seen before. Carolyn was like an East Indian spice trader who was introducing me to a new and exotic world of flavor that I'd never even imagined.

I took the book from her and leafed through it three times. A random thought came to mind.

"Why are you smiling?" she asked.

"Oh, I'm just fascinated." I didn't tell the young woman from Charleston that the real reason for my smile had nothing to do with Kandinsky. Although I was interested in her mentor, I was actually thinking that she was terrific and as different from Val as night is from day. Carolyn was, in fact, the opposite of Val. Val, a blue-blooded Northeastern extrovert, put on the airs of being a free woman, whereas Carolyn, a simple country girl, had to conform to the dictates of her family and what was expected of a Southern woman in those days. But Carolyn was the freer and bolder spirit of the two. I experienced that firsthand in her gutsy question to the headmaster after his introductory lecture. She wasn't afraid to make waves. Both Val and Carolyn were passionate about art. Even though Carolyn's passion was predictable and consistent landscapes, she made art whenever and wherever possible. Creating was her reason for being.

Although Val's was more avant-garde, impulsive, and erratic, her passion was strangely conventional. Val envied those who made art and made excuses for not making a commitment to herself as an artist. She surrounded herself with artists; purchased art and even, at times, tried to wear it. It came to me that possibly she was afraid; afraid of expressing what was inside her; afraid of standing alone. As I thought about how opposite Val was from Carolyn I began to see something I hadn't previously wanted to accept: Val's limitations and how I just might be wasting my time with her. That afternoon on the quad in Sarasota there had been no *terremoto*. Nonetheless, my world had still been turned upside down.

XXXX

Over the next few days, everywhere I went I imagined things and people painted with a brightly colored swirl or splash of paint. Everything I saw I imagined upside down. I even had a fantasy of turning Val upside down and painting her in brilliant shades of green, orange, and blue. I couldn't wait for the school day to be over so I could get home and paint on my own. Oddly enough, I began to use new colors and color combinations that I had somehow overlooked in the past. I was at peace, something I wasn't accustomed to. It probably sounds strange to you, but I honestly felt I had fulfilled my promise to Val.

A few days later, something very bizarre occurred. It was a first for me. I had dinner at my bungalow, cleaned the kitchen, and retired to read before bed. No matter what I did I couldn't concentrate. After twenty minutes I got so anxious I couldn't sit still. I tried to think of what was bothering me. Was it Val, DeWitt, or maybe Carolyn? I couldn't come up with any explanation, so I closed my book. *Maybe a hot shower will help*, I thought. I was on my way to the bathroom when I stopped at the easel I had set up for myself near the front window that looked out onto the street. It was about ten o'clock when, without thinking, I picked up a horsehair brush and my palette. Before I knew what had happened, hours had passed. The sun was just rising. That day I awoke to a different watercolor world of pastels, shadows, and infinite possibilities.

A few hours later I drove to school and looked everywhere for Carolyn. I finally found her just where we had spoken the first time. She was sitting on the same mound of grass on the quad. "Hiya," I said breathlessly. "I want you to be the first to know."

"What are you talking about, Jake?" Carolyn asked.

"I have made up my mind."

"Made up your mind about what?" She looked puzzled.

"I have decided to quit school."

She sat forward with a shocked look on her face. "Does this mean you're giving up on your art?" she asked.

"No, no, nothing like that; it's high time I dive deeper into it. I think you are my muse. Teaching me about the Armory Show, introducing me to Kandinsky . . . It all got me thinking. You see, I need to cross more borders of my own. It's time I turn some things upside down in my life before it's too late."

Shortly after that conversation I quit art school. You might say it was a rash and impulsive decision. But I don't think so. I believe I got all I could out of that place and it was time to move on. Although the school bore the name of a Ringling, I was almost certain quitting that school would not hurt my career with the circus. I did write Val and explain my decision. I felt it was the right thing to do.

The only certainties in my life at that point were that I was going home for about six weeks until I would report back to Ringling Bros for our opening at Madison Square Garden and that Harry and Daisy would visit me in El Paso for a few days on their way to California for some movie deal. I was stepping out into the unknown, flying by the seat of my pants, so to speak. I hadn't remembered feeling that alive in a long time.

CHAPTER 25

Hari Kidd

"Last Light," Jake Erlich

Driving from Sarasota to El Paso in early March, I had no way of knowing that soon my hometown would become a nexus for me; a place of power where strange forces would converge for an unexpected transformation. Truth be told, I almost never met the key player in that transformation. His name was Hari Kidd and he would become my mentor.

A few weeks after I got back home, Mama first talked to me about him and the possibility of taking his art classes. That morning, I was sitting at the breakfast table with Papa and feeling pretty blue.

The bravado I had felt when I decided to leave the Ringling School of Art had faded away, replaced by gnawing self-doubt. I spent most of my time second-guessing my decision, worrying how Val reacted when she found out, and missing Carolyn and the Dolls. Since I had returned to El Paso I had received letters from all my friends but Val. I figured that she didn't write me because she was upset and disappointed when she learned of my decision.

The only bright spot in my gloominess was looking forward to Harry and Daisy's upcoming visit to El Paso. In those days, just about everything seemed negative, including the unlikely possibility of working with some local-yokel art teacher.

"Is Hari Kidd that *meshugana* who wants to make a WPA project out of painting all the stores from the Stanton Street Bridge to the San Jacinto Plaza pastel colors?" Papa inquired.

"That's him," Mama answered. My ears perked up.

"Yeah, that one's a strange bird. I saw him walking around downtown in bright blue, silk pajamas and multicolored *huaraches*."

This guy sounds like he belongs in the circus or the Big Spring Asylum, I thought to myself.

"And I've heard he has several mistresses in Juarez," Papa added.

It was odd to hear my conservative parents gossiping, particularly about a man they wanted to be my teacher. Mama glanced at me with a worried, disapproving look on her face. "On second thought, Jakey, I'm not so sure I want you to study with that man."

I felt relieved at my mother's apparent change of heart. Mama stood up from the table and quickly walked to the kitchen counter. She took the dish towel from its resting place on the white ceramic duck's head that was nailed into the wall next to the sink. After sixty seconds worth of aggressively drying the remaining wet plates in the dish rack, she threw the towel down on the kitchen counter with the same determination of a judge hammering his gavel. Papa and I looked at each other, raising our eyebrows but not daring to speak. Mama had come to some kind of a decision. I anxiously awaited her ruling. It turned out that any relief I felt at not having to meet the flamboyant art teacher was premature.

"I did promise his mother," she said, looking over her right shoulder at me. "A promise is a promise."

My father smirked. There would be no appeal from Mama's court.

That's just what I want to do, I thought, *spend the precious few weeks I have till the circus season starts fulfilling my mother's social obligations.*

XXXX

Just one day after Mama had first told me about him, I met Hari face to face. He was a real character and it was quite an experience. Hari was standing in the drawing room of his mother's home. They lived on River Street, just a few blocks away from my folks' house. You can imagine how happy I was to be there. Suffice it to say, I went along just to please Mama. I would have rather been anywhere else—and I do mean anywhere; even at the dentist.

I remember walking up to the two-story house clutching two of my paintings that I'd finished in Florida under my arm. They were each wrapped in brown paper. *This joker's probably one of those typical purple-mountain painters that I detest like the plague,* I thought. I could easily visualize his art classes: full of stiff old ladies and toothless codgers, and maybe a few socialites, all painting exact replicas of the same boring plate of bruised apples. I bet their paintings could have rolled off a production line with few, if any, detectable differences between them.

When Mama knocked on their door I was still lost in thought. I was sure that that art teacher's students felt painting was a hobby, like knitting; not a passion, like it was for Carolyn. None of them felt compelled to paint.

None of them needed to paint like they needed to breathe like Frida Kahlo and Diego Rivera. Looking back on it, I was feeling holier-than-thou and pretty full of myself.

"Jake, this is Mrs. Kidd and her son, Hari," Mama said as we stepped into their house and nodded at each other. Mrs. Kidd, a petite woman with her gray hair done in a Gibson girl bun, was dressed in a white lace apron that came down below her knees. Underneath it she wore a blue, high-collared, floral-print dress.

"Come on, Dora, let's leave the boys alone." Either Mrs. Kidd sensed the tension in the air and chose to ignore it, or she was just oblivious. As the two mothers moved to the kitchen, I smelled a strange combination of oil paint, potpourri, and flour wafting from Hari's mother.

After they walked away, neither of us said a word. Hari just stood there looking as unhappy as I felt. I studied him carefully. The most pronounced feature in Hari's appearance was his head. It was huge. He had chiseled cheekbones and a prominent hooknose that made him look like a falcon. Hari was about five foot two, with tufts of thinning blond hair sitting atop a massive forehead. His smoldering, black eyes darted around the room as if he were hunting some hidden prey. I almost forgot to mention that Hari wore a red kimono with a large, embroidered, ferocious-looking yellow dragon on the back. Under the robe, he sported a black paint-stained T-shirt and wrinkled black trousers. He was barefoot.

This oddball would fit in with the circus all right, I thought, repressing a smile. I couldn't imagine what my poor mother must have been thinking when she arranged that get-together. Then without even a by-your-leave he walked over to the steps just off the entryway and started climbing up the stairs. I didn't know what else to do, so I followed him.

When I reached the landing of the house's second floor, I realized that whatever walls had been there when the house was originally built had been demolished, leaving a huge space that became Hari Kidd's studio. There were easels set up all around the room supporting oil paintings at various stages of completion. The white walls also had paintings and sketches mounted on them that were framed ornately, simply, or not at all. Some of the floor space was covered by beige canvas drop cloths blemished with splotches of paint like Hari's T-shirt.

Hari busied himself picking up a few paintings that were on the ground and placing them on a large pine worktable that sat in the middle of the studio. Finally, he looked up at me as if acknowledging my presence for the first time. Then he pointed at the two paintings covered in brown paper that I carried under my left arm. That morning Mama had insisted I take them. Reluctantly, I complied, but at that moment I wished I hadn't brought them. That fellow didn't exactly inspire any confidence.

"What's that?" he asked, breaking the painful silence. Hari spoke in the domineering tone of someone who is used to getting what he wanted. Instead of waiting for a reply, he motioned for me to bring my paintings to him. I took a cautious step closer. He reached out and grabbed hold of one side of the brown-paper-clad paintings. I held on to the other side, refusing to let go. Hari glared at me, and then for some strange reason, I let go.

Like a five year old would tear open a birthday gift, Hari immediately began ripping off the brown paper and throwing it on the ground. Then he abruptly stopped, took a step back, and pointed his index finger up at me.

"Are you interested in learning to paint women with pretty, red lips?" He spoke in a contemptuous tone. I remember being shocked that he would address me in that scoffing voice so soon after we were first introduced.

"No sir, not a bit," I answered him politely, angry at myself for tolerating his rudeness. Then Hari continued unwrapping my paintings. The only way to describe what happened after he finished is that he devoured them with his eyes. One after the other, he drew the paintings close to his face. Then he pushed them away. Then he turned them upside down. It felt like he was looking for some code hidden in the dried paint. For the next fifteen, awkward minutes he didn't say a word. As he examined my work from every angle imaginable, I felt terribly vulnerable at having my paintings judged by someone I didn't know and didn't like.

I wished I had never agreed to come here, I said to myself. I had expected that that morning I'd feel bored, maybe even disdainful, but not nervous and insecure. Before I knew what hit me, I had an awful case of the jitters. After watching him silently inspect my work for what seemed like an hour, I couldn't take standing still anymore. So I walked around his studio and tentatively eyed the paintings on the walls, on the easels, on the table, and on the floor. I was not prepared for what for I saw. I was totally amazed. *If these are his, it's certainly not purple-mountain painting*, I thought. The work was some of the best I'd ever seen. His use of shape was flowing and avant-garde, and his colors were innovative and dynamic. The themes were romantic. Hari's paintings had a strange effect on me. I lost myself in them and overlooked the fact that in the same space, a stranger was critiquing my work. I almost forgot that I was nervous.

A few minutes later, as if he were lifting a great weight, Hari slowly raised his head and began to talk, oblivious to where I was in the room. The art teacher's voice stirred me from my trance and my jitters came back.

"You understand this is by no means an invitation." As he spoke I walked back to where he stood. Hari placed the second of my paintings down on the pine table next to where he'd place the first one. Then he continued. "In order to accept you—or anybody else for that matter—as my student, I require total commitment; a promise that you will never study technique, but strive to embrace the truth that lies behind it, to see what is real beyond the surface." I didn't understand what the hell he was talking about but I was intrigued. Hari still hadn't said a thing, good or bad, about my paintings. I didn't have the slightest idea where I stood with him. "If I agree to work with a student, I will never teach him to paint to the market. I will guide that artist to look at things from all sides and then to express his inimitable self through color, form, and image." I didn't know what to say. "Is that understood?" he demanded.

"Ye . . . yes," I stammered. Then he turned his back on me so he faced the maple armoire that rested against the wall opposite the windows and pointed to the door. I guessed that meant I was dismissed. But I didn't care about his lack of manners. After seeing his paintings firsthand, I knew I had to study with this strange little man. I ran down the stairs moving so fast I almost tripped.

I found my mother and Mrs. Kidd still in the kitchen. Mama and I immediately made eye contact. She raised her brows, wordlessly inquiring what had happened. In a language that only mothers can hear, I nodded and silently replied I was done and it was time to go. After the obligatory thank-yous, we finally left. It was none too soon. As we walked out of that house I inhaled deeply, feeling as if I hadn't taken one breath since Hari shooed me out of his studio.

XXXX

"*Zug mir*, so how did it go?" Mama inquired on the way home.

"I really don't want to talk about it," I said. I stared down at the sidewalk as we walked on in silence. All I could think about were the myriad reasons Hari wouldn't want to teach me. After all, I was just a beginner and based on what I saw in his studio, he was a master. Judging by the way he acted, he didn't particularly take a liking to me or my paintings. Maybe he couldn't see beyond my height to any inklings of talent I might have. You know, after my conversation with Carolyn, I dreamed of studying with avant-garde artists. Although Lya once had told me that when the student is ready the teacher emerges, I had been certain that there was no way on God's green earth that could happen in a place like El Paso. Could Hari Kidd possibly be my mentor? That unlikely scenario was just too good to be true. I couldn't let myself believe it.

For the next few days I was on pins and needles. I didn't eat or sleep, waiting to hear whether or not Hari Kidd would be my teacher. Finally, two days later, he called my parents' house in the late morning.

Mama answered the phone. "Hello, Mr. Kidd," she said.

I jumped out of my chair, unable to contain myself. "What is he saying?" I demanded. "Did he reject me?"

Mama put her finger up to her mouth to shush me. "I understand. Thank you for your time." She turned her back on me and hung up the phone. It seemed like an eternity until she turned around again. I braced myself for the worst. I imagined his rude response: "*I'm not interested in working with a circus freak.*" Then I thought of how he'd possibly let me down easy. "*A neophyte artist like your boy would be best served with something more basic. Maybe he should look into art class at the high school or the women's club.*" Mama turned around.

"Jake, be careful what you ask for." I locked at her impatiently. She gave me a half-smile. "Your classes will begin next Monday morning. You're to meet with him in his studio from nine a.m. to noon, five days a week. The cost is two dollars."

Unable to contain myself, I grabbed Mama, swept her off her feet and gave her a big bear hug.

"Put me down, Jakey! You'll break my ribs," she said, laughing.

Besides Val's visit to Sarasota, I don't remember ever looking forward to anything with such anticipation. But to be honest, I was also still fearful. What if after we worked together he told me I wasn't cut out to be an artist?

In class, we would both paint. He'd talk; I mostly listened. During my initial session he said something I've never forgotten: "In order to express yourself in art, first you have to see, know, and understand what lies beyond the superficial. While others use their eyes like cameras, I want your eyes to become fingers that explore, caress, and feel; that know the world by making love to it." That day and throughout every class, whenever I painted he asked me what I was feeling and where in my body I felt it. No one at the Ringling School of Art had ever done anything like that. "Don't get me wrong, thinking is important and you'd better believe I'm going to get you to think differently," he said during one of our sessions. "But thinking is not nearly as important as what you feel. You feel images. You feel colors. You don't only think them. They speak their own language. Eventually people will realize the wisdom of emotion."

I often picture him standing in the warm winter sunlight that streamed in through the large bay window in his studio. For our classes he typically wore a black, corduroy beret and a white smock stained with yellow, blue, and burgundy that, if framed, would have been a collector's piece. "If you want to touch the people who see your work, let those emotions flow through you, from that giant soul of yours, down those tremendous arms, to your gargantuan fingers, through that puny brush and out onto the vacuous canvas." I loved how he spoke. He said things I'd never heard or even thought about. Often he'd surprise me. One day he pulled a large tomato out of his pocket. "What do you see?" he asked.

"It's a tomato," I answered without thinking.

"No! No!" he corrected me vehemently. "Damnit to hell, if you want to be a painter you have to learn to observe things from more than one point of view." He held the tomato up to the light as if in awe and wonder, and began to explore it from every possible angle. "We're not Renaissance artists with a fixed and limited vantage point painting exact replicas, are we?" He didn't give me a chance to respond but charged ahead with his lesson. "Are we impressionists, still with a single point of view, entranced by the dance of color and light? No, we're not. If you truly want to be a modern artist, as you've said, then you must see things from multiple perspectives; from every which way imaginable." Hari held the tomato in front him as if he were Hamlet speaking to Yorick's skull. Then he took a bite out it. When he had finished eating it, he wiped his mouth with his sleeve and continued. "With me you will paint all the dimensions; the parts, the whole, the totality."

Hari would look out the bay window with the intensity of a man who could see the center of the sun and not go blind. Then he'd walk across the tongue and groove oak floor to where I was painting. As he ambled toward me he'd swing his arms in a strange, restrained way. I remember thinking that he moved like a rusty gate. It seemed the gods had bound Hari's upper body and, like a mythic hero, he was fighting to free himself. Later I would learn that he suffered from some kind of a neurological condition. The doctors thought it might be encephalitis. I recall how his paint-stained fingers scissored my forearm. He'd squeeze me hard, as if what he was about to say would be the last words he would ever utter and that I would ever hear. "Art is not about calipers and engineering, Jake. It's about heart," he once said.

Studying with Hari was night-and-day different from studying at the Ringling School of Art. My classes in Florida were all about creating exact reproductions and mimicking rigid, refined technique. Hari's classes were all about flexible thinking, multiple perspectives, feelings, and finding yourself in the work. Whereas DeWitt demanded I hold my brush as he commanded, Hari insisted that I hold my brush however I was most comfortable. I think he wouldn't have cared if I painted with my toes, as long as I was truly engaged in what I was doing.

When we talked about art school and why I left, Hari explained that the type of rigid requirement for artistic realism demanded at the Ringling School of Art and many similar institutions actually dated back to sixteenth century Italy and the Counter Reformation. When he spoke about it, Hari's eyes flashed and his voice became angry as if he himself had lived at that time and his work had been scorned by the Holy See. He taught me that the Church saw the freedom expressed in art since the Renaissance as a threat to their authority. As he spoke to me he became more irate. "They wanted us to portray things in a straightforward and simple fashion. For them, art was a tool for communicating lockstep biblical images to the masses. The ecclesiastics tried to force artists to bow down to their definition of the divine and their plans to increase devotion. People like that are still threatened by anything that is different. For Christ's sake, we've been up in airships and we've built skyskrapers. Once you've been that high you can't deny what you've seen. In this day and age, how can anyone in their right mind expect an artist to have a simple perspective?" Hari pounded his fist on the worktable so hard that two unused canvases fell on the floor.

As he picked them up, I thought of the *yankis* that Cuco had mentioned and wondered at the perspective they must have had. At first, all of my teacher's talk about multiple perspectives was abstract and foreign. But over time, as Hari got me to expand and transform the way I saw the world and what I was painting, he also helped me to change the way I saw myself. The more time I spent with my teacher, the more I appreciated his passion for modern art. It was contagious. I came to understand why he made me swear to never let the fascists in the world keep me from expressing myself.

At one point, Hari told me about his travels abroad; in particular, his experiences with *Les Fauves* (the wild beasts) and what they taught him about color; his fascination with the expressionist painters and their articulation of emotions; and most recently his time with the cubists and their experimentation with the dynamics of form. Once, after we had talked about his adventures in Europe, Hari became very somber. "A nightmare is coming, Jake," he said. "I'm certain of it."

Besides being a fine abstract artist, he turned out to be a great but complicated teacher and a dear friend. Hari not only inspired me in too many ways to count, but he also taught me things about painting—like chroma, value, hue, and vibrating edges—that transformed my work. He was an artist's artist who painted like no one else in El Paso at the time or since. He was an innovator of modest circumstances who supported himself by writing songs, stories, and illustrating books. I would learn that Hari had attended one of the best art schools in the country, the Pennsylvania Academy of the Fine Arts. Unlike the Ringling School, that was an institution that embraced modern art. While Hari was studying in Philadelphia, he—as Carolyn had—actually attended and had been moved by the Armory Show.

Despite the picture Mama painted of Hari as an accomplished teacher, it turns out I was his one and only student. After the way she built him up and tried to sell me on taking class with him, I thought he must have had at least twenty students. I didn't have the heart to tell her.

I now understand that at first, like I had done with so many others, I idolized him. But as I got to know Hari and we became friends, besides all his talent as an artist and skill as a teacher, I saw that he had his dark side. One morning I came into his studio for my class and the thick, gray, wool curtains that were normally open in the sunny room were drawn. The darkened room smelled stale and acrid. I found my teacher huddled in a corner. A semicircle of empty *mescal* bottles surrounded Hari as if they were some kind of frontier fortress, a Great Wall of Mexican whiskey. I crouched down next to him. My teacher was unshaven and his clothes looked like he'd slept in them. He didn't appear to be breathing. I thought Hari might be dead. Then he whispered something. I couldn't make out what he was saying so I leaned in closer to him. He opened his eyes and looked up at me.

"Jake, I have monsters in my head." Then he closed his eyes again and tears ran down his cheeks and on to his paint-stained smock. Hari's words and his tears shook me.

I wanted to fling his wall of whiskey bottles aside and force him to tell me about his monsters; but I also wanted to shield my teacher and friend from any further pain and humiliation. I felt embarrassed for him and for me. Like one of Noah's sinful sons, I had uncovered my teacher's nakedness. In retrospect, I think I idolized people like Hari because I couldn't stomach their imperfections. Back then, I couldn't tolerate my own.

For the next few minutes I just kneeled there in the shadows, watching him. Hari had fallen off his pedestal. I imagined myself running away and quitting my classes. But I didn't.

We never spoke about that incident. I remember thinking how hard it must be for someone like Hari, someone who didn't fit in . . . especially in a place like El Paso. After all, west Texas in the 1930s wasn't exactly the Left Bank. I wondered if he had ever had a brotherhood of freaks where he could find some peace and acceptance. Did he have a lover in whose arms he could escape? I had heard many rumors that he was a *mujeriego*, a womanizer, but I never met or saw one of his paramours. It wasn't pity I felt for Hari. I think it was more like a tender shoot of compassion that sprouted from my own fledgling self-acceptance. Though I was thirty, I think I was finally starting to awaken.

"Let's get you cleaned up and to bed," I said, lifting him off the ground. I don't think Hari's impact on me occurred despite his demons. I think he inspired me so strongly because of them.

Hari's spells, as he called them, reminded me of my own black times when I had to be alone. In the past, I rarely saw or allowed myself to see that negative, shadowy side in anyone else. Those few times in Hollywood or Ringling Bros when I encountered someone else with dark spells, it was too painful of a reminder of my own and I was compelled to get away from them as soon as I could. I must have felt that I could escape myself by running away from another person who was like me. Maybe it was because I respected Hari and his ability so much, or for some other reason it would take Solomon in all his wisdom to understand, but whatever the explanation, when I met the monsters in Hari's head, I grew a bit more accepting of my own. I guess that's the sign of a true teacher. He got me to see things I had previously missed and experience feelings I didn't even know I was having.

It might have been his words, or maybe it was his art. But most likely I think he had that effect on me by being unafraid to be himself.

XXXX

We had been studying together for about a month when a letter arrived that upset the applecart. I'm pretty sure it was a Saturday morning.

Dear Largote,

That frog of a husband of mine and I will be traveling through your fair city on our way to San Francisco next Friday so he can visit the mansion of some rich cabrón *in Hillsdale who bought some of my paintings. I think our train gets in around noon. We thought it would be great fun to stay overnight in El Paso. Can you make reservations for us at a nice hotel? Please call or wire me at the Statler Hotel in Detroit to let me know things are all set.*

Con cariño,

Frida.

P. S. Your friend Val will be traveling with us. It was supposed to be a sorpresa. *She made me promise not to tell you but I'm awful with* pinche *surprises.*

F. K.

After I read that letter, all my old feelings and ambivalences about Val, the long-toothed ghosts I thought I'd exorcized, came rushing back. Though it pains me to admit it, despite all that had happened—my disappointments and my pronouncements—I couldn't wait to see her. If she was traveling all this way, maybe there was still hope for us. Then again, maybe I was just deluding myself.

When I re-read Frida's letter, two realizations sunk in. First of all, judging by the combination of exhilaration and nausea I felt, I was far from over Val. Then I also remembered Harry and Daisy's plans to visit me on their way to Hollywood. It struck me that Frida, Diego, Val, and the Dolls would all visit El Paso the same star-crossed weekend. *How will I ever deal with that strange cast of characters?* I wondered. I probably would have invested more time and energy wrestling with that that dilemma, but I was already late for my class with Hari.

XXXX

It was next to impossible to concentrate that day. Hari must have realized something was wrong because he suggested we break early and take a ride to town for lunch. Spending a little social time with my teacher outside of the studio sounded like a great idea and a welcome distraction from my anxiety and worry about my upcoming visitors. Despite his demons I looked up to Hari and respected his wisdom. I thought our lunch that day might afford an opportunity to ask Hari his thoughts and any advice he might offer about Val.

I decided it was best to approach my mercurial teacher in a roundabout manner. I waited until we'd almost arrived downtown before I broached the subject. "My friends are coming to El Paso next week. I was wondering if we could all get together. I wrote them about you. It would be great for you to meet face to face."

"Who is coming to town?" Hari asked.

"Remember my friends Harry and Daisy Doll, my closest circus pals? They'll be stopping here on their way to Hollywood, where they're going to be auditioning for a Tod Browning movie."

"Who else?"

"Well, two artist friends are also coming. I know you'll want to meet them. We became acquainted back in New York." I had mentioned my connection with Frida and Diego once before, but on that occasion Hari had abruptly changed the subject. Now that they were traveling to El Paso, I couldn't wait for them to meet. "Their names are Diego Rivera and Frida Kahlo. They're going to visit a client near San Francisco," I said as we drove past Saint Patrick's Cathedral.

"Those two?" I looked over at him across my Buick's backseat. I was surprised and puzzled to see him making a face like he'd bitten into an unripe persimmon. "I'm going to take a pass on that one, Jake. You know I'm not a very social person."

I knew he was making excuses. I had been certain he would have wanted to meet the infamous Diego and Frida. "Hari, I have a feeling you have more to say. I'm curious what you think about them." But he didn't. I made a right turn onto North Oregon.

"Curiosity killed the cat, my young friend."

"Well, I am curious."

"If you must know, I'm only interested in meeting two of your guests: Harry and Daisy Doll."

"Why is that?"

"They sound interesting and genuine. I believe they've made the best of a great burden."

"I'm shocked. I thought sure you'd have wanted to meet Diego Rivera and Frida Kahlo. After all, you have so much in common. Talk about burdens; Frida's spent her life in agonizing pain from her accident."

"I know she has," Hari said. I signaled to make a right turn on San Francisco Street and stopped to allow the mule-drawn streetcar that locals called the *tranvía* to pass. Once it was safe to proceed, I finished the turn and Hari continued what he had been saying. "But we don't have one damn thing in common. They're both Communists. One day, after too many people have died, the world is going to wake up to what a mistake that whole ugly business is."

I saw a parking place in front of Zork's Hardware and pulled into it. I looked over at my teacher. "I didn't know you were so conservative."

"There's a lot about me you don't know." Hari nodded his head. "Diego Rivera and Frida Kahlo are show-offs."

"Show-offs?"

"I like their art, but I hate the look-at-me pieces in their lifestyle and all the sycophants in that sick cult of personality they call an entourage."

"Come on, Hari, you're not exactly low-key. I mean, you wear silk pajamas and colored sandals around town."

"I know! I know! What a paradox," Hari continued. He had a sly smile. "Maybe I'm envious. Maybe I don't like them because I'm not as successful as they are. Maybe I don't like them because they remind me of me. Whatever the hell the reason, the two of them make me as uncomfortable as a rash in a whorehouse. So when they come to town you can count me out."

I was flabbergasted. Hari was full of surprises. As he opened the door and started to exit the car, I knew I had to get up the gumption to ask him what I really wanted to know and had been avoiding. "My friend Val will also be here. Remember, she's the one who helped get me the scholarship to art school." During one of our classes, in passing, I had briefly mentioned my infatuation with her.

"Oh yeah, the married broad," Hari said.

I couldn't tell if his tone and choice of words was innocent or judgmental. "What about meeting Val?" I asked.

"I'm not interested in saying how'd-ya-do to some tart who's giving you the runaround," he said bluntly.

I flung my door open and got out of the car in a huff. You know, it's really important to have a friend you can confide in and who cares enough about you to always tell you the truth. In my life, Hari was one of those people. But just because somebody's words are true doesn't make them any easier to stomach. Hari looked at me, as if inviting an argument. I sensed the resolve in my teacher's voice, bit my lip, and didn't say a word. As we crossed the street and walked through San Jacinto Plaza to get to Lupe's *Taquería*, I hated Hari.

The two of us must have made for quite a sight. All eight and a half feet of me dressed like Pecos Bill, complete with snakeskin boots, a red bandana, and silver belt buckle, and Harry in his yellow silk pajamas, straw sun hat, and sandals.

"Get a load of the freaks."

When we heard those words pierce the plaza's peaceful façade, we both spun around. A half-dozen drunken, young dog soldiers, likely on a pass from Fort Bliss, stood about ten feet away, glaring at us. It was evident they were looking for trouble. One of them hurled a bottle and it shattered, spewing beer and glass at our feet. I charged toward them. Hari grabbed my arm, restraining me. The soldiers instinctively stepped back. They appeared to be sizing up the consequences of escalating the confrontation. I thought about Eisenbeis, the rube in Madison Square Garden, the jerk who tried to hurt Harry Doll in Chattanooga, and all the countless bullies who'd crossed my path over the years. I clenched my fists tight, preparing for battle. *It stops here*, I thought. I shot a dirty look at the one who threw the bottle. *He's the one I'll take down first*, I thought. Then the young troublemakers whirled around and walked quickly away from us in the opposite direction.

For a few seconds I believed I must have really scared them. Then two Military Policemen on foot patrol strode past us, offering another explanation for the soldiers' rapid retreat. The would-be altercation temporarily put the brakes on my negative feelings towards Hari and any investment I had in pursuing the subject of Val with him any further.

Over lunch, Hari and I talked about what had happened. "Why did you let those young bucks get your goat? After all, they just called us *freaks*," Hari said.

"You know, I've been in Ringling Bros sideshow for eleven years now. I'm glad to be a freak in the circus, and I don't mind when the other freaks use that word. As a matter of fact, I am proud of it. *Freak* is a badge of honor. But when outsiders use it, like those punks, the word is an insult." I pushed back from the table and continued. "I can usually ignore troublemakers. But they were slurring you. You're my teacher."

"It's just words, Jake," Hari said, repeating himself. "They don't know who we are. They don't know one goddamned thing about us." Then he took a sip of his coffee to let me know that was all he had to allow on the subject.

I hemmed and hawed and got very quiet. I wanted to say it but I just couldn't. As the words started to come out I swallowed, as if I could digest them and avoid what I feared would happen next. *You cannot ask him that, Jake*, I warned myself. *Maybe he'll feel humiliated or maybe even insulted.* I started to sweat and got very anxious about what might happen next.

"Jake, what's wrong? Are you feeling sick?"

"It's nothing . . . "

Hari scooted closer to the table and looked up into my eyes. "Come on, Jake. Don't bullshit a bullshitter."

"Hari, there is something . . . there's something I . . . "

"Out with it, man," he demanded impatiently.

"Okay, okay. I've been wanting to ask you . . . " I said haltingly. Hari hit the table with his fist, as if the impact of his hand would stop me from choking on my thoughts. "How does a man like you handle living in a place like this? I mean, how do you fit in?"

I was shocked that I'd actually asked him. He sat there staring at me with the same intensity he had looked at my paintings when we first had met. I had not felt this uneasy around him since we were introduced four weeks earlier in his mother's drawing room. Certain that I offended him, I squirmed in my chair. *Why couldn't I just keep my trap shut?* I could count the people I'd been that straightforward with on the fingers of one hand. My stomach churned, and it wasn't from Lupe's chicken tacos. Hari got an impish grin on his face and looked amused.

"Well, Jake, that's a complicated question." *Here it comes,* I thought, preparing to deal with the consequences. "I've made my peace with El Paso."

A few years later I would think about that very conversation when I learned that Hari had been beaten within an inch of his life by a drunk in a run-down bar just off South El Paso Street.

"My mother is here, and El Paso is a pretty place what with the Rocky Mountains, the Sierra Madre, the desert and all. I like the different cultures here, too." His face softened as he spoke. "The weather is good. You know, my spells are worse where there are weeks at a time without sunshine. But really, more than anything, El Paso's just a place. I've come to see that if your Paris isn't in El Paso it won't be in Paris either." I sat back, took a deep breath, and sighed, relieved at not having provoked Hari's wrath or harpooned his pride with my honesty.

"Jake, where's your Paris?" Hari asked a few second later. His question demolished any sense of relief I'd felt. Something about it cut through all my layers of pretense.

"That's a tough question, Hari," I finally answered. "I don't think I've found my Paris."

"So what do you think your Paris would be like?" Hari asked quietly.

I hesitated. I hadn't allowed myself to fantasize like that. My life had pretty much been spent doing what was necessary and letting fate, like a runaway horse, take the lead. There didn't seem to be a whole hell of a lot of choices for me. At that instant, I felt a deep, scorching sadness, as if scalding steam had escaped from a subterranean hot spring somewhere deep inside me. Oddly, that melancholy gave form and color to my words. "My Paris would be a place where I totally belong and where I'm free to be myself. For a while I thought I found it in Hollywood. Then I thought it was in the circus. Then I thought it would be in art school or with Val," I answered, looking down at the table.

Hari got out of his chair and quickly moved toward me. I wasn't sure what he was going to do. "I think your Paris wasn't in Hollywood or Sarasota. I don't think it was in the circus. I don't think you'll find it leaving the sideshow or in the arms of some unobtainable woman. I'm not saying those places aren't important, but I think you'll find that your Paris," he paused and put that crooked index finger of his right hand in the middle of my chest, "is here."

I felt warmth where Hari's finger touched my sternum. His words reverberated inside me and took my breath away. I blinked away tears. "And Jake, I have one more question, and I don't expect an answer. Why would somebody like you, somebody who was born to stand out, worry so much about fitting in?"

I didn't know what to say. Long after our lunch was finished and for many years since, Hari's question has stayed with me.

CHAPTER 26

South El Paso Street

Circus World Museum, Baraboo, Wisconsin

Six days later at about half past eleven, I was at Union Depot impatiently waiting for the last train from Dallas. Earlier that afternoon, I had greeted Harry and Daisy when they arrived in El Paso on their trip from Florida. When I checked with the ticket agent he said thunderstorms outside of Abilene had delayed Val, Diego, and Frida's train by about two hours. That gave me plenty of time to get the Dolls situated at the Hotel Paso del Norte, where everyone would be staying. It was the nicest place in town. The Paso del Norte was famous for its twenty-five-foot-wide dome ceiling of exquisite emerald, sapphire, and ruby-colored Tiffany glass. If I close my eyes now I can see that dome and the hotel lobby it covered filled with sleepy-eyed, cigar-smoking cattlemen reclining in huge, brown, rawhide chairs and sofas that seemed to swallow them up.

That Friday night I found myself pacing back and forth at the depot, imagining what I would say to Val when she arrived. *Should I hug her? What if she gives me a kiss?* I practiced how I would introduce her to my parents and the strategy I would use to parry any uncomfortable inquiries about her past, our friendship, and the whereabouts of her husband. I buttoned my plaid Pendleton to avoid the chill in the air that I had not noticed earlier that evening. Then I looked at my wristwatch, trying to estimate how much longer I would have to wait, and noticed it had stopped. Carefully removing the gold Elgin with a specially made extra-extra long, black lizard-skin band, I wound the tiny bezel between my massive thumb and forefinger.

As I strapped my watch back on I wondered how Val would act toward me. Would she be affectionate or cool? Would she treat me like a mere acquaintance, even though I had passionately kissed her the last time we parted? Did I need to worry about being discrete? After all, her husband wouldn't even be there. I wondered why I was so focused on Val and even thought about why she had agreed to make this trip anyway. I didn't want to read into it, but perhaps Val coming to El Paso meant there was a chance she really cared about me. Then again, maybe she wouldn't even show up. That would certainly be consistent with Val; predictably unpredictable. I wondered if normal-sized people's relationships were that complicated. I tried to prepare myself for the worst.

At just past midnight, the Sunset Limited finally pulled in. A dozen sleepy, disheveled travelers disembarked. The train belched a bank of steam from its steel underbelly, making the scene dream like. As the exhausted passengers made their way along the platform, they all stared at me. A few even pointed. I ignored them, looking for Val.

The last person to climb down from the train was Frida. I was stunned to see her beautiful, long hair harshly cropped short, like a man's. Val and Diego were nowhere in sight. Unable to stop myself, as if I could will another passenger to appear, I kept looking past Frida into the bank of slow-rising steam that now gradually dissipated into the cool midnight air. Frida hobbled over, dropped her textile travel bag, wrapped her arms around my legs, and gave me a big hug. I imagine if Frida hadn't been crippled by her streetcar accident and I wasn't that tall, she would have jumped into my arms. But as my father always said, "If my sister had *baitzim* (balls), she would have been my brother."

I was so tense I didn't really feel Frida's embrace. I just patted her on the shoulder, still looking around for Val. "Oh, Jake, I'm so happy to see you. My friend, you are a sight for sore eyes." Frida looked like she'd been crying. I wondered why. "I know. I know. I can read your mind," she said, misinterpreting the inquisitive look on my face. She squeezed my forearm with one hand while clutching her textile suitcase with the other. I remember the large gold, green, and scarlet image of *Tlaloc*, the goggle-eyed, Aztec storm god, embroidered on her valise. I wondered if *Tlaloc* had a hand in the rains that had played havoc with the trains in west Texas earlier that day. "My friend, *el largote*, is wondering about the whereabouts of that ugly frog I sleep with," she surmised. "Well, that hideous lump of clay had to make an unplanned trip to Mexico City to consult with some *pinche* Communist or *puto* of an *industrial*."

As Frida spoke, all I could think about was Val. I wanted to interrupt her and ask where she was, but I couldn't take that liberty. After all, Frida was still a relative stranger that had yet to prove she could be trusted. There was no way I wanted to let on I was troubled by the whereabouts of her married friend. But I couldn't help myself. The anxiety was too much for me.

"What about Val?" Her name impulsively pushed its way past my better judgment and I immediately regretted it.

Frida looked away and muttered, "She didn't wire you?" I shook my head. "*Esa niña diabla* . . . that damned girl. At the last minute she said she just couldn't get away."

That's it? She just couldn't get away? I thought.

Then Frida turned, made eye contact with me, and smiled. Her smile seemed put-on, as if it were meant to placate me. "Val said to tell you, *que lo siente*. She is very sorry that she's not here; that you would understand."

Yeah, I understand all right, I said to myself. When Frida shared Val's message her tone didn't fit the words she was uttering. Her tenor was biting, as if she resented the role she had been scripted to play. But there was something else in her voice. Her remark was meant to be empathic, but the way she said it made me uneasy. I was already disappointed, and now I felt attacked, as if Frida's words were thin camouflage for something else. But I couldn't be sure what it was. In so many ways that Mexican artist—like most women I had ever met—was an enigma. My confusion about Frida's tone of voice didn't divert me for long from my negative reaction to the news about Val. If I were to tell you that it made me sick to my stomach, I wouldn't be lying. That's probably why I forgot to ask Frida about her radical haircut. I'd find out soon enough what was behind that craziness. I grabbed her bag and we walked inside the depot to collect the rest of her luggage.

On the short drive to the hotel it took my best acting job to not let on to Frida just how awful I felt. Suffice it to say that after I got her checked in and went back to my folks' house, I didn't sleep much that night.

XXXX

Early the next morning, I dropped by the Paso del Norte to meet my friends. I noticed they were not yet in the lobby, so I approached the registration desk.

"Has a Ms. Val McPhearson checked in?" I asked the clerk. I know it sounds crazy; like a child's wishful thinking, but somehow I fantasized that Val might have taken an early train and come in to surprise me.

"No, sir, we have no such person staying at the hotel." I felt silly asking a question for which I already knew the answer. I just nodded, said thank you, turned around, and walked to the elevator to wait for my friends. As I stood there waiting, I just couldn't get Val off my mind. I walked back and forth in the lobby and deliberated about how to explain her absence to the Dolls. Don't ask me why, but I was genuinely embarrassed that she hadn't come to El Paso. I didn't want to bring it up, and hoped they wouldn't ask.

Harry and Daisy were the first to come downstairs. He was comfortably dressed in white, linen trousers—perfect for the heat—a white cotton shirt with the sleeves nattily rolled up, two-tone white and brown shoes, and a white Panama straw hat with a black band. Daisy wore a yellow cotton dress with bluebirds embroidered on each shoulder, and dark brown, patent leather walking shoes. She carried a tan handbag. The Dolls had such a sense of style. The three of us stood near the elevator, waiting and chatting.

"Those damn Nazis are going to start another war," Harry fumed, opening the folded newspaper he carried in his right arm and pointing to the headline: "Hitler Supports Violent Demonstrations in Austria."

"That's just what we need," Daisy said. "As if this Depression isn't enough. I'm so worried about Lya." As she spoke, her brow wrinkled and her voice cracked. "Things just keep getting worse over there. I don't know what she's going to do. I wish to God she'd never gone to Germany."

"I know, Daisy. It's *nisht gut* (not good). I'm worried too," I said, trying to console her. I took the newspaper out of Harry's hand and began to read the article he referred to as if I could find balm for our anxiety about Lya by reading the facts about how bad things actually were.

Daisy reached up, grabbed a corner of the paper, and yanked it lower so she could read it as well. She looked up at me, realizing that if she could see the print it was too low for me to make it out. "Ah," she said in frustration, pushing the newspaper forcefully away with the back of her right hand . "So did the rest of the crew get in all right?" Daisy asked as I scanned the paper.

It sure didn't take her long, I thought nervously. "Frida Kahlo is the only one who came," I explained. "The other two had commitments and just couldn't make it."

Daisy shook her head and frowned. "I know you were especially looking forward to Val showing up." Daisy paused and looked out of a large picture window in the hotel lobby that faced a construction site across the street, where a maverick by the name of Conrad Hilton would shortly open his second hotel. I was uncomfortable with her compassion. "For the life of me, I can't figure out what he sees in that broad," Daisy said, as if addressing everyone in the lobby. "He's such an intelligent man; good looking too; but so dense about women. Maybe someday he'll wake up and smell the coffee." She sounded like my mother.

"What are you talking about, Daisy?" I asked, not doing a very good job of hiding my irritation with her. I think Val was a welcome target for Daisy's ire at the Nazis and an outlet for her fears about Lya.

"Why are you wasting your time with her? There are plenty of gals in this world who know how to appreciate and would even give their eyeteeth to have a special man like you."

"Like who?" I challenged.

"A woman like Lya," she responded, glaring up at me. I couldn't believe Daisy would mention Lya and me and romance in the same breath. "She's a good woman who wouldn't disappoint you like that high-society dame," Daisy insisted.

"I'm not disappointed. I couldn't care less," I said a little too angrily, batting the air with my right hand as if I was swatting a fly. Daisy shook her head in disapproval of my reaction. Then she looked toward a centerpiece of fresh gardenias floating in an oversize bowl on an end table close to where we were standing. Harry clucked his tongue and gave me a sly wink. Could they both really see Lya and me together as a couple? I winced at the image of the world's tallest man and the world's smallest woman in an embrace.

Harry and Daisy were midgets and my closest friends, but the idea of becoming lovers with a little person . . . Was that some kind of joke? What she was saying was almost impossible for me to fathom. It seemed unnatural. I wonder why I had such a harsh reaction. Could it be that I was just as prejudiced as all those awful rubes that over the years I'd come to despise?

Daisy turned back around and walked up to Harry. "Me thinks the gentleman doth protest too loudly," she said forcefully enough for anyone in earshot to hear.

"Jake, are you really not disappointed about Val?" Harry asked intently, cutting through the mustard. I looked down and hesitated as I struggled to formulate an answer to his question. After all, I had confided in Harry about how disappointed I was when Val had to cut short her trip to Sarasota . . . I didn't want to lie to my friends but I also didn't want to open the topic up for discussion. I sure as hell was disappointed. But to tell the truth, in those days I was disappointed and depressed about many things in my life. Normally, I just swallowed those feelings and tried to put on a happy face and make the best of it. Then something like Val not showing up would come along and smack me between the eyes, reminding me of the pain in my life that had been there since I was seven, and the whole goddamned house of cards threatened to come tumbling down.

"Well, are you disappointed or not?" Harry pressed me.

"I . . . I—" Before I could say another word the elevator door opened. Frida hobbled out.

"Jake, we need to talk sometime today. It's important," Harry said as Frida approached. I wondered what he had on his mind.

Frida was striking. She sported a plain, white gauze dress traditional for Mexican peasants, a bulky, yellow ceramic parrot necklace, and bright blue sandals. She limped up to me and held her arms out wide for a hug. Normally, I would have immediately reciprocated. However, something about her tone the night before put me off, so that morning reluctance replaced habit. But once she put her arms around my legs and squeezed, I had no choice. I bent down and forced myself to give her an obligatory, reciprocal *abrazo*. Daisy shot us a disapproving look.

"*Hay*, Jake you're dressed like a *chivero*; complete with a *cachucha de sopapilla*," she said, looking me up and down and pointing at my cowboy hat. I was wearing the twenty-gallon Stetson especially made for me and one of my favorite cowboy outfits. Judging by Frida's lightness and wit, I wasn't sure whether or not she felt the stiffness in my body when we hugged and if she understood its message: that I didn't particularly want to be close to her.

"Harry and Daisy, this lovely flower is my friend, Frida Kahlo. I'm sure you must have heard of her. She's a wonderful artist," I said, doing my best to hide my ambivalence.

"It's nice to meet you," Daisy said as Harry nodded in agreement. But the suspicious look on Daisy's face did not match her cordial words.

"That was Spanish, right? What did you just say?" Harry asked, apparently oblivious to what was going on with Daisy.

"Frida is referring to my cowboy garb. She said I'm dressed like a sheepherder, complete with a hat that looks like a pointy, fried Mexican pastry. If you haven't already noticed, though she's a Mexican, she's kissed the Blarney Stone." The four of us laughed, but for me it was forced. "Shall we?" I asked, gesturing to the door.

As we walked through the lobby, Frida stepped closer to the bowl of flowers on the end table. We all stopped to see what she was doing. Frida nimbly reached into the bowl, fished out one of the larger gardenias, shook it a few times, spraying several drops of water into the air, and then proceeded to pin the white and gold flower behind her right ear. Then she squatted down next to Daisy. "Don't you worry *querida* (sweetheart). I have no evil intentions toward your precious big man." Then she straightened herself up and sashayed towards the lobby door. The look on Daisy's face was a combination of astonishment and anger that only one woman can provoke in another. I worried whether or not those two would get along.

We all walked outside past Pepe, the old, skinny Mexican with a long gray handlebar mustache who worked as a bellhop. He was a permanent fixture at the Paso del Norte. You could almost always find him standing just to the right of the large, brass-framed glass doors that served as the hotel's main entrance. Pepe's right shoulder drooped almost half way down to his hip. Some people said the deformity was the result of a birth defect. Others said it was from an awful injury. Whenever I saw someone with a deformity like that, it was second nature for me to picture them on a platform in the sideshow. Another local legend had it that the droop in Pepe's shoulder was a result of a bullet taken fighting with Pancho Villa at the Battle of San Andres. As we moved past him that morning, he was stowing a rich rancher's scuffed luggage in the trunk of west Texas's only Duesenberg. It always amazed me to see how easily Pepe handled heavy suitcases that were almost as big as he was.

"It's about twenty blocks to the South El Paso Street Bridge. We can take the *tranvía* or we can walk," I said.

"On a gorgeous spring day like this, I absolutely think we should walk! What about you, kiddos?" Harry asked.

"Let's walk," the two women said in unison. Then they eyed each other and smiled uncomfortably.

"Then walk it is," I said. "Follow me." My friends were only in town for a little while and I had planned a very busy morning for them. I was glad of it, hoping that all our activity wouldn't give me a chance to obsess over Val's absence.

XXXX

After we walked another block I stopped. "On this spot in 1881 Marshall Dallas Stoudenmire gunned down four men in five seconds. Then I pointed across the street to an old bar on the ground floor of a chocolate-colored building with bay windows. "That used to be called the Acme Saloon," I said doing my best to be a good tour guide. "In 1895, that famous gunman John Wesley Hardin was shot dead there."

"*Was machte* (what's cooking), Jake?" a voice yelled from the far side of South El Paso Street. It was old man Zeitner. He was wearing a denim apron and sweeping the sidewalk in front of his hardware store.

"Hello, Mr. Zeitner. My regards to the missus!" I yelled back, but kept walking. "That guy ran guns to Zapata," I whispered to my friends. Frida nodded approvingly.

"Really?" Daisy asked. She and her brother stopped, wide-eyed, and stared at old man Zeitner as if they were seeing the legendary, mustached revolutionary himself.

I was trying really hard to entertain my friends; too hard. It was what Black Jack Pershing might have called a *diversionary tactic*. Though I wasn't acting in a flicker or appearing in the sideshow, I was, nonetheless, performing. I had been performing so long in so many different venues that sometimes it was hard to tell when I was on or off stage. It came to me pretty clearly that my act that morning was a way to avoid feeling how disappointed I was about Val. Maybe that's what all those years in Hollywood and with the circus were about; performance as a ticket out of pain. I wondered what my life would be like if I didn't perform; if I didn't try so hard to avoid and hide my melancholy.

As the four of us walked along the sidewalk we passed Mr. Blaugrand's store, the old Imperial Furniture Company. I looked in one of the picture windows at a display of mirrors.

"Did you hear? Lou Adler's not coming back next season," Harry asked. Harry vigilantly scrutinized my reaction.

"No, I didn't. Why is he leaving?"

"Some say he's tired. But rumor has it there's a problem with his liver."

Before I ever met Val or even dreamed of being an artist, I'd watch Lou painting in the backyard. Sometimes that famous clown who had taught me so much about kids would even paint while he still had his makeup on between shows. Lou loved to paint clowns. There was always something so sad about the faces he captured on canvas. I would miss that old clown and, now that I was painting, the opportunity to talk with him about my art.

As we walked on past Blaugrand's store, I imagined myself not as a movie actor or a sideshow trooper, but as a giant circus clown. I visualized myself sitting in front of one of the mirrors in Clown Alley after a show, pulling off my big red nose and scrubbing away the white greasepaint. In my fantasy, after I removed all my makeup no reflection looked back at me. There was nothing there. I was invisible. I'd been in one type of show or another so long that if I didn't perform, I wondered if I'd disappear. I wouldn't only be invisible but worse; I'd be all alone. That idea made me shudder.

Walking on toward the border, I felt a bit wobbly. Harry bringing up Lou had unsettled me. I'd been pushing the decision about whether or not to leave the circus out of my mind, but now Harry brought it back into clear focus.

Staying in the sideshow was no longer dictated by my family's finances. Since I'd been home I had realized that Dad had clawed his way out of bankruptcy, paying back every single penny he owed, and the store was doing better. Because they couldn't convince any relatives to leave Europe, my folks also no longer needed my financial help with that. Now I was free to choose whether I would stay or leave Ringling Bros. But with that freedom I started to obsess again about how I would earn a living if I stopped performing.

Maybe I'd move to Mexico. After all, in those tough times I'd heard many stories of crazy and not-so-crazy *gringos* who moved south of the border where they could live on the cheap. That made me think of the time a few years before, when Clyde Ingalls sent me to Chihuahua as a part of a public relations stunt. I was to meet a young, seven-foot *Tarahumara* Indian from a small village called La Misión in Barranca del Cobre, the Mexican Grand Canyon. Besides getting my photo in the Mexican press, Ingalls wanted me to evaluate the girl as a possible attraction for our sideshow.

It was a big deal for the locals. They billed it as *La Junta de los Gigantes*, The Meeting of the Giants—the Tallest American and the Tallest Mexican. The governors of Chihuahua and Sonora even attended, as did journalists from as far away as Mexico City. I remember they brought the Indian girl to town from the mountains on a wagon decked out with flowers drawn by two white mules. That was the first time that giantess had been in a big city. It would have been impossible for her to travel with the circus. I mean, the poor thing could barely walk. She was a slow, sad girl of about sixteen. When one of the reporters told me about her life, I understood why. There was no way she could stay with her family, who lived in a cave on the side of a mountain. She couldn't ever play with the other Indian children who passed their time kicking a small wooden ball up and down steep, rocky trails. So her community had shunned her; said she must have been cursed by the gods. The family brought her to the priest at the small church in La Misión. He let her stay in a toolshed next to the cemetery. The locals shunned her, too. To them she wasn't just a freak—which would have been bad enough—but worse, she was also an Indian. I often wonder what ever happened to her.

I shook my head to bring myself back from that memory. I was glad it was barely eight a.m. and most of the stores on South El Paso Street weren't yet opened. If they had been, I would have been lassoed into chewing the fat with a least a dozen merchants— among them, Jews, Mexicans, and Chinese, all friends of my family—and we'd never get to Mexico.

As we strolled on, Harry and I talked. I was relieved to see that Frida and Daisy were finally chatting as well. The four of us stepped into the street to cross Paisano Drive and stopped short as an old, green, flatbed Ford packed with crates of freshly picked Hatch chile peppers turned left in front of us. I swore I saw Norma Schroeder, the grocer's daughter, driving. As we started moving again Harry began to talk.

"When I mentioned Lou Adler, you got a very strange look on your face. Did that remind you of your predicament?" Harry asked. I looked at him quizzically. "You know . . . about your future with Ringling Bros," Harry explained as the two of us stepped out of the street onto the opposite curb. Daisy and Frida followed a few paces behind.

Harry's question made me uncomfortable. I was already upset enough about Val's absence. I really didn't want to get into a discussion that would just make me feel worse. "I know it's been on your mind. Have you made any decisions yet?" He wouldn't let up. Harry looked at me, demanding an answer. I felt I had no choice but to say something. I glanced at him then looked away.

"No, I really haven't. I thought I was going to leave, then I needed to stay in the show to help my folks out financially. But I think that's all cleared up now."

We walked by a two-story, gray, granite building with a cheap façade of two Ionian columns. My brothers had told me that Mrs. Rosensweig ran a cathouse in there. I debated whether to say anything about it to my friends, but chose not to. After all, the Dolls were teetotalers, and contrary to what every Tom, Dick, and Harry thought about show people in those days, they were very old-fashioned in their values.

"Harry, you've been with the sideshow longer than I have." I decided the best defense was an offense. "How have you stayed there so long?" I asked. "What's your secret?"

"You know, there have been plenty of times when I was fed up with the whole damned thing, but you see that little blonde bringing up the rear?" Harry looked over his left shoulder at his sister. "Daisy helps me find the strength to soldier through those doubts. It's my family, Jake. That's what drives me through the rough patches. I guess it's the glue that keeps me stuck in the freak show." Harry stopped walking and so did I. Then he tugged on my pant leg with the passion of a *padre* yanking on Sunday morning church bells. "You need somebody too, Jake," Harry said gazing up at me. "Even eagles have to come down to earth to eat."

I nodded, but didn't say a word. I wondered if I would ever meet that special person. It seemed that everybody—my mother, my father, my brothers, Frida, Val, the Dolls—had plans for my future. I needed to come up with my own.

CHAPTER 27

Juarez

A few minutes later, the four of us walked across the stone bridge located at the end of South El Paso Street that spanned the Rio Grande and served as the international boundary. At that time of year in El Paso, the Rio Grande—the liquid edge between two nations—consisted of little more than a trickle of water. It was hard to believe that about fourteen years before I had almost drowned in that river. Crossing the border between Texas and Mexico that morning, I finally felt my head clear of its Val-induced fogginess. I even felt a bit exhilarated.

"I cannot believe how close Mexico is," Daisy commented.

"Poor Mexico, so close to the United States but so far from God," Frida remarked. As she spoke I looked down and saw my giant shadow cast by the morning sun against the cracked outer wall of an old adobe building we were passing.

"That's profound, Frida," I said.

"*Ni modo*, I didn't say it. I stole those words from that bloody *cabrón*, that damned dictator that tried to destroy my country. Porfirio Diaz, may you rot in hell." Frida spit on the sidewalk.

We stopped in the shade of the awning that hung over the picture window in the front of Sidransky's Curio Shop. I watched as a young nun in a starched black habit herded a flock of neatly pressed youngsters past us. The nun and the children had dark complexions like the young giant I met in Chihuahua. But unlike her, the nun and the children were *mestizos*, the mixed blood offspring of conquering Spaniards and vanquished Indians. Though they came to be the majority of those who populate that place, those mixed blood children, like mixed blood children everywhere, were outsiders, never fully accepted. Maybe that's why I felt so at ease in Mexico, a land made up of outcasts, like me, who never fit in.

The nun and the children were halfway down the block when she suddenly stopped and stomped back toward us. Then the nun stormed up to Frida. Her determined demeanor abruptly changed. As she humbly dropped her gaze to the sidewalk in front of Frida, I noticed the children, staring at us and particularly at me.

"*¿Hay, eres Señorita Frida Kahlo, la estimada artista y esposa del famoso Diego Rivera* (Are you Frida Kahlo, the great artist and wife of the famous Diego Rivera)?" she asked in a breathless, reverent whisper.

"*Si, soy yo* (Yes, that's me)," Frida responded, almost giggling, clearly caught up in the nun's excitement.

"*Es un milagro* (It's a miracle)!" She said making the sign of a small cross in the air in front of her chest. "*Me encantan sus retratos* (I love your paintings). *Los ví en una exhibición en un museo en El D. F. cuando visité a mi mamá el año pasado* (I saw them in an exhibit at a museum in Mexico City when I visited my mother there last year)." As the nun spoke, Frida smiled and seemed captivated by the attention. "*Son muy especiales.* (They are very special). *Su talento es un regalo de Dios* (Your talent is a gift from God)," the young nun said hurriedly, gazing upward to the sky. As she glanced up I could tell she took sight of me because she looked startled and stepped backward. She crossed herself again. I noticed the children were restlessly moving around but still gaping at us.

Frida reached out and took the nun's hand. I couldn't tell if she was trying to calm the woman or capture and hold her attention. "*Disculpe la molestia, que Dios la bendiga.* (Excuse the bother and God bless you)." The nun spun around, took a few steps back toward her charges, stopped, and stared back over her right shoulder, first at Frida and then up at me. She turned back around and stood like a statue, frozen there for a few more seconds. I imagined that she was reciting some special prayer that Catholics are commanded to say when they see a rarity of nature. Then the nun stomped back to the children with the same determination with which she had approached us and herded her flock onwards.

"I see you have fans," Harry said.

"Yes. I guess there's no rest for the wicked," Frida replied, with not a little pride.

"It's starting to get hot. We'd better get moving," I suggested. "Frida, you've lived in Mexico and the United States," I said as we began walking again. "If you had to sum up the differences between Americans and Mexicans in a few words, what would you say?"

Frida thought for a minute, ran her fingers through her cropped hair, scratched her head, and finally replied. "*Los Mexicanos*, they know how fragile life is. The Americans are working hard to forget it."

Harry and Daisy laughed. I smiled.

The rest of morning was spent seeing two of my favorite landmarks in *Ciudad Juarez*: the bullring and the central market.

Our first stop was *Banderas plaza de toros*. The bullring was smaller and more intimate—if you could use a word like intimate to describe such a place—than others I'd seen. In *Banderas* during *las corridas* you were so close to the life and death struggle of the bullfight that you could almost smell the bull's, or sometimes the *torero's*, blood on the sand. At that hour of the day we had the whole place to ourselves, which made the experience a bit eerie.

All told, we were there about three-quarters of an hour. The first part of our visit was very unpleasant. For several minutes, we had to walk through a narrow, dimly lit tunnel that led to the stairs to the seats. The ceiling was so low that I had to bend at the waist to not hit my head on it. It sort of reminded me of that passageway I told you about that I took to get away from Clyde Ingalls in Madison Square Garden. Once we finally got out of that damned tunnel, we climbed up the rock and mortar stairway to the top row on the sunny side of the round structure. Climbing those steps wasn't easy for any of us. Then we sat down on a rough wooden bleacher.

"This place reminds me of the circus," Harry said after we had sat in silence, resting for a few minutes.

"Why is that?" I asked, gazing down at the arena where, over the years, too many bulls had died to even count.

"It's the shape of the place. It's laid out in a circle."

I nodded. "Sitting up here makes it easy to visualize the original circus," I said. "You know, the Roman Circus where they raced chariots and lions ripped Christians to bits."

"Maybe that's why they slaughter animals in places like *Banderas*," Frida added. "In this show, it's the Christian's turn for revenge." She laughed, but no one else did.

"It's a little too warm for me," I said after we'd been sitting there for a while.

"For me, too," Frida replied.

"If it's okay, we'd like to spend a few more minutes here. It's not every day we get to see a place like this," Harry said.

"Sure, take your time," I replied. Frida and I stood up, made our way to the stairs and slowly began our decent. I noticed it was much more difficult for her to climb down the steps than it had been to climb up them. I offered my hand to help her and she pushed it away abruptly. After about twenty steps I stopped, removed my Stetson, took a hankie out of my pocket and wiped away several drops of sweat that had formed on my forehead. Because of how she had reacted to my attempt to help, I never let on that I was stopping to let her rest.

"Did it bother you when that nun recognized you?" I asked, trying to make conversation.

"Bother me? You silly man, it doesn't bother me. I love it." Her tone was dismissive. Her answer made me uncomfortable and made her seem arrogant. I thought back to Hari Kidd's admonition about Frida and Diego. "Celebrity is a reward for all those lonely hours of toiling in my studio all alone. It's like *mezcal* and religion. It intoxicates me, makes me think I can tolerate my misery; makes me think I'm somebody else, that I'm going to live forever." She sighed a deep, sad sigh. The sadness made her seem vulnerable and more human. "I'm sure you like being famous, too. What about all the *señoritas* that want to get to know you up close and personal—if you know what I mean—because you're famous and not like everybody else?"

I paused and, for what seemed like a long time, didn't say anything. I wondered if my fame was behind Val's interest in me. "Not really. Fame is not important to me," I finally said. "You see, I wish, just once in my life, I could go somewhere and not stand out."

Frida looked at me and shook her head. *"Ay, eres loco, larguito querido* (You're crazy, my dear big friend)." Then she continued to climb down the stairs.

At that moment, I realized that Frida didn't understand what I was talking about. Though she'd had more than her fair share of pain in life, she hadn't had to deal with the unwanted stares since she was seven. For me, anonymity would have been a godsend. For her it would have been a curse.

After a few more steps she stopped again. "You know that *monjita*? I bet she grew up on a *ranchito* (small ranch) with a *borracho* (drunk) for a father and a *María* for a mother who tolerated his *chingadazos* (punches) and brutality," she continued. "Bless her. If that nun had stayed home she would be married to some *cabrón* who couldn't keep his pants on." Frida sounded so sad and angry. "Now she's married to the Christ and not a drunk. She serves holy water and communion wafers instead of tequila and tortillas. At least she has a lover that's faithful. But you know what happened to him."

I wondered about the real reason for Diego's absence. I could feel the pain behind her sarcasm. Then it came to me. Though I was a giant and an artist, Frida Kahlo just saw me as a man, like any other man. She was unable to distinguish between me, Diego Rivera, and all the others who had scarred her.

I looked up and noticed that Harry and Daisy had begun to climb down the stairs. With their little legs it was challenging to make the descent. Harry tenderly took Daisy by the hand. He might have been trying to help her so she didn't tumble down the steps, or it might have been a display of brotherly kindness. Whatever Harry's intent, that caring gesture stirred a longing and loneliness in me. I looked over at Frida. At that moment, I saw vulnerability in her that I had seldom, if ever, seen before and never saw again. I wanted to reach out and hold her. But as the Dolls approached, I watched her stifle her softness with what looked like a sneer.

I was the last one to walk down the remaining steps to the exit. Just before I reached the bottom, I hesitated and, once again, gazed out onto the arena where a sudden gust of wind sent dust devils flying in different directions across the dirt space. I waited there for a moment longer. *Bullfights draw crowds to see men try to master what they fear most: that which they cannot control,* I thought. Then I took another step down to the bottom of the stairway and turned into the labyrinthine tunnel that led to the exit from the bullring. Harry, Daisy, and Frida were nowhere in sight. The passageway, which had been lit— though just dimly—when we entered, was now in total darkness.

Making my way slowly and cautiously alone in the darkened bowels of the bullring, I heard a voice in my head: *You and all the other freaks in the sideshow are mistakes that nature herself cannot not even control.*

It was taking much longer to get out of that place than it had taken to get in. I started to feel frightened. Reaching out like a blind man, I felt the tunnel's rough plastered surface. The confined space made me feel trapped. *I'll never, ever be free of my body, my thoughts, and my memories,* I thought. At that instant I became a seven-year-old boy soon after I started my monstrous growth. I lay in my bed, drenched in sweat, haunted by a night terror. I felt my heart race just as it had then.

The damning voice in my head continued its rant. *From the four corners of the world the promoters collect mistakes like you, put them in a circus, and sell tickets to rubes, who for a meager twenty-five coppers can feel more secure about what they cannot control. Like the bulls that die in this place,* I thought, *we freaks rarely, if ever, leave the ring alive. Will I?* I wondered.

To the best of my recollection, that's when I tripped on something in my path, stumbled, and almost fell, just barely managing to maintain my balance. *Calm down and wait for your friends to come back in the tunnel and find you before you hurt yourself,* I commanded. I ignored my own advice, took a deep breath, and forced myself to keep going. *I'm not a gladiator, a condemned bull, or nature's mistake,* I thought as I moved farther into the darkness.

"I'm much more than that!" I said forcefully, loud enough to echo off the tunnel's stone walls, as if there were someone there to hear my confession.

After another hundred or so steps, I saw rays of daylight ahead. When I finally exited *Banderas*, my three friends were waiting for me in the midmorning sunshine.

"What happened to you?" Daisy asked.

"I thought we might have to send Max Drummond to the rescue," Harry added.

"Oh it was nothing, I answered. "For a minute, I got lost."

XXXX

I was feeling a bit overwhelmed by what had just happened, so I led my friends back to *Avenida 16 de Septiembre* in silence. I was glad we were headed to one of my favorite places in Juarez; it was a place where you could buy anything and everything imaginable. Wouldn't it be nice if I could purchase a solution to all my worries there?

"Where are we headed now, Jake?" Daisy asked, breaking my silence.

"The *tianguis*," I replied.

"The tian . . . what?" Harry asked.

"We're going to Juarez's central market. Follow me."

When we finally reached the sidewalk in front of the place, Daisy was accosted by a one-eyed, one-legged beggar on crooked crutches that looked so ancient they might have been used by an injured *conquistador*.

"Señorita, ayúdeme. Por favor, pesos para comida (Lady, help me. Please, money for food)." The beggar, whose clothes looked more like grease-stained rags, stared down at her like a coyote looks at a cornered rabbit.

Harry moved between them. "Not so fast, buddy."

The beggar shifted his gaze to my little friend and scowled. He started to raise his crutch as if he was going to strike him. Harry stepped back, made two fists, and crouched into a boxer's stance, shielding Daisy from the crippled predator.

That's when I moved forward; making sure the beggar could see me with his one good eye. *"¿Hay algún problema, señor* (Is there a problem, sir)?" I asked.

"No, no hay ningún problema (No, there is no problem)," the beggar said as he quickly stepped back.

"Un momentito (Just a minute)." I reached into my pocket and handed the bum a dollar. The beggar hobbled away. I stood there looking after him, and Harry took a handkerchief out of his pants pocket and wiped his brow.

"Why did you give that son of a bitch anything, Jake?" Harry asked.

I didn't answer for a moment and just watched Daisy straightening her skirt. "Daisy, are you okay?" I inquired.

"I'm fine! I'm fine!" she insisted.

"I bet he's a faker and that under that patch his other eye works fine," Harry said.

"It's nice to finally see a *caballero* (gentleman) that will defend his lady," Frida said emphatically. Her tone telegraphed that it had been a long time since any man had defended her. At that instant I understood why she had chopped off her hair. I wondered if I persisted trying to connect with Val I'd end up chopping something off.

We continued to the main entrance of the market, the dusty air giving off a fragrance and a stink. It smelled of life and death, a wide-open window to the magic and uniqueness of that special place. As they say, *Mexico Mágico* (Magical Mexico). *That's another reason why I love Mexico*, I thought. It's a place that is so different that, at least for a little while, it lets me forget how different I am.

I held open the market's large mesquite wooden door for my companions. As we entered, I surveyed my friends filing by and thought that the four of us represented our own country, not a country like the United States or Mexico, but a country of freaks, living at the margins; a country of those who don't fit in anywhere but with one another.

We walked into the teeming market and I thought of the security I felt in that fringe state and the price I paid for that security. I wondered if traveling with the circus was a distraction for me. I wondered about the other distractions in my life. Maybe my craziness about Val and all the sadness I felt about not connecting with her the way I wanted was just one giant diversion. Frida smiled up at me knowingly. I wondered if she could read my thoughts.

While we wandered through the huge *mercado*, the aroma of fresh corn tortillas and the sound of *carne asada* sizzling in strange oils and the occasional putrid smell of overripe produce grabbed hold of my attention. I thought of how everything has its allotted time—fruit, vegetables, fame, people, and even memory—and how the only thing that has no limitation is love. It was odd. The deeper into the market we ventured, the less I thought about Val and the circus.

The four of us rambled past stands covered with orange, red, and green tropical fruits, purple flowers, huge stalks of bananas, and mountain-grown vegetables that I rarely, if ever, saw on the other side of the river. On the next aisle we saw cages with scarlet Costa Rican macaws, yellow and black fire-billed toucans from Chiapas, and light-blue canaries from Colima. That *tianguis* had an inimitable power to bring you into the here and now. It made me want to savor every breath; the sweetness and the stink.

After a few minutes we walked through a section of the market where herbal cures were sold. Something gave me gooseflesh.

"This place gives me the willies," Daisy said as we moved by an old, toothless woman who sat next to a table covered by some kind of desiccated green plant and bottles and bottles of dried, dead crickets, flies, and frogs. She was dressed in black and stared intensely at a small silver medallion that she clutched in her left hand. I imagined that the medallion bore the engraved likeness of some saint she prayed to for protection from all that she feared.

"This is the place to get a custom-made love potion you can slip into Val's martini. The big-city *señorita* won't stand a chance," Frida said, attempting to be funny. Even though her remark felt cruel, I stopped and weighed her suggestion. The old woman looked up at me from her meditation. She beckoned me with a gnarly finger to come back. I spun around and ran to catch up with my friends.

A few minutes later, in one of the smaller stalls, we came upon a poor and humbly dressed *Huichol* Indian sitting on the ground and selling some of his art. He had a leathery, wrinkled face that made him look much older than his years. His once-colorful native garb was now sweat-stained and faded. The *Huichol's* worn huaraches blended with his brown, bare feet. Something about that Indian and his art—maybe it was how out of place and time they seemed—drew us all into the booth. I was the first to step in for a closer look, but Harry and Daisy, and finally Frida, who had been enjoying a colorful display of *piñatas* in the next booth, followed.

"If Clyde Ingalls got a look at this guy he'd sign him up for the sideshow faster than Seabiscuit makes the clubhouse turn." Harry, now standing next to me, grinned and elbowed my knee as he spoke.

In his tiny booth, the *Huichol* displayed several string paintings. In three dimensions they captured peyote-induced quests that shaped his traditions. My three friends walked around, looking at those colorful creations. The looks on my friends' faces reminded me of what I must have looked like the first time I wandered around Hari Kidd's studio. I'd seen string paintings before, so they didn't draw my eye. However, an unusual piece of this man's art instantly attracted me. As I walked toward it, the Indian stood up from his place on the ground and quietly approached.

It was large—about three feet by four feet—and had an irregular, circular shape. The piece, which eventually magnetically drew each of our interests, was fashioned from shiny beads that were the vibrant colors of the fruits and flowers we had just seen in the market. The multihued beads had been skillfully positioned on a wooden board and held in place by beeswax. The mosaic was unlike anything I'd ever seen.

"*¿Hablas español*?" I asked, having previously encountered indigenous people in Juarez who spoke *Nahuatl* or some other native dialect, not Spanish.

"*Seguro que sí, señor* (Yes sir, for sure)." He grinned and answered with an accent that must have predated the Spanish conquest.

"*¿Qué es la imagen* (What is the image)?"

"Pues, es el eclipse del sol."

"He says it depicts a solar eclipse; the coming together of sun and moon," I translated for my friends.

The mosaic made me think about how, for some, the daytime darkness that is the outcome of opposites intersecting during an eclipse is frightening. For them, it is a time to hide from the gods and the evil they might be hatching. I glanced at the artist. For some reason I thought of Hari Kidd. Maybe it was because Hari and this *Huichol* created such unique art. I imagined what it would be like to experience an eclipse, a time that day suddenly becomes night, with my teacher and with the *Huichol*. I considered that for both men the eclipse would be a sacred, transformative time that would move them to create. I wondered if the *Huichol*, like Hari, had monsters in his head, and if eclipses exorcized them.

Harry, Daisy, and Frida walked on to another booth but I continued to contemplate the beaded mosaic. The *Huichol* stepped closer. *"Los polos opuestos se están juntando, ¿Te gusta? ¿Lo quieres comprar?* (The opposites are coming together. Do you like it? Do you want to buy it?)" I remember perceiving the coming together of the opposites the *Huichol* referred to not as the sun and the moon, but as a rare community made up of a giant, a family of midgets, and a half-Russian, half-crippled, bitter Mexican artist. I wondered if Val would ever be a part of that community. Would she and I, opposite in so many ways, ever come together in a sacred eclipse, or was she just a hallucination inspired by the drug of my loneliness?

"Sí, me fascina . . . para gozar pero no lo voy a comprar (Yes, it fascinates me . . . to enjoy, but I'm not going to buy it)."

I stepped out of the booth and caught up with my friends. A few minutes later we left the market. It was early afternoon by the time we crossed over the bridge to U.S. side. The four of us pilgrims were pretty tired, so we mostly walked in silence. Harry and Daisy carried the souvenirs they'd purchased: two Mexican black sombreros and a pink and white papier-mache *piñata* in the shape of a donkey that was as big as they were. Frida kept stopping and looking back over her shoulder toward Mexico, as if she'd left something there.

As we walked, I looked at the Dolls and contemplated if I'd ever have a companion. Looking at Frida, I wondered what I'd be willing to sacrifice in order to keep one.

Leaving Mexico that day, I felt ill at ease. I considered the boundaries, bridges, and borders I'd encounter next. I wanted to have the courage to leave whatever needed leaving behind.

On the way back to the hotel, we stopped by Geneva Loan and I introduced Frida to my folks and my little brother, Myer. Over the years, when Ringling Bros came to town, Harry and Daisy had met my family. But that was the first and only time Frida met them. That was also the first time any of my friends besides Carolyn—my pal from art school—had been exposed to my art. The two oil paintings they saw were hanging on the walls of the store. One portrayed the midway from a giant's perspective and the other presented the scene of a bull man trotting a string of Indian elephants into the arena for the spec.

"These are really good!" Harry said.

"Jake, I'm genuinely impressed," Daisy added.

Frida just looked on in silence.

"The intensity of your color . . . those vibrating edges. The world really needs to see your work," she finally said. "I have an idea. I have to talk with Val about it," Frida added cryptically. In light of her tone the night before, her kindness confused me. The mention of Val's name put me on my own vibrating edge.

"What are you talking about?" I asked.

"Never you mind, *largote*. Never you mind!"

In a few weeks I would understand just what she meant.

CHAPTER 28

Santa Fe

"Franciscan Friar," Jake Erlich

Speeding up a snaking curve on a mesquite-covered, obsidian mesa called La Bajada Hill, I felt powerful; a sensation to which I wasn't accustomed. You might think it odd that someone of my size would see himself as powerless, but that's exactly how I often felt. But not during my recent classes with Hari Kidd, and not that afternoon as I drove toward Santa Fe. Despite being a movie and circus celebrity recognized around the world who had the strength to hurl a football a hundred yards like a spiraling bullet and shatter a man's jaw with a gentle tap, I didn't have the power to make that special person materialize, the one who would free me from the dungeon of this giant's life. Maybe that's why I had such high, if unrealistic, hopes for Val and me. But swooping up the high desert in the foothills of the snowcapped Sangre de Cristo Mountains, commanding the invisible herd of mechanical horses that powered my Town Car to do my bidding, I forgot all of that, if just for a while.

It was the beginning of March 1937, and I was on the first leg of a photographic safari and a sorely needed vacation. Hopefully a few days in the majestic surroundings of northern New Mexico would help me make sense of everything I had on my mind. After all, Santa Fe had a reputation as a healing place, at least for the tuberculosis sufferers who started coming there around the turn of the century. Maybe that treasure of adobe architecture would be healing for me, too. You see, I was still plagued about what to do with the rest of my life. My father's trip to Poland, the trip that forced me to re-sign with Ringling, was a bust. Papa couldn't convince even one relative to leave. Most of them thought Hitler was a joke. If they only could have known what I know now, so many would have taken Papa's offer and saved themselves. That painful truth would haunt my family for the rest of our lives.

As I told Harry Doll a few weeks before in El Paso, staying in Ringling Bros was no longer a family obligation. I was committed to the sideshow for just one more season. I worried about what I would do the next time Ingalls approached me to sign a new contract. If I decided to quit the circus, how would I break the news to my parents? What with their bankruptcy, the state of the economy, and the dangerous mess in Poland, they had too much on their plate for me to bother them with my problems. I also wasn't at all clear about where I stood with Val. When she left Sarasota, and when she didn't show up in El Paso, I thought I was ready to let her go. But then, fed by memories of the kiss we shared on the steps outside of Dean's, I made excuses for her and wanted to give her another chance. Despite all of the things I was confused about, one thing in my life was crystal clear; I wanted to continue painting, sculpting, taking pictures, and writing. I might not have mentioned it, but on the trip home from Sarasota I had begun writing some verse. Late one afternoon, after I helped him hang some new paintings in his studio, I shared a couple of my poems with Hari.

"The long shadows in your words speak loud and clear to anyone who has ever felt different," he said. Even now I recall how Hari looked at me and shook that big head of his. "You know, Jake, I've heard of people with secrets in their past hiding in the circus; even some that are on the lam, but what is a poet like you hiding out there for?" I had no answer.

Driving along toward Santa Fe I was distracted, thinking about that still-unanswered question, when three huge crows flew past my windshield and soared over a high desert arroyo that stretched from one mesa to the next. I finally had come to the conclusion that self-expression was something I needed in my life. It wasn't so much that I painted, sculpted, shot pictures, or wrote poems for accolades. More than anything, I did it for myself. Now that I had started, I couldn't stop. It was like breathing; I just had to do it.

XXXX

It turns out, not through any planning or intention of my own, that I only stayed in Santa Fe for just a day. But I did get some great shots at the weekly farmer's market in the colonial plaza. That's where I found the Franciscan friar who would be the subject for one of my favorite photos. Later, that portrait won a gold medal at the annual Southwest Photography Contest.

On the cold, steel-gray morning when I first spotted him, his ancient face was framed by a rough, black, woolen cloak. As I recall, he was scurrying by me, headed toward a booth where a young, plump Indian woman was selling Mexican hot chocolate and autumn-red ancho chiles. When I walked over to where he was standing, the cold air made me shiver. I smelled an approaching storm and the delicious aromas of chocolate and fire-roasted chile.

One of the myriad things Hari spoke about in our sessions was that producing a masterpiece was not only a question of talent, but it depended to a large extent on how hard you were willing to work. Though my art allowed me to lose myself in the moment, I worked hard at everything I did, particularly photography. My photographs are classic black and white, moody images; the product of hours and hours in my darkroom. I approached every photograph, even the ones I shot on vacation, like the one of that friar, with tenacity, intensity, and—what Hari taught me is the most elusive discipline—patience. Hari had also said that creating a work of art required being in the right place at the right time and that depended, most of all, on listening to your sixth sense.

"What do you mean listening to your sixth sense?" I had asked.

"Pure and simple, it's paying attention to your instincts, Jake," he answered.

I guess because I'd made some serious mistakes like flattening that rube in Madison Square Garden, I told Hari I didn't really trust my instincts; that I did my best to ignore them, particularly powerful instincts like the anger that Val had stirred in me.

"You've become deaf, dumb, and blind to your intuition. It's your birthright, boy. Up until now you haven't ever been comfortable enough with yourself to be fully present. When you are, you'll begin to paint with all the colors on your God-given pallet," Hari had said.

When I saw that friar in the plaza in Santa Fe, I felt I was in the right place at the right time, and my intuition roared that he would make a great sitter for a picture. So I did something I had never done before. I walked right up to him, introduced myself, and asked if I he would pose for a photo.

At first, as most people are, he was taken aback by my size. Arturo—that was his name—was hesitant and very modest. "For your time, I'll make a ten-dollar contribution to your abbey," I said. He looked down, evidently still reluctant. "What is your favorite restaurant in Santa Fe?" I asked, sipping on a cup of cinnamon-and-almond-flavored hot cocoa I'd purchased from the Indian girl.

He glared at me as if he was suspicious about the intent of my question. "*Pues*, Coyote Grill," he answered reluctantly.

"And what is the best thing they make there?"

"*Enchiladas verdes con crema* (Green enchiladas with sour cream)." The suspicious look on his face was replaced by the countenance of a hungry man visualizing a plate of that savory fare.

"I will throw in a beer and a plate of enchiladas at Coyote's," I said, upping the ante.

"*Hecho* (Done)," he said, acquiescing with a smile. Then we walked across the plaza back to my hotel. The people at La Posada—the pink adobe inn where I was staying—were very accommodating. They let me set up my tripod right in front of the blazing stone fireplace in the lobby.

About one hour and a beer or two later, Arturo settled more comfortably in the chair and relaxed. Then he asked me a strange, unsettling question. "Are you Jewish?"

I recalled being asked the same thing by Frida Kahlo when she came to visit me in the sideshow in New York.

"Why do you ask?" Now it was my turn to be suspicious.

"I think it's because of your name. Anyway, you seem Jewish." I started to feel very uncomfortable. I didn't like where that conversation was going. Maybe he wasn't the kind, old friar he appeared to be. Maybe the alcohol had loosened the lips of a Father Coughlin-loving anti-Semite. Then the friar looked down at the ground and, as if he had the weight of the world on his shoulders, slowly turned his head up to me. "You see, *mis antepasados eran Judíos* (My ancestors were Jews)."

In a million years I never would have imagined those words to come out of that friar's lips. I cautiously moved out from behind my camera and tripod and slowly stepped toward him. His revelation and vulnerability and my own curiosity urged me closer. Arturo proceeded to tell me how his family had come to Mexico, fleeing the Spanish Inquisition. Then several years later, in a new, malignant incarnation called *La Purificación de la Sangre* (Purification of the Blood), the Inquisition re-immerged in Mexico. To avoid being burned at the stake or forcefully converted, his family came north with some of the *conquistadores*.

"My people settled in *Nuevo Mexico* and practiced their faith in secret. We and many others became what they called *marranos*; pigs, crypto-Jews." The friar took a swig of beer and wiped the foam from his beard with his cassock-covered right forearm. "Friday nights at sunset things got mysterious in my house. I remember *mi abuelita, que descanse en paz* (my grandmother, she should rest in peace) closing the curtains, lighting candles, and saying strange words. *Mi abuelito* would put a black skullcap on his head, like priests wear, and hold a silver goblet high in the air and say weird words as well. On their deathbed they whispered the appalling secret of our Jewish roots to my parents, who passed it to me. Since I've taken my vows to the church, I've left all that behind. But here in Santa Fe there are a lot of others who haven't. Anyway, my big friend, you may be a long-lost cousin."

We both laughed. I sighed. Not knowing what to say, I just smiled and nodded my head. Something about his story had made me tired and uncomfortable. I walked back behind the safety of my tripod and tried to refocus my camera. Moving the lenses to the left and right, increasing and decreasing the light that I would capture in my photos of Arturo, I reflected on how far people will go to hide who they really are. I wondered how far I would go to conceal myself. I wondered if, in fact, I had been hiding. All these years, playing roles in Hollywood, masquerading in the sideshow, and now pining for Val, was I a crypto-Jake; hiding my true self, whatever that might be.

Arturo seemed to notice my discomfort. He smiled kindly. "Are you all right, my son?" he asked.

"No, I have a lot on my mind," I said.

The revelation of his secret and his sensitivity to my discomfort produced an intimacy and trust between me and the Franciscan friar with Jewish roots. I imagined if I were a Catholic that would be the closeness I would need to speak to a holy man like Arturo in the confines of a darkened confessional.

I was moved to share some secret, private part of myself with the friar. I walked out from my refuge behind the camera, pulled up a nearby chair, and sat down in front of him. I spent the next hour telling Arturo about my life; the nightmare growth that started when I was seven, the back alleys and the taunts, my depression, my time in Hollywood and my blindness, my years in Ringling Bros, and my dilemma about whether to stay or leave. I even told him about Val. He listened thoughtfully, only pausing now and then to take a swig of beer.

After I finished unburdening myself, he sat there in silence. "There is something to this confession stuff," I joked, trying to lessen the awkwardness I felt and my fear that I might have said too much. *Is that all there is to it? I mean, you just spill your guts and you feel better?* I thought. But in all honesty, I didn't feel better. There was no catharsis; no magic cure. I mean, it was great to connect with another human being on an intimate and honest level like that, but I wanted more. I needed a lightning bolt of inspiration, a symbol, a sign or a divine message with answers to all my troubles, but none came.

The old friar squinted as if he were trying to focus on something in the distance. Then he put his hand on my right shoulder, shook his head, and smiled. "*Mi hijo, el tiempo es el mejor autor. Siempre cuenta con un final perfecto.* (My son, time is the best author. It always comes up with a perfect ending.)" Back then I had no idea what he was talking about and how wise he was, but it sounded like something you'd hear in a sermon; a nice attempt to put me at ease. It didn't work.

Later that afternoon, after I made good on my promise of an enchilada lunch at Coyote Grill, we parted on the sidewalk outside the hotel. Arturo took my hand.

"*Muchas gracias,*" I said as I looked down at him.

"*Que Dios lo bendiga,*" he replied, making the sign of a small cross just in front of his chest. "How you say, God bless you?" Later I would send him a copy of his photo; the one that earned a gold medal.

As I started to walk away, I heard Arturo call my name.

"Jake, if you are planning any travel from Santa Fe, you'd best leave early *mañana* (tomorrow morning). We're expecting a *tormenta* (storm). They say it's going to get bad. You don't want to get caught in a storm in these mountains. It can be treacherous. Remember, if you get caught on ice and the car starts to swerve, keep your foot off *los frenos* (the brakes)."

XXXX

Taking the old friar's warning and the black clouds on the horizon that I saw at sunset to heart, I left before dawn the next day for my day trip to Raton. I wanted to get there by late morning and get on the road back to Santa Fe before dark. My only stop in that little town nestled on the border between New Mexico and Colorado and the sole purpose of my day trip was a visit to the ranch where Rene Gillis, my friend that worked at Geneva Loan, had grown up.

You remember Rene; his nickname was Frenchie. For years I listened to his stories about how beautiful the ranch was. When he learned I was planning that trip he begged me to stop there and even wrote to his people to arrange a visit. Given the awful weather, if they hadn't been expecting me and if canceling was an option, I would have; but they didn't even have indoor plumbing or electricity, let alone a phone. As I drove out of town past the Pojoaque Pueblo, the predawn sky looked like black velvet. The storm clouds in the east made for a spectacular crimson sunrise. Soon I was gaining altitude, leaving behind the cougar-browns of the high desert and driving through an evergreen forest of *piñón* pine, spruce, and fir.

Gente supone y Dios dispone (People suppose and God disposes). Or the Yiddish version, *Menshe tracht unt Gut lacht*: (Men talk and God laughs). Those proverbs happen to be my favorites, but they especially come to mind when I think back on the accident. Despite everything that happened that awful day, including almost losing my life, for reasons I could never have fathomed at the time, I'm glad I made that trip.

I arrived at the cut off for Frenchie's ranch by ten. It was idyllic setting complete with jagged, snow-capped peaks, a winding, caliche-red dirt road that snaked over rolling pastures blanketed with herds of sheep, and rock bridges that traversed rushing, icy streams. After about twenty minutes I pulled up to a small stone ranch house with a sod roof. Next to the ranch house stood a large, rough-hewn, cottonwood corral holding four horses; two of them were black, the others a palomino and a pinto. The horses, still in their winter coats, galloped back and forth, frisky in air that was so chilly you could see their breath.

The ramrod of the outfit and the only one in sight was an old, potbellied Mexican cowboy with a thick beard and wide-set, friendly brown eyes. His name was Enrique. When he came out to greet me he was wearing a weathered *vaquero* hat, a patched, woolen navy-blue vest, and worn dungarees tucked into his mud-caked, calf-high boots. As soon as I saw him, with the same certainty I had felt about Arturo the day before, I knew taking Enrique's picture was a must. Later, that photograph would also garner a gold medal.

I took several shots of him; some in front of the corral, some on the porch of the ranch house and one in an alfalfa field with a backdrop of mountains and afternoon sunshine briefly splitting the clouds. I had planned to leave after I put my tripod and camera case in the backseat of the Buick, but Enrique kept drawing me into conversation. He was a pleasant sort of fellow and very interesting; a regular almanac of facts about the area and a wealth of stories about Frenchie. He wanted to show me places on the spread where Frenchie had gotten into mischief as a boy when he had just arrived from France. Then he told me about the time cattle ranchers had fired their rifles at Frenchie, him, and the herd of sheep they were shepherding.

"*Vaqueros y chiveros, mezclaban como agua y aceite, siempre eran enemigos* (Cowboys and sheepherders mixed like water and oil; always enemies)," he said. I was genuinely interested, but my attention kept being drawn to the threatening storm clouds on the horizon. *At this rate I'll never get out of here,* I thought. As it was, I didn't leave the ranch until around three.

Driving back to the main road, I noticed that the black clouds I had worried about had now descended to the point that they swallowed up the snow-covered mountains I had marveled at on my morning drive. Quicker than day turns to night, the scenery changed from majestic to ominous. I felt a sudden drop in the temperature. The air had turned so cold that just before I came to the county road, I pulled over, parked, and put on the heavy overcoat, gloves, hat, and muffler I'd stashed in the trunk. Though it was only half past three, the sky had grown dark. The wind started to howl. Heeding some primitive instinct, I sped up. Then I saw a pair of shelter-seeking eagles land in a tall pine tree on the side of the road. If I had any sense, I would have turned back and found shelter at the ranch. But I didn't.

At first, the snow flurries were sporadic. Then they grew heavier and heavier, dumping larger and larger snowflakes on my windshield. My wipers were barely able to keep up. I could hardly see through the fogged glass, so I reached forward to the dashboard and switched on the defroster. It didn't seem to work. Something was wrong. I rubbed the inside of the frosty windshield with my gloved hand. That was awkward, considering I had to reach it all the way from the back seat of my custom-made car. I had made jokes about that Town Car; how it took a team of attendants to park it and how no one else but me could drive it. But at that moment, the challenge of maneuvering the machine I depended on to get me safely out of the mountains was anything but funny.

The storm I tried to evade in Santa Fe had snared me. I was too far from Raton to turn back when the blizzard finally hit. *I'm in a white out*, I thought, clutching the steering wheel. I had to strain to even make out the black asphalt just a few feet in front of my fender. I couldn't see a damned thing. *Slow down*, I said, or more accurately, screamed to myself. Although it was below freezing outside, and none too warm in the car, I was sweating. I'd never driven in those conditions before.

I could feel my heart beat harder as I strained to see. Then I heard a horn and a loud noise to my left. I saw the silhouette of an old pickup barrel by me. As the truck passed a plume of slush and snow hit my windshield and completely obscured what little vision I had. I jerked the steering wheel hard to the right. The Buick started to skid, but I yanked the wheel to the left. Thank goodness I remembered Arturo's admonition and I kept my foot off the brakes. It was lucky I was going so slowly or I would have lost control of the car and ended up in the deep ravine on either side of the road. God knows what would have happened then.

I was so frightened after that that I slowed down to a crawl. Finally, I calmed down. *At this rate I'll never get back to Santa Fe*, I said to myself. The blinding winds had slowed though snow still fell steadily. A half hour later I finally felt comfortable and safe enough to pick up a little speed.

It happened so fast. Out of nowhere, an elk the size a horse darted in front of me. I slammed on the brakes and jerked the steering wheel. That time, it wouldn't respond. The car started to violently swerve and skid. I yanked the wheel with all my might but it did no good. In my panic I slammed on the brakes again. Out of control, the car careened off the road and down the steep embankment. I hit a tree stump. The Buick flew into the air and flipped over. I heard the sound of smashing glass. As the car tumbled, I cracked my head against the window and felt a sharp stabbing pain run through my legs.

I had been through so many things in my life: my monstrous growth, the accident on the set in Hollywood, my blindness, and my suicidal depression. Now, if there had ever been any, there was no doubt; fate was my hunter. Seconds before I blacked out, I was sure that my frozen, mangled corpse would be found on the side of a snowy mountain, just off the road from Raton to Santa Fe.

CHAPTER 29

The Wreck

"Vaquero," Jake Erlich

It must have been a bad dream, I thought. Trembling from the cold, I peered into the darkness and struggled to remember where I was and how I got there. As I tried to stretch my cramped body out and couldn't, it came back to me. I hadn't had a nightmare. It really happened. There had been a blizzard and a terrible wreck.

"Help! Help!" I panicked, screaming louder and louder as if someone would hear me. Little by little, I put the pieces together. My car had careened off the road and was now buried in a snowy, steep ravine on the side of a mountain somewhere just over the New Mexico state line. It was impossible for me to extend my arms and legs because I was pinned between the ceiling and the floor, upside down, in the crushed cabin of what once had been my Buick Town Car.

Nobody's ever going to find me. I'm going to die here, I thought. In the darkness I visualized my funeral. My mother, father, brothers, Rabbi Roth, the Dolls, Frank Buck, and even Clyde Ingalls were all staring into my open grave. I noticed Val was nowhere in sight.

Seeing my own funeral—or perhaps it was the snowstorm's sub-zero cold or the violent trauma—made my teeth chatter. When the shivering finally stopped, I was so exhausted all I wanted to do was sleep. Recalling a Jack London story in which a man craves sleep just before he freezes to death, I fought to keep my eyes open. That's when I got a whiff of it; the smell of gas leaking from somewhere in my wrecked car was ominous. I was certain there would be a fire and an explosion, and that I was going to burn to death. Even in the freezing cold, I was sweating. Instinctively, I kicked at the windshield. A stabbing pain ran from my thigh to my ankle. I had no choice—pain or not, I had to get out of that wreck then or I never would. I kicked the windshield again; that time as hard as I could. The whole car lurched. I stopped for dread I'd send what was left of the Buick—with me trapped inside—hurling down the rest of the ravine.

I weighed my options and realized there was no alternative. I began to kick again. That time I didn't stop. I booted the glass for several minutes until I finally heard the windshield crack. After a few more seconds of kicking, my bloodied legs, like those of a breeched, gargantuan newborn, pushed their way into the icy night. I felt some relief but it was short lived.

When I struggled but still couldn't free my torso, I knew it was no use. I was trapped. The pain, exhaustion, and loss of blood overcame me; I passed out.

XXXX

I'm not sure how much time elapsed before a gravelly voice in the darkness revived me.

"I'm sure I see two of them trapped inside. This one must have tried to kick his way out." Along with that voice, two small, golden beams of light penetrated my shattered windshield. The light splintered into hundreds of tiny, rainbow prisms as it shined through the smashed glass and bounced off fragments of dust and an occasional snowflake. I wondered if I was dreaming.

"We better move fast! I smell gas and this thing's liable to blow," someone else warned.

"Help! Help me!" I said as loud as I could.

Something heavy struck what was left of my windshield. I automatically jerked my head in the opposite direction and a sharp pain shot through my neck. The snow and wind that surged into the car stung my cheeks and made my shivering intensify even more than before. The voices and the beams of light turned out to belong to the New Mexico state policemen who saved my life.

"Don't worry, you two, we'll get you out of there," the rescuer said as he struggled to pull me out of the wreck by my legs. When he couldn't, he crawled into the car next to me and tied a rope around my chest. As both officers heaved and yanked with what seemed like all their might, I reached out in the darkness, felt the handle on my camera case, and clutched it tightly. I winced and screamed when they finally hauled me out of the wreck under the hood of the car and dropped me in the snow, but as if that case contained some magical amulet I'd quested a lifetime to find, I never let go.

"Listen, buddy, I know it hurts like hell, but we've got to get you away from this wreck. With all this snowfall and ice, it's likely to slide down the rest of this mountainside and take us all with it," one of the troopers warned.

"It's okay," I replied, nodding my head. "I'm ready when you are." Then the two of them dragged me up the side of that ravine through the snow. They had to stop several times along the way to rest.

"I've never seen anybody as big as you," one of them remarked, struggling to catch his breath.

"You're as heavy as a horse," the other cop added, wiping the sweat from his brow with his gloved hand. They'd almost lugged me all the way up the ravine back to the county road when I heard a rumbling, cracking sound. The officers let me go and I fell into a snow drift. The three of us stared back down the precipice. Then I heard what was left of my car careen into the ravine, slam into something, and burst into flames. For a few seconds the light from the ball of fire lit up the night, allowing me to see the faces of my rescuers for the first time. That's when I passed out again.

The next thing I knew I was laying on the floor in the back of an ambulance. "You're okay now. Just try to be calm. We'll get you to a doctor as soon as possible," the state trooper said in a kind voice. Then he patted my shoulder and covered as much of me as he could with several blankets.

It took all my strength just to bend my knees so they could close the ambulance doors. I was so exhausted that I didn't even have the energy to thank that cop for rescuing me or even to nod. What I remember most about that wreck wasn't the pain from my injuries but being grateful to be alive. I don't think I had truly been grateful to be alive like that for almost twenty-four years, since I was a normal-sized six-year-old kid.

For the ride to the hospital, the trooper sat on the stretcher next to where I lay on the floor. Over the wailing of the siren, just before I blacked out again, I heard him declare to the ambulance driver: "Mack, we couldn't believe there was only one guy in that wreck. My partner and I would have sworn on a stack of Bibles we saw at least two full grown men in there."

XXXX

If it wasn't for how bad I hurt, I would have chased the whole goddamned lot of those quacks the hell away from me. You see, for the two weeks I was laid up in St. Francis Hospital in Albuquerque, there was a never-ending parade of doctors in and out of my room. There were young ones, old ones, teachers, and students, some specializing in areas I never heard of or that had little or nothing to do with me. No matter, it seemed like every sawbones in the western U.S. found his way into my cramped quarters to poke and prod the freak. I didn't have much use for any of them. You see, since they misdiagnosed my blindness back in Hollywood as klieg eyes, I doubted what any of them said. I probably knew more about gigantism than all of them combined.

So when I met Dr. Lazarus, the physician in charge of my case, I had my doubts. Although he had a Jewish name, he had a swarthy complexion. He wore a white lab coat and in one hand he carried a stethoscope and in the other a lit cigarette. He smoked Pall Malls, just like Harry Doll.

Dr. Lazarus sat down at the foot of the two hospital beds they'd pushed together to accommodate me. I remember his fingers were yellow and he wheezed when he spoke. He was balding and appeared to be about fifty-something. I thought my doctor looked as bad as I felt.

"It's mostly soft tissue damage," Dr. Lazarus said. "You've torn all the muscles that connect your pelvis to your spine and you have a terribly sprained neck and back. But you're lucky to be alive." He coughed, cleared his throat and continued. "You need a lot of bed rest."

"How much bed rest, Doc? How long do I have to stay in the hospital? When can I go back to work?" As I asked my questions, I noticed the unbelievably long ash on the end of his cigarette.

"I'm not sure, but conservatively speaking I would say you'll be with us at least two more weeks. As for bed rest, I strongly recommend that you take another three months off."

Three months off? What a laugh. Who does he think I am, Rockefeller? I'm supposed to report to Madison Square Garden for the season opener in less than a month, I thought.

"Doc, there's no way I can do that. I have got to get back to work or I'll lose my job." After all the problems getting me to sign my contract last season, I knew I was already skating on thin ice. Ingalls would have a coronary if I asked him for ninety days to heal a sore back.

"Well, if you do return to work, it will be against medical advice and at your own peril." It wasn't his authoritarian tone or my general dislike of doctors that stopped me in my tracks, but rather his use of that nasty little word. *Peril . . . peril . . . what does this guy mean by peril?*

"One more thing: I saw irregularities in some of your blood work."

"Irregularities? What kind of irregularities?" I was alarmed and automatically began thinking about all the other giants I knew who were younger than I was and had already bitten the dust.

"I'm sure it's nothing, but some of the blood tests showed some other possible problems. While you're in here for your pelvis, neck, and back, we'll look more closely at everything else just to be sure there is nothing wrong with you."

"Well, I really don't have much choice in the matter, do I?" I answered sarcastically. Dr. Lazarus didn't respond. He just stood up, patted my leg, and walked out of the hospital room. As he did, the huge, skinny ash on the end of his cigarette dropped to the floor. In retrospect, I think my sarcasm was a way to disguise how scared I was about what was happening to my body and what I was going to do with however much life I had left.

I spent the next few days following doctor's orders and bouncing between extreme boredom, gnawing worry, and excruciating pain. I'm not proud to admit it, but the truth of the matter is that while I was cooped up in that hospital I forgot all about the gratitude for being alive that I had experienced in the ambulance. I was so uncomfortable and feeling pretty damned sorry for my self. It's funny; on the side of that snowy mountain, when I thought I surely was going to die, whether or not I had a shot at Val, and whether or not I'd continue with Ringling Bros didn't seem to matter much. When I had time on my hands in that hospital, they became urgent concerns, demanding my attention, filling up just about all the vacancies in my mental real estate. To escape my obsessive fretting, I read any newspaper or magazine the nuns who ran the place would bring me, cover to cover, at least three times. I read about the massing of Japanese troops in Manchuria and the growing Nazi war machine. When I read those awful things, I couldn't help but worry about something else; if and when would my friend Lya and her family be able to get out of Germany.

I was so bored and so down in the dumps you would have thought that when I finally had visitors I would have been grateful as hell to see them. But that's not at all how it played out. As a matter of fact, I was downright rude; a real horse's ass. Let me tell you what happened.

Five days after I was admitted, my parents, Ben—who was home on a visit from Los Angeles where he was practicing law and Myer, took the half-day drive up from El Paso to see me. I'm ashamed of how I treated my family that night. When they burst into my room around eight o'clock, I was watching the shadows on the wall and trying to sleep. The only light illuminating the depressing space came from a small lamp on my bed table. I must have looked six shades of pale and sadness. They were happy to see me. For one of the first and only times I can remember, the feeling wasn't mutual. The day before, when Dr. Lazarus told me my family was coming, I had been excited for their visit. But when they showed up at the hospital, I wasn't. You see, I was in so much pain, drugged up on morphine, and so full of self-pity, that I didn't want to talk. To avoid them, I even pretended to be asleep. But they still wouldn't leave. They just stood there staring at me. Afterward, I wondered if Mama really knew it was all an act.

That night, when she finally kissed my forehead I felt too guilty to continue with my charade. Feigning waking up, I opened my eyes and yawned. I was immediately sorry I did.

"How long have you been here?" I asked. That's when they bombarded me with a million questions about the wreck and what the doctor had said about my condition.

"I really am too tired to get into any of that," I answered curtly. Then Mama took the large wax-paper-covered plate Myer was carrying out of his hands.

"I brought your favorites," Mama said, uncovering about a dozen pecan *schneckem*. The sight of those pastries, which were, in fact, my favorites, nauseated me. I pushed them away. Mama, Papa, even my brothers all looked wounded, as if the whole clan had baked the *schneckem*. I wondered if Dr. Lazarus had a pill to stop the guilt I was feeling.

"We also brought you some things to read," Ben said, laying a few magazines on the nightstand next to my bed.

"Some letters came to the house for you," Myer added, taking an envelope from his rear pocket and setting it down on my lap. The stylized handwriting and the detailed drawing of a hummingbird on the envelope drew my attention. Without thinking, I reached for it. I saw that the letter was from Frida Kahlo and quickly tore it open.

There was no way I could have predicted or prepared myself for what was written in it. As I read the letter, I immediately understood the cryptic remark Frida had made a few weeks before in El Paso when she saw my paintings at my parents' store. Now I knew what she had in mind when she insisted that the world needed to see my art and what she was up to when she said she had an idea and needed to talk it over with Val.

It seems that Frida and Val were personal friends with J. John Hutchinson, a patron of the arts in New York and the owner of the Delphic, a famous Fifth Avenue art gallery. That was the same gallery where Val and I attended Diego's exhibit. You remember, that was the night I smacked my head in the subway on our ill-fated date. Well, to cut to the chase, at Frida's insistence Val had contacted Hutchinson and told him about me and my work.

"What's the matter?" Ben asked after I finished reading and set the letter down in my lap. "You look worried."

I didn't have an answer for Ben's question, and I wasn't in any mood to discuss my feelings. I just needed to be alone so I could get a grip on why reading that letter had disturbed me so much. After all, it was good news but it felt like I had just received a death sentence.

"I don't really want to talk about it," I answered honestly.

"There you go again with the 'I don't want to talk about it' routine." The concerned look on Ben's face had transformed to anger. "What the hell has gotten into you? What do you mean you don't want to talk about it?" Ben challenged.

"Don't you speak English? What part of 'I don't want to talk about it' don't you understand?"

Ben took a step toward me. Papa stood up, blocking my older brother's path. "Sha," he commanded. "I think Jake is tired and doesn't feel well. We'll come back and see you tomorrow when you're more rested," Papa announced as he herded Mama and my brothers out of the room. After they left I immediately felt awful for chasing my family away. I mean, they had just driven all day from El Paso to see me. To distract me from my guilt, I tried re-reading Frida's letter. It helped, at least for a while.

Dear Larguito,

You have been invited to present a one-man show at the Delphic in Manhattan! Our friend at the gallery, J. John Hutchinson, has spoken to your teacher in El Paso and seen photos of your work. He was impressed. He needs your response as soon as is convenient.

Con cariño,

Frida

Even though it was the second time I'd read it, I still couldn't believe my eyes. In a little over a month so much had happened. Besides being shocked, that bolt from the blue brought a wave of self-doubt, anxiety, and flat-out terror. *I'm just a rank beginner. I'm not a real artist. I'm a phony, an imposter. Nobody will come,* I thought. *I only have about a dozen paintings and two sculptures to my name. I don't deserve this. A one-man show in New York in a little over six months; how in God's name will I ever get it together? And even if I could assemble a show, my work is not good enough. There must be some mistake. There is no way I can do it. It's out of the question.*

"What were they thinking? I'm turning it down," I said aloud in that empty hospital room. I folded Frida's letter and stuffed it back in its envelope with finality.

XXXX

By early the next morning when I expected my family to return to the hospital I had adjusted my attitude. I'm not sure why—maybe it was my guilt or maybe it was the good night's sleep I had. Maybe it was because I didn't take my pain medicine that morning. For whatever the reason, I realized I had been truly glad to see my family when they came to visit the evening before. When Papa was the only one who walked through the door, I was surprised and concerned. "Where are Mama, Ben, and Myer?" I was sure that I had offended them.

"They'll come later, but I wanted to have a chance to talk with you alone first; you know, man to man."

"I'm so sorry for how I acted last night," I said as Papa stepped closer to my bed.

"Don't give it a second thought. Mama and I know you weren't yourself yesterday. And your brothers . . . well they love you. They'll forgive you."

I have often thought and worried about how my condition had impacted my parents, but until that morning in my hospital room I hadn't really taken into account how everything that had happened to me must have affected Ben and Myer. Maybe it made them grow up early—too early. For the first time, I began to think about what it must have been like for them to have a brother like me; a brother who required a great deal of Mama and Papa's attention and limited financial resources. Did they have to hide their troubles for fear it would hurt our already emotionally over-taxed parents? Did they have to step up and be good boys, acting old for their years when maybe they didn't want to? As Papa spoke to me that morning, I wondered if Ben and Myer secretly resented me.

Papa pulled up a chair and sat down next to my hospital bed. "Last night your mood seemed to sour when you read that letter," he said.

"I guess it did," I answered. I felt I owed him an explanation. "You remember Frida Kahlo, that Mexican artist who came to the store a few weeks back. She walked with a limp."

"The one with the gardenias in her hair?"

"That's right," I said. "Well, she and another friend arranged for me to have a showing of my art at a fancy gallery in New York this coming fall."

"*Mazel Tov!* What great news." Papa stood up and patted my shoulder.

"Hold on, Papa! I'm not so sure I want to do it."

Papa looked puzzled. "Why in the world wouldn't you?" he asked. "I would think you'd be thrilled."

I explained all of my doubts: doubts that I wasn't good enough, and doubts I couldn't get everything ready in time. I also admitted that I felt like an imposter and not a real artist.

"I'm no expert, but I love your paintings. They each tell a story," he said. "All our friends who have seen them hanging in the store like them, too! Eli Krupp even wanted to buy one." I was surprised. The idea of someone actually paying their hard-earned money for my art was hard for me to believe. "That teacher of yours, Hari Kidd, he really likes what you do. I mean, Mama told me you're the only one in all of El Paso he's ever selected to be his student," Papa asserted as he sat back down. "Jakey, I know this art show business is a real challenge for you," Papa added. I nodded. "From great challenges come great possibilities," he said. "It's like that Spanish prayer Cuco told me the priests taught him to say before every wrestling match: '*Del agua mansa líbrame Dios, que de la brava me libro yo* (Free me, oh Lord, from the stagnant water, that in the raging torrent I may save myself).'"

Papa's words gave me chills. He had the gift of knowing just what to say. For several seconds the two of us didn't utter a word.

"I almost forgot," Papa said, interrupting the silence. "Something else came for you in the mail. We didn't get a chance to give it to you last night."

With that, he stood up, reached into the breast pocket of his coat, pulled out a wrinkled envelope, and handed it to me. The letter was from Hari Kidd. I opened it carefully and read it several times, just as I had Frida's letter. Hari first wrote his wishes for my speedy recovery. Then he quickly got to the point:

I hope it is okay with you. At your Mexican friend's request, I put together a portfolio of your work and sent it to New York. I've also been in touch with a Mr. Hutchinson, the gallery owner who wants to show your art. A few days ago, Frida Kahlo wired me the fantastic news. The Delphic has agreed to exhibit your paintings and sculpture. Congratulations!

Frida believes you're probably overwhelmed by the idea. That woman may be a lot of things; you know how I feel about her. But she is perceptive. I'll bet you dollars to doughnuts that when you read about the offer you had major doubts and tremendous uncertainties. You and I have only worked together a relatively short time, but with every fiber of my being I know that although you may not feel ready, your work is ready.

New York is just the place for you to show it. Life is short, my friend, and time does slip away. Don't pass up this opportunity.

Best regards,
Hari Kidd

Reading my teacher's words of encouragement felt good, but I still wasn't convinced. As you have probably figured out by now, self-confidence was never one of my strong suits. Although Papa asked, I chose not to share the contents of Hari's correspondence. He didn't pry. I know he understood and respected my need to keep some things to myself. He just nodded knowingly, kissed me on my forehead, and said he'd be back later that afternoon. Then he left.

At about three o'clock, he returned with the rest of the family. On that visit and on all the rest of their visits to the hospital I did my best to put the art exhibit in New York out of my mind and enjoy my time with them. Whenever I'd begin thinking about it, I'd force myself to think of something else.

Two days later, on the morning that my family returned home, after all the good-byes, Papa bent down and whispered in my ear. "Jakey, promise me you won't make a rash decision about whether or not to accept the offer; promise me you'll think about it."

"I promise," I whispered back.

"Whatever you decide to do, son, don't do it for the family. Do it for yourself."

XXXX

For the remaining week I was hospitalized in Albuquerque, I couldn't push the matter out of my mind. As a matter of fact, all I could do was lay there and pass the time fretting about whether or not to do the art exhibit at the Delphic. I knew that by the time I left that hospital, the gallery would need an answer. I started to feel like the walls in my hospital room were closing in on me. That's just how I felt after the crash in my upside-down Buick on the side of that snowy mountain.

Every time I visualized the art show I ended up having the same two awful fantasies. In one nobody attended. In the other, the gallery was packed with cruel rubes who, over the years, had tried to taunt me. It seemed that no good could possibly come from me agreeing to participate in that exhibition at the Delphic.

XXXX

When I wasn't worrying about the art show I was thinking about Val. Whether or not I exhibited my work in New York, she had done a very nice thing for me by interceding with the gallery owner on my behalf. I wondered what that meant about her feelings for me. I visualized Val's look of disappointment when she would hear that I had turned down the show. Especially after leaving art school, that would be a slap in the face. How many of those hits would it take to torpedo any remaining chances I might have with her?

Because of all that worry and my persistent pain, my nights were mostly sleepless and my days were interminably long. I bet it sounds strange, but if it wasn't for the tests Dr. Lazarus ran on me, my boredom, worry, and pain would have driven me out of my mind. It was actually the results of those tests that got me to finally make my decision about the art show.

Late one afternoon at the end of my second week at St. Francis Hospital, Dr. Lazarus stepped into my room and closed the door behind him. "Mr. Erlich,

I'm discharging you today," he said in a matter-of-fact tone.

I sat up and groaned. "You're what?" I felt a stabbing pain in my sacroiliac. Dr. Lazarus had my undivided attention.

"I'm discharging you today," he repeated. "You still have a severely strained back. But I'm more concerned about something else." He paused for several seconds, took a drag on his ever-present cigarette and exhaled the smoke, which seemed to hover around his face like a curtain. "The follow-up tests we did on your kidney function indicate the beginning phases of kidney disease. I suggest you follow up with a specialist to confirm my diagnosis. Do you have any questions?"

Kidney disease, I thought. *What the hell is he talking about?* I had many questions. As I'm sure you know now, if something else doesn't get me sooner, kidney failure will probably be the end of me. But that was the first inkling I had that anything was seriously wrong. It was a harsh reminder that my days really were numbered. At that moment, I was too excited about getting out of that damned hospital and too frightened about what the doctor might answer to ask all my questions.

Two questions did make their way through the blur of emotions swirling around in my head. "If there was something wrong with your kidneys, Doc, where would you go for help?"

"I'd go see Dr. Fishbein at Mayo Clinic in Rochester. He's the number one nephrologist in the field," Lazarus answered without hesitation. I reached for a pencil and pad on my bed table and wrote down the kidney expert's name. Then I turned to a new piece of paper and quickly jotted down an address and a brief note.

"One more thing, Dr. Lazarus," I said, tearing the note I'd just written off the pad and handing it to him. "Can you please have someone send this telegram?"

The telegram was to Hutchinson in care of the Delphic Gallery in New York. I had decided to accept his offer. It's funny. When you're faced with the cold, hard facts that you're already naked, terror of being embarrassed doesn't make any sense.

After the doctor left the room with my note in hand, I had a change of heart. "Dr. Lazarus!" I yelled. But he didn't hear me. By the time I got up and moved into the ward, he had disappeared. I slumped back in my bed, worried that it was too late and resigned that, come what may, I would

CHAPTER 30

Dr. Morris Fishbein

"Under the Big Top," Jake Erlich

Two weeks later, Dr. Lazarus's recommendation to seek out special help for my kidneys led me to Mayo Clinic in far-off Rochester, Minnesota. I was able to get my appointment so soon at Mayo because of my parents' good friend, I.B. Goodman. He had been going to the clinic for years to treat his sugar diabetes. When my folks told him about my situation, he made a personal call to his doctors and told them about the Texas giant with kidney problems and a sore back. The physicians at Mayo Clinic jumped at the chance to examine me.

It's not that I wasn't accustomed to worrying about my health, aches and pains, and being uncomfortable. Hell, I lived with that every day of my life. But this was different. You see, after I left the hospital in Albuquerque, for the first time, I had started to feel weak, and that bit about my kidneys was truly alarming. Ringling Bros new season would start in a few short weeks. If my health didn't improve, how would I ever be able to travel with the show?

By the time I arrived in Rochester, I was really sick. I had started to run a low-grade fever, had no appetite, and no get up and go. The pain in my back was so bad I could barely walk. To treat me, they used a combination of hot mineral baths, massage, and the latest medicine. But it turns out that damned kidney disease business was worse than I thought. The terrible pain in my lower back was from my kidneys, not from the accident.

"You have a serious kidney infection," Dr. Morris Fishbein said in a somber tone while we sat in his office.

He was short—like Dr. Lazarus—but thin, with pale, almost translucent skin. I imagined he spent his free time in the medical library and never, ever saw the light of day. I wondered why all my doctors looked so unhealthy. Fishbein usually didn't say much. When he did speak to me he was calm and composed. He was a real gentleman who spoke in quiet tones with a Boston accent. Fishbein was a natural healer. He inspired confidence. Maybe it was because he had a very soothing voice. There was something medicinal about just being in his presence. He made me understand why in ancient days, medicine, magic, and religion were all intertwined. Dr. Fishbein also had a poker face that masked his feelings; a trait he was born with or that had been beaten into him in medical school. But I did get an emotional reaction out of him.

"Well I'll be goddamned!" he exclaimed as he walked into the room and saw me for the first time. In a space where he was used to seeing one exam table he saw me filling the two that had been lined up, end to end, to accommodate me. I took an instant liking to the man. Soon I would have one of the most profound experiences of my life because of him. And it didn't have a thing to do with my health.

"It's really a lucky thing you had that wreck and your doctor in Albuquerque caught this," he asserted, sitting behind the small desk in his office during our subsequent meeting. I wondered if luck really existed, or if it was all just meaningless chaos. That thought, and what the doctor said next, frightened me. I drummed my fingers on his desk.

He picked up one of my X-rays and held it to the light. "With a big man like you, your kidneys have been doing a yeoman's work. It's amazing they lasted this long. If we hadn't started to treat this kidney infection now, it would have progressed rapidly and the outcome wouldn't have been good."

"What do you mean by 'wouldn't have been good?'" I asked so quietly that I wondered if the doctor heard me, and if I really wanted to hear the answer to my question.

"Your kidneys are sick, but at least we can treat them. Mr. Erlich, with a reasonable degree of certainty I can say that without care it wouldn't be long before your kidneys would have failed. You know, a person can't live without their kidneys."

"Are my kidneys going to fail?" I asked.

"I really don't know. All I can say is your kidneys are in bad shape. They're going to require careful monitoring. I can't tell you if or when they're going to fail and I cannot make any promises about your future. There are no guarantees for any of us." I found myself squeezing the sides of my chair. "But for now we will get your kidney infection under control and get you back on your feet."

I sighed and relaxed my grip. Over the years, most of the doctors I saw gave me scary prognostications where my gigantism would lead and about my life span. It appeared to me that they felt the length of my life would end up in direct but opposite proportion to the length of my body. So whenever doctors talked about my health, I did my best to take it all with a grain of salt. But there was something about how Fishbein said, "If it progressed, the outcome wouldn't be good," that let me know, whether I took his words with salt or pepper, that was exactly what was going to happen.

XXXX

By the time I left Mayo Clinic I was feeling much better, so it was a bit easier to not worry so much about my health. But every bit as important to me as the medical care I got at Mayo, were the lifelong friends I made there. One was Dr. Fishbein. The others were strangers I met late at night as they crowded round the baby grand piano in the bar at the Caylor Hotel while I played and we all sang songs. In those few late-night hours over cocktails, we all became intimate as cousins, related by pain, worry, and fear of what Mayo's medicine-men would find wrong with us and what, if anything, they could do about it.

XXXX

Shortly after I departed from Rochester, I received a strange request from my new friend, Dr. Morris Fishbein. It turns out ours would not be the typical doctor-patient relationship. My kidney specialist would end up depending on me as much as I depended on him.

Let me explain. Two weeks after I was discharged from Mayo Clinic, I received a special-delivery letter from him. When the carrier delivered the doctor's missive, we had just started our month-long opener at Madison Square Garden.

Dear Jake,

I must tell you what a pleasure it was to make your acquaintance. I hope you are in good health and spirit.

I find myself in a difficult and unenviable situation. I am a physician who needs a favor from his patient. You are in a unique position to help me and the venerable American Medical Association. Besides my work at Mayo Clinic I am the editor of the Journal of the American Medical Association. I, another doctor, and our association are being sued for libel. Perhaps you know the plaintiff; his name is Robert Wadlow. The other doctor is Charles Humbred of Missouri who, I have been informed, you have already met.

Dr. Humbred submitted an article on gigantism to the Journal that we published last year. Wadlow and his family interpreted that article as being libelous. Now they are suing us. I hate to ask, but I don't know where else to turn. Will you assist us?

If you are at all amendable to help, please let me know. Of course, for whatever reason, if you are not available or interested in this matter, I will understand. Whatever you decide, this will in no way impact our fine friendship and my professional commitment to providing you with the utmost medical care possible.

I remain your humble servant.

Sincerely yours,

Morris Fishbein, M.D.

Chairman of the Department of Nephrology

Mayo Clinic

Right then and there, without thinking about it or weighing the consequences, and despite the fact that my experience with Dr. Humbred had been most unsettling, I impulsively decided to help my friend. It just felt like it was the right thing to do. I would soon wish I had thought the matter through more carefully. From what little I knew about Wadlow and his family, I didn't much care for them but I don't think that's why I decided to lend Fishbein a hand. And based on most of my experiences with doctors, I couldn't have cared less about the venerable American Medical Association. Pure and simple, my intention was to help a friend. But you know what they say: The road to hell is paved with good intentions.

XXXX

I'd met Dr. Humbred, a coroner from Barnard, Missouri, back in '35. He had approached me and introduced himself after the spec during a three-day run in St. Louis. I remember that when I shook his hand it was cold and clammy, like the skin of Joe Blaugrand's pet corn snake that I held once when I was a kid back in El Paso. Humbred told me he was a medical man with a lifelong interest in gigantism and that he would like to interview and examine me. Even though he presented his credentials and licenses and a long list of references, he gave me the creeps.

Humbred was a tall, skinny, Ichabod Crane of a man who resembled someone who spent his time working with dead people. There was no way I wanted to be poked and prodded by an undertaker with a medical degree. My intuition was to send him packing, but my conscience, in the name of advancing science and medicine, compelled me to help him out. As a compromise, I agreed to the meeting but not to the examination. He seemed displeased, but grudgingly agreed.

I spent the following afternoon with Humbred, being interviewed and filling out forms. His windowless office was dark and dusty. The smoke from a burning cigar in the ashtray on his desk could not hide the telltale smell of formaldehyde that permeated the place. Humbred's office was filled with an old rolltop desk and two worktables piled high with magazines. Those tables also supported several huge jars that held scary-looking pickled body parts. Although it was supposed to be a doctor's office, I heard buzzing and thought I saw a fly or two in the dim light. The room had floor-to-ceiling bookshelves packed with hundreds of musty old books and photos. Humbred even had a skeleton that was well over eight feet tall hanging from a butcher's hook behind his desk.

"What is that?" I asked, pointing to the skeleton.

"Oh, you want to know about that, do you?" One of his skinny fingers emerged from the dirty white lab coat he wore and pointed at the skeleton. "That's my prized possession." There was a sinister tone in his voice. "It comes all the way from England. It originally hung in London's Royal College of Surgeons."

I wondered what nefarious activities had resulted in Dr. Humbred coming to acquire it. The way he looked, I wouldn't for a second have doubted he was a grave robber. "The skeleton stands eight foot, four inches; almost as big as you are." Humbred stared at me through beady, half-open, Gila-monster eyes. At any moment I thought he might thrust his tongue out and capture one of the flies buzzing around the room. I detected a sense of envy in him, as if he longed to have all eight and a half feet of me hanging on that butcher's hook in place of the smaller skeleton that was hanging there. "Those bones belonged to an Irishman named Charles Byrne. And there is quite a story that goes with them." Humbred didn't hesitate for an instant to gauge my interest in the tale, but plunged ahead. "I purchased this skeleton from the family of a famous English anatomist by the name of John Hunter. Hunter sought Byrne's bones for his medical museum, as did a swarm of others." I couldn't fathom why anyone would want to own someone else's bones. "Byrne knew he would die young. I'm sure you are aware, most giants do."

He looked me up and down with not the least shred of sensitivity for how those words might affect me. I swallowed hard. Humbred smirked and continued. "Well, the Irish giant feared if his doctors got hold of his remains they'd dissect him; something he loathed happening." As Humbred spoke I shuddered. I could just imagine this creep doing the same to me. "In 1783, just before he drank himself to death, Byrne arranged with his pals to spirit his body to the Irish Sea, weight it down, and hurl it into deep water." Humbred abruptly stopped speaking and walked over to one of the worktables in the middle of his office on which sat several large bottles that contained body parts soaking in a brown, murky liquid. He took hold of one of them and repositioned it, as if he had found it to be out of some bizarre order that only he comprehended. Then he strolled back to the skeleton and me. "Where was I? Oh yes, yes . . . After word spread that Bryne had died, a rabble circled his house." As Humbred spoke, I visualized that crowd as harpooners circling a giant whale. "It appeared that Byrne had outsmarted the scientists, but Hunter paid off his friends and got his body anyway. And if they hadn't, I wouldn't own it today." Humbred spoke with a self-satisfied arrogance, emphasizing the word *own*. He had the look on his face of a child who never shares his toys and loves having what everyone else does not. The story disturbed me. I felt anxious and I couldn't wait for the interview to conclude. "Would you like some coffee, Mr. Erlich?" Humbred offered.

"No, thanks." I worried that if I consumed anything in that awful place, it might be laced with a Mickey Finn and I'd never wake up. I'd end up in some creepy doctor's office hanging on a meat hook.

Humbred was a real pain in the ass; kept pushing to let him examine me; didn't want to take no for an answer. I got the feeling he was eyeing me like one of Buck's hungry tigers eyes a piece of horsemeat in the cage boy's hand at feeding time. As soon as I could, I made my excuses and got the hell out of there.

XXXX

About a week after I agreed to help Dr. Fishbein, a messenger delivered a note summoning me to a meeting the next morning with his attorney. The lawyer's office was just off Columbus Circle near the park in a stately brownstone. Standing outside on the sidewalk, I read the shiny brass plaque engraved with the names of the firm's four partners set in the side of the building. My appointment was with Honeywell, the first lawyer listed. Like all the other names on that sign, it sounded Anglo-Saxon—better said, gentile. I wondered if Jews would ever be accepted into the halls of those highfalutin law firms. They certainly weren't welcomed at the Ivy League schools that supplied most of their recruits. Even though I was there to help my friend, that gray Thursday morning when I walked into the mahogany-paneled office I felt like the atmosphere of the place was alien. It was somewhere people like me didn't belong. By the time the trial went down, I realized that my intuition was right.

As his secretary escorted me to his office, I felt I was being led into the inner sanctum of some secret temple. Honeywell, a short man in his mid sixties with wavy, white hair slicked straight back, Valentino style, appeared from behind a costly desk that seemed like it was built for someone twice his size. He was dressed in an expensive, black, three-piece suit. As the little man moved toward me I noticed the gold chain that bounced off his rotund belly.

"Hiram Honeywell is the name," he said, stretching out his stubby arm and exposing a French cuffed shirt and a gold cuff link. "You must be the one and only Jake Erlich." The attorney reminded me of someone, but I couldn't recall whom.

My mother had warned me to be wary of silver-tongued strangers who are easy with the compliments. "Thanks so much for agreeing to come in today." The lawyer's grandfatherly smile couldn't hide his fierce eyes. I got the sense that Mr. Honeywell was a competitor who had received and given his share of hard knocks. If I wasn't careful, he'd take me out with an uppercut I never saw coming. "Mr. Erlich," the lawyer said. "I don't want to waste your time, so let me blunt. I need your help with Wadlow's suit against Dr. Fishbein." His directness put me a bit more at ease. "How much do you know about this litigation?"

"I know very little about it. But I'm really in the dark about what I can do to help." I didn't have the slightest idea why Fishbein, Humbred, and the AMA's high-priced mouthpiece needed me Still, I knew I wanted to help my friend out of a jam.

"Let's start from the beginning." I towered over him, but in a lawyerly ritual of dominance he led me to a large, dark-green leather sofa that rested against the far wall, and motioned for me to sit down. When I sank into it we were eye to eye.

"In 1936, Humbred—with whom I know you are acquainted—wrote an article about gigantism that appeared in the Journal of the American Medical Association. *Time* magazine ran some excerpts from it. The piece was critical of Robert Wadlow." Honeywell paused and looked at me as if to ask, *"Are you listening?"* I nodded and he went on. "Although Humbred never actually used Wadlow's name, referring to him instead by his initials, R.W., it was as clear as the results of Roosevelt's last election who he was writing about."

Honeywell had a folksy, disarming way of speaking, but I still didn't trust him. It felt like he had told this story many times before and I was just one of many audiences for whom he had performed. "When we deposed young Wadlow, he testified that on a rainy, dismal day Humbred showed up, unannounced, at his family's home and demanded to examine him." I rolled my eyes. After the unpleasant experience I had with Humbred, I could easily visualize that scene. "Wadlow told us that he had just returned from college." For some reason, when Honeywell said *college*, I was surprised. Not because Wadlow wasn't bright; I didn't know him well enough to make that determination. But I had just assumed that people like us—Wadlow and me that is—didn't do normal things like go to college. I guess maybe I was envious.

Honeywell told me how that evening Wadlow was cold and wet and the family was eager to sit down to supper. Wadlow's family reluctantly let the doctor in. In my mind's eye I easily pictured the scene; Humbred being pushy and obnoxious like that. After all, when I met him in St. Louis, that's exactly how he had behaved with me. I didn't let him in my house or anything, but that day in St. Louis, against my better judgment, I talked to that toad.

"Mr. Honeywell, what in that article would have made the Wadlows so hopping mad that they would sue him, Fishbein, and the AMA?" I asked. Honeywell sat back in his chair and met my eyes. For the first time since I had entered the lawyer's office, I felt he wasn't just going through the motions, and that he recognized another human being in his presence.

"Well, that gets to the heart of the matter, doesn't it?" Honeywell asked. Then he opened a file that was on the table, removed what appeared to be a copy of a medical journal, and leaned toward me. He moved in a slow, deliberate choreography. I wasn't sure if he was trying to create a sense of drama, intimacy, or he wanted to make a point. "Humbred referred to R.W. as a freak of nature, unintelligent, with a 'surly, morose, and indifferent' personality." He enunciated and emphasized each adjective with precision and flair. Honeywell gazed down at the journal as if he were reading, but I had the feeling he had the contents committed to memory.

All the world's a stage, I thought. Besides being a pugilist and barrister he's as much a showman as I am. Something about seeing this battle-hardened attorney as an actor made me more comfortable. I sighed and relaxed.

"Humbred wrote that Wadlow demonstrated a 'lack of attention' . . . that he 'responded slowly to stimuli' . . . that 'all functions we attribute to the higher center of the frontal lobes are languid and blurred' and that he was 'apathetic, unfriendly, disinterested, and antagonistic.'"

Honeywell sat back and folded his arms. For a second I thought he might have been expecting applause. To say the least, that article was not flattering. I could understand why Wadlow and his family were furious. Although I recognized Honeywell's act, I still wasn't sure what he was after so I kept my thoughts to myself and just nodded my head.

"Now the Wadlows are transferring their rage to dollars and cents. They're suing Humbred for $100,000; Fishbein and the AMA for $500,000; and *Time* for $1 million." Honeywell frowned and knit his bushy eyebrows together in an arc. That's when I realized who that old lawyer reminded me of; the frown gave it away. He looked like Emmett Kelly, John Robinson's show's melancholy clown, "Weary Willie," who dressed like a hobo. *Underneath his costume of fine clothes, bravado, and lawyerly skill, lies the secret to why he's so formidable,* I thought. *Honeywell is driven by a deep sadness. Maybe beneath all that polish he feels like a tramp that's never fit in, too.*

"Wouldn't you agree that based on what's happening right now with the Depression and all, that's a hell of a lot of money?" Honeywell asked.

I nodded in agreement but I still wasn't clear why I was there. My uncertainty and the need to be on guard started to make me uncomfortable again and my stomach churn.

"Mr. Honeywell, I still don't understand what precisely you want me to do," I said, no longer able to maintain my silence.

The old lawyer held up his left hand, as if he were a halfback stiff-arming a tackler. "I promise I will get to that, but for now, please be patient. Would you like a cup of tea, some water, or perhaps—" he winked at me, "a snort of something stronger?"

"No, nothing, but I do have to perform in a matinee this afternoon."

"I understand," Honeywell added. "What exactly do you know about young Wadlow?"

I sat back and paused. I reported how he was said to be the tallest man in recorded history, and that he performed with Ringling Bros only twice. Both were stadium shows; once in New York and once in Boston. I also shared that he wouldn't set foot in the sideshow. Honeywell grunted his disapproval. He grabbed a yellow pad from the coffee table and jotted something down. I hesitated for an instant and then continued. "Wadlow would only appear in a suit and tie; and the troupers, particularly the freaks, didn't like him. We felt he was standoffish and unfriendly." I felt that the attorney already knew what I would say and that he asked his question just to maneuver me for what would come next.

"I noticed you used the word *freak*. Does that term bother you?" he inquired.

"Bother me? What do you mean, 'bother me?'" I asked, trying to buy time to figure out where he was headed.

"Is it pejorative? You know . . . an insult?"

"That's what the performers in the sideshow call themselves," I answered, dodging his question.

"Does the word *freak* bother you, personally, Mr. Erlich?"

I felt cornered. "Why do you ask?" I continued, not waiting for his answer. "What does how I feel about circus slang have to do with my friend's case?" I tried to beat Honeywell back with my own questions.

"It has everything to do with it," Honeywell countered. His voice grew louder and his tone shifted from calm persuasion to irritated impatience. "Please, just answer my question," he insisted.

"No, it doesn't," I said, just this side of exasperated.

Honeywell nodded as if he agreed with me, leading me farther down the garden path."Mr. Erlich, we want you to testify at the trial."

"You want me to what?" I asked. I could feel my heart beat faster. He still hadn't answered my question. *What am I getting myself into?* I wondered.

"To testify for the defendants," the lawyer repeated. "We will ask you about your relationships with Dr. Fishbein, Dr. Humbred, and Wadlow. But most of all we want to talk with you about your work in the circus. We want a giant at the defense table. We want—excuse the expression—our own freak to counter Wadlow's claims."

I didn't like the sound of that. "How will that help?" Now I was torn between my desire to help Fishbein and my fear of what would happen if I testified. This had transformed from a favor for a friend to something dangerous; something that could hurt me; something that would expose my private life in a courtroom. My thoughts raced. *Would I make a fool of myself? Would I be embarrassed? Would I be manipulated into saying things I didn't want to say?*

"Don't concern yourself. That's what they pay me for. I'll take care of everything,"Honeywell said, as if he could read my mind. Then he abruptly stood up, removed a gold watch from his vest, and opened it to check the time, signaling that our interview had come to an end.

When I stood up, my head started to swirl and I almost lost my balance. Unaware, Honeywell guided me to the double doors and shook my hand good-bye. I felt confused, anxious, and worried, with a world of more questions than when the meeting began. *Would I be a human sacrifice on this high priest's alter?* I wondered.

"One more thing, Mr. Honeywell," I said, stopping and turning to face him. "Dr. Fishbein is my friend and I have agreed to help him out but . . . but . . . I won't lie," I said, giving voice to my worry.

"That's what I'm counting on," the old attorney said as he escorted me out of his inner sanctum. I left Honeywell's building in a daze.

CHAPTER 31

The Trial

Photo by Edward Kelty, with permission of Alan Siegel

"Wait up! Where's the fire, Jake?" I turned to see a tuxedo-clad Harry Doll trot up behind me. "Where in blazes have you been?" he asked.

"Oh, I dunno," I said, looking past him.

"That's a load of horseshit." He pointed his index finger at me. "We haven't seen hide or hair of you for the past week." He sounded angry, as if I had offended him.

"It must not be easy to be friends with a mug like me," I said.

"See here, Jake, Daisy and I know you well enough to tell when you're slipping into one of your dark spells. Now spill the beans. What's troubling you?"

"I've got things on my mind," I replied. I didn't want my friends to be angry with me, but at the same time I didn't want to say too much. As you can probably tell, back then, when it came to my troubles, I was a very private person. Mixing in, particularly when I was down, took real work. Most of the time, I didn't have the energy for it.

"Does it have to do with that goddamned trial?" As Harry continued to interrogate me, I wished I'd never mentioned it to him in the first place. "I don't know why in the hell you ever agreed to help that doctor out. What's in it for you, anyway?" he demanded.

"Hiya, fellas!" Daisy interrupted, unaware of our intense interaction. She sallied up to us, dressed to the nines in her sapphire-blue chiffon getup. I noticed that she clutched a piece of stationary in her right hand. "I've got a letter here from Lya. It came today," she said, out of breath. "Well, if it isn't the long-lost Jake Erlich," Daisy added. "We used to know him; even thought of him as a friend."

I half-smiled at her sarcasm. Harry and Daisy had me dead to rights. Since the matinee the day I had met Fishbein's attorney, and throughout the next week, I had been lost in worry about the trial, the art show, and all the awful consequences I imagined were sure to result. I had been avoiding the Dolls, Frank Buck, Clyde Ingalls, and everyone else I normally talked with. During those seven days, my fears pursued me like a five-headed dragon. I couldn't stop the thoughts racing through my mind. In the name of a new friend that I hardly knew, I had agreed to testify as a sideshow expert; a resident freak, so to speak. I had also agreed to a public display of my art, something I had previously felt very protective and insecure about. The more I mulled it over, the more I felt incapable of either task. Though I had always felt like an outsider, now insiders like Honeywell, Fishbein, the American Medical Association, Humbred, and Hutchinson wanted me to play on their team. I wasn't sure I fit in with any of them.

"To tell the truth, I've been tense about testifying," I said.

"Jake, why do you worry so much? Every freak and all the other troopers that know you would swear that you're the most articulate guy in all of Ringling Bros," Daisy said, trying to comfort me. Then she got a quizzical look on her tiny face and bit her lower lip. "Is there anything else troubling you, Jake?" she asked. "Maybe something you didn't mention?"

There was something else on my mind, but I wasn't about to share that information with her. One of the things that had been weighing heavy on my mind was Val, but I knew she was a taboo subject. I was certain there was no way I could talk to Daisy about her. If I complained that I still had not received a letter from Val, even though it had been over a month since I had agreed to do the exhibition at the Delphic and set a late-October date for the show, Daisy would have been furious. She would have wanted to crucify her.

Speaking of letters, I'm ashamed to admit it, but I must not have really wanted to know what was in Lya's letter. I knew it contained a litany of the awful things that were happening to her and her family; things that I could do absolutely nothing to prevent. For months there had been little correspondence from our friend. Most of the information I got came from the papers and newsreels. Every time I read or saw something about Germany, scary pictures and premonitions came to my mind of what would happen to her, her family, and my *mishpacha* in Poland. Now that I had the opportunity to finally hear, firsthand, what was actually going on, I wanted no part of it. It took a while, but later I realized how much I actually missed that tiny woman. How terrible and frightening it must have been for a fine person like Lya, fending for herself in a place like the "New Germany," with its beautiful men and women and trains that arrived and departed on time, but a place where those who were different had to constantly be on guard.

I was terribly uneasy about Lya's predicament. I didn't want my concern to add to the worry I knew was eating at Daisy and Harry. But, much more than that, I hated how weak and useless the whole situation made me feel.

Standing there with my friends, I grew more and more anxious by the second. Talking and thinking about Lya had made me feel worse. I couldn't help it. The only thing I knew to do when I felt that way was to run. That's what I had done for most of my life; that's what I had done the previous week, and that's what I was compelled to do at that instant.

"You know, you two, getting ready for the trial and for my first art exhibit take time," I explained. "I need just about every second for those challenges, so I can't waste any of it lollygagging around here. If you'll excuse me..." I spun around and started to stomp off. Even though my feelings pressured me to get away from them, I realized, clear as daylight, I was being curt to my closest friends in the circus; people who genuinely cared for me. I intuited that my abruptness would draw Daisy's attention like the smell of a fugitive from a chain gang draws a bloodhound. So I hesitated, turned back around, and forced myself to smile through my anxiety. "I'm sorry. I'll do my best to be more available."

"There's about as much chance of that happening as there is of finding snowballs in hell," Harry said, shaking his head. I walked away again, not realizing I had never even asked to see Lya's letter.

I should have. Maybe learning more about the dangers Lya faced and spending more time with my friends might have lessened my own troubles. As it was, I felt trapped between my ears. I'd lie in bed at night, tossing and turning, my mind bombarded with nightmarish images: A spotlighted Honeywell in whiteface and ragged clothes sitting in the center-ring sawdust in a court of clowns; Val as a decrepit, lonely old woman who had never made up her mind whether to stay with or leave her husband; Wadlow crying as he read Humbred's cruel manifesto, his smartly pressed, brown business suit and flowery silk tie watered by a downpour of giant tears; Lya running from an evil presence lurking in granite shadows; a family plot with a plain gravestone barely visible in one of those harsh west Texas dust storms that came every March and blotted out the sun.

I felt helpless, overwhelmed, and I didn't know where to start. I wondered which one of those damned dragons' heads would be the first to sink his teeth into a mangy giant that wasn't as good a friend or artist as others made him out to be. Thank God I had my palette, easel, some canvases, a few horsehair brushes, and plenty of oil paint with me on the circus train, because, for a fortnight, I didn't sleep much.

XXXX

It seems that Harry knew me better than I knew myself. You see, despite my promise, I continued to avoid my friends. Once, when I was walking in the backyard, I saw Major Mite coming and I dodged into Clown Alley where I hid out until he passed; another time I hightailed it when I entered the bull yard and saw Frank Buck talking to one of his tunnel boys. It took a while to admit it, but I realized that hiding out came naturally to me, just like running. I had started hiding out in alleys back home when I was a kid and, at thirty-one, I hadn't stopped yet.

But something about getting the subpoena changed things. Receiving that formal, written notification calmed me down, if just a bit. I guess I realized I couldn't run and I couldn't hide from what I had to do. As with my size, I had no choice in the matter. Come rain or shine, like it or not, the trial would begin in three weeks at the Federal Courthouse in St. Joseph, Missouri, and I would have to testify.

XXXX

I took an overnight train from Louisville, where we had just finished a two-day stint. Everyone in the crew besides me was relieved to get out of that town. We almost had a blowdown there the night before. That was a rare occurrence that time of year and that far north. I guess I was still pretty reluctant to go to St. Joseph because I had a sixth sense that once I got there, I'd be facing a blowdown of my own. The rest of the crew made the jump to Cincinnati after I left them. As I watched four powerful locomotives heave, grunt, and finally haul the Ringling train—all one mile of it—out of the station, I couldn't believe Clyde Ingalls had actually let me go. If it hadn't been for the subpoena, I think he would have had a conniption when I asked for time off. As it was, he was none too happy when I told him about it. But circus folks—and Ingalls was no different—tend to avoid confrontations, or anything that smacks of it, with John Law. I guess it's part of the culture that goes back to mud show days, when wanted roustabouts and runaway kids were holed up in the circus and we had to grease coppers' hands to stay out of hot water.

I arrived in St. Joseph, road-weary and sweaty, late on the afternoon of July 8, 1937, the day the trial began. As I recall, it was very hot and muggy, the kind of heat that makes you grimy and gets you craving a shower the minute you step outside. *I'll never get used to this damned humidity,* I thought as I packed myself into the back of a taxicab.

On the short ride from the train depot to my hotel, I noticed, despite the heat, a number of people picnicking and children playing in the park. It seemed like a weekend or a holiday, but it wasn't. The sidewalks were crowded and butchers were selling popcorn and hotdogs. I wiped the sweat from my forehead. *I could sure use an Eskimo Pie,* I thought.

The atmosphere reminded me of the circus, though there was no Big Top to be seen. I felt the electricity in the air that hovers just before a circus parade and wondered what the ruckus was about.

Glancing at the rearview mirror, I noticed that the cabbie kept looking at me; but I was used to that. He finally spoke up. "Ain't this some ta-do?" I just nodded. "You must be coming in for the trial," he said.

I smiled thinly but didn't respond. Honeywell had advised me to avoid the locals and particularly the press.

The taxi driver chuckled. "Folks been lined up to get into city hall since six this morning. Yesterday, I drove a bunch of reporters from the train. Some of 'em came from big-time papers all the way in St. Louis and Chicago."

I sighed and looked out my window at the crowded sidewalk. My time in St. Joseph would turn out to be more of a circus then I could have imagined. A few minutes later the cab driver dropped me at the Rubidoux Hotel and I ducked in as quickly as I could to avoid the crowds.

After checking in and unpacking, I was hungry so I went downstairs and walked across the lobby to the dining room. Off in the corner, I spotted Glenn Hyder eating alone. He was a seven-foot giant, a gruff sort of fellow who walked with a pronounced limp that was almost rhythmic. I recall hearing he had a bum knee. In his youth, he had worked as a carnie and a boxer. He had the cauliflower ears, flattened nose, and slightly punch-drunk way about him to prove it. Glenn had a head of gray hair, and at forty-two had outlived every giant I knew. Hyder had traveled with the Al G. Barnes outfit until they folded then, before he retired, he did some work with Ringling Bros. That's when we had met. As I walked toward him he stood up. The full-sized linen napkin tucked into his collar looked like a tiny tissue.

"Glenn, don't tell me you got shanghaied into this mess!" I said.

"We'll, I'll be damned. If it ain't my friend Jake." We gave each other a hug. For others in that dining room, the two of us must have looked like Kodiaks in mortal combat.

Glenn explained that he had also been called to testify for the defense. It seems a few years back he'd been interviewed by Humbred as well. *Honeywell never mentioned another giant.* I wondered what other cards that slick hobo had up his sleeve.

"Do you still have that cigar store in Kansas City?" I asked.

"I sure do. It keeps me in long johns and chewing tobacco. You've got a good memory, Jake," Glenn said as the two of us sat back down at the table strewn with his half-eaten chicken dinner.

"It's good to know there's life after the big show," I said. Here was a giant who actually had left the circus in one piece and seemed to be surviving nicely on his own. "How did you get into this mess?" I inquired.

"I'm here strictly for the do-re-mi. I can use the scratch," he replied. Maybe he wasn't doing as well as I imagined. "And you?" Glenn asked.

"I'm here to help a friend," I answered.

Glenn laughed. "Well, you know what they say, buddy. No good deed goes unpunished." He ripped a drumstick from the chicken carcass on the plate in front of him and took a bite. It looked like a scene I had shot in *Jack and the Beanstalk* when I was back at Century Comedies. All that was missing was Baby Peggy hiding under the table and me mouthing the words *"Fe, Fi, Fo, Fum! I smell the blood of an Englishman!"* Glenn roughly wiped his mouth with his napkin and went on to tell me how he had gone down to watch the proceedings and what had happened earlier that day at the trial. As we were speaking, the waitress came up. I ordered a steak dinner.

"Well, Jake, the rumors about us are flying around this berg. Reporters have been interviewing guests in the hotel. Somehow they've gotten wind that a couple of giants are in town for the trial." Glenn picked up his copy of that morning's *St. Joseph Gazette* that was resting on the ground next to him. "'One,'" Glenn said pointing to me, "'is supposed to actually travel with the circus. He is being kept in strict seclusion.'" We both laughed. "How's Cliko doing?" he asked. "And KooKoo the Bird Girl?"

"Everybody in the show is fine. There have been no dramatic transformations since you left," I said.

"Is Clyde Ingalls as cantankerous as ever?" he asked.

"You can say that again."

"And you're still at it," he said, shaking his head.

"Year in, year out; a freak's life is a freak's life," I philosophized. For a second I wondered if the only way I would ever leave that life would be feet first.

"Please give my regards to the whole kit-and-kaboodle," Glenn added. Then he got a more serious look on his face. "Have you read the article that stirred up this hornet's nest, Jake?"

I nodded my head. "Have you?" Glenn nodded. "What do you think about what Humbred wrote?" I inquired.

"That doctor ain't gonna make any points as a diplomat, that's for sure. If they sent him to talk to Adolf Hitler himself, there'd be no need for peace talks. We'd be throwing blows before tea time." Glenn shook his head. "I mean, what Dr. Humbred wrote ain't the kind of thing you would want to share with your family and friends. In Iowa, where I was reared, those are what we call fighting words," Glenn said.

I nodded. "Did anything exciting happen in the trial so far?" I asked. I reached out and took a gulp of ice water from a glass that had been placed in front of me.

"Well, it was pretty boring. They didn't even get goin' until four o'clock; had to try some counterfeiter first. I guess when times get tough one remedy is to print your own greenbacks." Glenn took a heaping forkfull of mashed potatoes and peas and shoved it into his mouth. The fork looked miniscule in his hand. "When things finally got rolling they only had time for one witness."

"And that was?"

"Wadlow's mother, Adie."

"How did that go?" I asked.

"She was pretty darned upset. It was sad; really sad. Well down the road to pitiful."

"Why? What happened?" The waitress brought over my dinner and set the plate directly in front of me. I took a bite of steak. It was tough as shoe leather and none too tasty, but in my time on the road, I had eaten much worse.

"To hear her tell it, that Humbred is really something. He showed up at suppertime, unannounced, demanding to examine her son; didn't even say he was a doctor or an expert on giants. The son of a bitch didn't even have a doctor's bag; all he carried was a measuring tape and two scrapbooks."

"Sometimes those doctors and scientific types have their own particular plans. They can be absentminded," I said, pointing at Glenn with my fork. I wondered why I was making excuses for somebody like Humbred.

"He never even told the Wadlows that he was writing an article. In fact, the old lady said she didn't find out about it until a young fella with the Alton newspaper telephoned and told her husband, Harold. They both decided to keep it a secret from Robert."

"Why in the world did they hide it from him?" I asked.

"One of the lawyers asked her the same question. She said they were certain it would hurt him. I don't know Wadlow from the man in the moon, but if somebody wrote that article about me it would have hurt like a kick in the crotch," said Glenn.

I put my knife and fork down, wiped my mouth, and pushed back from the table a bit. I didn't feel much like eating anymore.

Glenn went on to tell me that Adie Wadlow broke down and sobbed when she testified about how her son had cried after he read the article. For a few days, he stayed in his room and he didn't even eat.

I squirmed in my chair. I had experienced that kind of self-imposed exile in your own room. I'd been chained up like that before.

In retrospect, I know it was pretty damned distressing for me to reflect on that young giant's reaction and his mother's tears. It was too close for comfort. The sadness of it all felt contagious.

"You know, Wadlow's not one of my favorite people," I said, trying to stir the conversation in a different direction.

"Is that why you're here?" Glenn asked.

"I told you, I'm here to help a friend," I answered in a voice that barely masked my annoyance.

There was an awkward silence as I thought about what Glenn had asked. *Why was I really here?* I wondered. He finished his chicken dinner and I just stared down at the cut-crystal salt and pepper shakers in the middle of the table. The waitress approached and looked down at my plate: "You left half that steak, mister. Is there something wrong with it?"

"No, everything's fine," I said. "I guess I'm not as hungry as I thought I was."

After paying the bill, Glenn and I made plans to meet the next morning to attend the trial, said good night, and parted. When we left the dining room, I was preoccupied. I felt confused and half-hearted about my decision to participate in the trial. I was also anxious and uncertain about my testimony. Instead of going directly back to my room, I stepped out of the lobby and bought the evening edition of the *St. Joseph News-Press* from a paperboy. The case was front-page news in that rag, as well. The headline read: "Courtroom Packed by Crowd Desiring to See Tall Youth." The unmistakable article and accompanying photo sat in the middle of the page, nestled between pieces about Mrs. Clark Gable suing for a divorce, Admiral Leahy telling the Senate of the need to improve fortifications on Guam, and a raucous American Nazi Bund rally in Chicago that ended in fistfights and a near riot.

I scanned the Wadlow story and read how the federal courthouse was being renovated, so the trial was being held in the chambers of the city council, and how that morning throngs of people lined up outside the doors to get a peek at what was happening. By nine thirty, when the trial began, there hadn't been a seat to be had in the whole place.

As I walked back into the hotel and waited for the elevator, I read about Mrs. Wadlow's testimony. What most drew my attention were not the printed words but the photo of Wadlow with his mother, father, brother, and sisters on the bottom of the front page. They were all standing together in a park somewhere. The Wadlows looked like any other family. The only difference was that Robert towered over rest of them, just like I did in similar photos of my family and me. It came to me that, even though I had seen the young giant with his father in New York and in Boston, I had never pictured him as a part of a family.

Later that night in my cramped hotel room, before I turned off the little ceramic lamp on the table next to the two beds that had been laid end to end to accommodate me, I reached for the paper I had just purchased. That time I read the front page story, word for word. I read how Adie Wadlow felt Humbred's malicious words had scarred her son. After I finished reading, despite being exhausted from a long travel day, I still couldn't sleep. I couldn't stop imagining my mother on that witness stand in Adie Wadlow's place, and how awful she would have felt if the same thing had happened to me.

XXXX

The next morning, I met Glenn in the lobby. Then we pushed through crowds of rubbernecks all the way to city hall. Glenn wore his signature top hat, a tweed Edwardian jacket, and a red ascot tie. I dressed more conservatively in a navy blue three-piece suit. Neither one of us dressed for the weather. Glenn carried a folder that held some notes he had jotted down to review before he testified. All I carried was my sketchbook and a few drawing pencils.

"It looks like they're giving something away for free!" Glenn remarked as we got closer to the courthouse.

I laughed. "Would you look at all these kids?" I added. "Must be some kind of school holiday."

"No, I'm afraid not, Jake. I think they either closed the schools or they are all playing hooky to come and see you, me, and Wadlow."

When Glenn and I walked by the bailiffs into the council chambers, the uneasiness I felt did not match the festive atmosphere in the air. Once inside, I noticed that the council chambers had been converted into a temporary courtroom. A rail ran through the packed space, separating the spectators from the participants in the trial, just like footlights separate the audience from players on a stage. All the seats were filled with people dressed in their Sunday best, women wearing hats and gloves, men with coats and ties. The children that were present looked like they had been scrubbed and polished the night before. Though it was still morning, it was already hot and stuffy in that room. The only circulation came from the open windows and one tired ceiling fan.

Glenn and I found the specially built, uncomfortable chairs on the aisle of the first row that were placed there and reserved for us. They were situated several feet behind the table where Fishbein, Humbred, Honeywell, and another younger fellow who looked like an attorney all sat. At a table across the room I saw Wadlow, his father, and their attorney. I felt overwhelmed. The whole thing seemed unreal. To calm down, I took a deep breath. Then I opened my sketchbook and began to draw.

Shading, straight lines, hatch marks, and highlights—I roughly fed the page's hungry white space with No. 2 graphite. I worked feverishly, trying hard to forget the throng of gawking rubes in the council chambers, and the worry I wouldn't do a good enough job when I testified and that I'd end up hurting my new friend and humiliating myself. Things were just getting started and all I could think about was when it would be over. For a few minutes I was apprehensive that other people might be bothered by what I was doing. But I pushed those concerns away and lost myself in my drawing.

Only occasionally did I take the luxury to stop sketching and look up. Then, ever so briefly I'd peer through the ocher morning light that flooded the council chambers to the wall where the model for my sketch hung. It was a blue, gray, and black portrait of Justitia, the blindfolded goddess of justice, grasping her scale in one hand and her sword in the other. When I did look up, Justitia glared back, accusing me with her sightless eyes.

A gavel and an old law book rested on the judge's bench, which was placed against the rear wall just in front and below Justitia's painting. The bench was flanked by flags; on the left, the stars and stripes, and on the right the white-starred and red-, white-, and blue-striped Missouri state flag. The witness stand was placed to the right and the jury box to the left. Later, I would learn that the jury for the Wadlow trial was comprised of merchants, farmers, a salesman, an insurance man, and a lumberjack.

At exactly 9:30 a.m., Judge Merrill E. Otis pounded his gavel three times, calling the proceedings in that makeshift federal courtroom to order. He was a small, heavyset man with a bulldog's square jaw and stern demeanor. Judge Otis let it be known that he expected decorum. "This is a big crowd. You are all welcome, but I will tolerate no tomfoolery in my courtroom," he demanded.

After the lawyers for both sides made their opening arguments, as I recall, Jason Randolph, Wadlow's silver-tongued attorney, called a string of witnesses. I continued to draw, not paying too much attention to what

I was doing. I listened as doctors and teachers who had been called to testify countered Dr. Humbred's every claim.

"Even though at six months of age, he already weighed thirty pounds; and by the time he was eighteen months old, he weighed sixty-two pounds; and when he started kindergarten he wore a suit that was made for a seventeen-year-old boy, the lad developed mentally and emotionally as other boys his age. And what's more, Robert was a child with a high degree of mentality," Dr. Barr, his pediatrician at Barnes Hospital in St. Louis, said.

As well adjusted as they made Wadlow sound, I wondered what lurked in the shadows for him. Had he ever wanted to end it all, like I had?

"Contrary to what the Journal of the American Medical Association states, his hands are not deformed. From an artistic standpoint, they are beautiful," added Dr. Behrens, another physician at Barnes. "He is an alert, quick-minded youth who likes to play ping-pong, Chinese checkers, and who enjoys fishing and swimming," the doctor added.

As the witnesses testified I could barely stay awake. The pencil felt heavy in my hand. Every movement of my wrist took more and more effort. I was exhausted. I think what had tired me was the feeling that I was the one on trial; that my fate would be decided in that crowded courtroom.

"Robert was a normal, average student who made good grades. He had an above-average score on his intelligence test. He neither asked for nor got any special privileges other than a custom-built chair we provided," testified Mr. C.C. Hanna, the principal at Alton High School. When I heard that, I stopped drawing and looked up. *Nobody ever built me a special chair at El Paso High,* I thought.

That morning I learned that Robert was the photographer on the high school yearbook staff. Before that, I hadn't realized we had a love of photography in common, or anything else besides our height. I also discovered from Irene Degenhardt, his sophomore English teacher, that he loved to read books by Scott like *The Lady of the Lake* and *Ivanhoe. He sounds like a romantic,* I said to myself.

"They're doing everything they can to make this kid look normal as cherry pie for Sunday dinner," Glenn whispered. I looked at Glenn and shook my head in agreement.

But Wadlow, Glenn, and I, are anything but normal. How could we be? I thought. "When did it become a federal offense not to be like everybody else?" I said a few seconds later. "He may be a pain in the ass, but is that a crime?" I murmured to Glenn.

"What's that?" he asked, unable to hear my questions. His voice was loud enough that three spectators turned and stared at us. I held up my index finger to my lips and shook my head to end the conversation. But the chatter didn't stop in my mind. I looked down and erased an errant line I'd drawn that didn't fit my creation. *I'm an errant line in God's creation*, I mused.

Listening to witness after witness talk about Robert Wadlow's normalcy, I felt somehow disconnected from those around me in the courtroom. I pictured that rainy day in upstate New York when Val and I stopped for breakfast and ended up running for our lives from the fanatics at the eugenics rally and all their talk about sterilization and a world where anyone who was different would be eliminated.

Slowly the caricature I was drawing in my sketchbook took shape. It wasn't the likeness of Justitia, but yours truly as a gargantuan Chinese coolie, balancing a yoke of heavy water buckets on his neck. In one bucket I carried Humbred and in the other Wadlow. The burden was intense. *What strange surprises can leap out from a blank piece of paper,* I thought.

CHAPTER 32
Blind Justice

Jake and Cliko the African Bushman, circa 1935

At noon Judge Otis banged his gavel and said we would take a one-hour lunch break. It had been a surprisingly stressful morning for me. "I feel tuckered out," I said as Glenn and I walked out of the council chambers.

"Why do you think you're so beat?" Glenn asked.

"I don't know. I must not have slept too well last night." The two of us stepped from city hall into the midday heat and were blinded, not by the sun but by the fiery flash of photographers' cameras. Like a troop of mercenaries lying in wait, half a dozen journalists ambushed us.

"Hey, Jake, why are you here?"

"Are you going to testify?"

"Whose side are you on?"

The questions came in a barrage, like machine gun fire. Glenn and I pushed through the onslaught as best we could without saying a word. Making our way down the steps, the crowd from the trial flowed around us as if we were two huge islands in the nearby Missouri River. Once we found a little daylight, we hightailed it across the street to the park. I took off my suit coat, loosened my tie, and undid the top button of my shirt, which was so tight it almost cut off my circulation. Glenn took off his coat as well.

We didn't talk much. After a lunch of egg salad sandwiches and ginger beers that we bought from a butcher with a cart, I sprawled in the thick grass for a *siesta*. Glenn sat down next to me. I hoped that the stand of elm trees and a gazebo just behind us would provide enough shade to let me drift off and keep any onlookers away. When I closed my eyes, I kept seeing the exploding photographers' flashes. They were like the echo of lightning on a pitch-black west Texas night.

I fell into a deep sleep and woke up with a start, having no idea where I was. A towheaded, freckle-faced boy in coveralls, who could have easily passed as a Huckleberry Finn look-alike, was crouching down next to my legs. His name was Tommy Higgins and he was gnawing on a piece of grass. He would grow up to be editor of the local paper. Years later, he wrote me for my recollections about the trial to include in a book he was doing about the short, sad life of Robert Wadlow.

Well, staring up at that kid, I thought for sure he was going to ask me for my autograph, but he didn't. Instead, without even a *how do you do*, in a tone that demanded a response, he asked me something else.

"How big are they?"

I propped myself up on my elbows. "How big are they?" I repeated his question, not at all sure what this budding journalist was talking about.

Then he moved so he was standing directly in front of my feet, which, from my point of view, eclipsed about half the length of this cub reporter's legs.

"Your feet, mister. What size are they?" he demanded.

"Twenty-six and a half," I replied without a thought or hesitation. Normally when I shared that tidbit, especially with children, I got looks of awe and amazement. Not that time.

"Why, that's nothing!" he said. "Robert Wadlow wears a thirty-seven. I betcha I could rig a sail to one of his shoes and cruise to India or Siam," Tommy said with a far away, Marco Polo look in his eyes. "You know, mister, you ain't that big compared to Robert."

It's strange to admit and it's petty, but at that instant I felt threatened. I thought back to the evening, long ago, when I wandered into the sideshow tent in El Paso and everybody and their cousin saw that I was a full foot taller than Big Jim Tarver. I understood that I must have threatened Big Jim as I felt threatened. I wondered if Big Jim compared himself to me when I snatched his crown and claim to freak show fame as the world's tallest man. Who was I anyway, if not the tallest man in the world? Then a strange, unsettling question peppered my mind. Besides the size of his shoes and his height, was Wadlow bigger than me in other ways? How big was that young giant's integrity; his courage and his determination? How did I measure up?

Tommy Higgins didn't say another word to me. Having conveyed his message like Hermes, he spun around and sauntered away.

"That boy's got some nerve," Glenn said with a laugh. I was silent and just watched him walk off and disappear into the crowd that was milling around on the sidewalk.

I glanced at my wristwatch. It was 12:55 p.m. We'd have to hurry to get back to city hall before the afternoon session commenced. I got up and wiped a few blades of grass from my shirt and pants. *A size thirty-seven . . . that is something,* I thought as Glenn and I made our way through the park.

In my mind's eye, I sailed back thirty years to our house on Fewel Street in Sunset Heights. I was sitting in a kitchen chair with my father kneeling in front of me. He glared at me and then at the Buster Browns he clutched in his hands. Then he shook his head. "Jake, that's impossible." Papa's angry tone and the harsh look on his face are engraved in my memory. As an adult I know that my father's reaction was just a mask for his dread about the troubles the high-tops Mama had bought me just two weeks before that no longer fit portended.

Papa was right to worry. That was the beginning of it. At age seven I didn't fit in those Buster Browns. As time went on, I had to struggle to fit in anywhere else.

Walking through that park with Glenn, returning to the trial, I saw boisterous, picnicking families and couples arm in arm out for a romantic stroll on the sidewalk. Like a knife in the belly, I felt just how alone in the world I was. I didn't fit in with either side in that trial; neither with Fishbein, Humbred, and the AMA; nor with Wadlow. I didn't fit in the freak show either. But as much as I was dissatisfied and unhappy with my life in the circus, at that moment I longed to be back there. At least when I was on the platform I could hide my distress. I worried that when it was my turn to testify, the lawyers, the judge, the jury, and everyone in that room would see my naked despair and I'd be more cut off than ever.

"We'd better step on it or we'll be late," Glenn insisted, walking faster. I picked up the pace to keep up with him, but I was disoriented, lost in a thick fog of memory and worry.

I stepped off the curb. The next thing I knew, Glenn yanked me backwards. "Watch out!" he yelled as he grabbed my arm and jerked me out of the path of a Hudson barreling down on us. *Ahuga! Ahuga!* The driver honked at me. "For the love of Mike, be careful," Glenn demanded.

We were in such a hurry when we climbed the steps and re-entered city hall that I had trouble catching my breath. At that point I was so fixated on how I'd perform as a witness that I didn't even notice there were no pesky members of the third estate milling around to bother us. The reporters were already inside waiting for the performance to begin.

"This guy Wadlow's a regular hero in these parts," Glenn said as we entered the council chambers and found our seats.

Before I could answer, the bailiff bellowed, "All rise. The honorable Judge Otis presiding in the matter of Robert Wadlow versus Dr. Morris Fishbein, Dr. Charles Humbred, and the American Medical Association."

I looked over at Humbred sitting at the defense table with Fishbein, Honeywell, and the other high-priced lawyer. Humbred appeared mousey and as if he were trying to retreat into his suit, which looked two sizes too large. Later in the trial, Honeywell would do his best to paint him as a dedicated and committed doctor who only wanted to understand all he could about gigantism to further scientific understanding. I don't know; maybe he was. But from what I'd heard, read, and experienced myself, that dedication and commitment might have blinded him to the harm he could do. After all, we were people, not cadavers; at least not yet.

As I saw him sitting there, a darker thought crossed my mind. *He's a little guy. Maybe he uses his measuring stick to feel big.* I was sweating more than I had out in the midday sun. I wondered if I had been too quick to agree to testify. *Maybe I don't agree with what's happening here,* I thought. *Maybe Honeywell's using me to sell tickets to this sideshow.*

It was stuffy and uncomfortably crowded in the chambers of St. Joseph's city council on that sizzling summer afternoon. After an hour of testimony that all blurred together, I scanned the faces that surrounded me. Most of them were perspiring and looked heavy-eyed. We all were united in our craving for a nap. Some even nodded off. One bald gent in a green bow tie three seats down began to snore until the old woman sitting next to him elbowed him back to consciousness. Judging from how expertly she placed her elbow in his ribs, I'd bet she was the missus.

"Your honor, the plaintiffs call Mr. Robert Wadlow to the witness stand."

The crowd stirred and murmured. It was positively electric in that room. That was exactly what many of the observers and reporters had come to see and hear. I sat up, as did Glenn and the sleepy man in the bow tie and his wife.

Maybe now I'll get a better idea about this kid. Up to this point I haven't much cared for him, I thought. When I met Wadlow in Madison Square Garden, and later in Boston, he was aloof and none too friendly. All told, I was with him no more than a few hours. I really didn't have much information about him to go on. But like everybody else in Ringling's sideshow, based on what we saw and felt in the little time we were with him, we had concluded we didn't like him much.

XXXX

When Wadlow stood up, a veil of silence fell over the courtroom. It seemed as if those present were amazed that someone so big could stand, or that nature had created a man so much taller than they were that they had no alternative but to freeze in horror or in awe. He leaned on the silver-handled, oak cane he clutched in his left hand, and with determination uncomfortably tottered his stooped body to the witness stand. I felt that everyone held their breath to see if he would make it without falling. If a colossus like him were to fall, I imagined it would shake city hall with such seismic force that the walls would tumble down and the roof would collapse, killing all present—a Midwestern saga; Samson comes to Missouri. An entourage of two husky bailiffs preceded him, carrying his specially built chair. They looked like eunuchs bearing a throne, heralding the arrival of some Oriental potentate. Wadlow moved slowly, every step a struggle. Watching his bowed and almost twisted posture, I sighed and wanted to look away but couldn't. As I recollect, I wasn't amazed, frightened, or disgusted by what I saw, but something was definitely stirring in me. I couldn't take my eyes off him.

"Oh my Lord." Someone gasped.

Bang, bang, bang. Judge Otis walloped his gavel down on his bench. "Order; order in this court. If there is one more outburst like that, I will have this room emptied."

I'll be goddamned; he's grown even since the last time I saw him. Then again, maybe I didn't really see him before. He's much bigger than I am. He's the biggest man I've ever seen, I thought, just like everyone else in the room; just like all those hundreds of thousands of circus fans had, over the years, thought when they came to see me on the platform, in the spec, or in the parade. Though Wadlow refused to set foot in our sideshow tent, at that moment, in the midst of the trial, it was as if all of us in the council chambers were viewing our own personal freak show and Wadlow was the star attraction.

Wadlow sat in silence, waiting for his attorney to begin asking him questions. I felt jittery and my shoulders ached. *What is he going to say now? And why am I so damn tense?* I wondered.

XXXX

It was clear that his lawyer's questions and Robert's replies were carefully crafted to portray an affable young man libeled by an insensitive doctor. Wadlow described how, despite people's stares, he strived to live a normal life. The sound of his voice articulated more than the words he spoke. It was a haunting sound; the kind you never forget. His voice was very deep. But something about it reminded me of the sound a frightened child, lost and alone in a cavern, might make; a sound that let you know that it was dark and cold and he was running out of air. It was an echo of an echo that no one would understand while there was still time to save him.

When asked about his pastimes and hobbies he replied with a boyish grin, "I like taking photos and I like to fish." *He likes photography and he likes to fish, just like me,* I thought. *We've got things in common.* I imagined spending time with Wadlow, showing him the pictures I took of that old Mexican cowboy in Raton at the ranch where Frenchie grew up. Then, like he was the son I'd never have, I'd take him to a secret spot near the middle fork of the Gila River and teach him to fly-fish.

"Tell us what happened when Dr. Humbred visited your home." Randolph adroitly changed the subject.

Wadlow reported how he had been polite and accommodating to Humbred. "My parents always taught me to be respectful and, even though I was wet and tired, I was polite. More polite and respectful then he was. I let him measure my arms and legs and shoulders. But then he didn't want to leave."

After about half an hour, Randolph asked his final question: "Robert, what happened when you read Dr. Humbred's article yourself?"

Wadlow paused, took off his glasses, and cleared his throat with what sounded like a minor roar. Then he hesitated, as if trying to locate something in his memory or avoid the pain that was lashed to it. Except for a cough here and a sneeze there, the room was silent. That was the only time during the whole trial it was quiet enough to make out the electronic dots and dashes of the telegrapher in the cloakroom sending out updates to wire services and papers around the country. Wadlow slowly replaced his glasses and began to speak. The crowd, myself included, collectively sat forward and held our breath.

"When I saw those mean words and lies in print, I broke down. I cried and cried. I retreated to my room. I didn't eat or return to my family for two days."

In a scene repeated around the council chambers, the man with the green bow tie shook his head. His wife quietly sobbed and wiped the tears from her eyes with a linen hankie. Wadlow spoke with that odd mixture of sorrow and rage I know too well. The spectators hung on every word. At that moment, the men in the jury and just about every other soul in the place looked as if they were ready to grab Humbred, Fishbein, and their big-city lawyers and string them up to one of the sturdy elm trees in the park across the street. In those days, if Fishbein and Humbred had been darkies, that would have been a foregone conclusion. That's why I was so damned surprised by what happened.

"We rest our case," Randolph said, gazing at the jury.

By the time Wadlow finished testifying, it was already five p.m. *When will they finally get to me?* I wondered anxiously. The afternoon sun shined low through the large, open windows on the west side of the room. Strange shadows cast odd shapes across the space and onto the wall behind the jury; uninvited witnesses from other, silent realms that longed to be heard.

Wadlow started to stand up. So did Honeywell. "Please stay seated, Mr. Wadlow. I have a few questions of my own."

"Mr. Honeywell," Judge Otis interrupted, "given the late hour, we'll stop for the day. You can pick up with this witness in the morning." I watched as the courtroom emptied, wondering what tomorrow would bring.

XXXX

Though hours had passed since the trial had ended for the day, I hadn't calmed down a bit. I remember that evening the air was very still and the temperature hardly dropped. I was so hot and agitated I didn't eat any dinner. When I returned to my room for the night, I tried to but I couldn't focus my attention. Then I paced for a while. Nothing helped me relax. So I decided to turn in early. It was impossible to sleep. I got up, walked across my hotel room, and stared out the open window into the night, hoping whatever was upsetting me would be swallowed up by the constant buzzing of the cicadas. But it didn't work. I wondered what was disturbing me so much. I knew I was worried about my testimony. But I felt sure there was more to it than that. I knew that whatever was at the root of my distress was nothing new. It had been prowling there for a long while, just out of consciousness; a wily predator waiting to pounce. That wasn't the first time.

Occasionally over the years that feeling had even materialized as an image. Once the image took shape, it crept across the border through the barbed wire and past the corrals, into my dreams or the daylight. Then I'd get a fleeting glimpse of it before it fled back into the rocks. It was a stealthy cougar. *If only I could have captured it in a photograph or painting that I could hold in my hand,* I thought. I was certain that whatever was at the root of all this was dangerous and uncontrollable yet oddly familiar. I peered into the darkness and had a fleeting impulse to hurt myself; to hurl my body out of the window into the night before whatever lurked there grabbed me. I took a step back.

I walked back across the dimly lit hotel room to get a drink of water from the half-empty glass I left on the dresser. That's when I saw my reflection in the little mirror that was centered there. I rubbed my eyes. Then it all flooded back.

A torrent of disturbing images of Wadlow deluged my mind; especially him struggling to drag himself across the council chambers to the witness stand. Until that moment I never really understood it. Being at that trial and spending more time with Wadlow, I finally saw that mountain lion up close and personal. You see, if my fate hadn't been to fall from a speeding car and go blind, and if my doctors hadn't inadvertently shrunk my tumor with X-rays, I would have kept growing. I would have ended up like Wadlow, or worse. Maybe my beef with that kid was not about whether or not he was a pain in the ass, or whether he wore a suit and tie instead of a costume, or whether he wouldn't set foot in the sideshow tent.

Truth be told, everybody that had attended the trial would admit that they couldn't help but stare at Wadlow. For some it was fascination or awe, or the allure of what is freakish. Like everyone else, I couldn't look away. But I also couldn't look at him for more than a few seconds because Wadlow was a giant mirror for me that reflected a frightening image of what might have been and what still might be.

CHAPTER 33

The Clash of the Titans

"The Blow Down," Jake Erlich

The next morning, waiting for the proceedings to begin, I was too nervous to even draw so I stashed my pad under my chair. Even though Honeywell had prepared me, I still felt antsy about the questions he and Wadlow's lawyer would ask me. I had volunteered to testify to help my friend Fishbein. I was committed. I gave my word and knew what was expected of me. We'd even meticulously reviewed what I would say again that morning at breakfast. But still I felt painfully uncertain.

The trial started at 9:30 a.m. sharp. Judge Otis walked in and everyone stood up. Then the bailiff called Robert Wadlow to return to the witness stand.

Honeywell began his cross-examination with a question that was really more of a statement. "Mr. Wadlow, at what age did you first realize you were not normal?" I didn't listen to Robert's reply.

When I heard the word "normal," I found myself a scared, seven-year-old child in Dr. Epstein's exam room. *If he keeps growing like this, by his eighth birthday he'll be close to six feet. I don't know what's going to become of him. We're not looking at the development of a normal child here.* The insensitive doctor's words hung there, as though I could still clearly hear them.

"Mr. Wadlow, would you please walk over to the jury box?" Seeing Wadlow drag himself across the room brought me back to the trial. Wadlow stepped, shifted, and swayed toward the jury. In some strange courtroom choreography, they all simultaneously lifted their chins and dropped their heads back to watch him. "Observe how Mr. Wadlow walks. A long pendulum swings slower than a short one." Honeywell sounded like a sideshow blower.

It's so sad. The kid moves like a lame camel who has seen one too many seasons, I thought.

"Now Mr. Wadlow, so the jury can see the tops of your hands, hold them out with your palms facing the floor." Wadlow complied. The size and shape of his hands and the circumference of his fingers took even my breath away. I looked across the room and saw that some of the men in the jury shook their heads in wonder. Honeywell held up his own hand and pointed out the differences not only in size but in the rock-like shape of the knuckles and the yellowish color of Wadlow's skin.

As Honeywell continued to speak, I felt it was me he was talking about and not Wadlow. I covered my left hand with my right and then uncrossed them and slowly sat on the tops of both hands, hiding them. It was clear to me that Honeywell was aiming to point out how different Wadlow was from everyone else in that council chamber.

Next, continuing to call attention to Wadlow's freakishness, the defense did something that had never been done anywhere in the long history of jurisprudence.

"I would like everyone to walk to the Missouri Theater," Honeywell said.

The crowd murmured. Glenn turned to look at me. "What does this carnie have up his sleeve?" I shook my head. I had an uneasy feeling, yet Glenn and I, along with everyone in that room, including the judge and jury, rose and paraded two blocks down the street. Once we got to the theater, young ushers with little pillbox hats guided everyone but Wadlow, Glenn, and me to their seats. The three of us stood in the back so as not to hinder anyone's view. I thought Wadlow might look across at us but he just stared straight ahead, not even acknowledging our presence. The trial continued.

"Gentlemen of the jury, please watch the screen carefully and determine for yourselves how normal Mr. Wadlow is."

Then the houselights went dim and I heard a familiar sound from my Hollywood days, the *clickety-clack* of a movie projector's electric motor. I half expected to see myself on the screen. But the giant on display wasn't me. It was Robert Wadlow. All of us watched newsreel footage of Robert at various stages in his life: Robert as a young boy, Robert in the Boy Scouts, Robert in college, and Robert at the Texas State Centennial. Each new bit of carefully edited film added layers to the story of his abnormal development. All of the shocking images displayed and emphasized that, though he tried not to be, Wadlow was as different as black is from white and as freakish as they come.

When the movie was over, we all trudged back through that God-awful heat and humidity to city hall. Glenn and I walked in silence. I didn't feel much like talking. I don't know about Glenn, but for me, the images we'd just seen of Wadlow's early years stirred ghosts from my past.

When the trial resumed, Honeywell's arguments took a different tack as he cunningly moved to counter the claims that Robert was friendly and outgoing. One of the witnesses he employed to tell that story was a distant relative named Eugene Wadlow, a physician in St. Joseph. "Why, I know Robert to be quite shy, bashful, taciturn, and unpleasant," he said. As I recall, he used the word *curmudgeon* to describe him.

Then the mouthpiece called Roger Sanders to the witness stand. He was a beefy doorman from St. Louis. "A few years back, I was at an air show out at Lambert Field. Robert Wadlow was signin' autographs and lettin' people take his picture for two bits. I snapped a photo without askin' and he popped me a good one in the face; knocked me backward. I figure I must'a flown ten feet." Spectators' laughter and chattering filled the council chambers.

"Order! Order in this room or so help me, I'll have it cleared," Judge Otis demanded. As he pounded his gavel I harked back to that night in Chattanooga when I broke that bully's jaw. I recalled how great the pats on the back I received from my fellow troopers felt. I also recollected the awful scolding I got from Clyde Ingalls.

Once he made his point, further isolating Wadlow, the attorney shifted his focus to establishing Humbred's credibility. "Dr. Humbred is the American authority on gigantism," he said to the jury, placing his thumbs under the lapels of his suit.

Doctor . . . How can they call that son of a bitch a doctor? I wondered. *He's got the bedside manner of a rattlesnake.* I shuddered as I recalled my creepy experience in his office and the giant skeleton that hung behind his desk.

"And besides being the leading expert, he possesses the nation's outstanding library on the subject," he continued.

"As if owning books makes you an expert," I whispered to Glenn. Honeywell never even called Humbred as a witness, choosing instead to use prominent doctors to frame his assertions. Then he did the same thing for Fishbein and the American Medical Association. *He's trying to make you feel that if you disagree with Humbred, his article, or the American Medical Association you're as dumb as bag of hammers,* I thought.

As the morning wore on I must have realized that it was only a matter of time until they called me to the stand to testify, because I began to feel more and more agitated. I was supposed to be the defense's star witness, but at that moment I strongly disagreed with the false picture Honeywell had painted of the obnoxious pathologist whose article had kicked up this mess. Feeling claustrophobic, I tugged on my tie, fidgeted uncontrollably, and worried that I was on the outskirts of panic. I needed some fresh air. I glanced at the man in the green bow tie and noticed the sweat dripping down the side of his face. The walls started to close in on me. Glenn looked at me, puzzled.

"Are you okay?" he asked.

"I gotta get out of here," I whispered. Even though I was in the front row and leaving would have drawn all kinds of unwanted attention, it got so bad that I stood up and started to walk out. It seemed that everyone in that room turned to stare at me. That's when Judge Otis banged his gavel and called an hour recess for lunch.

XXXX

During the break I kept to myself and didn't eat a thing. Glenn approached me with a sandwich and a soda pop and I waved him off. I paced around the park at the most rapid clip I could muster, struggling to compose myself. Although the exercise helped, for the life of me I couldn't stop those damned jitters.

At about a quarter to one, everyone started to stream back toward city hall. I wanted to head in the opposite direction, straight out of town, and not stop until I reached Cedar Rapids. But I knew that wasn't an option, so I did the best I could to pull myself together.I found a spigot in the park, opened it up, and splashed water on my face and the back of my neck. That would have to do.

The afternoon session began with Honeywell calling Glenn to the witness stand. He spoke as a firsthand expert on gigantism and about being examined by Humbred. Looking around the room as Glenn testified—better said, regurgitated the scripted lines Honeywell had fed him—I realized there were no more witnesses to be called but me. When Honeywell finished with Glenn it would finally be my turn to speak. I squirmed in my oversized seat.

I did not want to disappoint Dr. Fishbein, or for that matter, Honeywell. As a matter of fact, I didn't want to disappoint anybody. Maybe that was my problem. If somehow I did skip town I imagined what Papa would say.

How could you do such a thing? It was not honorable to change your mind and, at the last possible minute, renege on your commitment. But I couldn't stand Humbred and how he had treated Wadlow and me. I felt Humbred wasn't a good man and I didn't like how Honeywell was trying to turn everyone against Wadlow, painting him as less than a freak. I was so confused about what I should do. The possibilities gave me a splitting headache. But it was really too late to run. I hated being out of control like that. *Why did you ever agree to appear at this goddamned trial?* I asked myself.

I saw Honeywell turn toward the judge. "Your honor, the defense calls its last witness, Mr. Jacob Erlich."

Before I knew it, I was frenetically up and out of my seat, moving toward the witness stand on a caffeinated mixture of anxiety and anticipation. Anybody who watched would have sworn I moved with little of the strain and struggle Wadlow had exhibited. But I honestly can tell you that on the inside I labored every bit as much as Wadlow had.

Honeywell slowly approached me where I sat on the witness stand. For some reason I imagined that the high-priced legal eagle was about to dry-gulch me. Honeywell stepped closer and smiled disarmingly. "Please state your name for the record."

I scanned the room and answered softly, "My real name is Jake Erlich, but I'm known as Jack Earle." The intensity on the faces of the folks in the courtroom made me even more edgy.

"Would you please speak up? I can barely hear you," Honeywell asked.

"Yes, sir." I nodded and cleared my throat.

"Mr. Erlich, what do you do for a living?"

"For the last eleven years I have been employed as a performer with the Ringling Bros, Barnum and Bailey Circus."

"What exactly do you do with the circus?"

"I work in the sideshow."

"And what do you do in the sideshow, sir?"

"I'm the giant."

"And what are your duties as the giant?"

I shifted uncomfortably and felt the sweat gathering behind my neck. "I work as one of the freaks in the sideshow. My responsibilities are to sit or stand on the platform and let the fans look at me as they walk through the sideshow tent. I march in the circus parade when we first come to a town. I also perform in the opening and closing spectaculars, and in the parade of freaks. Sometimes I put on a shooting exhibition. I also sell lead replicas of my ring and postcards with my picture on them."

"Mr. Erlich, in your testimony you just used the word *freak*. Is that correct?"

"Yes, it is."

"Do you have a problem with that word?" The lawyer inquired.

"I've been called worse," I answered, without hesitation. The court broke into laughter. Judge Otis reached for his gavel but before he could use it, the room quieted down. I sighed and relaxed a bit. I liked making people laugh. Reporters would later write that my testimony that afternoon was articulate and funny. But at that moment, I certainly didn't feel that way.

"Mr. Wadlow has taken issue with the word *freak* being used to describe him," Honeywell said pointing across the council chambers at Wadlow.

"Well, I don't. It used to bother me but not anymore. You see, this is my work." I sat forward. I had carefully rehearsed that portion of my testimony. I knew exactly what I was going to say. I liked that kind of predictability. And, what's more, I believed strongly in what I was saying. As I felt more confident, my voice grew louder and a bit more forceful. I looked around the room and noticed that all the members of the jury were staring at me as I spoke. I wondered what they must be thinking.

"People outside our world, the do-gooders, the common folk, might not understand, but being a freak in Ringling Bros gave me a chance; a place to make my stand. It's not just me, but the same thing applies to many of my friends who travel with the show. The sideshow is our ticket. It's a chance to make a living we wouldn't have had otherwise." I paused. "Without the sideshow, I don't know how many of us would survive. We'd be out of work, in snake pit asylums, flat broke, penniless. We'd be on those bread lines, selling apples; homeless, beggars, or worse!" I took a breath and sat back. I felt like Rabbi Roth must have after he gives a sermon and worried that I had sounded too preachy.

"Are you acquainted with Dr. Humbred?" Honeywell asked, changing the subject.

"Yes, sir, I am."

"When did you first meet him?"

"I met him in St. Louis once a few years back. As I recollect, it was in the summer of 1935."

"Would you say he is an expert on the condition of gigantism?"

Randolph shot to his feet. "Objection, your honor! Mr. Erlich is not a physician or a scientist. He cannot possibly establish Dr. Humbred's expertise." Randolph had made the same objection when Glenn testified. As Wadlow's lawyer spoke to the judge, I recalled the pungent stench of formaldehyde in Humbred's office and the sad story of the Irish giant who ended up as a skeleton on a hook. Then Honeywell was on his feet too.

"Your honor, Mr. Erlich is indeed an expert on the condition of gigantism. He has suffered with it since he was seven and he has been examined by doctors all across the United States. He does have something to say on the subject and, as such, his opinion of Dr. Humbred should be heard." Honeywell and Randolph formed a semicircle in front of me. I imagined them to be the same harpooners I had visualized hunting for Byrne's leviathan body.

Bang, bang. Judge Otis walloped his gavel. "Objection overruled."

"Go on, Mr. Erlich," Honeywell commanded.

"Would you please repeat the question?" I asked.

"In your opinion, is Dr. Humbred an expert on the condition of gigantism?"

"Yes, sir. He told me about all the giants he'd examined and that he had written articles on the subject. He showed me his collection of photos and books on gigantism. He even owns a skeleton of a giant."

Honeywell paused, spun around, and walked back to the defense table where he picked up a legal pad and scanned it. He seemed like an actor on a stage. I smiled to myself and wondered if this slick, high-priced lawyer reminded anyone in that room besides me of Weary Willie.

"Do you know Robert Wadlow?" The attorney asked.

I hesitated. My inner smile disappeared. I was hoping Honeywell would ask me something about Humbred as a man; a human being. Then I would have been relieved to say how pushy and insensitive he was. I was hoping Honeywell would inquire what I thought about the words Humbred used to describe Wadlow in the journal article. Then I could have upbraided him as a cruel and insensitive lout who should have his typewriter shoved where the sun doesn't shine. But Honeywell never asked what I thought about Humbred as a man or what I thought about the journal article. My answers to those questions would never be known until now. My feelings and thoughts about Humbred and the journal article about Wadlow would linger, locked in a sealed vault, buried with all my other regrets, where things I wished I'd said or done when I had the chance but didn't remain entombed.

"Mr. Erlich! Please answer the question." Honeywell's demand brought me back to the proceedings.

"Sorry, I lost my train of thought," I said.

"Do you need me to repeat the question?"

"No, sir, I don't," I replied. "I met him at Madison Square Garden in 1936 when he first appeared with the circus. Then, a few weeks later, I ran into him again during our arena show in Boston," I replied.

"Would you say Mr. Wadlow was friendly?"

"Well, I only tried to talk to him that one time."

"I'm looking for a simple *yes* or *no*." The lawyer snapped at me with more intensity than I expected. "On the occasion that you spoke to Wadlow, was he friendly?"

"No, sir, I can't say that he was. I tried to make a joke—you know, one giant to another. I asked him, 'How's the weather up there?'" There was a bit of laughter in the room. Judge Otis's glare was enough to silence every spectator in the council chambers. I hoped I didn't hurt Wadlow with what I was saying, but it was the truth. "Wadlow didn't laugh or smile," I continued. "He didn't acknowledge me. He just walked away."

"Those are all the questions I have for this witness."

I felt like I had more to say about Humbred and Wadlow, but to be honest, at that moment, more than anything, I was relieved that I was almost off the hot seat. Soon I would be finished.

I looked up and saw Honeywell sit down. A few feet away, Randolph was conferring with Wadlow at the plaintiff's table. I sighed and hoped Randolph wouldn't want to ask me any questions. Honeywell had said he probably wouldn't. After all, Randolph had not cross-examined Glenn.

So when I saw Randolph stand and walk toward me, I was alarmed. The knot in my stomach tightened. Randolph gave me an artificial smile, just as Honeywell had. "Mr. Erlich, I only have one question for you." Then he paused, stroked his chin, glanced at the jury and then back at me. "How tall are you, sir?"

I couldn't comprehend what he was asking. It was a simple enough question, straightforward and all, one I had been asked thousands of times. But in the context of that trail, for the life of me, I couldn't comprehend what Randolph was getting at. For as much as I understood his question, he could have been speaking to me in Swahili.

"Mr. Erlich, how tall are you?" he repeated. The friendliness that had seasoned his words the first time he asked rapidly dissolved into thinly cloaked irritation.

I looked at Randolph with what must have appeared to be a puzzled expression. I felt defensive, my heart drumming like a tom-tom.

Randolph's eyes narrowed. He looked at me with audacity and continued, not waiting for my answer. "Mr. Erlich, you may not be aware of this but the defense has been using you as a pawn in a clever scheme to distance the jury from Robert Wadlow and to discredit him. They trot you out like a prize pony doing tricks for the crowd. They demonstrate how easily you move, and how friendly, funny, and articulate you are and how you have no aversion to the epithet *freak*. But, sir, I think you may have ulterior, nefarious motives of your own. Don't you?"

"I object, your honor!" Before I could say a word Honeywell had shot out of his seat, like Zacchini out of his cannon. "What relevance does Mr. Erlich's height have to do with this trial?" He spoke forcefully, his voice bouncing off the walls of the council chambers.

"Explain your reasoning, counselor," Judge Otis commanded. Randolph approached the judge's bench but spoke loud enough for everyone in the council chambers to hear.

"Mr. Erlich made it crystal clear to us just now that he earns his living in Ringling Bros sideshow as the tallest man in the world. He's made a point of telling us if it weren't for the circus he'd be destitute and living on the streets," Randolph said. He began to pace back and forth, reminding me of one of Frank Buck's tigers at feeding time. At that instant I felt that I was the one on trial. "When Robert Wadlow came on the scene, that title was threatened." As he spoke, I recalled my encounter with the young boy the previous day in the park, how he had compared me to Wadlow and the difficult questions I'd asked myself after that meeting. Randolph turned, pointed at me in a hostile way, and continued with his indictment. "Then Mr. Erlich lost his place in the sun. He was being replaced by a younger and taller rival. So, your honor, Mr. Erlich has other fish to fry here at this trial. He hopes to shame my client in some pitiful attempt at retaining his pathetic place with Ringling Bros."

His words stung me. I wondered if the pain I felt was because the lawyer's accusation was true. My throat constricted. Not knowing what to say or think or how I felt, I was overwhelmed with doubt. Then finally from somewhere at my core I asserted myself. *No! No,* I thought. *That son of a bitch is twisting my words.* My face felt hot. *How dare he challenge my integrity?* I grabbed the wooden arms of my chair and squeezed so tightly my hands turned a bloodless white.

"Objection overruled. Mr. Erlich, answer the question," Judge Otis demanded.

"Your honor, I have nothing against Robert Wadlow. I have done nothing here but tell the truth."

"How tall are you Mr. Erlich?" Judge Otis asked in a stern tone. As he spoke I felt degraded. *How tall am I? How tall am I?* My temperature rose even higher. They were trying to pigeonhole me. They saw me as less than a man and dishonest at that. What difference did it make if I was ten feet tall or two feet tall? It came to me that Randolph, Honeywell, the judge and jury, most of the people in that room, and even Val for that matter, couldn't have cared less about what I had to say. They couldn't really see me for who I was, much less even hear me. They didn't perceive me as a feeling, thinking man, but as placeholder in the record book of human oddities. I shook my head. I had had enough!

"Your honor, we are more than feet and inches. We are human beings. Don't define us by our height. We are more than that!"

The courtroom was quiet for what seemed like a long time. Then people began to murmur. Judge Otis looked down at me incredulously from his perch. Finally he spoke.

"Mr. Erlich, that speech is all well and good. Save it for Sunday school!" He held his gavel up in his right hand and shook it as if he were threatening to hit me with it. "Frankly, I don't care how you define yourself. You work as a giant don't you? You're paid a salary based on your height. Is that correct?" I bit my lip and wondered what I had done. I couldn't focus. "Is that correct?" Judge Otis repeated himself. He couldn't hide his rage at my defiance behind the decorum of a black robe and the veneer of legal precedent.

"Yes, sir," I finally answered. "But maybe not for long," I muttered under my breath.

"What was that?" he asked.

"Nothing," I said. I clenched my teeth like the oppressed everywhere once they have said too much.

"For the last time, unless you want to spend ninety days in our jailhouse for contempt of my court, answer the damned question. Let's get on with this."

I let go of the arms of my chair and my hands balled into fists. I wanted to tell all of them to go to hell. Later I came to understand that it didn't matter how they defined us or what I said. It didn't matter if they were deaf or blind, because the words I uttered on that witness stand were really meant for me. What really counted in that courtroom was how I saw myself.

"I am eight feet, six and one-half inches tall." I'm sure my voice was red with anger.

"How tall is Robert Wadlow?" Randolph asked rapidly.

"I believe he is just shy of nine feet," I answered.

"He is actually eight feet, eleven and one-half inches tall," he added, correcting me. "That's all I have for this witness." Randolph turned and walked back to the defense table.

Before he even sat down Honeywell was standing in front of the judge. "I would like to redirect, your honor." Judge Otis nodded. "Mr. Erlich, I have a few questions."

Now what? I thought. But by that point I was numb and didn't really care.

"Did Mr. Wadlow's appearance with Ringling Bros threaten your livelihood in any way?"

"No, sir, it did not."

"Why do you say that?"

"Because he only appeared in two shows; one in Madison Square Garden and one in Boston, and then, to the best of my knowledge, he quit."

"Do you hold any grudge or bare any ill will or envy for Robert Wadlow?"

"No, sir. As I said, I don't particularly like the man, but I do not wish him any harm." At that moment I knew beyond knowing that I truly wished Wadlow well.

"Thank you. That's all."

"You may step down," Judge Otis said.

On the long walk back to my seat, I was disoriented. At first I gazed down at the ground, almost embarrassed or afraid to look up. Then I slowly lifted my head. Like a sailor lost in a squall looks to a lighthouse, I searched the room for some sign of approval, recognition, or human connection, some proof that I wasn't alone, that I belonged. I didn't look to Fishbein, Honeywell, or even Glenn. I'm not sure why, but I found myself looking at Wadlow. He avoided my eyes and stared straight down at the table where he sat.

When I finally sat down, I remember Glenn patting me on the back and saying I had done a good job. Then the intensity of what had just happened began to sink in. I squirmed as I realized why I had been subpoenaed as a witness. Randolph was right. I had been used as a pawn, a norm, a huge tool to define and protect the status quo. And I didn't like it.

XXXX

In the summations that followed, both attorneys reminded me of sideshow talkers flinging hyperbole at a crowd of rubes. The two of them used as much exaggeration as Ringling Bros when they made me wear platform shoes and sixteen-inch-high velvet hats.

Randolph was first to speak. For sixty minutes he did his best to show that Humbred's article was full of untruths and that his client had been maligned and injured by it. I remember that he began his speech by saying Humbred had tried to portray Robert Wadlow as a Frankenstein. He reviewed the testimony that Wadlow was normal in every way with the exception of his height. As he addressed the court, I thought about Frankenstein and wondered if the movie studios and the circus had manipulated the public to see me as aberrant, as a monster, too.

Then it was Honeywell's turn. He spoke for an hour as well. To say he was dramatic and bombastic in his closing arguments would not be an overstatement. All I recall were the last words he uttered to the jury: "A just decision means weighing the facts on the day that Dr. Humbred visited Robert Wadlow. Justice requires balancing carefully the claims Wadlow and his attorneys have made and the refutations we have put forward." Randolph enunciated and accentuated the words *just* and *justice*.

As he spoke I reached down under my seat and picked up my sketch-book and pencil from the place I had stashed them that morning. I opened the pad to my drawing of Justitia and scribbled the words "blind justice" on top of the page. I gazed at the caricature I had created and wondered, *Is it justice or a flip of some cosmic coin that determines who will be normal and who will be born without arms and legs or a dwarf or giant; who will find peace and acceptance as an ordinary man and who will be hounded for being a freak?* I felt alone, angry at the fates, and strangely, I also felt free; freer than I had felt in as long as I could remember.

It was about half past five when Honeywell finished his summation and sat down. Then Judge Otis spoke to the jury. He stipulated key points that needed to be proven to demonstrate that Wadlow had, in fact, been libeled. He said that he felt that thirty different declarations in the journal article had offended Wadlow.

"Gentlemen, there are only a few of these statements that in and of themselves are defamatory in nature," Judge Otis explained. "The first has to do with the use of the word *freak*. The others have to do with wording in the following statements—" One of the men in the jury sneezed, interrupting the judge. "God bless you," Otis said and continued: "'That fate has fashioned him on so preposterous a scale,' 'his expression is surly and he is definitely unfriendly and antagonistic,' 'his hands are startlingly enormous,' and finally, 'his fingers are double-jointed and curl up into bizarre and gruesome positions.' The question for you, gentlemen of the jury, is whether or not these statements were true on June 2, 1936, the date on which Dr. Humbred examined Robert Wadlow."

XXXX

Three quarters of an hour had passed since the jury had retired to consider their decision. Glenn and I were standing outside on the steps that led up to city hall, getting some early-evening air. I was exhausted but happy the day was winding down. We both felt it was wise to stay close just in case there was a verdict. I was booked on an eight o'clock train to Wichita where I was to catch up with the circus for the Saturday matinee the following afternoon.

"If the jury is out much longer, I will have to leave before the verdict," I remarked to Glenn. "That's something I really don't want to do."

The sun was just setting in marbled lavender and pink. I gazed up from where we stood to see a flock of crows flying low across the pastel horizon. Just then several reporters ran by us, up the steps, and into the building. One of them almost knocked me over.

"Hurry up!" Glenn said. "The verdict must be in and it's only taken a little over fifty minutes for their decision." We scrambled up the stairs and into to the council chambers. The jury had already filed in. Glenn and I found our seats just in time to hear Judge Otis.

"Mr. Forman, has the jury reached a verdict?"

A skinny old man in red suspenders with gray hair pomaded in place stood up. A hush fell over the room. "Yes, your honor, we have. In the matter of Wadlow vs. Humbred, Fishbein, and the American Medical Association, we find for the defendants."

"No! No!" cried several spectators. People seemed distraught.

Judge Otis hammered his gavel hard.

I was stunned. I thought for sure the jury—made up of locals who had lionized Wadlow as a hero—would have crucified Humbred and, by association, Fishbein and the AMA, but they didn't. The words of Arturo, the old Franciscan friar I had befriended in Santa Fe, came to mind. *"Mi hijo, el tiempo es el mejor autor, siempre cuenta con un final perfecto* (My son, time is the best author. It always comes up with a perfect ending)." *What kind of a perfect ending is this?* I thought. Perfect for young Wadlow, perfect for Fishbein, the AMA, and Humbred, perfect for me? It had been a long and strange road that had led me to that trial: my unhappy childhood in El Paso, my days at Century Comedies, my blindness, my travels with Ringling Bros, meeting Val, my time at the Ringling School of Art and classes with Hari Kidd, my car wreck in New Mexico, and then Mayo Clinic. There were circles within circles, but what would come of all this? I had no answers; no clear sense of direction. At that moment nothing made sense to me. Everything felt chaotic.

I took a deep breath and let it out; not so much with relief that the trial was over but with determination. Despite my uncertainty there was something I knew I had to do. It was already 7:20 p.m. I would have to rush.

I shook Glenn's hand good-bye, stood up, and moved quickly toward the exit. As I made my way through the throng of spectators down the hall to the staircase, I saw Wadlow and his parents huddled against the wall, talking to a reporter. If not for my size I would have been stuck in the sea of slow-moving people, all trying to get from the hallway to the street. If not for Wadlow's size I never would have spotted him.

"We're not done with this fight," I heard Wadlow shout as I got closer. True to what he said to the reporter, within a few days the Wadlow's appealed the decision. Within a month Wadlow and his family would lose that appeal as well.

I made my way to where Wadlow's mother, father, and siblings stood in a bevy, like quail frightened by a coyote.

"Robert! Robert!" I shouted over the clamor. "Can I have a word?"

I shouldn't have been, but I was surprised and saddened by what happened next. His father tried to pull him away from me. Their disdain was evident. Wadlow and I stood, like two skyscrapers towering over the fog, facing one another above the crowd. Looking at him there in the hallway, I wondered if Cuco would have described Wadlow, the tallest man in the world, as a *yanki*. You remember, that's a man who looks down from above and sees things others do not. I wasn't sure about what Cuco would have called Wadlow, but it came to me at that moment, for the first time, that a person's height has absolutely nothing to do with his ability to see.

"What is it, Erlich? Haven't you already done enough damage?" he asked, violently pushing away the air in front of him as if it were me.

"Listen, Robert, I just want to say, no hard feelings."

"No hard feelings? No hard feelings? Right!" Wadlow snarled. He made no effort to hide his rage. It was as if he blamed me for all that had gone wrong that day and in the rest of his life. Then he spun around and, as quickly as is possible for a nine-foot man in a crowd, tottered away on his cane with his family in tow.

Wadlow didn't give me a chance to say all that was on my mind. To be honest, I wasn't sure what I wanted to tell him but I felt the need, in some way, to connect with him again. Sadly, I never got the chance. As I watched the world's tallest living man hobble down the hall to the elevator, I was strangely moved. His rudeness and antagonism didn't bother me. I understood. I had indeed changed my opinion of him after our negative encounters in the circus. It's funny, but when I changed my view of Wadlow, I saw myself in a different light as well. Maybe Wadlow wouldn't be my choice as a friend. But for me, he was a teacher of sorts and deserved my respect.

At that moment, I had no way of knowing that I would never see him again. Six weeks later, while making an appearance at the Forest Festival in Manistee, Michigan, Robert Wadlow developed an infection caused by blisters from a poorly fitting leg brace. The infection caused a high fever, and within a few days he died. I tell you now that I owe Robert Wadlow more than I can say. I didn't realize then how much he had impacted me and how our brief time together at that trial would soon change my life forever. Wadlow became a hero and mentor who helped orient and align me for a giant step into the unknown.

CHAPTER 34

The End of the Magic

DELPHIC STUDIOS

724 Fifth Avenue, New York City

EXHIBITION OF PAINTINGS

BY

JACK EARLE

MAY 4th TO MAY 17th

1 9 3 6

Program from Jake's show at the Delphic, May 1936

Because of my responsibilities in the circus and all the energy I put into getting ready for the art show after the trial, I didn't have much free time. But what little free time I did have was haunted by thoughts of Robert Wadlow's untimely death. The condolence letter I wrote to his family soon after I heard the news didn't help. Based on how the Wadlows had responded to me after the verdict, I doubted they had ever even read it.

Despite—or maybe because of—my sadness about the young giant, I experienced something I'd only had brief glimpses of before. I began to feel a buoyant, burning urgency to be productive with pastel blue and green watercolors and the bright reds, yellows, and muted greens of oil paints, with fresh alliterations and couplets, finishing touches for my new book of poetry, and with chunks of gray clay for my latest sculpture, an homage to another freak, my friend Cliko the African Bushman.

I wasn't driven, as I'd been in the past, by the fear that time was running out for me; I knew sooner or later it would. In that way I was no different than an ordinary-sized man; both of us had to deal with the realization that one day it would all end. I was driven by something else. The quote from Proverbs that hung on the wall in Papa's office: "Give me a heart of wisdom, oh Lord, that I may number my days," became my mantra. Those words rang like cathedral bells in the space behind my eyes, waking me from a thirty-one-year slumber. I didn't know how much time I had left and I didn't want to squander it. I was eager to fill every waking second of every minute with breath and life and color; touching and being touched.

I walked over to the open window and inhaled the crisp, early-evening air of an October sunset in Manhattan. I looked down at the sidewalk twelve stories below and watched the bustling traffic. It was hard to believe that a little over a year before in a similar room in that same hotel, in a midnight's dire straits, I had almost jumped to my death. I turned away from the window and gazed at the tuxedo neatly laid out on the two beds that the staff at the Algonquin had pushed together for my stay. In about an hour I would celebrate the opening of my one-man show at the Delphic. It seemed like yesterday that I was lying in my hospital bed in Albuquerque after that awful car wreck reading Frida's letter with the offer to do the exhibit. The time since then had blown by as fast as shadowy rain clouds on a west Texas monsoon afternoon. Then the phone rang, startling me.

"Hello, Jake?" I heard Harry Doll's unmistakable voice on the other end of the line. I was sure he was calling with some last-minute congratulations on the milestone I would celebrate later that evening. It made me so happy when I discovered that he and Daisy took time off from Ringling's four-day run in Cleveland, as I had, to travel to New York for my big night. My mother and father, Ben, and Myer had come in for the event. Frank Buck, Frida, and Diego would be there, too. Even Clyde Ingalls was supposed to show up. There must have been some public relations angle he was trying to work I had thought when I first heard about him planning to attend.

I couldn't spend much time schmoozing with Harry since Val was coming to the hotel to pick me up soon. I looked forward to the romantic midnight dinner she'd promised we would celebrate with after all the people at the show had left. When Harry called, all I had on was my half-buttoned shirt. I needed all the time I could muster to get into my monkey suit, a skill I'd never quite mastered.

"Hiya, Harry," I replied. "I don't have much time to talk."

"Jake, I have some bad news. You'd better sit down." His normally vibrant tone was replaced by one with the gravity of stone. Without thinking, I sat down on the bed. I immediately wondered if Daisy had taken sick.

"What is it?" I asked. I heard my voice quiet, as fear of what I would soon learn clenched the muscles in my chest, my throat, and my jaw.

"Lya is dead." I dropped the receiver on the ground. I struggled to pick it up. My hand trembled as I tried to hold the phone to my ear. "Jake, are you there?" Harry asked.

"What did you say?" I ignored his question, not wanting to believe what he had said.

"We were so worried about her. When Lya didn't respond to our last few letters, Daisy contacted her people in Germany. Her family in Dresden just sent us a cable."

"Harry, what in God's name happened to her?" I was numb. It all felt so unreal.

"God had nothing to do with it. Lya was murdered," Harry said. "The Nazis arrested her and put her in an asylum. It was a trumped-up charge.

All the police would say was that they were enforcing Hitler's euthanasia laws. Then they shipped her to a concentration camp where they killed her."

I still couldn't believe what Harry was saying. I felt a weight on my shoulders that seemed to grow heavier by the second.

"Daisy is devastated. I don't know if we will be there tonight. We'll see. I've got to go." Then, before I could say another word, the phone went dead.

I got up and walked over to the window and opened it as wide as it would go. *I will never see her again,* I thought. I leaned out as far as I could and looked down. I hesitated for a moment. "No!" I screamed. My voice echoed off the other buildings. Then I began to wail. Tears flowed out of me in a torrent, down my cheeks and onto my half-buttoned tuxedo shirt. I wept for Lya, I wept for Robert Wadlow, and I wept for me. I wept for injustice; for what might have been and for what never would be. A flood of bittersweet memories poured over me. At once the news of Lya's death made me nauseous and dizzy, while it also ignited and sharpened my recollections.

Finally my tears stopped. Not so much because I was done crying, but because I was exhausted. I looked at my wristwatch. It was 6:15 p.m. Now there were only a few minutes to get myself dressed and down to the lobby to meet Val. I really did not want to go to my opening, but that event was being given in my honor and there was no way I could cancel, especially at that late hour. No matter what had happened to her, I knew Lya would have never wanted me to miss my art show.

I forced myself to walk across the room. I moved slowly, as if in a stupor. Then I gazed into the mirror that hung over the dresser and struggled to button the collar of my shirt. It would not close. My huge fingers lost all coordination. In frustration I pulled and tugged at it, sure I'd tear the damned thing. I thought of the ancient custom of ripping your cloths upon learning of a loved one's death. Shards of memory reflected back at me from someplace deep inside that felt shattered.

How pretty Lya looked the first time I met her; her angry eyes when she let me have it at the telegraph office; her grace and elegance; the way she flirted with me that afternoon in the sideshow when Frida had come for a visit; how available she was and how I'd shut her out. Lya was open to me like few other people in my life had been. She was certainly more available than Val. I felt I'd been such a fool and now it was too late to do anything about it.

Finally the collar pin slipped into place. After I buttoned the remaining studs in the shirt, I reached for my black bow tie. The feel of the smooth black satin reminded me of something I'd all but forgotten. It occurred in San Antonio three years back. All the freaks had been invited to Hertzberg's Circus Lover's Annual Gala. It was a formal affair. I had asked Lya to lend me a hand getting ready. While I crouched on my berth in the circus train, she stood on tiptoes, perched on a chair in front of me helping tie the same bow tie. She was so gentle and caring. How I wished Lya were there to help me that night. I began to sob again. Then I flashed back on other memories and my tears continued to flow: our late night games of gin rummy in the pie car, her wise and tender counsel, her insight about my dreams and how deeply she listened. Now Lya was dead.

The sound of the phone ringing shook me.

"Mr. Erlich?" A baritone brogue articulated my name. I felt confused and couldn't place the voice. As if the caller sensed how puzzled I was, he identified himself. "It's Scotty, Ms. Val's chauffer. We are parked just in front of the hotel, sir." I looked at my watch again. It was six thirty. I had lost touch with the time. Now I was late. Disoriented and feeling rushed, I grabbed my tuxedo coat and made my way out of the hotel room. I don't know how I did it, but somehow I finished tying my tie in the elevator.

Just as Scotty had said, the Pierce-Arrow was parked in front of the Algonquin. Scotty, dressed in his chauffer's cap, tunic, and polished, knee-high boots, stood on the curb holding an umbrella, guarding the opened passenger door as I stepped out of the lobby into the drizzle. "Good evening, Mr. Erlich," he said. I nodded and contorted myself into the back of the car.

The two times I'd previously ridden in that limo there was no separation between the passenger cabin and the chauffer. Things were different that night. A mahogany partition separated us from Scotty, sealing Val and I off in our own private world, a privileged experience only the wealthy in limos and the dead riding to the cemetery ever know.

I wondered if Val would notice I'd been crying. She was dressed in an elegant, beaded white gown and matching headband and heels. She was smoking a cigarette and had a pouty look on her rouged face. Val turned, gave me a peck on the cheek, and looked away. As numb and hurt as I was, I knew something was wrong. Val looked upset. I debated telling her about Lya. It was painful, but I realized it was too risky to share my sorrow with someone who was, at best, only occasionally receptive to what I felt or needed.

As I sat back in the glove-leather seat, Val picked up the in-car intercom that looked like a telephone. It rested on a small console between us made of wood that matched the partition.

"Scotty, please take a roundabout way to the Delphic so Jake and I can have a few extra minutes to chat." We drove for several blocks and didn't say a word. Typically, I would have broken the silence with solicitous questions, but that wasn't a typical night and I felt anything but solicitous. Crosstown traffic seemed particularly heavy. Several times it ground to a halt.

"I had a fight with my husband," Val finally explained after a few minutes had passed. "I will have to meet him for dinner. I am so sorry to cancel at the last minute like this. I promise to make it up to you."

She moved close to me. Her perfume was normally intoxicating, but not that night. Val put her left hand on my thigh, the other on my cheek. Then she reached across, grabbed my tuxedo jacket, and pulled me down to her level to kiss me on the lips. I stiffened and turned away.

"What's wrong, Jake?" she asked. I heard a muffled ringing sound from the same phone Val had used to communicate with Scotty. Val abruptly scooted away and answered the phone. "Yes, Scotty, I understand," she said. Then Val listened intently for about a minute. "Do what you think is best." She hung up. "Scotty says there's a terrible traffic jam. He thinks there must be some big event at Madison Square Garden."

A few seconds later when the limo stopped, I partially opened the rear window, looked out, and noticed that Scotty was speaking to a cop in a yellow rain slicker who was standing in the middle of the street. I rolled my window farther down and could just make out what they were saying.

"What's going on, officer?" Scotty asked.

"Aw, it's a big deal at the Garden. They're expecting over twenty-thousand people inside and maybe that many on the sidewalk and in the street, as well."

"On the sidewalk and in the street?" Scotty asked.

"Yeah, they say there may be trouble. It's a rally of the Nazi Bund." When I heard the word *Nazi* my skin crawled. "Fritz Kuhn, the front man for the Third Reich in America, and some guy named Moseley are supposed to talk."

"Who is Moseley?" Scotty asked.

"I dunno," the policeman replied. Then the car in front of us lurched forward. The cop reached for his whistle and blew it to get the line of cars going again. "Move it along now, mack," he ordered.

Scotty put the limo back in gear and we slowly inched ahead. I remembered last year's incident when Val and I had to run from the eugenics rally. Moseley was the demagogue haranguing the crowd in the park. On that excursion Scotty and I had passed Camp Siegfried on the way back to the city from Val's horse farm. I recalled how that place gave me the creeps. Now I understood why.

Traffic was still crawling along. I felt trapped. The back of the limo reminded me of the inside of a coffin. I couldn't breathe. Yet again, Val was yanking my chain, promising and not following through. At that instant I saw Val like I had never seen her before. I wasn't hurt or angry. I just felt sad for her. Val was like a watch whose fine, jeweled movement had stopped after it had been dropped on the ground. It came to me that even the finest watchmaker in the world couldn't get it started again. In my heart of hearts I knew Val craved freedom but she didn't know how to free herself. She was like me when I felt trapped by who I thought I was and by what I thought I could or couldn't accomplish. *I've already wasted too much time with her*, I thought.

"That's enough," I said. Though I spoke out loud my words weren't intended for Val. They were meant for me.

I sat forward and knocked loudly on the mahogany partition that separated us from Scotty. Val looked puzzled. A few seconds later I heard a cranking sound. The wooden wall that had isolated Val and me in the surreal, stuffy world in back of the Pierce-Arrow slowly lowered. As it did, a rush of fresh air filled the passenger cabin. I sat forward.

"Scotty, would you please let me out?" I asked. Scotty slowly pulled the limo to the curb. I gazed over at Val. At that instant she looked like a lost and stunned little girl. I opened my door. She grabbed hold of my arm.

"It's raining out there," she said.

"I know, but I don't care," I replied. "Val, your life is a train wreck. Life is so short." I reached over and kissed her on the cheek. "Good-bye and thank you for everything," I said and pulled myself free.

When I got out of the limo and straightened my spine, I was able to finally breathe again. I began hoofing it towards the Delphic, oblivious to the light rain that was falling. I strode down the crowded sidewalk and dodged the passersby, some of whom stopped to stare at me. *I'm really alone,* I said to myself.

After about a half a block, I paused, thinking about Val and her life; tragically orphaned at a young age, married to a wealthy, controlling man who was old enough to be her father. She was really talented but only dabbled in art as a pastime. There is nothing wrong with that, but when you have her gift it is a colossal waste. What troubled me most was that in her art, and for that matter in every other aspect of her life, Val avoided any and all semblance of commitment and real passion because that would have meant she had something to lose. *Maybe I'm afraid, too,* I thought.

I glanced over my shoulder for one more look. A cloud of exhaust and raindrops almost obscured the Pierce-Arrow like a foggy curtain. The limo just sat there at the curb, a huge metal animal frozen in terror, unsure which way to go. I turned back around and continued to walk. After a few blocks I started to think about Lya again and reached up to wipe the wetness from my eyes and cheeks. It was hard to tell if it was raindrops or tears. *I'd rather be alone than running after the crumbs of a paper cake,* I thought.

I had thirty blocks to cover and I was already late. While I hurriedly made my way to the gallery, the rain stopped. I thought about time; how the days seemed to drag on in the circus and how I couldn't wait for them to end. But since I started to paint, sculpt, take photographs, and write, time had shrunk and even disappeared. There never seemed to be enough of it.

When I passed Grand Central Station, it came to me that I'd soon be reenacting the same old script; the one I revisited year in and year out. Clyde Ingalls would approach with my contract for next season. I'd stall, put him off, and avoid him until he gave me an ultimatum. He always made the same threats; said I'd end up homeless or in some mud show. *It's funny,* I thought, *I want to avoid the circus every year but when it comes to my art it's different. I don't think I've ever avoided anything about it.*

I dodged a yellow cab at Park and Forty-Fourth. The cabbie started to honk his horn and stuck his head out the window as if to curse at me. After he looked at me he thought better of it and sped away. I had four more blocks to go. I looked at my wristwatch. I was already a half hour late. I jogged the rest of the way.

XXXX

The Delphic was a classy gallery and that night it was packed with a classy crowd of well-heeled people in tuxedos and ball gowns. I cannot remember a time when I saw more sequins. But besides the patrons of the arts and the high-society types you might expect to see, there were also stage door johnnies and showgirls, several circus aficionados, and well-dressed gangsters and their better-dressed molls. I think I spotted a couple of professional ball players dragged out for a night of culture by their wives. *The excitement in this place does not match my mood,* I thought as I hesitantly pushed my way into the crowd, most of which was now staring at me.

The attention started to make me nervous when I heard a familiar voice. "*Felicitaciones, largito* (Congratulations, big boy)." It was Frida Kahlo with my brothers in tow. It appeared we'd all purchased our tuxedos from the same tailor. Frida had met Myer on her trip to El Paso and he must have introduced her to Ben that night at the gallery. The three of them looked as thick as thieves. Frida, whose hair was still starkly cut, motioned for me to bend down. It saddened me that she no longer wore the bright colors and tropical flowers she had when I first met her. Now she dressed like a man. I missed her flamboyance. When I bent down she gave me a kiss on each cheek.

"Hey, little brother. *Mazel Tov!*" Ben said, stepping forward to give me a hug.

Myer appeared unsure of what to say or do at an artsy occasion like that so he awkwardly shook my hand. Then Frida led us toward the back of the place. It was strange, and I've often wondered why Frida never said a word about Val's absence that night. I think maybe she sensed that things between us would turn out the way they did; whatever the reason, she never asked and I never brought it up.

At the rear of the Delphic we came to the doors to a large salon that was as crowded as the room we had just walked through. There we ran into Diego chatting up some young thing in a slinky black dress. Diego acknowledged me but went on talking as if Frida and I weren't even there. I heard Frida growl. That was confirmation of the conclusion I'd come to in Juarez when we visited there together. At least in part, Diego's philandering and inattention had a direct connection with Frida's austere appearance. Based on what I observed it didn't seem their painful tango was going to change any time soon. Diego was saying something about capitalist pigs and the role of revolutionary artists. The girl looked starstruck.

"*Ay* that *cabrón*; he never changes. Diego never stops using art and politics to get in the pants of pretty *jovencitas* (young girls). Sometime I might just shoot that damned *gallo* (rooster)." Frida joked about a too familiar, too painful situation.

The four of us kept moving through the crowd. Finally we entered the salon where my paintings, my photographs, and a few of my sculptures were displayed under small spotlights. In front of each display I noticed several people looking at my work. Since Harry's phone call about Lya and my confrontation with Val, I had forgotten how preoccupied and worried I was that those who attended the exhibit would not approve of my art; that they would flat out reject it.

As I moved into that space, the mob of people parted for me like the Red Sea for Moses. When I got close to the first painting I saw Mama and Papa standing proudly in front of it. They were beaming.

As I approached, I banged my head on a low-hanging crystal chandelier. It almost knocked me to my knees, immediately replacing any pride I felt with more embarrassment than pain. I did my best to regain my composure.

"Are you all right?" Mama asked. "Let me see," she commanded, not waiting for my response. I bent down and she examined my forehead and gave me a kiss on the scalp.

I wished I could have felt as genuinely happy as they were, but I wasn't. I couldn't bring myself to tell them about Lya's death. There would be time for that later. For obvious reasons, any feelings I had about my parting of the ways with Val would have to remain my secret. I did my best to not let any of that sadness show. Once again I called upon my acting skill to mask my feelings . . . *Some things never change,* I thought. But to be honest, despite my sorrow, right then and there I did experience some sense of accomplishment. Still, everything seemed so unreal, as if everyone was there to honor someone else.

The painting my folks were looking at was an oil that I had titled *The End of the Magic*. How appropriate, I said to myself. In reds, greens, purples, and grays, *The End of the Magic* depicted a Ringling Bros circus wagon drawn by four white Percherons. A family warming themselves by a fire watches as the draft horses haul the wagon out of town. I gazed around the salon and saw small and large groups of people transfixed, facing each of my paintings, photos, and sculptures. Some pointed and seemed to be talking about them; some crouched in front of the art; some just stood there, as if they were daydreaming. I honestly couldn't say that everyone in that crowded gallery liked my work, but they did appear to be engaged and some seemed to be moved. I wished Hari Kidd could have been there to have seen that.

I felt a tug on my sleeve. It was Papa. "Jakey," he said. I bent farther down to better hear him. "Just because they're looking doesn't mean they're laughing."

Papa's words gave me goose bumps. I remembered the last time he had uttered them. I was just sixteen and we were walking to Century Studios for my first day of work in silent pictures.

I looked around the room again. That was the very first time I can remember that the big show was what I'd created and not my height. At that moment, I thought about Robert Wadlow and his struggles to be normal; how he never wore a costume or appeared in the sideshow tent, how all he wanted was to be an advertising man or a lawyer. It's too bad he never had the chance. Even at thirty-one I wasn't sure what *normal* meant. But the closest I had ever felt to it was when I lost myself creating something: a painting, a photograph, a sculpture, or a poem.

I'm not exactly clear why that night at the Delphic I got the courage to finally do it. Maybe it was Lya's death or the breakup with Val. Maybe it was the excitement of the art show. Maybe it was a combination of all three. I mean, in the past I'd certainly fantasized about it, talked about it, and spent many a sleepless night thinking about it, but until that night I never had the balls to actually do it. Whatever the reason, I realized what I had to do when I spotted Clyde Ingalls in the middle of the room talking with two guys I didn't recognize.

"Excuse me," I said to those gathered around me. "I've got something I need to take care of." I took a deep breath and marched across the room. When Clyde saw me he stopped what he was saying and looked up.

"Fellas, this is Jake Erlich, the *artiste* who created all of this; the tallest man in the world and the star of Ringling's sideshow. Jake, this is Jordan

Douglas. He's a reporter for the *New York Times*, and this is Pat O'Hanlon from the *Herald*."

"Hello, gentlemen," I said to the reporters. They nodded back. "Clyde, can I have a word in private?"

"Why, Jake, you know we have no secrets from our friends in the press."

"Are you sure?" I asked.

"Absolutely," he answered adamantly.

"Okay. Next first of May, I won't be coming back to the circus."

Clyde's jaw dropped. He looked flabbergasted, grabbed me by the arm, and pulled me from the reporters. "But I . . . Why, Jake? Don't you know there's a depression going on? Do you want to end up living on the street?"

Or in a snake-pit asylum or working in some awful mud show? I said to myself, completing the monologue I'd heard so often before.

"I know, Clyde. I appreciate your concern. But don't waste your breath." I cut him off. "I've thought it through carefully. There's little time and I don't have any to waste." Ingalls looked baffled but I didn't care. "I know in life and especially for somebody like me, there are no guarantees. I'm not sure what I'm going to do next, but I've got to take my shot."

He looked stunned and stood there completely speechless. "Clyde, you and I have had our rough patches." I said, putting my hand on his shoulder and continuing. "Last year when I nailed the fan in front of Gargantua's cage, my yearly bouts of indecision about signing contracts, and when my dark spells got the better of me and I'd disappear. I want to thank you for your patience. All in all, the circus has been wonderful to me. It's been a home. I've made great friends there. Ringling Bros has opened many doors, but now I need to walk through some different doors. It's time for me to write a new chapter in my book."

After I said what was on my mind—for once uninterrupted by the convincing sideshow master and salesman *par excellence*—I reached out and grabbed his right hand and shook it. "I wish you the best."

As I walked away from him, I felt weightless. But I still had one more thing I had to do. A few minutes later I found my parents. They were standing amidst about a dozen others in front of the photo I'd taken of Arturo, the Franciscan friar, in Santa Fe.

"Mama and Papa, I need to talk with you."

"Jake, it's going to have to wait. Before you say a thing I need to tell you something," Papa insisted.

"Mama and Papa, I—"

"*Sha*, listen to Papa," Mama said, silencing me as only she knew how to do. I was rankled that I would have to wait to finally tell them what was on my mind. I could hardly hold myself back.

"There's a rumor going around that there are two people here tonight from the Metropolitan Museum of Art," Papa said. "People are saying they want to buy a painting or two and a sculpture for their permanent collection. The word is they're very impressed with your art."

I was shocked, almost numb. I stumbled for something to say and felt overwhelmed. My first show and a major New York museum wanted to buy some of my art—during the Depression yet.

That's when I looked at the door and saw Harry and Daisy enter the room. They were arm in arm, Harry tenderly supporting his sister. Without uttering another word to my folks, I walked toward my two little friends. As I got closer, I noticed that they both had been crying. Despite how upset they were, they had come out to honor me anyway. I felt even more moved. The only thing that could have made the night more perfect was if Lya could have been there.

When I reached them I kneeled down. "I'm so sorry about Lya," I said, swallowing hard to hold back my tears. Harry nodded his head and held up his hand to hold the overwhelming sadness at bay and stop me from saying any more. "It means so much to me that you're here," I said.

"You don't need to say a word, Jake," Daisy replied.

"We wouldn't have missed this for the world," Harry added. Then my two friends each gave me a kiss on the check.

"We'll talk later," Daisy said. "But first we want to wander around this place and see what all the fuss is about." Then they turned around and wandered the gallery on their own.

Now, a different kind of tears than the ones that had fallen previously that night started to well up in my eyes. They weren't tears of sorrow, but of gratitude. I was grateful for my family, teachers, and friends. I couldn't believe how lucky I was.

Despite how moved I felt, I still had a nagging urgency to tell my parents about my decision to leave Ringling Bros, as if my courage to do that would soon wane. I couldn't wait any longer. Unable to put it off a second longer I walked back to where my parents were standing.

"Mama, Papa, I have . . . "

My father got an amused look on his face. "Are you going to ask our permission to leave the circus or are you going to tell us you did?"

I was perplexed. "I was going to tell you I did."

"We know, son."

I shook my head and smiled at how needlessly worried I'd been. I realized that my mother and father had grasped more about me than I'd ever given them credit for. As I'd changed my views of what I was and wasn't capable of, they must have, too.

I felt relieved. My eyes wandered across the gallery and I thought I saw a young woman who looked like Carolyn. Even though I knew it couldn't be her and it was just wishful thinking, curiosity got the better of me. You see, Carolyn was on the very short list of people who were important in my life but were not able to be present that night at the Delphic. When I had invited Carolyn she told me she would be taking exams the week of my opening and it would be impossible for her to attend. As I approached the young woman she turned around. There was no mistaking her million-dollar smile. I could not believe she was there. Carolyn threw her arms around my legs and gave me a warm hug.

"I'm so goldarn proud of you, Jake," she said.

"I've really missed you." I was amazed at how unguarded I was with that woman.

"I wouldn't have missed this night for all the tea in China. But don't get a swollen head. I didn't come north of the Mason-Dixon Line just for your opening."

"Now you've peaked my curiosity."

"After you left the institute it got me to thinking about why I was there in the first place. I gave them my notice last week."

"You what? What about your need for your parents' support, and your worry about their approval, and all that stuff about Southern ideals of what a young woman's supposed to do with her life?" I asked.

"When I read what you wrote me about your teacher, Hari Kidd, and his experience at the Pennsylvania Academy of the Fine Arts, I asked myself what in holy hell fire I was doing wasting my time in Sarasota." As she spoke she seemed to get more animated, moving her hands and arms like she was conducting an orchestra. "Well, I wrote them and applied.

When they saw my portfolio they arranged for me to get a grant from some old robber baron to cover my tuition and living expenses. Classes start the first of next week." Carolyn winked at me. "I bet you didn't realize you were such a trendsetter. But I sense something is wrong. Are you okay? Have you been crying?" she inquired.

This woman is really tuned in to me, I thought. That was an experience I wasn't accustomed to. It felt good.

I told her about Lya's death and that I had, in fact, been crying.

"I'm so sorry." Carolyn took my hand and squeezed it. We stood there for a moment or two and didn't say a word.

"We'll talk about it later. Maybe over dinner?" I suggested.

"I'd love that," she answered. We did talk about it later that night. After all these years, I still miss Lya. At times I miss her terribly. But like the harvest moon that shined over the city the night of my opening, and everything else in this life, the intensity of my sadness and regret waxes and wanes.

"I want to know more about you," I said, changing the subject. "How did your folks react to your decision to change schools?"

"Not another word about me. This is your special night," she said adamantly. "Right now, I need to tell you I'm impressed with your work, Jake." My face felt flushed. "I hope you realize that you're not just entertaining the people here tonight with your art; you're moving them—me included. I particularly like this one," she said, pointing to a simple self-portrait done in maroons, greens and grays that was displayed nearby to where we were standing.

"Why is that?" I asked. Her comment surprised me and made me curious. "It's the only image in the whole exhibit that has nothing to do with the circus."

"I realize that," she said. "Looking at it, I'd never know that the artist's model was anything other than a normal, sweet man with intelligent, caring, yet sad eyes." I smiled at Carolyn and kissed her hand. "I'll find you when this shindig's over," she said. "I don't want to miss a thing." Then she spun around and walked away. At that moment I stood taller and felt stronger than any time I could remember.

My new sculpture of Cliko, the one that ended up at the Metropolitan Museum of Art, was displayed next to my self-portrait. I stepped toward it and stopped. As I glanced at the bronze figure, because of my height I was also able to notice that a small spotlight meant to draw attention to that sculpture also cast my shadow against the barren wall behind it. Then I looked across the crowded gallery and saw something I've never forgotten. At that instant, I caught sight of how the many spotlights in that space that were intended to highlight my art also cast the shadows of several spectators on the salon's walls, as well.

How strange shadows can be, I thought. At times we hide things there we don't want to see. Sometimes shadows are the stuff of nightmares, obscuring the light. Monsters, like the ones who murdered Lya, spring from them. Yet from the same mysterious darkness the inspiration for my paintings, poems, photos, and sculptures sprouted; bending the light to new perspective; giving my life different color, shape, and form, meaning and promise.

The faint shadows on the gallery's walls gave us all something in common, making us constituents of a strange, ephemeral community; each unique, separate, a specter, oracle, prism—an elusive reflection of something more than we knew. That's how I came to understand that my shadow, though longer than the rest, was not alone.

EPILOGUE

Watercolor, Jake Erlich

July 25, 1952

Dear Mr. and Mrs. Erlich,

My name is Elizabeth Reardon. I was one of your son Jake's nurses at Hotel Dieu Hospital. That is where I got to know him during one of his many hospitalizations. Jake called me Liz. Over time your son and I became good friends. When I learned of his untimely death I knew I had to write to you.

I worked the late shift at the hospital. Often I would sit in his room and we would talk until the early morning hours about his life, my life, and everything you can imagine. He even read me some of his poetry.

In one of our first conversations I shared with him that I was very homesick. You see, when I met Jake I had only recently graduated from nursing school in the Midwest and moved to El Paso. To cheer me up he suggested we sing together. Please try to visualize that wonderful scene in the darkened ward of the old Hotel Dieu; coming from one of the rooms you hear the melodious voice of your sweet Jake and yours truly quietly singing "On the Banks of the Wabash, Far Away," and "My Old Kentucky Home."

During one of our many late-night chats, I told Jake that mine was one of the few Catholic families in the Indiana community where I grew up. I shared with him how every day my brothers and I would take back alleys to avoid the Protestant kids who called us *Cat-lickers*. When Jake heard that he got keyed up. He told me that we had that in common; that he also had to take back alleys. But when Jake took back alleys it was to avoid the children who threw rocks at him because of his height.

I was so moved hearing about all he'd been through. I tend to be a shy person and when I first moved to El Paso I was having a terrible time making new friends. When I told Jake about my dilemma he sat up in bed. Mind you, with his kidneys failing and all, and his need for so many transfusions, that was no small feat. I will never forget his words to me. "Liz," he insisted, grabbing my arm, "you have to get ahold of yourself.

People don't know you're shy and lonely. You have to reach out to others." Jake knew what I was going through because he'd been through the same thing. He refused to let me just feel sorry for myself. And for that I'm eternally grateful. But more than what he said, what most moved me about Jake was that though he was terribly ill, he was more concerned about me than himself. Your son was a great man, and I miss him.

When I stopped working nights I would come back to Hotel Dieu before my shift started to take my friend Jake for a walk. I remember how he rested that massive right hand of his on my shoulder as we strolled through the halls. I can still feel it. You know, it wasn't heavy or anything; it mostly felt reassuring. On our walks, whenever we passed a doctor or nurse or patient, I remember how Jake would stop, look down at them, and smile. I know Jake went through a lot. But let me assure you, he never lost his dignity.

I don't know if you are aware of it, but shortly before Jake died, he gave me one of his paintings. I treasure it as one of my most prized possessions. That magnificent watercolor in blues, whites, and turquoise shows a tiny sailboat braving blustery waves on a glorious, stormy day. Whenever I look at that painting I think of your son; all that he struggled with and accomplished and how he never gave up.

I now work the early shift and have to leave my house while it's still dark. As I make my way down to the hospital from Sunset Heights, where I live, I look up to the east at the magnificent west Texas sunrise and whisper, "Hiya, Jake! How's the weather up there?"

My prayers are with both of you at this time of loss.

Liz Reardon

"The stars at night affirming man's infinitesimally tiny stature . . ."

Jake Erlich
1906–1952

AUTHOR'S NOTES

"Blustery Day," Jake Erlich

The Long Shadows is based on the life of my uncle, Jake Erlich. Many of the incidents recounted in it are true and were shared with me by my father, Jake's parents (my grandparents), and countless relatives and friends, many who have since passed away. When word spread that I had undertaken this project there was an outpouring of interest that Jake's story be told.

Uncle Jake died on my third birthday, but as I grew up he continued to play a role in the warp and woof of the life of my family. His paintings, sculptures, and photos he took, along with photographs of him in silent films and in the circus, decorated the walls of our home. On special occasions there were always stories about Uncle Jake. As children, we were quick to grab for Volume G of the *World Book Encyclopedia* and show friends Uncle Jake's picture along with an illustration of Goliath under the heading "Giant." When I became an adult I would tell Jake's story informally to friends and share it during presentations at my children's school. I continue to make keynote speeches about his life to motivate others. I even share stories about him with my patients who feel down and out because they are different.

It is my fervent hope that Uncle Jake's life story will serve as an inspiration: to understand that we are all freaks in the sideshow of life; to appreciate the debilitating and freeing power of our perspective; and to view human differences as sources of inspiration and creativity.

Writing *The Long Shadows* has been a gift and an honor. For that, I am truly grateful to Uncle Jake.

Here are the facts as they were told to me firsthand or as I discovered them in various secondary sources.

Jacob Reuben Erlich was born on July 3, 1906 in Denver, Colorado. He was premature, weighing only three and a half pounds at birth. Due to his diminutive size and limited weight, his doctors were concerned that he would not survive his infancy. At the time, the Erlich family consisted of his father, Isadore; his mother, Dora; and his older brother, Ben. Five years later, my father, Myer—the youngest of the Erlich boys—was born.

In 1912, due to hard economic times in Colorado, Isadore moved the family to El Paso, Texas. According to firsthand accounts, Jake had a normal childhood until he turned seven. That is when his parents noticed he was growing so fast that they had to buy him a new pair of shoes every two weeks. His feet would eventually grow to a size twenty-six and a half. His mother was quoted as saying that she thought Jake grew an inch every night. Jake would later learn that he was suffering from acromegaly, a condition characterized by large feet and hands, a protruding jaw, abnormal growth of the long bones, and profound height. Those who suffer from acromegaly usually have a benign tumor that has formed on their pituitary gland. That tumor affects the secretion of growth hormone. Acromegaly is very rare, impacting about three to four out of every million people. When acromegaly strikes before puberty, as it did with Jake, it is even rarer. Then it is called gigantism. Today gigantism is treated with medication and surgery. Those were not options for Jake, who was looking at a death sentence by his early twenties. By the time he was eight years old, Jake was six feet tall. According to his teacher at Vilas Elementary School, when he finished the sixth grade he was seven feet tall.

During Jake's childhood he almost drowned in the Rio Grande. My father told me a man from Mexico saved him by his hair. Then that Good Samaritan stole Jake's shoes. In one version of the story my grandfather had to pay a ransom to get those shoes back.

Jake had to deal with constant taunts, teasing, and cruel tricks. To avoid this hostility and the rocks that were often thrown at him, he began taking back alleys to avoid people. When Jake entered his teens, feeling helpless and hopeless to do anything about his growth, he became very depressed. To cheer him up my grandfather took him on a fishing trip to Santa Monica, California.

There are two versions of how Jake was discovered by Century Comedies. In the version I included in the novel (which my father told me), Jake and my grandfather were met on the pier after a day of fishing by two talent scouts, Zion Meyers and Jerry Ash. In another—which I found in Diana Serra Cary's autobiography, *Whatever Happened to Baby Peggy*—he was discovered by the director Fred Fishbach during a studio tour.

My father reported that Jake made more than a hundred silent films at Century Studios. In an extensive search of film archives I have only been able to find forty-eight titles. It should be noted that over the years, many silent films were destroyed and many may have ended up in film archives in eastern European countries that, until relatively recently, have been inaccessible. Thus, Jake may actually have made more movies. During his time at Century Studios, Jake—who was given the stage name Jack Earle (also spelled Earl)—appeared in several films with the famous child star, Baby Peggy.

Century Studios was run by the Stern Brothers, who were brothers-in-law of the famous producer and president of Universal Studios, Carl Laemmle. The stories recounted in this book about Julius Stern were either told to me by Diana Serra Cary or I found them in magazine articles about Jake. The story of the confrontation with the chauffer after Zion Meyers rear-ended his limo actually occurred. The interactions with the waitress at The Napoli were based on a story Diana Serra Cary shared that her father, Jack, had told to her. During the mid-twenties Jake's name was included among the relatively few people in the *Blue Book*, a list of noteworthy Hollywood celebrities. The party at the Cocoanut Grove depicted in this novel was fictionalized. However, Johnny Manos was said to have stashed stuffed monkeys in the palm trees at the Cocoanut Grove and Lionel Barrymore was reported to have released live monkeys in that nightclub.

During the filming of Jake's forty-ninth film he fell fourteen feet from a speeding funny car. After he had crashed into the asphalt, a piece of wood attached to a camera boom on the same automobile broke loose and hit him in the back of the head. When he regained consciousness Jake had a fractured nose and blurred vision. Within a few days he went totally blind. Jake's physicians deduced that he must have a tumor that was pressing on his optic nerve. Actually, the tumor that caused his gigantism had grown to the point that it caused him to lose his sight. Jake's doctors decided to treat his condition by bombarding his skull with X-rays. Eventually his tumor shrunk and his vision returned. Besides some temporary weakness brought on by the X-ray therapy, he was left with two noteworthy side effects: Jake never had to shave again and he stopped growing. If this had not occurred, Jake would have kept growing, and he most likely—as was typical with other giants at the time—would have died within a few years.

The question of Jake's height is controversial. Most of the people I spoke with in my research who actually knew him and most secondary sources said he was eight feet, six and one-half inches tall. One of those people I interviewed was Fred McDaniel, the son of Pete McDaniel, the undertaker who had to special order Jake's nine-foot-long coffin and who was one of the last people, if not the last person to see his body. Mr. McDaniel told his son that Jake completely filled the coffin's custom-made, eight-and-a-half-foot interior. There are some secondary sources that say Jake was nine feet tall. There are also several sources that report his height at seven feet, seven and a half inches.

As a part of his convalescence from his blindness and X-ray treatments, Jake returned to rest at home in El Paso. The incident at El Paso High School where Jake opened the classroom door via the lintel did occur; as did the escapade where his younger brother sneaked out of the synagogue to see the Four Horsemen of Notre Dame and his father emptied the place when he yelled, "Myer! Myer!" which the other congregants heard as, "Fire! Fire!"

While Jake was at home recuperating, Ringling Bros, Barnum and Bailey Circus came to town. There are two versions of how they discovered Jake. In one, Jake's friends took him to the circus sideshow. In that version of the story it was clear to everyone in the tent that Jake was a foot taller than Big Jim Tarver, who the circus had billed as the world's tallest man. In the other version, Clyde Ingalls heard about Jake and came to his home to see him firsthand. In either event, Jake was offered a contract to become a professional giant and he signed an agreement to travel with the Ringling Bros, Barnum and Bailey Circus.

Jake's closest friends in the circus were the Doll family. Jake met Harry Doll in 1926 the night of his first appearance during Ringling Bros opening at Madison Square Garden. The interchange between them reported in the book actually took place. Gargantua was a gorilla and a major attraction while Jake was with the circus. The incident in Chattanooga during which a fan grabbed Harry Doll and Jake spun the bully around, gave him a tap, and broke his jaw did occur.

When the circus came to El Paso, Jake's parents would invite his friends from Ringling Bros over for Sunday dinner. That created quite a spectacle and traffic jam as the locals drove or walked by my grandparents' Kansas Street home, trying to get a better look at the circus celebrities lounging on the porch. During one of those trips to El Paso, Jake took the Doll family on an excursion to Juarez. On another trip Jake was reported to have met with a Mexican giantess. Besides the Dolls, Jake was good friends with Lya Graf and other circus personalities including Major Mite, Cliko the African Bushman, Frank Buck, the Flying Codonas, and Lou Adler. Jake also worked for a time in Europe with the Mills Circus. There are some unsubstantiated rumors that he served as a spy for the United States before World War II.

On a visit home to see her family, Lya Graf was arrested and executed by the Nazis. The Germans justified that murder using their euthanasia laws, but Hitler had supposedly ordered her arrest personally after he saw a newspaper photo of Lya Graf and J.P. Morgan. In that photograph—which was originally intended to be a publicity stunt—Lya was posed sitting on J.P. Morgan's lap. It turned out that Morgan's bank had just turned Hitler down for a loan for his war machine and he was furious. It should be noted that besides the Jews, Gypsies, mentally ill, and developmentally disabled that were executed by the Nazis, ten thousand people were murdered for the crime of being little. The Nazi philosophy of racial purity was influenced by the teachings of the eugenics movement, which had its genesis in England and the United States. Major General George Moseley was a prominent figure in the eugenics movement and Fritz Kuhn was a major player in the German Bund (the American face of Nazi Germany) in the United States.

The story of Jake first trying his hand at sculpture in the menagerie in the basement of the old Madison Square Garden is true. I do not know the name of the woman that he saw doing the sculpture of one of the animals there that got him started in the visual arts. My father did tell me that she was the wife of the president of a major oil company. I have no idea if there was ever any romance between her and Jake. However, as a result of that chance encounter and the woman's fascination with him and his raw talent, she and one of the Ringling Bros arranged for Jake to have a scholarship to the Ringling School of Art. Jake attended art school but he hated the classes. He felt they stifled his creativity. Jake decided he was more interested in modern art and left the school. He found like-minded artists in El Paso to study with on his own, including Hari Kidd and Emilio Cahero (a muralist and student of Diego Rivera). In interviews with those who knew Hari Kidd, I learned that he did, in fact, want to paint buildings in downtown El Paso pastel colors and that he would wear colorful silk pajamas around town. Jake was his only student at that time.

In 1936, Jake had a one-man art show at the Delphic Gallery on Fifth Avenue in Manhattan. Around that time, Diego Rivera also showed his work at the same gallery. One of the pieces included in Jake's exhibition at the Delphic was a sculpture of Cliko the African Bushman. That sculpture is now a part of the permanent collection at the Museum of Natural History in New York. Besides painting and sculpture, Jake was an award-winning photographer and a poet. The title of his book of poetry is *The Long Shadows*. It was published in 1951.

Jake was a first-class marksman with a pistol and 410 skeet gun. According to Bob Phillips, a gunsmith in El Paso and a friend, Jake's skeet gun was a gift from Winchester Firearms and his pistols—ivory handled, .44 caliber Peacemakers—were a gift from Colt Industries. Charlie Askins, a border patrolman and a world champion pistol shot, was reported to have said, "Jake is good enough with a pistol that, if he wanted, he could be a world champion." Mr. Phillips told me about Jake putting on a shooting exhibition in the circus.

Jake taught himself to play the piano and the saxophone. He also studied dance with Karma Dean in El Paso. She wanted him to go on the road with her as a professional dancer. Jake did dance professionally on the vaudeville circuit where he also sang and played the piano and the saxophone. Later Jake would sing on the radio, as well. In the 1920s he did public relations work for and appeared in some of the earliest rodeos in Arizona. When World War II broke out, Jake wanted to join the army to fight the Nazis. When the armed forces turned him down, he helped the war effort by speaking and selling bonds.

At eight feet, eleven inches in height, Robert Wadlow was the tallest man in recorded history. He appeared with Ringling Bros while Jake did. However, unlike Jake, Wadlow would only appear under the Big Top and he never wore a costume. According to my father and others I interviewed, unlike Jake, Robert Wadlow was not well liked by the sideshow performers. He was reported to only have appeared in the circus in New York and in Boston for the 1936 season.

In 1937 the infamous article about Wadlow by Dr. Charles Humbred appeared in JAMA, the Journal of the American Medical Association. At the time, the editor of the journal was Dr. Morris Fishbein. Excerpts from the article appeared in Time magazine. In 1938 the Wadlows sued Humbred,

Fishbein, the American Medical Association, and Time magazine for libel. Jake and another giant appeared as witnesses for the defense. Jake testified that he earned his living as a circus giant and that he had no problem with the word *freak*. The Wadlows lost that suit and a subsequent appeal. Robert Wadlow died on July 15, 1940. It is interesting that a few months later Jake retired from Ringling Bros. As a result of the Wadlows' suit, the ethics of medical research changed. After that trial doctors began to take more responsibility for how they treated and wrote about the human beings they studied.

Jake was a committed Jew. He had a special chair on the aisle in B'nai Zion Synagogue in El Paso where he would sit and pray. He was described as a very spiritual person. Wherever he was in the world, every week Jake would do two things: call his parents and visit a synagogue.

In 1951, as Jake's kidneys started to fail, he returned to El Paso to be with his family. On one of the many hospitalizations that followed, he befriended a young nurse who worked the late shift. Her name was Betty Snyder. As Jake's condition worsened he took up watercolors, giving the paintings to his friends. Recognizing the inevitable, my father had to special order Jake's coffin. On July 18, 1952, Jake died of kidney failure. Those who attended the funeral said it was the largest in El Paso history. The back of the hearse had to remain open to accommodate the coffin. Those who dug his grave had to redo it, making it long and wide enough. Even in death, Jake was bigger than life.

In preparing this book, I read every bit of research I could find about Jake and interviewed anyone and everyone who knew or remembered him. Just about everything I read and everyone I spoke with initially mentioned Jake's kindness; his creativity; his painting, poetry, photography, singing, saxophone, and piano playing; his dancing; his acting; his gourmet cooking; his business acumen; how good of a bridge and poker player he was; his storytelling; his skill with a skeet gun, pistol, and fly rod; his sense of humor; and what a wonderful friend he was. In the words of Dean Jennings, a good friend and writer, "It seems that Jake's height was the least significant thing about him."

My mother told me that when I was about three, just before Jake died he asked me to give him a kiss. "I can't reach you, Uncle Jake," I said. In writing this book Uncle Jake has reached me. I hope he's reached you, too.

~A.E.

About the Author

Andrew Erlich, PhD, is a prominent Scottsdale, Arizona-based clinical psychologist, author, and nationally-known speaker. His newest book, *The Long Shadows*, is a real-life novel about the remarkable life of his beloved uncle, Jake Erlich (also known as Jack Earle), an accomplished artist, silent film star, circus performer, and, at an astonishing eight foot six, one of the world's tallest men. Dr. Erlich spent ten years researching and writing the book, which he describes as a labor of love. He says his uncle's life was an inspiring example of human resilience and transcendence in the face of adversity.

Dr. Erlich is the author of two previous books, *Selling to Latinos: Building a Bridge to Understanding,* and *Exploring Culture: Cultural Overviews and Insights.* He is also a popular motivational speaker and educator whose speaking engagements include *Freeing the Giant, The Yoga of Change*, and *Cross-Cultural Success*. In 2010 and 2011, Dr. Erlich was awarded the prestigious *"Top5 Speaker"* designation by Speakers Platform, one of the nation's most prominent speaker's bureaus. He also earned the *"Platinum Speaker"* designation offered by Meeting Planners International.

To learn more about Jake
and experience more of his art
visit www.thelongshadowsbook.com